THE GREAT BETRAYAL

The Great Betrayal

THE STRUGGLE FOR FREEDOM AND
DEMOCRACY IN THE MIDDLE EAST

FAWAZ A. GERGES

PRINCETON UNIVERSITY PRESS

PRINCETON & OXFORD

Published by Princeton University Press
41 William Street, Princeton, New Jersey 08540
99 Banbury Road, Oxford OX2 6JX

press.princeton.edu

Library of Congress Cataloging-in-Publication Data

Names: Gerges, Fawaz A., 1958– author.
Title: The great betrayal : the struggle for freedom and democracy
    in the Middle East / Fawaz A. Gerges.
Description: Princeton : Princeton University Press, [2025] |
    Includes bibliographical references and index.
Identifiers: LCCN 2024040978 (print) | LCCN 2024040979 (ebook) |
    ISBN 9780691176635 | ISBN 9780691189598 (ebook)
Subjects: LCSH: Middle East—Politics and government—20th century. |
    Middle East—Politics and government—21st century. | Middle East—
    History—20th century. | Middle East—History—21st century. | Middle East—
    Social conditions—20th century. | Middle East—Social conditions—
    21st century. | BISAC: POLITICAL SCIENCE / World / Middle Eastern |
    HISTORY / Middle East / General
Classification: LCC DS62.8 .G457 2025 (print) | LCC DS62.8 (ebook) |
    DDC 956.04—dc23/eng/20241211
LC record available at https://lccn.loc.gov/2024040978
LC ebook record available at https://lccn.loc.gov/2024040979

British Library Cataloging-in-Publication Data is available

Editorial: Eric Crahan, Rebecca Brennan, Rebecca Binnie
Production Editorial: Elizabeth Byrd
Jacket: Karl Spurzem
Production: Danielle Amatucci
Publicity: James Schneider (US), Kate Farquhar-Thomson (UK)
Copyeditor: Shazia Amin

Jacket Credit: ASSOCIATED PRESS

Printed in the United States of America

10 9 8 7 6 5 4 3 2 1

To Bassam, Annie-Marie, Hannah, and Laith

CONTENTS

Preface   ix

Acknowledgments   xiii

Introduction: The Struggle for Political Change and
Social Progress   1

1 The Original Sin: The Formation of the Arab State System   21

2 The Great Betrayal: What Was Promised and What
   Was Delivered   35

3 Rhetoric versus Reality: The Contradictions of the
   Colonial State   50

4 Life after Independence: The Search for a
   Foundational Myth   68

5 The Collapse of the Foundational Myth: Where It All
   Went Wrong   89

6 From Colonialism to the Cold War: The Subversion of
   the Postcolonial State from the Outside   114

7 The Winter of Discontent: The Pauperization of the
   Arab People   141

8 How and Why Did the Middle East Fail to Achieve
   Its Potential?   162

9 The Nation versus the *Umma*   190

10 The Subversion of the Nation from Within and Without   220

11 The Arab Spring Crushed   244

12 The End of Empire, or Is History about to Repeat Itself?
   An Empire by Proxy   261

   Conclusion: Reimagining the Middle East   292

                          Notes   307
                          Index   353

PREFACE

I HAVE WORKED ON THIS BOOK on and off since 2010, trying to answer a recurring question posed by my students: Why has the Middle East reached this seeming low point after a century of state- and nation-building? My students have been eager for some explanation as to why the people of the Middle East have been systematically denied self-determination, representation of their voices in the halls of power, and just and effective government. What explains the chronic instability in the Middle East? Why is there so much turmoil, instability, and anger in this region? How do we make sense of the frequent foreign interventions in the region's internal affairs, intensifying geostrategic rivalries and rampant militarism, spreading political authoritarianism, and rising extremism?

One of the flaws with many contemporary approaches to the Middle East is that they focus almost all of their attention on the rulers and elites. But as the 1979 Iranian Revolution, the 2010–2012 Arab Spring revolts, and the toppling of the Assad regime in Syria in December 2024 should have taught us, focusing on elite politics provides a skewed view of societal currents, blinding us to what may be happening in the day-to-day of Middle Eastern politics.

Although this book covers political elites and leaders, it goes further by integrating a grassroots perspective of key events and watershed moments in Middle Eastern history from the first years of the colonial era through the present day. The book does so by foregrounding the experiences, desires, and agency of the common people, the nonelites who are neglected by much contemporary historical scholarship on the region. I try to present a fuller picture of how Middle Eastern peoples see themselves and the world around them. After more than three decades of teaching and writing on Middle Eastern affairs, I know that there is a fierce thirst, and urgent need, for historically critical accounts of those affairs—accounts that do not suggest that the region is a monolith but that study its nuances systemically and comprehensively.

Reviewing a century of history was not a simple task, and I did not want to recycle outworn tropes or repeat Eurocentric and sometimes Islamophobic explanations as to why certain conflicts have occurred or dictatorships have arisen. Instead, my goal has been to pursue a deeper understanding of the dreams of the people of the region for an inclusive, open, free, and peaceful society. In other words, I have sought to inquire and make sense of why their dreams have been repeatedly thwarted.

Making the story of the Middle East and North Africa accessible to the nonspecialist, my analytical framework is built around the interaction of three key forces within the context of prolonged conflict. The first force is the constant and intense intervention by foreign powers in the region's internal affairs. The second is domestic authoritarianism. The third is the agency of everyday people in the region. The mutually reinforcing programs of external intervention and authoritarian governance helps explain why the people of the Middle East have been excluded from developing representative government and obtaining basic human and civil rights protection.

If there is one primary conclusion that I have reached based on a lifetime of study, it is that the future of the Middle East will ultimately be determined by the massive and growing Arab and Muslim youth population, not by the dictators who rule over them. The fifty-four-year dictatorial Assad dynasty (father and son) in Syria is a case in point. Against great odds and after thirteen years of a devastating war in Syria that cost hundreds of thousands of lives and almost destroyed the country, many in the West and in the region had written the Syrian revolution off and declared Assad the winner. Yet in 2024, it took the Syrian people only two weeks to seize their country back from Assad and reclaim their freedom and dignity. The swift fall of Assad stunned the world and showed the resilience of Arab agency. The rulers may receive a disproportionate amount of attention and media coverage, but this outsized focus only distorts reality and obscures both the causes and solutions to the many problems that plague the region and its peoples.

As I write this preface, Israel's war in Gaza in the wake of the October 7, 2023, Hamas attack has emerged as a major global crisis, rocking the political status quo and threatening to trigger a wider regional conflict. At the precise moment when Western powers as well as Israeli and Arab autocrats were set to celebrate an expansion of the Abraham Accords, which were premised on ignoring the question of Palestine, this topic has been thrust to the center of regional and global politics. The long-standing quest by Palestinians and the many other peoples of the region for dignity, respect, and self-determination is once again at the heart of regional politics, reminding all that unresolved questions from the past still animate and haunt the politics of the contemporary Middle East.

In the pages that follow, I hope my readers will discover how the politics of the past can give way to a politics of the future, particularly if there is a commitment to empowering progress from the bottom up instead of trying to impose it from the top down.

ACKNOWLEDGMENTS

FIRST AND FOREMOST, I want to thank my students, both former and current, at the London School of Economics. Their probing questions, genuine care for the Middle East and its peoples, and their conviction that the world can be made better has given me hope that if we learn from the mistakes of the past, we need not be bound to repeat those mistakes. In this book, I have sought to critically examine the Middle East's past century to understand why the dreams of its peoples for an inclusive, open, free, and peaceful society have been so elusive, and I hope that one day their dreams are made real.

I owe a great intellectual debt to my doctoral research students at the London School of Economics, who provoked me to rethink some of my own views about the Middle East. There is insufficient space to thank them all. Of note, however, are Dr. Anissa Haddadi and Ms. Noor al-Bazzaz, who assisted me in my research, as well as Ms. Nour Eid, who reviewed the manuscript and the endnotes.

My thanks also go to Dr. Oussama Kanaan for reviewing chapter 9, and Dr. Mustafa Menshawy for reviewing chapters 1 and 2. Dr. Jan Wilkens of the University of Hamburg provided comments on the introduction, and Ms. Jessica Jiji proposed additional important edits. Dr. Andrea Dessi, a former doctoral student and now assistant professor at the American University of Rome, read the manuscript and offered valuable feedback. Dr. Nicola Degli Esposti of the University of Padua helped improve the flow and consistency of the narrative. As a rising scholar of the Middle East, Nicola provided important insights that strengthened the arguments.

As always, I am thankful for the intellectual generosity of Professor Nader Hashemi at Georgetown University. Time and again, Nader critiques my ideas, motivating me to think harder and to challenge my own arguments. Emeritus Professor Avi Shlaim at Oxford University closely and critically mined the first three chapters.

Of the many colleagues who read the book, the assistance of the historian M. E. McMillan stands out. Margaret went beyond the call of duty, synthesizing and organizing most of the chapters, greatly enriching the narrative and strengthening the arguments. Her vast knowledge of Islamic and world history helped sharpen my analysis.

I am appreciative of Jennifer Lyons, my book agent and a dear friend. My editors at Princeton University Press, Rebecca Brennan and Eric Crahan, suggested ways to tighten the manuscript, and I thank them for that.

This book is dedicated to my children, Bassam, Annie-Marie, Hannah, and Laith. Their commitment to justice inspires me daily.

After graduating from Yale Law School, Bassam has spent the past five years fighting for the housing rights of low-income Americans, and he has clerked in both the state and federal judiciaries in the United States. After obtaining her master's degree from the School of Oriental and African Studies in London, Annie-Marie has been striving to advance global education. She began as a Teach for America corps member in Miami-Dade, Florida, and now works as the executive director of Teach for Lebanon in the United States, helping to ensure that Lebanese schoolchildren have access to talented educators.

After Hannah earned undergraduate and master's degrees in sociology, criminology, and in social work from the University of London, she has pursued a career in social work, supporting those in the toughest circumstances. Laith just completed his master's degree in biology at University College London, graduating at the top of his cohort, and has embarked on a medical career.

Finally, my wife, Nora, has been my toughest critic but also my rock-ribbed and loving companion. I could do very little without her.

Introduction

THE STRUGGLE FOR POLITICAL CHANGE
AND SOCIAL PROGRESS

"KINGS ARE THE SLAVES OF HISTORY," Leo Tolstoy famously declared. History's great protagonists, its drivers, are the ordinary people who too often get overlooked. Nowhere is this truer today than in the Middle East. Unlocking an understanding of their influence on events will open the door to greater comprehension, positive engagement, stability, and prosperity in the region and beyond.

War and Peace, Tolstoy's masterful chronicle of Russian life during the Napoleonic Wars, stands as a warning against distorting reality with neat explanations that disregard the countless multitude of causes and actors shaping events. "To study the laws of history," he argues, "we must change completely the object of observation, leave kings, ministers, and generals alone, and study the uniform, infinitesimal elements that govern the masses."[1] I am convinced that modern history should focus on the causes that generate political power, which, according to Tolstoy, derive from the work and actions of the people and their universal strivings.[2]

The fault lines and conflicts of the Napoleonic Wars that provide context for War and Peace are far less complex and sweeping than those prevailing in the Middle East and North Africa today. The application of Tolstoy's golden rule underscores the need to acknowledge the complexity and even chaos of developments in the region, and stands as a reminder to eschew explanations that reduce humanity and people's struggles to the facile but false notions of ancient hatreds, Islam's incompatibility with democracy, tribalism or sectarianism, or to the actions of kings, emirs, and strongmen.

Mainstream discussion of the Middle East in the West has mainly focused on rulers and elite politics to the exclusion of society down below. But as the 1979 Iranian Revolution, the 2010–2012 Arab Spring revolts, and Hamas's attack on Israel on October 7, 2023, taught us, focusing on elite politics gives us a skewed view of societal currents and blinds us to what is happening in the real world of Middle East politics. This book uses historical sociology as a methodological and conceptual framework, utilizing historical sources to make general statements and arguments of a theoretical nature about key events and watershed moments in the past one hundred years. It is written in the historical tradition with both a bottom-up and a top-down focus, which aims to show the struggle of everyday people against local and external actors for self-determination and justice.[3] My goal is to provide an inside-out story of how Middle Eastern peoples view themselves and the world. It is a book of interpretation that can be read by nonspecialists and used as a textbook to understand the modern history of the Middle East and the roots of instability in this region. While many theories of political science and international relations analyze today's affairs through abstract generalizations, historical sociology focuses on local context, deploying the scholarship of historians to answer questions relevant to the world we live in. If, on balance, social scientific theories have failed so far to explain "what is wrong" with the Middle East, it is imperative to ask ourselves what "went" wrong.

Tempting though oversimplifications may be, there is no "one cause fits all" to explain the current turmoil in the Middle East and the likelihood of collective action and political change. With so many forces and groups jockeying for power and advantage in the region today, it would be arbitrary and simplistic to look for a single cause. For example, do economic vulnerabilities like abject poverty and high unemployment among youth explain instability in the region? How about the role of autocrats and repression in fueling extremism and terrorism? Or does the "oil curse" and black gold in the Middle East leave the region prey to intense and repeated intervention by the Great Powers? What about geostrategic rivalries and structural vulnerabilities like the prolonged Arab-Israeli conflict? Is it the fault of European imperialism, the global Cold War, or America's attempt to resurrect empire in the region? How about the huge social dislocations borne by Arab countries through the neoliberal reforms urged by Washington-based institutions such as the International Monetary Fund (IMF) and the World Bank? Do all these causes or a combination of them help explain socioeconomic underdevelopment and deepening political authoritarianism in the Middle East?

These questions do not lend themselves to easy, straightforward answers. The Middle East is in a transitional moment that reflects the enduring impact of the colonial legacy and the bloody path of nation-building as seen elsewhere in the Global South. The region is also witnessing a redefinition of social norms and undergoing upheaval as a result of intensified competition for space, resources, and survival rather than coexistence. Far from being frozen in time and space, the Middle East surprises us with its constant change and sudden shifts. The region's fluidity, variability, and volatility are difficult to quantify or compartmentalize. This book uses the terms "the Arab world" and "the Middle East" interchangeably. The broad generalist tone adopted in this book is not to suggest the region is a monolith but to show instead that the Middle East is a region whose problems must be addressed in a systemic way. In the following chapters, I will point out the differences and specific circumstances of regional states as well as unpack some of the terms mentioned in this introduction.

The more time I spend in the region, the more skeptical I am of those who offer tidy answers to the region's chronic instability. Anyone doubting the uselessness of simple solutions need only pay a visit to the vast graveyard housing disproved political science theories that met their end when applied to the Middle East; these abstract grand theories like modernization overlooked the complexity of the regional context and its historical-sociological specificity.[4] That is why I caution my students against being lured in by the temptation to apply neat, rigid arguments instead of the messier and conceptually elastic approaches necessary to grapple with complexity.

Notwithstanding the colonial origins of states and borders in the Middle East, one hundred years later these lines on the map have broad public support. Several generations of Arabs have been raised as Iraqis, Jordanians, Lebanese, Palestinians, Syrians, and Yemenis and have been educated in these postcolonial states. These new national identities have deep roots. Even in the collapsed states of Iraq, Libya, Syria, Yemen, and others, there is little public support for redrawing the borders. The plight of the Kurds falls outside of this framework, as does Al-Qaeda and the Islamic State, which also envision remaking of the Middle Eastern state system, including borders. In short, most people in the region accept the current nation-state framework. What they desire is more effective and accountable governance. The rallying cries of millions of protesters during the two waves of the Arab Spring revolts (2010–2012 and 2018–2019) revolved around citizenship and taking the state back from dictators-for-life, not sectarianism tribalism or secessionism.

Much ink has been spilled on the Middle East, but history is about more than examining past facts; it demands asking how historical events are still present and relevant today, and whom they affect. The famous German philosopher Georg Hegel once aptly pointed out that "in our language the term *History* unites the objective with the subjective side . . . it comprehends not less what has *happened*, than the *narration* of what has happened."[5] There is no substitute for firsthand knowledge of everyday people in the Middle East, their hopes, fears, and aspirations as well as their struggle for justice, freedom, and a dignified life. We historians have forgotten the subject of our study, as Tolstoy reminds us, which is the collective will and agency of the people, as well as the causes behind the manifestations of political power.

To insist on the complexity and specificity of the historical trajectory of the Middle East does not mean neglecting the existence of dominant "threads" of interrelated issues. These "threads" help us organize and synthesize our knowledge of the region and make sense of it. This book's analytical framework is built around the interaction of three key forces within the context of prolonged conflict. The first force is the constant and intense intervention by foreign powers in the region's internal affairs, initially by formal empires and later by informal ones.[6] The second is the local trajectories of governance developed in different forms of traditional and modern authoritarianism. The third is the agency of everyday people in the Middle East. Making sense of the interactions of these forces requires that we consistently keep in mind how the first two forces, of foreign intervention and domestic authoritarianism, benefit from and actively propagate prolonged, violent conflict. This historical layer of prolonged conflict runs throughout the book and provides the backdrop against which all three key forces operate.

There is a puzzle at the heart of this book: How and under what conditions might collective action and political change take place in the contemporary Middle East? And why is there so much turmoil, instability, and anger in this region? This investigation will be structured by considering the three key forces foregrounded in this book—foreign intervention, political authoritarianism, and the agency of the people—and the theater of prolonged conflict that shapes each force and their interactions.

Foreign Intervention and Dependency

Since the early nineteenth century, Western powers have repeatedly intervened in the Middle East. Driven by imperial ambitions and the desire for military and economic expansion, they have presented the Arab-Islamic world as an exotic, irrational, and inferior cultural Other in need of a "civilizing mission." The pretext for intervention is usually national security, cited to cover more complex motives. These include, depending on the time, control of the region's strategic location, its natural resources, access to its markets, backing allies like Israel and the Gulf states, social engineering experiments like America's invasion and occupation of Iraq in 2003, and preventing rival global powers from gaining a foothold.

This pattern of repeated and intense foreign intervention in the region's internal affairs continues today. The end of imperial politics has been predicted many times, but in spite of the tumultuous events that have rocked the region over the past century, it has not yet happened. As a set of practices and an ideology, imperial domination and control has proven remarkably durable, nimble, and dynamic. The colonial experience derails and disrupts a country's normal social, economic, and political progression, leaving deep and lasting scars.[7] The Middle East has not recovered from the social, economic, and political devastation caused by European imperialism.

Besides this toxic legacy, colonialism did not really end with the formal independence of Middle Eastern countries following World War II. Western intervention has persisted, prolonging colonialism under different names and disguises. From the 1950s until the late 1980s, the United States and the Soviet Union also fought proxy wars in the newly decolonized Global South, including in the Middle East. Casualties among American and Soviet citizens were relatively low—but in the proxy societies they were staggering.

In my recent book, *What Really Went Wrong*, I argue that the impact and effects of the global Cold War on the newly independent Middle Eastern states and societies was transformational. The region was reimagined as a Cold War chessboard, leaving a legacy marked by weak political institutions, fragile sovereignty, lopsided economic growth, and political systems prone to authoritarianism. Washington's decision to roll back Soviet communism and its desire to build a new informal empire frustrated early efforts by the first generation of postcolonial leaders in newly independent nations. The Cold War also polarized the Middle East into two rival camps—pro-Western and nonaligned—forcing decolonized leaders to shift focus and priority away from development and institution-building to geostrategic competition and rivalry.[8]

The worst legacy of the Cold War was to deprive people of the Middle East of their right to self-determination. From colonial times to today, Western (and Russian) covert and overt military interventions repeatedly undermined internal societal forces seeking to bring about alternative forms of progressive governance but strengthened compliant dictators. The lingering impact and effects of colonial and neocolonial processes is discernible not only in the ways actors within the Middle East think about their past but also in the persistence of colonial narratives and in the old European (and later American) attitudes toward the region. Colonialism did not just retire into the sunset. It reproduced itself through indirect means of control, making sure to preserve the vital economic and geopolitical interests of the imperial powers, particularly oil, military bases, and arms deals.

Although the United States can no longer unilaterally impose its will and dominate the Middle East, it has been trying to compensate for its relative decline and retrenchment from the region by setting up an empire by proxy. US decision makers seek to assemble a new regional grouping, which will include Israel and pro-Western Arab states, whose raison d'être is containment of Iran and ultimately regime change in Tehran. America's empire by proxy aims to lead from behind and provide its local partners with weapons, intelligence, leadership, and logistical resources, whereby they defend themselves and do the heavy lifting.

It is precisely the region's many riches and strategic assets that attract so much unwanted interference. In the past 100 years, trillions of petrodollars have been recycled and invested in the West, deepening the material ties—or, more precisely, the dependencies—that bind the region to the global capital and financial markets.

That is why the role of the Great Powers is so central to understanding how we reached this point of organic crisis in the Middle East. Of all explanations, the international level of analysis helps us make sense of why the region is marked by dependency, political authoritarianism, weak democratic forces, geostrategic rivalries, and rampant militarism and extremism. The story of the Middle East in the last 100 years cannot be fully told without accounting for the preponderant role of external actors (be it the colonial European powers or neocolonialist America), which made pacts with local autocrats and strongmen. Both the borders of some Middle Eastern states and their institutions were set up by white men in smoke-filled tea rooms in Western capitals, as was the establishment of Israel in the heart of the Arab world. Those outside forces never eased their grip on what they set up with the deliberate goal of maintaining control, disregarding the interests and aspirations of everyday people in the region.

While European colonialism exercised direct territorial control, after World War II the right to self-determination and sovereignty could not be so openly violated. Nevertheless, the United States used informal means to tame assertive Middle Eastern leaders like Iranian prime minister Mohammad Mossadegh and Egyptian president Gamal Abdel Nasser and to financially reward local collaborators and friends like Shah Mohammad

Reza Pahlavi of Iran and the Saudi royal family. The means were different, but the effects were the same. What emerged from this was a policy of backing authoritarian strongmen in the name of stability, which has become a cardinal rule of how Western governments deal with the Middle East today.

Unlike other regions, Middle Eastern states and peoples, with few exceptions, have not been left alone to determine their own affairs. Unceasing foreign meddling by Western powers has exacerbated the region's problems and undermined territorial sovereignty and independence. Local leaders who resist Western hegemony do so at their peril. Mossadegh lost power and his freedom in August 1953 after he nationalized oil and sought to use natural resources to modernize the country. In the second half of the 1950s, Nasser narrowly escaped a similar fate to Mossadegh's because he pursued a nonaligned foreign policy and mobilized economic assets to lift millions of Egyptians out of severe poverty. Half a century later, Iraqi president Saddam Hussein met a fatal end after he dared to challenge America's hegemony in the Gulf.

Despite their stark differences, what Mossadegh and Hussein shared in common was a defiance of Western (American) imperial ambitions and a desire to act independently. The United States, together with Britain, deposed both Mossadegh, a democrat, and Saddam Hussein, an autocrat, under the pretext of combatting Soviet communism (replaced later on with Islamist extremism) and defending stability. The result is that Iran's and Iraq's political and developmental trajectory was altered, empowering radical and revolutionary ideologies like Shia and Sunni puritanical Islamism.

One hundred years after the end of European imperialism, Arab states are as dependent on and subservient to foreign patrons as ever. Unlike the first generation of postindependence Middle Eastern leaders like Mossadegh, Nasser, and Saudi king Faisal, who defended the dignity of their people and nations, today's Arab rulers fear their people and depend on external support for political survival. Most lack popular legitimacy and authority, relying instead on patronage, cronyism, and coercion. More than a hundred years after its formation, the modern Middle East is still the most penetrated region in the world.[9]

With the exception of Turkey and Iran, Arab states in the Middle East have not attained either economic sovereignty or even basic food security. The neoliberal economic reforms known as the Washington consensus imposed by the IMF and the World Bank on many Middle Eastern countries in the mid-1980s and 1990s led to huge inequities and disparities.[10] And while these policies were applied across the Global South, the damage took a particularly heavy toll on the middle class and the poor in the Middle East. The ruling elite plundered both private and public sectors, defeating even the misguided intentions of reforms imposed by the international financial institutions and exacerbating the already-yawning wealth gap. The United Nations estimates that the Arab region's top thirty-one billionaires, all men, own almost as much wealth as the bottom half of the adult population.[11] Such massive inequality was exacerbated by the COVID-19 pandemic in 2020, the food crisis caused by Russia's invasion of Ukraine in February 2022, and Israel's war in Gaza and Lebanon in 2023–2024, which to date has killed and injured more than 150,000 Palestinians and thousands of Lebanese.

One of the great tragedies of the Middle East is the contrast between its near-total dependence on others and its inherent, indigenous riches— and here I do not only mean oil, crops, or other commodities but also the intelligence and ingenuity of its peoples. The region used to export food but can no longer feed its people, relying for its bread on wheat from Ukraine, Russia, the United States, and beyond. In fact, for all of its rich, fertile land, waterways, and millennia of farming and irrigation, the Middle East is now one of the most food-insecure regions in the world.[12] This could be explained by official neglect and mismanagement of the agriculture sector as well as water scarcity.

Yet, foreign intervention and colonialism are not the whole story about the dynamics that affect the everyday life of people in the Middle East.

Governance and the Global Setting

The story of the Middle East over the past 100 years is one of creeping and deepening political authoritarianism and gross economic mismanagement. While the Great Powers constantly intervene in the region's internal affairs either directly or indirectly, autocratic leaders who depend on external patrons for survival correspondingly exploit the specter of "foreign intervention" to whip up nationalist sentiment and hype up security fears. Turning the histories of foreign intervention like the Sykes-Picot Agreement into a discursive marker, not just a historical agreement, regional strongmen justified repression against dissidents and progressives by labeling them "foreign agents." An ironic twist considering who the real foreign agents are.

For example, the shah of Iran, who was installed in power by the United States, clamped down against Marxists and leftists, accusing them of being agents for the Soviet Union. Using similar tactics, the clerics in Tehran, the shah's successors, repress human rights activists and progressive critics under the pretext of foiling Western plots against the Islamic Republic. Saddam Hussein in Iraq and the Assad clan in Syria (father and son) demonized and terrorized dissidents as traitors to the homeland. Even President Recep Tayyip Erdoğan of Turkey has reverted to this scapegoating tactic to silence opposition at home and drum up religious and ultranationalist sentiment.

In "hot conflicts" and civil strife countries, such as Iraq, Israel-Palestine, Lebanon, Libya, Syria, and Yemen, local elites seek foreign intervention to gain strategic advantage over their domestic adversaries. External intervention in the region's internal affairs is perpetuated by self-serving rulers whose goal is to consolidate their authoritarian rule.

Since 1954, Lebanon's sectarian-dominated elite have jostled with each other to induce the United States, the Soviet Union, Iran, Israel, Syria, and other external actors to take their side. The post–Saddam Hussein politicians climbed to power in Iraq on the shoulders of US troops. As the Arab Spring uprising reached Syria in 2011, President Bashar al-Assad implored Iran and Russia to come to his rescue and put down a popular revolt against his brutal rule. On December 8, 2024, his brutal regime collapsed like ripened fruit due to the inability or unwillingness of Russia and Iran to continue propping him up. The swift downfall of Assad clearly shows that external intervention sustains domestic authoritarians and prolongs their reign.

This point cannot be overemphasized. While rulers benefit from their client status, citizens chafe. In a measure of the disintegration of public trust at home, these same citizens, due to their desperation, look abroad for salvation. It is truly a sad irony that ordinary people appeal to external powers to help them get rid of their repressive tormentors. Raised on a steady diet of anti-imperial sentiments and pro-Arab pride, this represents a remarkable departure from all that they cherish in a desperate bid to escape the injustice, repression, and poverty that works so well for those who are in power entirely at the expense of those who are not.

In 2011, many Libyans welcomed NATO's military intervention against Libyan ruler Muammar Gaddafi and subsequent regime change. Likewise, the Syrian opposition naively hoped that the Western governments might remove Assad from power, repeatedly urging the United States and Europe to do so. The Kurds of Iraq, Syria, and Turkey collaborate with foreign powers against the central authority in Baghdad, Damascus, and Ankara with no reciprocal consideration for the risk and sacrifice incurred. Following the explosion at Beirut's port in August 2020, which devastated much of the country's capital, more than 50,000 Lebanese signed a petition to place the country under the control of France, their former colonial master, for the next ten years. Forsaken by their Arab brethren and the world at large, the Palestinians turned to Iran and its local proxies for arms and finance in order to resist Israeli colonial rule.

I had never imagined that large constituencies of public opinion might condone and even lobby former colonial powers to return to the Middle East as liberators. That they do so, despite all the wrongs Western powers have done to the Middle East, is the strongest possible evidence of how badly Arab rulers have failed everyday people, violating the dignity of citizens with impunity and pauperizing the society as a whole.

Revisiting the choices and actions made by the local elites, who are backed by their superpower patrons, clearly shows these choices—not genetics, Arab exceptionalism, or a cultural defect—hold an answer to why the Middle East is a politically imploding economic wasteland. It is time to acknowledge the indigenous elites' share of the responsibility for the dismal state of the region.

Unlike the first generation of postindependence leaders who exercised agency in order to attain economic and political sovereignty, their successors have prioritized political survival and deepened their countries' dependence on foreign powers. Iran is a case in point. While Mossadegh

nationalized Iran's oil in 1951 and hoped to use the resources to modernize the country, his successor, the shah, who was installed in power by the
Americans in 1953, denationalized oil and allowed Western companies to
control the petroleum industry. The shah also tied his political fate to the
United States in return for military and development aid. Even if Western
support and oil revenues brought some money to Iran, under the shah
the country remained a commodity-dependent economy without any real
productive sectors. His political legitimacy was negatively affected, and
this set the stage for the 1979 Iranian Revolution.

Similarly, the early generation of postindependence Arab leaders must
now be turning in their graves. As the first leader of Egypt to rise from
the masses and become the president of the republic, throughout his rule
Nasser, like Mossadegh, aimed to rid his country of the legacy of imperial
control and gain full national sovereignty. In doing so, Nasser fought constant battles with the Great Powers, including Britain, France, the United
States, and the Soviet Union. In December 1964, Nasser lashed back at
American criticism and delays on economic aid to Egypt and publicly
reprimanded the US ambassador, Lucius D. Battle. He told him to "drink
from the sea."[13] "And if the Mediterranean Sea is not big enough," Nasser
went on, "we will give him the Red Sea to drink it, too." Nasser's rebuke
was the equivalent of telling the ambassador to "jump in the lake."[14] Im-
plying that President Lyndon B. Johnson was trying to attach strings to
its the United States' huge economic aid program, Nasser said Egyptians
were ready to tighten their belts in order to preserve their dignity and
independence. "The Americans want to give us aid and dominate our
policy. I say we are sorry. We are ready to cut our rations and minimize
the daily consumption so that we keep our independence," Nasser stated.[15]

King Faisal of Saudi Arabia was a very different man from Nasser in
terms of background and worldview and yet was equally determined to
build a strong and independent country. He reportedly let US secretary
of state Henry Kissinger have it after Kissinger implicitly threatened to
occupy the Saudi oil fields if the Kingdom did not lift the oil embargo in
1973. "You are the ones who can't live without oil. You know, we come from
the desert, and our ancestors lived on dates and milk and we can easily
go back and live like that again," said King Faisal to his US ally.[16]

Despite the many flaws of Mossadegh, Nasser, and Faisal, they were proud, defiant leaders. They never lost sight of the importance of achieving independence and dignity for their peoples. The first generation of postindependence leaders understood the organic links between gaining real independence and overcoming dependency and economic underdevelopment. Trying to do so, Mossadegh fell on his sword in a CIA-orchestrated coup in 1953. Similarly, Nasser faced political death by a thousand cuts in the June 1967 war with Israel, and Faisal fell to an assassin's bullets in 1975.

In a matter of years, those ancestors who lived on dates and milk were succeeded by a new generation of leaders that had to import staple foods and mortgaged their countries' independence in return for backing by the United States in order to retain power. Egypt and Saudi Arabia are cases in point. President Anwar al-Sadat and especially his successor, Hosni Mubarak, turned Egypt into a client state for the United States in return for military aid and political support for their regimes. His successor, General Abdel al-Fatah al-Sisi, has not fared better. Former US president Donald Trump jokingly referred to al-Sisi as "my favorite dictator."[17]

Similarly, although Saudi Arabia is now one of the wealthiest states in the world, it is increasingly dependent on the United States for protection against foreign threats. Saudi's dependence on its superpower patron breeds contempt and exploitation by US leaders. President Barack Obama called the Saudis "freeloaders." Obama forgot that the Saudis have pumped hundreds of billions of dollars into US coffers by purchasing arms, luxury goods, and treasury bonds. Trump went further than his predecessor by publicly humiliating his loyal Saudi ally. He boasted to supporters that Saudi Arabia and its king would not last "two weeks" in power without American military protection.[18] During his presidential campaign in 2019, Trump's successor, Joe Biden, warned Saudi Arabia that he would treat it like "the pariah that they are."[19]

The current tensions in US-Saudi relations is partly due to the assertiveness of the new Saudi leader, Crown Prince Muhammed bin Salman (known as MBS), who has de facto ruled the country since 2015. MBS has portrayed himself as a strong, independent leader in an effort to build up his popularity at home and prepare the ground for his smooth succession to the Saudi throne. His use of Saudi Arabia's economic power to regulate global oil prices angered the Biden administration. In Spring 2023, MBS upset US officials further by agreeing to normalize relations with Iran in a diplomatic deal brokered by China. However, MBS's actions are not aimed at building a real independent path for Saudi Arabia. Instead, according to US officials, MBS demands a new defense pact with the United States that secures a formal American commitment to defend Saudi Arabia with military force as well as advanced arms. In other words, the assertiveness by MBS and other Arab rulers does not challenge the foundation of Saudi and Arab dependency on the United States for protection and political survival. This symbiotic relationship between local leaders, their autocratic rule, and their foreign patrons is a key factor in sustaining political authoritarianism in the Middle East.

Bad governance and flawed leadership combined with structural factors help explain the wretched social and political conditions of Middle Eastern societies. The ruling elites who replaced the first generation of postindependence leaders did not fulfill their promises to deliver prosperity, justice, and freedom—and, most importantly, they failed to respect the dignity of everyday people. Instead of safeguarding national sovereignty, they relied heavily on external stakeholders to ensure political survival. They prioritized regime security at the expense of defending the national interest. Instead of promoting transparency, accountability, social mobility, and integration, Middle Eastern rulers set up one-party rule and eliminated all organized opposition. They deinstitutionalized the political and sectarianized it. Instead of strengthening the institutional ties that bind citizens to each other and the nation-state, these autocrats built expansive security apparatuses to consolidate their rule.

Although there are many wealthy Arabs, the Arab people as a collective are pauperized. The statistics on poverty, unemployment, the income gap, food insecurity, corruption, and stagnation in the system are shocking when compared to the natural wealth that many of these countries possess. For example, the Arab region is the only developing area in the world where income poverty rose in the last decade: in 2020, about one-third of the population, or 115 million people, were estimated to be poor, up from 66 million people in 2010. It also suffers from rampant inequality, with the wealthiest 10 percent of Arab adults holding more than 75 percent of total regional wealth, according to a recent study by the United Nations Economic and Social Commission for Western Asia (ESCWA).[20] Iranians do not fare better than their Arab counterparts. The regional economy is broken.

Cronyism has also led to state-sanctioned injustice, violence, and exclusion, thereby creating a pattern of alienation affecting the population.[21] In the Arab world, states sanction identity. Political parties are often formed on identity lines, with quotas for representation built into the system. This is ultimately destabilizing, though, because the state-carved identity lines are largely artificial and fail to reflect the natural society upon which state power actually rests. Even the one-party rule initially established by postindependence strongmen morphed into a cult of personality. The state steadily became synonymous with the predilections of the sole leader and a small, corrupt, and sycophantic inner circle.

The Agency of Everyday People

Historically, the intelligentsia stood as a vanguard for change and an expression of popular sentiment, but it has long forfeited that role. Since the late 1960s, pessimism and fatalism have taken hold of the Arab spirit. The mood of public intellectuals grew increasingly gloomy as they lost confidence in the future. The dominant narrative among Arab intelligentsia is self-defeating and despairing, surrendering its role as a vehicle of change. In the face of such corruption and disempowerment, many leading intellectuals chose or were forced to cross borders and settle in the very colonial countries whose past actions they rightly denounced.

With Arab intellectuals seized by pessimism, it is no wonder then that they played no discernible role in the two waves of Arab Spring uprisings, which were leaderless.[22] In contrast, everyday people stood up and filled the vacuum left by the retrenchment of intellectuals. If there is one lesson that we ought to draw from the struggles of everyday people of the region, it is their refusal to accept dictatorship, cronyism, and corruption as inevitable.[23] The history of the Middle East is as much marked by authoritarianism and state violence and exclusion as it is by popular insurrection against tyranny, a lesson often lost on Western commentators.

The first step in moving beyond a fatalism that only serves despotic elites is to abandon the tendency to see the people in the region as victims and passive spectators in a Shakespearean tragedy. Even after millions of courageous citizens have taken to the streets since 2010 to topple autocrats in the region, everyday people are still not taken seriously in the Western media commentary and coverage of the Middle East.[24]

It is no wonder that both writers and policymakers were caught napping when the Arab Spring uprisings burst out in 2010 and lasted till 2012. The media and Western analysts belatedly discovered that, after all, there is an Arab public opinion, and that political authoritarianism is not so durable. The Arab state system was not frozen in time and space, and tyranny was not destiny. Peacefully and inclusively, the millions of people who filled the freedom squares in Egypt, Libya, Syria, Tunisia, Yemen, and elsewhere called for freedom, justice, and dignity, earning the respect of the world. The Arab Spring uprisings showed us in real time that everyday people yearn for citizenship, political participation, and empowerment, and oppose autocrats, false prophets, and extremist ideologies.

The first wave of the Arab Spring was a rude awakening for many Westerners who saw the Middle East as a hotbed of terrorists who threaten their own way of life. But the people in the street were neither carrying Al-Qaeda's black flags nor burning US or Israeli flags. The uplifting stories of millions of peaceful protesters, young and old, men and women, poor and rich, were a reminder of the universal struggle of humanity for a better life. They were not divided by sect but united in purpose. No longer caricatures of "Arabs," these people revealed the shared longing for democracy, justice, and peace that is common to all.[25]

This may have moved some individuals in the West, but their governments were unresponsive. Bloody dictators like Assad and the House of Khalifa in Bahrain acted in collusion with regional and global powers, and exploited geostrategic rivalries, to shatter the dreams of millions of everyday people for a dignified life. The crushing of the first wave of the Arab Spring uprisings by Arab counterrevolutionary forces and their foreign patrons triggered civil strife and wars that still rage in Libya,

Yemen, and beyond, and fueled the resurgence of sectarian groups and militias like the Islamic State. This is another example of Arab despots colluding with foreign powers to maintain the status quo and to prevent any real change.

The voices of everyday people were muzzled and silenced for a while, prompting those in the West who had celebrated the Arab Spring to quickly pen its obituary. They were wrong to write off people's agency and consign the Middle East to a perpetual cycle of supposed Oriental despotism. Even for a region that has dominated world headlines for decades, today's Middle East is remarkable for its surprises.

To prove that the announcement of their deaths was premature, Arab uprisings roared back to life in a second wave in 2018–2019. Reverberating widely, it undulated in Algeria, Iraq, Lebanon, and Sudan, playing out on Arab streets, demonstrating that local agency is alive and that the struggle for representation continues. Millions of women, youth, and men today strongly challenge the status quo, reawakening consciousness among the larger citizenry.

Rather than starting from scratch, the new protesters drew valuable lessons from their predecessors in 2010–2012, especially the need to stay on the streets till the authorities respond to their demands and to face repression and even death without resorting to violence. The second wave, coming six years after the first wave, has given us a glimpse of the emergence of a new generation of freedom fighters whose aspirations revolve around social justice, political representation, and jobs. In Iraq and Lebanon, in particular, millions of protesters joined ranks from across the confessional and political spectrum to demand accountability, citizenship, and an end to the systemic corruption of the ruling elite.

Although the aspirations of the protesters have been crushed, activists and civil society groups acknowledge that the struggle to transform their societies will be long and fraught with setbacks. The struggle will continue, these freedom fighters insist. Indeed, we ought to listen to the hopes and fears of the people and learn from their struggles. As the following pages will show, this struggle for freedom, dignity, and sovereignty did not begin with the Arab Spring in 2010; it has been carried out since the onset of European imperialism in the nineteenth century.[26] For example, Hamas's surprise attack on Israel in 2023 has rocked the regional status quo and reminded the world of the unfulfilled quest by the Palestinians in the past 100 years for self-determination and freedom. This was also a reminder of how unresolved questions from the past still trigger wars and cause a humanitarian catastrophe.

With the exception of the rich, all sectors of society who represent a majority of the population are badly hurt, seeing their living conditions deteriorate further due to the turmoil and conflict that wrecked the region over the last two decades. A doctor in Syria who once commanded respect, lived comfortably, and contributed to society now struggles on a dangerous migratory journey to an uncertain and likely vulnerable future threatened by poverty, disease, and even hate crimes. Millions have lost their jobs and meagre subsistence incomes. Spiraling inflation coupled with a steep decline in the value of local currency has forced tragic choices onto millions: food or medicine? Stay and suffer war and a collapsed economy or leave your homeland and suffer discrimination and dislocation? Cling with hope to the vanishing past or set out for an extremely perilous future?

This was all before the emergence of the COVID-19 pandemic, which exacerbated the economic meltdown in several Middle Eastern countries, including Egypt, Jordan, Lebanon, Syria, and Tunisia.[27] For all the xenophobia surrounding the exodus of refugees from the region pouring into Europe, the vast majority stay there, hosted by neighboring countries and peoples in Jordan, Lebanon and Turkey, who display a spirit of Arab-Islamic generosity, which, silently but surely, saves lives there. A pandemic is lethal anywhere; a pandemic in a densely crowded refugee camp where water and soap are in scarce supply amounts to a mass death sentence for the vulnerable.

Pauperized and pressed between autocrats and extremists, for now, everyday people are preoccupied with survival. We have not heard their last roar, however. History has shown that the best way to defuse an opposition movement is not through force but by meeting its legitimate demands. Injustice is unsustainable over the long run because the human spirit—in the Arab world as everywhere—will ultimately risk safety to end it.

The region's rulers face a stark choice. Will they continue to rule by domination, divide-and-conquer tactics, and dependence on their foreign masters, or will they address the legitimate grievances of their people and their calls for justice, dignity, and freedom?

The first choice, almost too scary to contemplate, means more of the same failed policies, failed development, and even failed states, not to speak of the senseless loss of life and potential of the affected population. It would mean prolonged political instability, worsening terrorism, protracted civil wars, waves of refugees, and incalculable human suffering. This doomsday scenario will not only plague the Middle East but will also hurt Western and Asian states, which, in the global village, cannot isolate themselves.

The second option promises to arrest economic and cultural decline and end the political violence and civil wars that have ravaged the region. Building trust between governments and peoples would strengthen the resilience of both state and society, making them less dependent on external actors and less prey to foreign meddling and extremism. It could signal the beginning of the end of the hundred years' war for control of the Middle East.

Middle Eastern rulers resist instituting change at their own peril, as Bashar al-Assad belatedly discovered. It is not a question of whether protesters will achieve their aims but rather when. Yes, the process of political change will be fraught and difficult, but to avoid this will extract an astronomical cost in terms of lives, livelihoods, and stability.

In this effort, it will be helpful to remember the proud struggles of the region's peoples and the change that they have already achieved. As remarkable as the first Arab Spring was, taking pundits and experts completely by surprise, the second wave was even more noteworthy for arriving while the rest of the world had given up on the capacity of the region's people.

To envision a new future for the Middle East, one free of despotic rulers, settler colonialism, outside interference, and repressive governance, requires breaking with unimaginative and limited attachment to the paradigm of the status quo. The lockdown imposed by the COVID-19 pandemic, together with festering civil strife and wars, may have necessarily muffled the cries for justice, but nothing can silence them.[28]

The Struggle for Representative Government
in the Middle East

Reviewing a century of history in the Middle East is not simply a look back at the past hundred years; it is a journey into a deeper understanding of the region's dream for an inclusive, open, free, and peaceful society. And how and why this dream has been thwarted and the region's material, political, and spiritual capital has been squandered. An inside-out historical perspective on the Middle East helps us make sense of the contemporary moment there. Specifically, the yearning for self-determination is still out of reach for the vast majority of the population, and promises by Western leaders to support development and democracy ring hollow in the ears of many Middle Easterners.

Detangling the respective roles of internal, regional, and global actors in creating the current anti-democratic climate will open the way for explaining today's state of affairs and planning a new tomorrow. The future of the Middle East will ultimately be determined by the massive and growing Arab/Muslim youth population, not by the dictators who rule over them. This latter group gets a disproportionate amount of media coverage, thus distorting the reality of the region and the many problems that plague it.

In the pages that follow, readers will discover how the politics of the past can give way to the politics of the future, especially through empowering change from the bottom up. This book examines the modern history of the Middle East by using the lenses of foreign intervention, political authoritarianism, and the agency of everyday people. The first two forces feed upon each other, triggering prolonged conflicts that act as the main constraints on social progress and change and systemically denying people self-determination. With an understanding that people drive history and shape the future, there is room for outside forces to support this process, motivated not by thirst for petro-dollars, influence, or markets for armaments, but by an awareness that respecting the dignity and agency of Middle Eastern people will benefit the entire world.

1

The Original Sin

THE FORMATION OF THE ARAB
STATE SYSTEM

MORE THAN TEN YEARS after the first wave of the Arab Spring uprisings in 2010–2012, the Middle East is a mess. From Libya to Yemen to Syria-Iraq and Israel-Palestine, no part of the Middle East is immune to the changes sweeping through the region. In front of our eyes, the fabric of the state system is coming apart at the seams. The human cost of this upheaval is catastrophic.

In the wake of so much change, it is not surprising to find a wide variety of opinions explaining the current crisis in the region. When it comes to the Middle East, historians fall into one of two schools of thought, divided by whether they attach weight to internal or external factors in assigning blame for the crisis.

The internalist school blames the Arabs for what went wrong after the defeat of the Ottomans. According to this viewpoint, the Arabs blew their opportunity to build a liberal political order first under the mandates system and again after they gained their independence. Within this school, there are various strains claiming to explain why the Arabs fail to progress toward real democracy. Conservative voices in the West emphasize the exceptional character of the Middle East, citing what they view as a tendency toward despotism in the region. Even worse, they claim the Arab world is structurally incapable of building and maintaining a viable state system. This school was exemplified by the late historian

Bernard Lewis, who asserted that Islam is incompatible with democracy and therefore any attempt to achieve it in Muslim society was doomed to failure. Others, like the late political scientist Fouad Ajami, contend that Arab political culture is inherently authoritarian, that Arabs are addicted to Oriental despotism, and that this explains why there has never been a liberal age in Arab politics even if there has in Arab thought. Yet another perspective holds that Arab nationalism is the fundamental cause of Arab failures, culminating in the defeat at the hands of Israel in June 1967. All of them agree that the course of modern Arab history was largely shaped by the local actors rather than by external powers.

The externalist school places blame on the British and French, tracing the origins of the current instability to an "original sin," namely the victors' peace imposed on the region following the defeat of the Ottoman Empire after World War I. This school argues that the victors designed the postwar territorial settlement to serve their own interests at the expense of the rights and aspirations of the indigenous Arab population. Because it was imposed from outside, this settlement was characterized by its lack of legitimacy. The externally imposed borders lacked legitimacy, the undemocratic political systems lacked legitimacy, and the colonial puppet rulers lacked legitimacy. In what might be called the "post-Ottoman syndrome," this foreign-made, dysfunctional system prevents the Arabs from achieving development, democracy, and peace. This analysis can be understood as illustrating an Arabic saying: Something that starts crooked, remains crooked.

Both of these schools of thought are limited. While it is absurd to suggest that Arabs or Muslims are incapable of democracy, or to deny that Arab peoples yearn for a voice and a vote just like the rest of humanity, it is also myopic to blame colonial powers for all of the region's problems because that, too, deprives the region's peoples of their role in shaping their own destiny. The reality is that a complex range of factors has combined to create a perfect storm. The monopoly of power—and the privileges that go with it—held by unaccountable elites in the region has led to a chasm-like disconnect between state and society, between power and the people. And the failure of these elites to address the genuine grievances of their people, together with massive economic mismanagement, has, in some quarters, fueled extremism. Worse still, repeated interventions by Western powers have exacerbated the situation by undermining local groups that were trying to bring about alternative forms of governance. These outside forces, by taking advantage of instability in the region to advance their own ambitions, have made a bad situation much worse.

My perspective differs from the two narratives that I briefly outlined above. I consider foreign intervention and the dependency that external control endangered central to understanding the modern Middle East. The period from the end of the Ottoman Empire to the present is littered with interventions by Western powers. The onset of colonial rule in the Middle East is best understood not as an isolated incident whereby an invading army conquered a country but as a *series* of asymmetrical encounters between colonial and colonized actors.[1] But this perspective diverges from narratives that focus solely on colonial powers and the assumption that the Great Powers were able to implement their agenda unopposed across the region. Foreign intervention in the region must be understood in a dialectical and continuous interaction with the establishment and spread of authoritarian politics. These two forces actively accrued legitimacy and control by undermining local institutional development and furthering the ongoing violent conflicts that devastated the region. To understand the Middle East in its complexity, we have to look at the "layer" of international politics against the backdrop of domestic politics and military confrontations.

The agency of the people could not overcome the asymmetrical encounters with colonial power and its local patrons.

After they arrived in the Middle East, colonial powers faced resistance from populist protests and different forms of contentious politics. But the asymmetrical character of the encounter meant the outcome was never in doubt. The decline of the Ottoman Empire allowed Britain and France to develop plans for a whole new system of rule in the Middle East.

To achieve this, Britain and France were at first helped by the region's new elites. At the time, Western powers were not seen as negatively as they are today. Many people had no reason to believe that their word was not their bond. The region's new elites who emerged after the end of the Ottoman Empire saw French and British involvement as necessary to help build the new political structures in which they would then play a pivotal role. Organized resistance to Britain and France did not coalesce until the implications of colonial rule became visible, and it became obvious the Great Powers had promised one thing and delivered another. To understand how this happened, we need to look at what the Great Powers first promised.

False Promises: The McMahon-Husayn Correspondence

At the start of the Great War, Britain was looking to find a credible ally in the Middle East, one that could challenge the long-standing legitimacy of the Ottoman Empire and its ruler, who was at the same time Ottoman sultan and Islamic caliph. The rationale was simple: as German influence was growing in Istanbul, "it was desirable that there should be a pole of Muslim attraction which should be independent or in the British sphere."[2]

This thinking, along with stories of a vast secret society of Arab officers in the Ottoman Empire preparing to revolt and establish an Arab caliphate in Arabia, Syria, and Iraq,[3] drew Britain's attention to Arabia and, in particular, to the Emir of Mecca, Sharif Husayn Ibn Ali. There was no better challenger to the Ottoman sultan-caliph than the guardian of the holy cities of Mecca and Medina, the two holiest sites in Islam, and who was himself a direct descendant of the Prophet Mohammad. Husayn was "an ambitious dynast" who did not rush to take sides either with the Ottomans or with his new supporters, the British. Instead, he bided his time as both sides vied for his allegiance.

The outbreak of war presented him with a unique opportunity. He was not averse to working with the British. He had, in fact, been considering it for years.[4] Since 1912, when the Ottoman Empire's "Turkification" policy was at its height, he had entertained the idea of founding a sovereign Arab empire with British military support.[5] Following the Ottoman Empire's alliance with Germany, the British played on these ambitions and encouraged them, albeit unofficially. In July 1915 Husayn began a correspondence with the British high commissioner in Egypt, Sir Henry McMahon, in which he set forth the conditions that might persuade him to enter an alliance with Britain and to launch a revolt against his own Ottoman government.

In the first correspondence between Husayn and McMahon, Husayn stressed the determination of the Arab people to obtain their political independence and that "the Arabs believe it to be in Great Britain's interests to lend them assistance and support in the fulfillment of their steadfast and legitimate aims to the exclusion of all other aims."[6]

For Husayn, independence was more than a vague aim. It was an absolute condition of his support. In his first letter, he made it clear that he wanted British recognition of independence for Arab countries[7] and British support for the proclamation of an Arab caliphate for Islam. In his letter, he also assured Britain that the future "Sharifian Arab Government" would "grant Great Britain preference in economic enterprises in the Arab countries."[8] Finally, Husayn's letter stressed his proposal would remain open for thirty days, during which an explicit rejection or acceptance should be sent back by McMahon on behalf of Britain.[9]

McMahon's initial response was equivocal. He refrained from either agreeing or rejecting the conditions set out by Husayn and simply reiterated the assurance previously given to Husayn by the secretary of state for war, Lord Kitchener, that Britain would support the independence of the Arab people. McMahon, however, did not go into the territorial borders of this independence. Such discussions, he said, were "premature and a waste of time on details at this stage, with the War in progress and the Turks in effective occupation of the greater parts of those regions."[10]

Husayn was not fooled. He saw past the vague formalities of McMahon's first letter and responded with an assertive statement that the question of frontiers had to be treated as fundamental. For Arabs, "these frontiers form the minimum necessary to the establishment of the new order for which they are striving." Husayn's letter repeatedly stressed that he was not speaking on behalf of himself as an individual, but as a representative of the Arab people.[11]

McMahon's next letter to Sharif Husayn would prove to be monumental. The letter begins by expressing regret at Husayn's misunderstanding of McMahon's willingness to delay discussions of frontiers and "having realized from your last note that you considered the question important, vital and urgent, I hastened to communicate to the Government of Great Britain the purports of your note."[12]

Sent on October 24, 1915, McMahon's response assured Husayn that Britain was prepared to recognize and support the independence of the Arabs within the limits that Husayn himself had demanded, subject to three significant reservations: first, the coastal areas "lying to the west of the districts of Damascus, Homs, Hama and Aleppo," which McMahon stressed were "not purely Arab"; second, regions affected by "our existing treaties with Arab chiefs," referring to the Persian Gulf areas of Arabia; and finally, regions "in which the interests of our ally France" limited Britain's freedom to act alone, namely Syria.[13]

In the end, Husayn felt he had no option but to write and agree to postpone discussions of the Syria issue until after the war. He was not willing to jeopardize the "alliance between Great Britain and France and their concord during the calamities of the present war." But Husayn did not leave it there. He asserted that "on the other hand—and this Your Excellency must clearly understand—we shall deem it our duty at the earliest opportunity after the conclusion of the War, to claim from you Bairut and its coastal regions which we will overlook for the moment on account of France."[14]

That McMahon was able to avoid Husayn's demand regarding Syria, and that he was able to do it in such a highly ambiguous way, would be the source of great controversy and debate in the interwar period.

The Sykes-Picot Agreement: "The Agreement of the Colonial Thieves"

The Ottoman Empire's decision to ally with Germany was a historic moment that would have far-reaching effects on colonial Britain's psyche in the Middle East. The loss of Turkey as a potential ally, as well as the failure of the Dardanelles Campaign in March 1915,[15] prompted the British government to set up the British Desiderata in Asiatic Turkey Committee.

Mark Sykes was among the members. In 1915, Sir Mark was thirty-six years old. A Tory member of Parliament (MP), he was a wealthy Roman Catholic who had spent time traveling in Asiatic Turkey and had published accounts of his journey.[16] Sykes, a caricaturist and a mime, was charming and restless in equal measure. His fascination with the East began at the age of seven, when his father took him on a trip to the Middle East, and his passion stayed with him into adulthood. As an undergraduate student, he chose to travel to the Middle East instead of completing his degree at Cambridge University.

His travels made him somewhat of a Conservative Party expert on Ottoman affairs, but "as Ottoman affairs had not played any significant role in British politics between 1911 and 1914, and as his party was out of office; Sykes was not well-known either to the public or to his fellow politicians."[17]

Lord Kitchener recruited Sykes onto the committee as his personal representative.[18] Kitchener was in search of a young politician who knew the Middle East and Sykes was one of only a handful of members of Parliament who claimed such knowledge.[19] It gave him an authority on the committee that went beyond his experience as an MP, making him "outspoken and opinionated."

It was Sykes who identified Iraq as the center of British aspirations, seeing it as an essential extension of the British Indian sphere of influence in the Near East. He also believed the British position in Iraq and British India required a direct line of communication to a Mediterranean port. In his view, Haifa-Acre further north in the eastern Mediterranean (then part of historical Palestine and now in present-day Israel) was the obvious choice even though his patron Lord Kitchener preferred Egyptian Alexandria[20] and British control of the city would challenge France's claim for the whole of Syria.[21]

At this point in time, however, neither Britain nor France was seeking a partition of the Ottoman Empire. Discussion over the future of the Middle East revolved around spheres of influences for the Allied powers with British influence in the south, Russian in the north, and French in the center.[22] The negotiations to secure these objectives began on November 23, 1915, when the French representative, François Georges-Picot arrived in London with the job of securing the best deal for France.[23]

Picot, the son of one of the founders of the Comité de l'Afrique Française, was an advocate of the French Colonial Party and an ardent believer in a French Syria.[24] Earlier that year Picot had launched a parliamentary campaign in Paris against ministers prepared to give Britain a free hand in the Middle East. He succeeded in having parliament adopt a report[25] on the partition of the Ottoman Empire that would see Mosul added to Syria.[26] Like Sykes, Picot had worked in the Middle East. For a brief period just before the outbreak of war, he had served as consul-general in Beirut. During that time, Picot established strong relations with the Maronite Christian leaders, a community France would pledge to protect. This was a politically significant relationship as European powers relied on the support of the elites of religious and ethnic minorities in the Middle East. They saw them as loyal and dependent constituencies.[27]

It was a strategy deployed not only in cosmopolitan Beirut with its diverse mix of ethnic and religious communities but also across the wider region. And it was a strategy with far-reaching ramifications. Syria and Iraq, two of the countries currently in crisis, suffered from this strategy from the outset. Colonial Britain and France deliberately used minorities in both countries to "divide and rule" and thereby maintain their own imperial influence.[28] In the process, they built communal tensions into the structure of the state and, whether by accident or design, set communities against each other. In Syria, for example, the French used the minority Alawite community (now among Bashar al-Assad's staunchest supporters) to head up the army, which would rule over a majority Sunni society.[29]

In their attempts to divide and conquer, the French went even further and attempted to co-opt the community by creating a ministate based in Latakia on the coast and in the Alawite highlands where notables were to rule in collaboration with the French administration.[30] The British were no different. In Iraq, they supported a Sunni monarchy over the country's majority Shiites. The relationship between the Great Powers and minorities, including Christian Copts and Druze, created tensions between communities, and fed a sentiment in the majority that the minority had collaborated with European colonial powers against the homeland. In these circumstances, communal cohesion became difficult to achieve, just as the colonialists hoped. A weak, internally divided state would be in no position to challenge the might of Britain or France. However, throughout the post-Ottoman Middle East, the British and French relied not only on religious and ethnic minorities, but also on the support of the leading economic classes—merchants and landowners—favoring them in a way that exacerbated social conflicts.[31]

The very logic of divide and rule used by colonial Britain and France, which has become a cornerstone of authoritarian power in the Middle East, is itself a recognition of the potential power of the people's agency. If their power was nothing to be feared, there would have been no need to so meticulously divide them and turn them against one another.

When Picot arrived in London in November 1915, Sir Arthur Nicolson, permanent under secretary at the Foreign Office, was in charge of the British negotiating team. Sir Mark Sykes was brought in to replace him in December after talks deadlocked.[32] In spite of his lack of experience in negotiating with a foreign government, Sykes was thought to be ideal for the job because of his travels in the Middle East and was known to be "pro-French" and reportedly spoke French. And "as a Roman Catholic himself, he was not prejudiced against France's goal of promoting Catholic interests in Lebanon."[33]

For Britain, the idea of allowing Palestine to fall under French influence was unthinkable for a number of reasons. As Sykes himself had suggested in the De Bunsen Committee, Britain wanted control of the Haifa-Acre bay to serve as an outlet from British India, through Iraq and out to the Mediterranean coast. In addition, Britain did not want France, or any other power for that matter, to establish itself in immediate proximity to the Suez Canal.[34]

France was not the only obstacle to Britain's ambitions in Palestine. The Orthodox Russian Empire also staked a claim to the Holy Land. Russia had a number of Christian religious sites under its care in Palestine and, because of this, had initially tried to claim a right over the Holy Land.[35] This demand triggered British and French opposition but, in order to reach a compromise, London and Paris eventually conceded to international administration of Palestine. As compensation for their compromise, the French received a large zone of "direct control" that stretched along the Syrian coast from southern Lebanon into Anatolia. British officials were less easily pleased.

While British diplomats succeeded in securing Sykes's goal of controlling Haifa and Acre, they failed to deliver on their ambitions of protecting their imperial interest in India by establishing "a belt of English-controlled country"[36] across the Middle East: a direct east-west land route from India through Iraq and to Palestine.[37] Another of Sykes's failures was his concession of Mosul to Picot. This was a crucial mistake in the eyes of many British politicians and diplomats as it meant giving up vast oilfields in the north of Iraq. Sykes's concessions on both Mosul and Palestine would later contribute to the unmaking of the entire Sykes-Picot Agreement. Sykes's plans have also been criticized as arbitrary, symbolized by his famous declaration in a presentation to Prime Minster H. H. Asquith in 1915 when he explained, "I should like to draw a line from the 'E' in Acre to the last 'K' in Kirkuk."[38]

Historian David Fromkin puts forward an alternative view of what exactly Sykes was up to. In his best-selling book *A Peace to End All Peace*, Fromkin suggests that Sykes was much more wily than he appeared: "In secretly planning to take Mosul, Picot was unaware that Kitchener and Sykes were secretly planning to give it to him. They wanted the French sphere of influence to be extended from the Mediterranean coast on the west all the way to the east so that it paralleled and adjoined Russian-held zones."[39] In other words, the French were to act as Britain's first line of defense should the Russians ever decide to go looking for access to a warm-water port further south. Whatever reasons Sykes had for the concession of Mosul, it would be a decision that Britain would later labor to reverse.

While the McMahon-Husayn correspondence and the Sykes-Picot Agreement were constructed independently from one another, there is evidence to suggest that Sykes was aware of the McMahon-Husayn correspondence before sitting down with his French counterpart.[40] The discrepancies between the Sykes-Picot Agreement and the McMahon-Husayn correspondence would later be a source of anger and recrimination between Arabs and Britain, particularly over the issue of Palestine.[41]

Husayn and the Arabs felt deceived by British officials who were making one set of commitments to them and an entirely different set of commitments to the French and another, as we will see, to the Jews. To this day, Arabs have neither forgotten the McMahon-Husyan correspondence nor forgiven Britain for what they see as treachery. The McMahon letters did not refer to the future of Palestine directly. Instead, they kept it so vague that it was not mentioned at all. But for Husayn and the Arabs, Palestine was not—and could never be—considered in the regions "lying to the west of the districts of Damascus, Homs, Hama and Aleppo."[42] For them, there was no question that it lay within the independent Arab area promised by McMahon. While McMahon's deliberate ambiguity meant Palestine's inclusion in the independent Arab area promised to the Arabs could not be proven, many commentators have since noted the geographically obvious: that Palestine is *south* of Damascus.[43]

Furthermore, the British were prepared to lie outright to the French to keep Husayn on side. Although some of Britain's contradictory promises were unrealistic and might have angered French officials, the British felt it was a price worth paying for Husayn's support and the continuation of the Arab revolt against the Ottoman Empire. As Sir Reginald Wingate, a prominent British general who replaced McMahon as high commissioner in Egypt in early 1917, put it: "After all what harm can our acceptance of his (Husayn's) proposals do? If the embryonic Arab state come [*sic*] to nothing all our promises vanish and we are absolved from them—if the Arab state becomes a reality we have quite sufficient safeguards to control it."[44]

No amount of British and French diplomatic cunning could mask the deception engineered against the Arabs. Unfortunately for the people of the Arab world, this was not the end. More false promises were to come. This secrecy contributed greatly to the feeling of betrayal and mistrust toward Britain and France in the Middle East, particularly from the Palestinians.

The Deepest Cut of All: The Balfour Declaration

The deepest cut was to come in the form of a short document that has changed the course of history in the Middle East and beyond. No colonial agreement encapsulates the betrayal felt by Arabs in the post–World War I period like the Balfour Declaration, signed on November 2, 1917.

British foreign secretary Arthur Balfour issued the document as a letter to Lord Walter Rothschild, a British Zionist leader. However, the real driving force behind the move was not Balfour but David Lloyd George, a former chancellor of the exchequer who was prime minister by the time of the Declaration.[45]

The letter was brief, and its wording was notably vague. It did not mention or advocate for a Jewish "state" but affirmed support for the creation of a "national home for the Jewish people" in Palestine.[46] The only reference to the rest of the inhabitants of the country was indirect. The missive stipulated that British support was contingent on the provision that nothing was done "to prejudice the civil and religious rights of existing non-Jewish communities in Palestine."

Left at that the document would have been nothing more than a promise made to an ally while at war, but Britain inscribed the terms of the declaration into the League of Nations' mandate for Palestine. In doing so, the imperial power had transformed a letter into a legally binding international agreement.[47]

At the time of the declaration, the Jewish population in Palestine was tiny, numbering only around 10 percent of the population. To protect and inscribe in law the rights of a minority community, Britain had de facto deprived 90 percent of the people who lived in Palestine of their rights. It had seriously undermined future avenues for their national self-determination.

Much ink has been spilled on the reasons behind Britain's decision, and there is no need here to rehash the historical record (for more on Balfour, see chapter 2). Suffice it to say that Balfour's blatant disregard for Palestinian national aspirations is cynically revealed in a memorandum he wrote two years after the declaration: "For in Palestine we do not propose even to go through the form of consulting the wishes of the present inhabitants of the country.... The four great powers are committed to Zionism and Zionism be it right or wrong, good or bad, is rooted in age-long tradition, in present needs, in future hopes, of far profounder import than the desires and prejudices of the 700 000 Arabs who now inhabit that ancient land. In my opinion, that is right."[48]

Balfour dismissed the agency of 700,000 Palestinian Arabs as hollow in comparison to the interests of the Great Powers. Back then and now the agency of the people in the region is hardly factored in the decisions of local autocrats and their superpower patrons.

Imperial calculations, rivalries, and self-interest were key drivers behind Britain's declaration. By backing the Zionist cause internationally, Britain sought to ensure the loyalty of what it saw as a major strategic ally at home and abroad. The Balfour Declaration also provided Britain with an opportunity to gain strategic advantage over France, its main imperial rival. Although the French might have been angry at the machinations of a Great Power rival, the Arabs were shocked by British duplicity and cynicism.[49]

To this day, Palestinians still hold protests on the anniversary of the Balfour Declaration that set out British backing for a Jewish homeland in Palestine. For Palestinians, Balfour is a historic moment that embodies a century of betrayal, loss, settler colonialism, and resistance. For them, that betrayal and suffering would be repeated over and over again in the decades that followed the declaration. "The war on Palestine passed the 100-year mark with the Palestinians confronting circumstances more daunting than perhaps at any time since 1917," noted Rashid Khalidi, a distinguished Palestinian-American historian at Columbia University, in his new book.[50]

The Past and the Present: What It All Means

These initial imperial interventions by Britain and France in the Middle East played a crucial role at the time and they continue to do so today. In the popular imagination of the Arab world, colonial Britain and France (Sir Mark Sykes and François Georges-Picot) castrated the region to ensure its impotence and submissiveness to foreign powers. A consensus exists among people regardless of their class, sect, or social background that the postwar borders of the Middle East militated against the economic development of the newly created small countries and made them dependent on foreign aid and tutelage for survival.[51] As a result, for the millions of people whose lives were most directly affected by Sykes-Picot, a direct line runs from the colonial moment to the current crisis. For these people, British and French promises mean nothing but betrayal.

The impact of these colonial processes has lingered and is discernible not only in the ways actors within the region think about their past but also in the persistence of colonial narratives. All of which suggests that even after formal territorial decolonization, these viewpoints have not been decolonized. The various colonial projects (from Sykes-Picot to Balfour) and postcolonial borders established the precedent of handing down rulings from on high, with no consideration of the common man or his desires.

Because of this, if we wish to understand the twenty-first-century Middle East and the crises it faces, we must first understand how that world was created. The purpose of revisiting this significant moment in the history of the Middle East is not to deliver an indictment of the borders drawn by Britain and France or, for that matter, to pass judgment on the performance of the old regimes or the colonial state. Rather, the goal is to demonstrate the enduring legacy of the colonial moment on both the frontiers and the institutions of the Middle Eastern state system, as well as on the imagination and psychology of the inhabitants. Equipped with this awareness, we can more fully understand the importance of the colonial powers in the construction of the Middle Eastern state-system construction and its impact on the life of the people and regional conflicts.

2

The Great Betrayal

WHAT WAS PROMISED AND WHAT WAS DELIVERED

THERE IS A CRUEL IRONY behind the creation of the modern Middle East. In spite of claims by Britain and France that they wanted to achieve a kind of "Arab statehood" and a "national home for the Jewish people," *neither* country envisioned a system of sovereign nation-states during their negotiations in 1916.[1] Rather than establishing independent nation-states, they used the "Mandate System" to consolidate imperial control of the region.

This system came about thanks to US president Woodrow Wilson's support for national self-determination and his rejection of territorial annexation by the European powers. When the League of Nations adopted this policy, people living under foreign rule welcomed it with enthusiasm. Their enthusiasm suited the European powers because London and Paris saw an advantage in "native rule." After the war, neither Britain nor France could rule their new colonial territories through their own armies and bureaucracies. They lacked the resources. Instead, the European powers relied on local elites to run the *internal* affairs of the Mandate territories, while they directly controlled foreign affairs but exercised a profound influence over decision-making through the close relationships they established with the new elites. The McMahon-Husayn correspondence is an example of this. The Sykes-Picot Agreement of 1916 is another part of this colonial approach, which saw Britain and France access new territories and resources, while minimizing the material and military costs of controlling them.

The relationships and precedents established by colonial Britain and France in these years established a pattern that resembles the ways that foreign intervention and domestic authoritarianism still interact up through the present. It is important to remind the reader of the book's analytical framework, which focuses on the interdependence of foreign intervention and domestic authoritarianism of today, with today's strongmen taking the place of those colonial local elites, who also depended on foreign powers to shore up their control.

The Sykes-Picot Agreement and the post–World War I peace settlements were not the first attempt by European colonial powers to partition the Middle East. On the contrary, the Sykes-Picot agreement and the San Remo Conference, which followed after the war, were the culmination of a dual aim. The first was a material-political aim to accumulate resources and wealth. This ushered in a long struggle among the Great Powers of Europe to establish a dominant position in the Ottoman Empire and to instrumentalize that influence against each other. From the nineteenth century onward, the Ottoman Empire and the greater Middle East therefore became a theater where rival European powers battled one another for supremacy.

The second aim was missionary: European powers believed it was their duty to civilize the "barbaric" Orient.[2] This belief rested on a colonial mentality that viewed non-Europeans as "other" people who were intellectually and morally inferior. It served to justify colonialism as both necessary and inevitable and it helped fuel Great Power competition over the spoils from the colonies. Because of increasing global pressure to justify colonial practices, it was crucially important to maintain the image of an "inferior other" as it enabled colonial powers to treat their colonies as exceptions and, as a result, not subject to the legal structures of the League of Nations. Instead of acknowledging the agency of the people, British and French officials depicted riots and contentious politics as evidence of the inability of local societies to respect the rule of law and maintain order. According to London and Paris, these societies therefore had to be controlled.

In describing the emergence of the colonial state system of the Middle East, this chapter will analyze key historical events through the three analytical threads or principles set up in the introduction. In this context, British and French colonialism represents the utmost expression of foreign intervention, which is the first lens that helps us to make sense of Middle Eastern politics. Colonialism will not be seen as an isolated, unilateral phenomenon but instead as a continuous process of interaction with local actors. This dialectical relationship between local rulers and their external patrons plays a critical role in framing political institutions and in the unfolding of the endless conflicts that continue to afflict the region.

The Imperial Tensions between Britain and France

France and Britain were far from united. Britain's entente cordiale with France was only the result of new alliances developing among the European powers in the late nineteenth century. Britain chose to stand alone for as long as possible, preferring to maintain an isolationist position. Britain's stance, however, began to change when industrial and naval competition with Germany increased. London's view of Germany as a threat to British interests finally led Britain to negotiate with France. In the course of those negotiations, the two countries sought to resolve disputes that had, until then, kept them entangled in a tense relationship for more than twenty years.[3] As part of their new relationship, Britain and France began to remake the Middle East.[4]

Under the entente cordiale, Britain agreed to give France a free hand in Morocco if France agreed to give Britain a free hand in Egypt. In its perpetual search for a "friendly prince"[5] in the Middle East, Britain was aware that gaining control over Egypt was vital to securing power over the Suez Canal and protecting the sea route to India. For France, Morocco was the gateway to French imperial territories further south in Africa. Power brokers in London and Paris saw the Entente as a win-win strategy: it secured, at no military cost, each country's sphere of interests.

The entente cordiale was later expanded to include Russia in 1907 in what could be termed as the second stage of partition in the Middle

East.[6] And again, the motivation was similar: to secure a sphere of interest at no military cost. Under the new Entente, Britain and Russia agreed to reduce their competition for influence in Persia by recognizing mutual spheres of interest. Russia would exercise power over the north of the country, Britain over the south, thus securing a land route from India to the Mediterranean.[7] This new deal "raised the specter of Great Power cooperation in dismembering the empire" and led the Ottoman Empire to strengthen its economic, military, and diplomatic ties with Germany.[8]

In a way, Ottoman leaders were correct about the threat posed by the European powers because the start of the war initiated the third stage of partition of the Middle East: a process that would reach its conclusion in 1920 at the San Remo Conference. Toward the end of the war, Britain increased its promises in the Middle East in a bid to maximize its position before the end of the war and any peace settlement that would follow. In December 1917, following the capture of Jerusalem by the British, General Edmund Allenby announced that Britain sought "the complete and final liberation of all peoples formerly oppressed by the Turks and the establishment of national governments and administrations in those countries deriving authority from the initiative and free will of those people themselves."[9]

Such promises exacerbated tensions between Britain and France because they appeared to undermine the Sykes-Picot Agreement, particularly France's claim over Syria. As far as the conqueror of Jerusalem, General Allenby, was concerned, Sykes-Picot set out that France was entitled only to those parts of Lebanon west of the districts of Damascus, Homs, Hama, and Aleppo—an interpretation vehemently rejected by France.

In October 1918 tensions between the two colonial powers reached boiling point when Allied troops destroyed Turkish resistance in Damascus. The British allowed Emir Faisal, Husayn's son, Lord Kitchener, and his Arab forces to be the first detachment to enter the city, thus declaring Damascus "liberated by the Arabs" and independent. Allenby then allowed Faisal to establish himself in Damascus and to set up an Arab administrative system and government. This bitterly disappointed the French who, thanks to Sykes-Picot, had expected to control inner Syria.

More disappointment for the French was to follow when British prime minister David Lloyd George sanctioned an independent Arab state in Syria under British sponsorship. Such a state precluded French occupation of the area and aligned the British with Arab nationalist aspirations. Lloyd George's decision was motivated by the new facts on the ground in the Middle East. For Lloyd George, it was Britain who won the war in Iraq and Britain therefore had a greater right to control it. This was supported by Allenby who warned France any attempt to mount a military takeover of Syria would lead to trouble with the Arabs. He went so far as to suggest the French would not be tolerated in Syria.[10]

From the end of the war to the San Remo Conference, Britain and France repeatedly attempted to resolve their dispute over Syria. In December 1918, Lloyd George and the French prime minster Georges Clemenceau met secretly in London to settle areas of disagreement before the Paris Peace Conference in 1919.[11] At this meeting the concessions made by Sykes on Mosul and Palestine would be corrected at the expense of Syria.

Clemenceau agreed on condition that the rest of the agreement be upheld and, more importantly, that Aleppo and Damascus be included, along with Lebanon, in the area under direct French control. Furthermore, Clemenceau and Lloyd George agreed that when oil production began in Mosul, France would receive a share of around 20 percent.[12]

The exchange between Lloyd George and Georges Clemenceau is revealing for what it shows about the colonial mindset and its blatant disregard for the interests of local people. The British and French prime ministers traded cities and countries like they were trading sheep. Britain's and France's dealing with Emir Faisal is a case in point.

The Betrayal of the Arabs

The Arabs, represented mainly by Husayn's son, Emir Faisal, worked tirelessly to ensure Britain delivered on the terms set out in the McMahon-Husayn letters. Emir Faisal was the commander of the Arab Revolt in 1916–1918 and, until the end of the war, he would have thought of himself as an ally of Britain and France. Faisal had spent much of his childhood in Istanbul and was elected to the Ottoman Parliament in 1913 to represent Jeddah. When he visited Damascus in 1916, Faisal was appalled by Cemel Pasha's repressive measures against Arab nationalists. This inspired Faisal to start communicating with members of secret Arab nationalist societies in Damascus and to take a leading role in the Arab Revolt.[13]

At the Paris Peace Conference, Faisal presented a memorandum in which he set out the aspirations of the Arab people and the image of a united Arab nation: "If our independence be conceded and our local competence established, the natural influences of race, language and interests will soon draw us into one people."[14] Such declarations were awkward for Britain and France. The colonial powers were more interested in dividing the spoils of the Ottoman Empire between themselves than granting Arabs unfettered self-determination, particularly if such self-determination led to the establishment of a united Arab nation.

The British and French might have been able to sideline Faisal at the peace conference but they could not ignore the Americans. US president Woodrow Wilson's Fourteen Points inspired people across the Middle East to dream of self-determination and independence. The twelfth point addresses Arab aspirations specifically and stipulated that "the Turkish portion of the present Ottoman Empire should be assured a secure sovereignty, but the other nationalities which are now under Turkish rule should be assured an undoubted security of life and an absolutely unmolested opportunity of autonomous development." This point together with Wilson's emphasis on national self-determination gave great hope to the Arabs. Wilson also suggested the formation of a multinational commission of enquiry to travel to Syria and determine the wishes of the Arab people there. France and Britain joined forces to thwart the plan. They declined to nominate officials to take part, effectively undermining the validity of what became known as the King-Crane Commission.[15]

The commission toured villages in Lebanon, Palestine, Syria, and Transjordan in June 1919. Arabs saw it as an acknowledgment of their aspirations and welcomed its delegates with a wave of enthusiasm and hope. In July 1919, the Syrian Congress wrote to the commission to explain their rejection of both the Sykes-Picot Agreement and the Balfour Declaration. The congress stated that "the fundamental principles laid down by President Wilson in condemnation of secret treaties impel us to protest most emphatically against any treaty that stipulates the partition of our Syrian country and against any private engagement aiming at the establishment of Zionism in the southern part of Syria; therefore we ask for the complete annulment of these conventions."[16]

In its findings, the King-Crane Commission largely reflected the aspirations of local people. The commission called for a single unified Syrian state with Faisal as king. It also recommended that Syria be placed under a temporary mandate but only for a limited period and purely for the purpose of providing support. And that the mandatory power should be the United States. Britain was the second choice. Finally, the commission noted that the Balfour Declaration's promises to establish a Jewish national home in Palestine and to respect "the civil and religious rights of existing non-Jewish in Palestine" could not be reconciled.[17]

But these recommendations were never implemented. The report was shelved without further consultation when it was presented to the peace conference secretariat in August 1919. It was only made public three years later. And by then, France and Britain had divided the remnants of the Ottoman Empire and created new facts on the ground. Denied self-determination, Arabs faced the full force of European colonialism alone. Colonial Britain and France systemically ignored the will of the Arab people and their aspirations for freedom and self-determination.

Britain and France now drew closer, if only for reasons of mutual convenience. On November 1, 1919, Britain declared its intention to withdraw from Syria and Lebanon and hand over power to France. This came as a shock to the Syrian people. The Syrian General Congress, whose hopes of independence had risen during the King-Crane Commission, took matters into their own hands and prepared to declare independence. The Declaration of Independence was based on the findings of the commission and proclaimed Faisal king of Lebanon, Palestine, and Syria.[18]

Unsurprisingly, the British and the French refused to accept both declarations. France prepared to occupy Syria. The fight for Syria came to a head in the Battle of Maysalun on July 24, 1920. The battle took place in

Khan Maysalun about 50 kilometers west of Damascus and was led by Faisal's minister of war, Yusuf al-'Azmah. A group of around 2,000 Arab volunteers joined the battle but were swiftly and viciously defeated by the colonial power.

In her important book, the historian Elizabeth Thompson refers to the actions of colonial France in Syria as the Western "theft" of Arab democracy. France and Britain crushed the nascent democratic experiment led by Emir Faisal, which included a liberal constitution that enshrined the rights of all people, Muslims and non-Muslims.[19]

The symbolic value of this battle in Syria cannot be underestimated. Despite the dramatic defeat of the Arabs, the Battle of Maysalun is celebrated in Syria and the wider Middle East as an iconic moment, a courageous rebellion against a powerful imperial power. It clearly shows the active agency of the Arab people against colonial control and domination.

Colonialism under a New Disguise: The Mandate System

Convened in April 1920, the San Remo Conference would eventually supersede and modify many elements of the secret Franco-British plan for direct rule over the Arab territories of the former Ottoman Empire What *did* survive of the Sykes-Picot Agreement were the understandings between France and Great Britain concerning their respective interests and spheres of influence across the heartlands of the Middle East. These understandings formed the basis of the San Remo Conference and were subsequently recognized by the League of Nations.

Arranged in a hurry, the San Remo Conference sought to strike a balance between the contradictory goals of colonial rule and the Allies' pre-armistice declarations recognizing President Wilson's Fourteen Points preventing the direct annexation of these lands.[20] The result was the birth of the Mandate System. The system granted the Allied victors administrative rights over the Arab lands of the former Ottoman Empire until such time as these countries were thought to be able to "stand alone." This decision was classic colonial ideology: the notion that Arabs were inferior and so needed "tutelage" from the advanced Europeans to be able to progress to the same level. It went against the wishes and aspirations of the Arab people.

The construction of the Mandate System also represented a "European change of heart": a novel approach to imperialism demonstrating that "Europe was no longer unreservedly imperialist in good conscience."[21] Britain and France were in the unique position of meeting and securing their strategic interests while paying lip service to the principle of self-determination. This form of "diplomatic doublespeak" persists to this day and is one of the main reasons for Arab distrust of the West. Over the course of the next few years, the League of Nations would recognize three mandates: the British Mandate for Palestine; the French Mandate for Syria including modern-day Lebanon; and the British Mandate for Mesopotamia or Iraq.

However, the actual implementation of these mandates was far from smooth. Revolts soon broke out in Syria and Iraq.[22] Imperial rivalry between France and Britain also contributed to the turmoil. It took more than three years for France and Britain to pacify their new territorial acquisitions, and it was only following these lengthy negotiations that the modern borders of the Arab Levant slowly began to emerge.

Needless to say, Arab opinion was distrustful of Anglo-French intentions. The Mandate period was "marked by recriminations over secret diplomacy and haunted by lingering visions of what might have been if Faysal's Syrian kingdom had been allowed to survive."[23] To Arabs, Britain had sacrificed Faisal at the altar of their imperial understanding with the French. Britain's promises to the Arabs during the war years were clearly not credible and had been designed to convince them to revolt against the Ottoman Empire. As time passed, Arabs became painfully aware of their role as pawns during the revolt. Having sacrificed their allegiance with the Ottoman Empire for the West, Arabs did not expect, nor could they comprehend, the betrayal that followed.

The contradictory and cynical nature of British policy in the Middle East was nowhere as evident as it was in Palestine. In 1919, Britain officially agreed to the idea of self-determination set out by US president Woodrow Wilson. To that end, the British backed Faisal's call for an Arab state in Damascus in spite of London's prior agreements with Paris. Yet, at the very same time, Britain flat out rejected Palestinian claims for self-determination in Palestine in favor of Jewish claims. As Balfour him-self explained: "We regard Palestine as being absolutely exceptional . . . and that we conceive the Jews to have an historic claim to a home in their ancient land; provided that home can be given without their dispossess-ing or oppressing the present inhabitants."[24]

Balfour's argument had one very clear message: the aspirations and opinions of the 700,000 indigenous Palestinian Arabs were of no conse-quence or significance.[25]

The founding fathers of the Zionist movement likewise paid hardly any attention to the future reaction of Palestinians to mass Jewish immigra-tion. They even invented the myth of "a land without a people for a people without a land." Theodor Herzl and the British-Jewish diplomat Chaim Weizmann (Russian in origin) barely mentioned the Palestinians in any of their correspondence and statements because they assumed the Pal-estinians would welcome the arrival of an advanced European commu-nity to develop their "backward" homeland.[26] Arabs and their supporters therefore see Israel as an extension of the Western colonial project. Israelis and their supporters, however, see the creation of the state of Israel as a return home. This difference in perspective is one of the (many) reasons the situation is so hard to resolve, but it is often overlooked.[27]

The British Mandate for Palestine was recognized by the Council of the League of Nations on July 24, 1922, and was subsequently amended in September of that year to account for the creation of Transjordan on the lands east of the Jordan River. The British Mandate for Palestine ar-rogated national rights exclusively to Jews who were at that time a tiny minority of the population. The word "Arab" or "Palestinian" does not actually occur in the Mandate or in the Balfour Declaration. Instead, Arab Palestinians are defined by negation, by who they are *not*: they are referred to as "existing non-Jewish communities in Palestine" even though at the time they made up 94 percent of the population.[28]

Between 1920 and 1923 France and Britain negotiated a series of ar-rangements that stipulated the boundaries between their respective Mandate possessions. Known as the Paulet-Newcombe Agreement or the Franco-British Boundary Agreements, these were approved by France and Britain in March 1923. The agreement set out the boundaries between the

Mandates for Syria and Lebanon, Palestine and Mesopotamia. But even this agreement was not final. The borders of "greater" Lebanon only became established in 1924. Other significant adjustments occurred to the borders of Syria and Iraq during the same period. The same was also true of Jordan (formerly Transjordan), where the eastern borders of the kingdom were established after 1923.[29]

In Iraq, the British Mandate System was recognized by the Anglo-Iraqi Treaty in October 1922. The treaty came about following the Cairo Conference, which was convened in 1921 after fighting broke out in Iraq and Syria against the Mandate powers. The Iraqi revolt against the British began as a peaceful movement in May 1920 and encompassed a wide cross-section of Iraqi society. But within a month it had developed into an armed revolt after Ayotallah Muhammad Taqi al-Ha'iri al-Shirazi issued a fatwa[30] declaring, "It is the duty of the Iraqis to demand their rights."[31]

From the beginning Arabs resisted French and British imperialism as well as settler colonialism by the Zionists. Far from dormant, Arab agency has been active against both colonialism and domestic authoritarianism.

Initially, the tribes enjoyed success but in the long run, Iraqi guns were no match for the military might of the British Empire. The revolt was quashed in October 1920 after the British began using warplanes against the rebels in an early example of carpet-bombing. To achieve their victory, the British had benefited from the support of a number of tribes and also from former Ottoman officers who saw their future best guaranteed by a British mandate. The Anglo-Iraqi Treaty restored greater, albeit nominal, independence to Iraq and recognized Britain's erstwhile ally Faisal as king in August 1921. This was the same Faisal who had ruled Syria for two months before being militarily defeated by the French colonial authorities and ousted.

The Cairo Conference saw another member of Faisal's family ascend another throne: the British installed Faisal's brother, Abdullah ibn Hussein, as regent of Transjordan, a newly created entity carved out of the British Mandate for Palestine. In his memoirs, Winston Churchill boasted he had created the emirate of Transjordan by the stroke of his pen, which is an example of "informal empire."[32]

The 1922 Anglo-Iraqi Treaty was superseded by another treaty in 1930 granting Britain greater economic rights in the country and laying the path to formal independence, which Iraq achieved in October 1932. The British Mandate for Iran, Palestine, and Transjordan, as well as the French Mandates for Syria and Lebanon, all entered into legal force following the ratification of the Treaty of Lausanne in July 1923.

Exceptions to the Rule: Turkey and Iran

In contrast to their Arab neighbors in the Levant, Turkey and Iran successfully managed to resist colonial construction and partition. Led by Mustafa Kemal, the Turkish war hero and veteran of the Battle of Gallipoli, Turkey overturned the colonial plans to divide its territory as set out in the Treaty of Sèvres of 1920. Similarly, Iran also escaped colonial partition, although Britain and Russia never quite gave up their ambitions in this oil-rich country and reoccupied it for a short period during World War II to protect Allied oil supplies.

But the Turkish and Iranian victories against colonial power were hard won. In the wake of World War I, the Allies were in no mood to give anything away. The Turks had to fight for their independence on the battlefield. With his military expertise, Mustafa Kemal proved the man of the hour. From then on, he was known simply as Atatürk, "Father of the Turks," in recognition of his role as the founding father of the Turkish Republic. The emergence of modern Turkey was officially recognized by the Allied powers in 1923.[33]

Dysfunctional and broken, the Arab states now stood in very stark contrast to Turkey and Iran, both of whom snatched victory from the jaws of the colonial powers and did not therefore experience direct colonial rule after the war. This contrast between what happened in Turkey and Iran and what happened in Arab lands has not gone unnoticed. Arab academics, politicians, and writers often compare the fragmentation and institutional fragility of the Arab Middle East to the constitutional coherence and institutional solidity of Turkey and Iran, two regional powers that fought for and preserved their territorial integrity.[34]

This is not, of course, to say that everything has been plain sailing in either Turkey or Iran. The military has long played a disproportionate role in Turkish public life, and it repeatedly stepped into the political arena to oust popular and unpliant politicians in 1960, 1971, 1980, and 1997. The most recent military coup attempt was in July 2016, when officers achieved the opposite of what they intended and ended up strengthening the power of President Recep Tayyip Erdoğan. Iran, first under the shahs then under the clerics, has not developed into a free and open society. Both countries face significant other problems, not least of which is the predicament facing their large Kurdish minorities, who feel like second-class citizens excluded from the mainstream.

Furthermore, Turkey and Iran have been affected by the colonial enterprise and the implementation of state-building in the region. In spite of an absence of direct European rule, Turkey and Iran have had to deal with the consequences of European social engineering in the region. Iran, which sought to nationalize oil in early 1950s and use the resources to modernize the country and lift its people out of poverty, triggered covert military intervention by the United States and Britain. Both Western powers staged a coup in August 1953 that ousted the legitimately elected prime minister Mohammad Mossadegh and installed the shah of Iran as an absolute ruler.[35]

The major difference, however, between Turkey and Iran, on the one hand, and the colonially constructed Arab states on the other, lies in how society was shaped *after* the lines were drawn on the map.[36] Free of outside interference, the leaders of Turkey and Iran at least had the chance to map their own future. Whatever mistakes were made were their own.

The Enduring Legacy of Colonialism

The long series of British and French interventions in the Arab world amplify the historical irony that "the Middle East" as we know it today was not made in the Middle East. It was envisioned and constructed in Europe through a variety of negotiations, agreements, and political processes in which actors *from* the region were, by and large, excluded.[37]

In the eyes of all the peoples in the region, the roots of the ongoing domestic political turmoil and regional instability are traceable to the postwar peace settlements and to colonial rule in the years between the two world wars. From its very inception, the state system in the Arab Middle East lacked legitimacy. It was seen as the product of colonialism. This widespread popular perception has endured and continues to shape the imagination of leading social movements in the region.

However, it is important to note that the rationale for the colonialism of European powers at times differs from how it was represented and reproduced in popular imaginations in the Middle East. The so-called Mandate System under the banner of the League of Nations and the spirit of US president Woodrow Wilson enabled and consolidated British and French control over the Middle East; the "Mandate" whitewashed colonial practices in more benevolent terms. The Mandate System also increasingly forced Britain and France to justify their colonial projects, particularly as people in the Middle East staged protests and armed revolts in order to get rid of domination. The agency of the Arab people forced the colonial powers to try to rebrand their project and appeal to the population.

A few recent articles by Western commentators and academics have aimed at "debunking the myth" of the Sykes-Picot Agreement and the impact of colonialism in general. These Western commentators profess to be "tired" of hearing about colonialism when trying to make sense of the violent storm raging in the Middle East and dismiss the impact of the colonial origins of the borders as an overplayed "myth."[38] These revisionist accounts underestimate the pervasive psychological consequences the colonial mandates have had on the people in the Middle East. Historical realities are important but the perceptions and constructions of history are just as significant.

Colonialism has left deep psychological scars on how Arabs see the outside world and define their relationship with it. Arabs' early encounter with the colonial European powers proved to be fateful. They lost faith not only in Europe but also with the very idea of representative democracy. Europe's betrayal of the Arabs convinced many that sinister conspiracies are a constant feature of international politics that shape their future and over which they have little control. Arabs mainly view the last 100 years of Western intervention in the region through the lens of "conspiracy," be it Sykes-Picot; US president Donald Trump's "Deal of the Century" for normalization of relations between Israel and the Arab states; or the unconditional support that his successor, Joe Biden, provided to Israel's war in Gaza in 2023–2024.[39]

People of all persuasions in the region assign significant weight to the colonial construction of the state system and its legacy. Over the years I have met a wide range of people—journalists, public intellectuals, students, small business owners, blue collar workers, farmers, fruit and vegetable vendors—who say the state system was rigged by the European colonial powers to their own advantage. They insist the seeds of the current failure of so many Middle Eastern states were sown in the secret agreements, particularly Sykes-Picot, that the imperial powers made during World War I and the postwar peace settlements. Arabs believe colonial Britain and France consciously partitioned their lands into small, unworkable states to facilitate their control of the region and its resources. The organic unity of "the Arab nation" was sacrificed at the altar of European imperialism, a claim held as an article of faith by millions of people.

Once the Middle East was carved up according to their wishes, all that remained for Britain and France was to find the forms and institutions of government through which they could maintain their control. In doing so, they would come up against the same obstacle time and time again: they did not have the consent of the governed. From the holy city of Jerusalem to the cosmopolitan hub of Beirut to the city of *A Thousand and One Nights* in Baghdad, people right across the region could not, and would not, forget that the new Middle East had been drawn up in secret, behind closed doors, at conferences on another continent, at their expense and against their interests. And that colonial Britain and France installed their loyal clients at the helm of the new states to do their bidding. The gap between the lofty rhetoric of the colonial powers and the dismal reality of how they governed would place a fault line through the very state structure those colonial powers were trying to build.

3

Rhetoric versus Reality

THE CONTRADICTIONS
OF THE COLONIAL STATE

THE FUNDAMENTAL CHALLENGE facing the colonial-sponsored state system unfolded in three very distinct, but interrelated, ways. First, it created elites that embraced global capitalism at the cost of social inequality. Second, it demanded the loyalty of people who had previously lived under different forms of social organization during the Ottoman period, emphasizing centralization and top-down authority along Western models. And third, it ignited major concerns and problems about the place of Middle Easterners in the wider world—an issue that still resonates today. Any one of these layers of problems might have been managed satisfactorily had it existed alone. But the parallel existence of the other two led to severe contradictions in social dynamics: complications that undermined both state-building and nation-building.[1]

For all of these reasons, from its very inception, the state system in the Arab Middle East lacked legitimacy and authenticity. Britain and France not only drew the lines on the map, they made the rules for everything else. They left no aspect of public life in these new states untouched. Everything from the structure of the states to the role of religion in politics, to the organization of the army and the economy, to the aspirations of the elites: all were shaped by London and Paris.[2] In doing so, Britain and France made sure they would continue to influence the conduct of the postindependence state that inherited the colonial state after the end of World War II.[3]

Yet, in spite of these complexities, many commentators often reduce the colonial impact to the newly drawn borders in the region as if those state boundaries—and nothing else—caused all the problems. In many ways, it was the deceit, the betrayal, and the hubris of authoritarian colonial rule that angered Arab populations the most. When conservative analysts reduce the issue to borders alone, it portrays Arab people as unable to cope with change. Or worse: as unprepared to govern themselves. This was not, and never has been, the case. The reality is, and always has been, that Arab populations were, and are, unwilling to accept foreign domination and settler colonialism. For example, from the 1920s to the present, the Palestinians have resisted Israel's military occupation of their lands.

But in opposing colonialism, Arabs faced overwhelming odds. They were up against nothing less than the new postwar world order. The League of Nations Covenant Article 22 stipulates that territories in the Middle East and Africa are "inhabited by peoples not yet able to stand by themselves under the strenuous conditions of the modern world."[4] This assertion was used to legitimize British and French colonialism in the Middle East but also to endorse a claim of Western superiority.

Nowhere, arguably, was this more evident than in Egypt. From 1883 to 1907, British Consul General Evelyn Baring, Lord Cromer, single-handedly ruled the land of the pharaohs. Nicknamed "Over-Baring" by the people who worked for him because of his imperious manner, he once infamously said "Egyptians should be permitted to govern themselves after the fashion in which Europeans think they ought to be governed." A roundabout way of saying Britain had no intention of allowing the future of Egypt to be decided by the Egyptian people. But thanks to the wiggle room written into the Mandate System, the colonial powers no longer had to worry about such an eventuality. They rigged the system so heavily in their own favor; they made sure there was no chance of it happening. And British officials in Cromer's old stomping ground of Egypt showed just how it was done.

To expose the multifaceted nature of colonialism and its consequences on local politics and societies, this chapter will examine the Egyptian case, arguably the first of the large Middle Eastern countries to be colonized. I will then show how these practices by colonial Britain were exported to the new Mandate states of the Levant in the 1920s and their long-term effects as well. The mutually beneficial relationship between the colonial patrons and the local rulers, as emphasized in the Introduction, developed in this period into a mutually reinforcing process of foreign influence and political authoritarianism.

A Case Study in Colonialism: Egypt

After World War I, an unholy alliance developed between the British colonial authorities and the Egyptian ruling family.[5] This unholy alliance of king and colonizer trampled over the will of the people. And just as Cromer intended, ordinary Egyptians were systematically deprived of the right to decide their country's future. Instead, they were forced to put up with a monarchical elite whose authority came not from the people but from their colonial masters.

Far from seeing themselves as puppets, Egypt's kings used the new status quo to consolidate their own position. Both for themselves and for the British, it was a win-win situation: the British conspired with the Palace to establish a royal autocracy and circumvent constitutional authority; the Palace conspired with the British to ensure the failure of constitutional politics and eliminate the opposition.[6]

By frequently intervening in the country's internal affairs and overseeing repeated violent assaults against protesters, the alliance between the British and the Palace served as a constant reminder to Egyptians from all walks of life that they were not in control of their country's destiny. United by grievances caused by the abuse of power and the lack of an inclusive vision for Egypt's future, a consensus developed on the need to replace the corrupt political class who had failed to defend Egyptian national interests or to deliver on the promises of independence and restoring national pride.

Deteriorating living standards across the Arab world compounded these political failures. Socioeconomic indicators declined. The rising cost of living fueled resentment, anger, and, eventually, underground armed opposition. Here, too, Egypt stands out as an instructive case for the entire region. The dismal social conditions that prevailed after World War II eroded whatever credibility the colonially backed ruling elite had left. Foreign corporations tended to employ foreign residents, leaving Egyptians "little chance of being employed in business houses."[7] High unemployment among the population fueled civil strife and popular grievances against the status quo.[8]

In this febrile atmosphere, even successful government policies such as the tripling of enrollment in state secondary schools and the doubling of enrollment at the Egyptian University did not generate public support for the government. And with increased education comes increased expectation. But the government did not deliver. Resentment also spread against the liberal-nationalist ruling party, the Wafd, as inefficient government services led ordinary Egyptians to lose faith in established avenues of political expression and reform.

These dynamics were further aggravated by a collapse in cotton prices in the early 1920s, with prices dropping tenfold from an index figure of 200 at the end of 1920 to only 20 in March 1921, a fall that led to a dramatic 10 percent decline in per capita income. This drop was felt most acutely among the *fellahin*, the Egyptian peasantry.[9] As the conditions of workers worsened still further during the Great Depression, Egypt faced a social crisis that resulted in "severe economic contraction."[10] The country's exports lost more than a third of their value between 1928 and 1933, partly because of a drop in the global price of cotton from US$26 to US$10 per kantar.[11]

This severe economic crisis could have been tackled, according to most political opposition at the time, with a comprehensive national development program based on land reforms and an expansion of local manufacturing. However, foreign interests continued to dominate *both* the economic and political realms. To make matters worse, instead of passing legislation to deal with the declining socioeconomic situation and to alleviate the suffering of the urban poor and agrarian laborers, the ruling political elite squeezed the emerging trade unions in a bid to weaken the workers' movement, which had long been a hotbed of Egyptian political activism.

The inflationary hardship caused by World War II accentuated these challenges even further and radicalized public opinion to such an extent that new groups with a more subversive and revolutionary tone appeared on the scene. The Ikhwan (the Muslim Brothers), an Islamist organization; Misr al-Fatat (Young Egypt), a faction sympathetic to European fascism; and the growing number of Egyptian communists were three examples of radical alternative politics that had already been active since the inter-war period but whose strength significantly increased after World War II. These movements were willing to use violence for political ends, drawing important support from an increasingly disaffected and disenfran-chised population.

In the midst of these challenges, the Wafd lost its way. Disconnected from its own support base, the Wafd, like the king, became more depen-dent on the British. With many corrupt and unscrupulous personalities within its ranks, the Wafd squandered its political capital. But the dam-age spread beyond the party itself. The Wafd was more than just the party of power, it was the guardian of liberal constitutionalism in Egypt. So when its fortunes fell, so did support and hope for a gradualist transition away from colonialism into a liberal and constitutional state.

In theory, Egypt's constitutional-based monarchy allowed for the for-mation of a ruling political community, but in practice, as was so often the case under colonialism, the situation proved very different. The Brit-ish and the Palace exercised control and often violated the spirit and letter of the constitution. The convergence of a deepening political divide with ever more grim socioeconomic conditions produced a severe crisis of authority and utterly discredited the ruling elite, including Egyptian capitalists who had originally aimed to challenge foreign enterprise and capital.[12]

The British and the king, the two most powerful political forces in Egypt, played a fundamental role in this failure.[13] From the outset, both regarded constitutionalism as a threat to their ambitions and spared no effort to thwart its advance in society. In the process, they successfully co-opted, or repressed, any political representatives elected by the populace, such as the Wafd Party. By doing so, they fostered a deep disillusion within the public toward liberalism and constitutionalism, a point worth re-membering when considering the historical causes of the lack of democracy in Egypt and the Arab world.

This inherent contradiction—the façade of a modern state with the infrastructure of a colonial one—was not confined to Egypt. It happened across the Arab world. Thus, what happened under the British in Cairo also happened under the British in Baghdad and under the French in Syria. However, a key difference between Egypt and other Arab lands is that Egypt's borders and identity had been set long before British occupation of the country in the late nineteenth century and was inscribed in its geography. But this was not the case for Arab countries of the Levant.

More of the Same: Iraq and Syria

Like in Egypt, Britain and France undermined the nascent constitutional process in Iraq and Syria in disregard of local nationalist sentiments. The newly established constitutional monarchies and new ruling elites were not free to govern without undue pressure from the Mandatory powers. The colonial authorities frequently intervened to prevent any meaningful change that could challenge their control. It was a policy that backfired on many levels. Britain and France ended up delegitimizing their local allies and undermining the very institutions they themselves had set up.

Iraq was initially considered the most successful of the British Mandates.[14] In spite of a popular revolt against the British in 1920 that was costly in blood and treasure, King Faisal was appointed in 1921 and a Constituent Assembly was elected in 1924. In 1932 a new treaty was ne-gotiated between Britain and Iraq that would eventually lead to the coun-try's (formal) independence and its admission to the League of Nations.[15] Yet in spite of this apparent success, the domestic situation in Iraq under the British Mandate was febrile, and tensions were building that would plague the country for decades to come.

One of the main problems faced by the Iraqi state was the difficulty of forming a new national army. In trying to recruit a cross-section of Iraq's society into the national army, King Faisal found himself facing opposition from the Shia and Kurdish communities, who objected to conscription "as to any government initiative they believed gave disproportionate power to the minority Sunni Arab community," including the many ex-Ottoman officers and military men who had served alongside Faisal in the Arab Revolt.[16] This lack of unity proved to be a source of great frustration for Faisal who notoriously declared: "There is still—and I saw this with a heart full of sorrow—no Iraqi people but unimaginable masses of human beings, devoid of any patriotic idea, imbued with religious traditions and absurdities, connected by no common tie, giving ear to evil, prone to anarchy, and perpetually ready to rise against any government whatever."[17] In Faisal's view, the army was the "spinal column for the nation-forming,"[18] and he made efforts to associate the Shia with the new Iraqi state, promising young Shia men an accelerated program of training and the chance of rapid promotion to positions of responsibility. Similarly, he ensured the Kurds received an appropriate quota of public appointments.[19]

Yet, in spite of Faisal's efforts to form inclusive state institutions, the post-Ottoman British-sponsored Iraqi state set in motion a series of events that would ultimately fuel the sectarian policies of the 1980s, 1990s, and beyond. The first Iraqi constitution of 1921 and the Law for the Election of the Constituent Assembly of 1922 made a dangerous distinction between "original" and "non-original" Iraqis. Iraqis were defined as "every Ottoman subject now residing in Iraq and not claiming foreign citizenship."[20] This left many Shias in a compromised position as they may have been registered as "Iranian subjects" prior to the formation of the Iraqi state due to their geographical location. Defining Iraqi nationhood in terms of "Ottoman subjects" might have been uncontentious at the time because many of Iraq's new political elite were ex-Ottoman officers and officials. However, that definition framed the Shia population as second-class citizens in their own country and set the stage for the future mass deportations of Shia Iraqis, whom the Baath government accused of being *taba'iyah Iraniyya* or (Iranian followers).[21]

Further fragmentation of the Iraqi social fabric came at the hands of the British. Minorities in Iraq found support and protection under the British Mandate. But this created tension within the wider Muslim community. The Assyrians, for example, who had served in the British military, faced a devastating backlash after Iraq's nominal independence. British favoritism had left sour relations between the Christian Assyrians on the one hand, and the Muslim Arabs and Kurds on the other, and when the British left tensions escalated first into an Assyrian revolt and, soon after, into their massacre around the town of Simele in 1933. Moreover, the British government put measures in place to protect the Jews of Iraq "against any form of local tyranny."[22] These measures strengthened the antiminority perception, particularly among Iraqi nationalists, that because Iraq's Jews had cooperated with the British, the entire community was "foreign." Colonial Britain and France used this divide-and-rule logic to cement their control of Arab societies and undermine the emergence of a unified Arab agency.

Colonial power was so deeply embedded in the new Iraq that not even the country's independence and subsequent admission to the League of Nations in 1932 represented an end to colonial rule in its entirety. British civilian and military officials and private corporations continued to undermine the legitimacy of the Hashemite monarchy, contributing to its eventual downfall in 1958. In 1940, when a coup d'état installed the pro-German Rashid Ali as prime minster, the British became concerned about a potential German threat to the oilfields. London wasted no time and by 1941 Britain was back in full military control of the country.[23] The backlash on the streets was violent and unrestrained. The revenge attacks against the Jewish community were the bloody climax of these protests in what came to be known as the Farhud pogrom. Eventually, the British established control (Many Iraqis believe that the revenge attacks against the Jews were deliberately staged by the British to distract attention from their reoccupation of the country). At any rate, the British removed Rashid Ali from office and replaced him with the veteran Nuri al-Said (his third time in the job).

But for Iraqis, the damage was done. And Britain's second stint in Iraq did even greater harm to its reputation than its original mandate in 1920.

The removal of Rashid Ali, who was later seen as a hero, along with Britain's decisive influence over the political elite and London's later support of Israel, contributed to the rejection of Britain as an ally and to the eventual overthrow of the British-friendly monarchy in 1958.[24]

The French fared no better in Syria. The French mandate in Syria was more turbulent than the British experience in Iraq. From the outset, France faced nationalist opposition in the cities and in the countryside. Unlike the British in Egypt and Iraq, the French mandate was not based on any treaty, but on military power, and for most Syrians it was therefore seen as an occupation. The French underlined this impression with their own behavior: they were anything but subtle in their rule of Syria.

One of the nationalist revolts against the French was led by Ibrahim Hanunu. A landowner and ex-Ottoman official, he had fought in the Arab Revolt and taken part in the Syrian General Congress of 1919. Disenchanted with the French occupation, Hanunu led an insurgency of almost 5,000 men following the French occupation of Aleppo in 1920.[25] The revolt was supported and funded by the Turks, who were engaged in their own struggle against France for the coastal region of Anatolia.[26]

The French deployed troops in order to quash the revolt and by 1921 Hanunu had fled to Jordan. It marked the failure of the nationalists' ambitions. For colonial France, the need to counter the threat of a unified nationalist movement now became a top priority. To do this, they devised a strategy of dividing Syria into four ministates. The four states became the State of Alawites, the State of Jabal Druze, the State of Aleppo, and the State of Damascus. This partition strategy ensured urban nationalists in Damascus and Aleppo could not join forces against colonial France. It also ensured the Alawite and Druze communities remained detached from nationalist ideas and came to view their interests as vested in the French Mandate.

The creation of four separate states, with four identical sets of institutions, was destined to fail because it was too expensive to maintain. From 1922, the French began cost-cutting. They started by shrinking individual state budgets and reducing the number of French advisers and the size of each state administration. Such cuts initially alienated the middle-level bureaucrats who became jobless, many of whom later joined the ranks of the anti-French opposition.[27] Further tax increases alienated a greater number of ordinary Syrians.

And all the while, the French remained intent on their "civilizing mission" and French officials attempted to impose French culture on a mainly Arab population. Schoolchildren were taught to sing the "Marseillaise" and schoolbooks were rewritten to reflect the French perspective on the history of the region.[28] French rule in Syria was perhaps best described by explorer Freya Stark, who noted that "it is ridiculous to call [what the French established in Syria] a mandate, for I believe there is not a Frenchman in the country who intends these people to govern themselves."[29] Indeed, the French repeatedly blocked attempts to move Syria toward independence until 1943 when, under intense British pressure, elections were held that resulted in a strong vote for independence.[30] But even then, the French were reluctant to acknowledge the strength of opposition to their rule. All of these practices led to a major insurgency in 1925, the Syrian Great Revolt, which took the French two years to subdue.

What the British experience in Egypt and Iraq and the French experience in Syria show is the emergence of a deep distrust between the rulers and the ruled. No matter what the British and French said to try and convince people otherwise, local people recognized the Mandates for what they were: nothing more than colonialism by another name.

While Egypt, Syria, and Iraq exemplify how people struggled with state-building and the creation of a "modern nation-state," two prominent examples from the region show another trajectory of colonialism: denying the Kurds and the Palestinians a state of their own. This denial has caused lasting geostrategic problems and deepened the crisis over identities and belongings. In a world where nation-states constitute the prime organizing structure of contemporary politics, this denial left both peoples in limbo and at the mercy of other people's interests.

The Kurdish Question

After World War I, the Kurds had been promised their own state by the Allies and, like the Palestinians, had been let down. The colonial powers had no use for the Kurds, and they lacked the means to resist an imposed settlement. While the Arabs nursed their festering wounds, at least 25 million Kurds were forgotten, their aspirations of a homeland crushed.[31]

The Kurds were the main losers of the postwar peace settlements. They were largely split up within four separate states: Iran, Iraq, Syria, and Turkey. Alone and in isolation, they bided their time, navigating the minefields of rival national identities, and hoping the postcolonial, postindependence state would establish an inclusive governing contract in which all communities would be treated equally as citizens before the law.

Following the end of World War I, as Iraq, Iran, Syria, and Turkey evolved into individual states, the Kurdish question began to diversify. While it posed challenges in all of these countries, the Kurdish situation varied depending on the political and social experience within each of the different countries.

In Iraq, for instance, the Kurdish community began showing signs of independence as early as 1921, when the city of Kirkuk refused to swear allegiance to King Faisal. At certain times, and particularly during the 1940s and 1950s when people and politics were influenced by the relative success of the Communist Party in the country's main cities, the Kurdish question took a back seat in Iraqi politics. Communism's ideas and ideals of internationalism appealed to many Kurds as a way of transcending local ethnic differences. However, the rise of Arab nationalism and the success of the Baath (Renaissance) Party and Saddam Hussein toward the end of the 1960s played a crucial role in redefining the Kurdish identity. Saddam's hyper Iraqi nationalism increasingly saw the Kurds as a threat to the unity of the country and frequently accused the Kurdish community of harboring separatist ambitions. The repression of the Kurds in Iraq culminated in the *Anfal* campaign and the chemical weapons attack on Halabja in 1988, which killed and injured around 15,000 Kurds.[32]

In Syria, the situation was slightly better, but not for long. Syrian Kurds make up around 10 percent of the country's population, and initially they enjoyed significant rights under the French Mandate as France used a "divide and rule" policy and allied with minorities in Syria, including the Kurds. In fact, the first elections held under the new Syrian constitution in the 1930s saw a number of prominent politicians from the Syrian Kurdish nationalist party elected.

After independence and the rise of the Baath Party in the 1960s, the position of the Kurds in Syria changed drastically. In 1962, around 120,000 Kurds were stripped of their Syrian citizenship. Many were now categorized as "aliens."[33] The Kurdish language was banned in schools and all forms of Kurdish culture prohibited. The Kurds were painted as "menacing" with their separatist ambitions highlighted as a threat to the Syrian nation and Arab nationalism. Stateless Kurds were not granted Syrian citizenship until April 2011, when President Bashar al-Assad saw it as a compromise for Kurdish cooperation against the popular revolt that was brewing against him.[34] In the absence of any form of political legitimacy, Assad, like the French before him, resorted to tactics of divide and rule.

Tragically, Iran, Iraq, Syria, and Turkey never fully integrated the Kurds into the body politic and never stopped suspecting them of harboring secessionist designs. Treated as second-class citizens and at times persecuted, a revolutionary nationalist current developed within elements of the Kurdish communities, eventually turning violent. Overall, the Kurdish experience within such authoritarian states contributed to a fierce determination for autonomy (or even a state of their own), where they would be able to run their own internal affairs, as opposed to being marginalized and excluded. Without it, the Middle East will not reflect the aspirations of millions of people who live there.

The Failure of the Liberal Constitutional Process

The drawing of the borders of the Middle East is only half the story of what went on in the region in the early part of the twentieth century. The other half is the double-talk and ineffective conduct of the colonial state. In the eyes of the people in the region, there was a massive disconnect between the lofty pronouncements so often made by the colonially backed state about open society, liberal constitutionalism, and participatory government on the one hand, and the top-down elitism and exclusion that characterized the day-to-day experience of government on the other.

The individuals who rose to political prominence in the new Mandate states were mainly those who had held positions of influence within the Ottoman system: local notables, ex-Ottoman civil servants, bureaucrats,

and former Ottoman military officers. And they did so with the full support and patronage of the colonial powers. To preserve order and maintain security and stability, colonial Britain and France relied on traditional
officials whose conservative temperament militated against radical change.
These officials had neither the vision nor the will or ability to be
nation-builders or to escape from the clutches of colonialism. In Iraq, for
example, ex-Ottoman army officer Nuri al-Said became prime minster
in 1930 for the first time. He would occupy the post a staggering *thirteen*
times after that. He was not the only person to think of the post as a second
home. Another ex-Ottoman officer, Abdul Muhsin al-Sa'dun, served as the
country's prime minister on four occasions.

Syria, too, had a revolving door of senior political posts. And here, too,
the main players were former Ottoman civil servants and local
notables: men like Mohammed Ali Bey al-Abed (finance minister, 1922;
president, 1932–1936) and Shukri al-Quwatli (the first president of postindependence Syria in 1943).

Not surprisingly, this "new-old" elite preferred continuity rather than
change. All of which ensured that certain patterns of Ottoman-style
political behavior and social attitudes carried on into the postwar era.[35]

There was, however, another way into the new establishment: the military. In their construction of the Arab Middle East, the colonial powers
emphasized security and control (the military and the police) at the expense of representative institutions and a vibrant civil society and political
economy. In fact, two-thirds of colonial expenses related to security
measures, with France and Britain giving priority to the establishment and
training of police forces, with the armed forces in Syria and Iraq, respectively, coming second.[36]

For instance, in 1920, the French Mandate founded a military academy in Syria, where local officers, mostly from Syria's Alawite community, were trained by the French and appointed to the Syrian Legion.[37]
The Syrian Legion and its members would go on to play a monumental
role in Syrian politics and in the military coups that would eventually
lead to the rise of Hafez al-Assad's regime in 1970. This emphasis on
security served the dual purpose of consolidating centralized authority in the hands of the loyal and pliant ruling elites, ensuring their

dependence on the colonial powers, while replicating the experience of European nation-building.

Yet the colonial powers were not always the most reliable allies to their local clients. Oblivious to rising nationalist aspirations and widespread public disillusionment, Britain and France dangerously undermined the legitimacy of their traditional allies through heavy-handed tactics and misguided policies. For example, in February 1942 the British publicly humiliated their client, King Farouk of Egypt, by encircling his palace with tanks and forcing him to appoint Nahhas of the Wafd Party as prime minister, a decision that weakened the king and alienated the population.

The majority of the population did not have a voice in the system and did not participate in the democratic rituals. Because of this, the public did not learn the civic lessons associated with liberal constitutionalism. This has had long-term consequences: not only does the liberal constitutional political model remain alien to many people in the region, but it has become synonymous with colonialization and Westernization. Seen as an exclusive club for a small and privileged elite supported by Great Powers, the liberal constitutional experiment had a short lifespan.

The postwar state structure in the Middle East was thus arguably doomed from the start. Aside from the inherent contradiction of independence that was not independent, the entire structure was flawed. As a model, colonial Britain and France used the Westphalian concepts of territorial sovereignty. This involved a monopoly on the use of force and centralized state-led development based on modernization theory, dispensing with informal local networks and practices and privileging urban centers at the expense of rural areas. However, the application of the Westphalian model to the Middle East was fictitious, as the countries were not really independent and capable of delivering intermediary services between the state and its population. This lack of institutional capacity, along with the emphasis on strengthening security institutions, allowed the colonial powers to unwittingly pave the way for the advent of the military ruler or populist strongman in Middle Eastern politics.

The Legacy of the Colonial State

The failure of constitutionally based monarchies and governments in Egypt, Iraq, and Syria deepened the divide between rulers and citizens. Arabs lost faith in the liberal spirit at the heart of the constitutional process. Instead, they turned increasingly to slogans of *asala* or authenticity, communitarianism, and authoritarianism. Some even turned toward fascism, when it gained momentum in the 1930s and 1940s, or revolutionary action as a more viable alternative for bringing about real change.[38]

But the two radical forces that were to dominate Arab politics were nationalism and Islamism. The anti-colonial struggle fueled these anti-hegemonic ideologies and, as a result, they gained more converts in the 1930s and 1940s. The new radical religious and nationalist movements were led by men like primary school teacher Hassan al-Banna, who founded the Muslim Brotherhood in 1928, and lawyer Ahmed Hussein who founded Young Egypt in the 1930s. Also, politically active at this time were army officers like Aziz al-Masri and Gamal Abdel Nasser in Egypt and the architects of the Arab Baath Party in Syria, Salah al-Din al-Bitar and Michel Aflaq. These leaders and groups were themselves byproducts of a period in which constitutionalism had been constantly abused and undermined by the kings, the British, the French, and the dominant local political parties.

This shift also contributed to the politicization of the private space, a change exemplified by the emergence of underground paramilitary organizations, such as the Muslim Brothers' al-Nizam al-Khass (the Secret Apparatus); Young Egypt's al-Qumsan al- Khadra' (the Green Shirts); and the Muslim Brotherhood of Syria, who later launched an armed insurgency between 1979 and 1982. In Iraq, the Shia Dawa Party and Kurdistan Democratic Party, both of which had a political and paramilitary front, are also examples of this phenomenon.

This new radicalism filled a void created by failing constitutionalism and found receptive ears among the masses who had had no economic and political stake in the colonially constructed liberal-leaning order.[39] Furthermore, the political establishment's failure to engage directly with the situation in Palestine created opportunities for the new, radical political

actors in Arab countries. The Arab defeat in 1948 fueled anger and disillusionment against the ruling establishments because it woefully exposed
the weakness of the armies and the lack of commitment to build effective
military institutions. Many young army officers held the postcolonial regimes responsible for their humiliation at the hands of the newly born
Israeli state. Nasser spoke for many young army officers in Egypt, Iraq,
Syria, and elsewhere when he noted bluntly in his autobiography that to
"save the homeland" from the grip of "wolves" became a personal mission
and a strategic priority.[40] From the ultra-right to the ultra-left, opposition
forces now turned to subversive and revolutionary methods to topple the
old regimes.

Coming from within, the revolts of the army officers sealed the fate
of the pro-British and pro-French monarchies and conservative rulers.
And they did so with widespread public support. Increasing public despair
with the status quo helped turn these armed conspiracies into full-
blown revolutions.

The authoritarianism at the heart of the imperial framework had
thus paved the way for the political authoritarianism of the postindependence state.

Why This Still Matters

As this chapter has shown, long after the mandates were established, the
influence of colonialism lingered. The historical formation of the Middle
Eastern state system continued to influence public perceptions and
the popular and institutional imagination of the postindependence state.
Hostile public perceptions of the postwar peace settlements, coupled
with the failed policies of the pro-British and pro-French monarchies and
the conservative elite in the 1930s and 1940s, doomed the prospects of
liberal constitutionalism. They also nourished and fed alternative modes
of radicalism anchored in identity politics and anti-colonialism.

Since the 1930s, one of the rallying cries of secular-leaning Arab nationalists and religious nationalists has been the urgent need to reconstruct the state system along more viable and authentic foundations. What
united these political rivals was a deep-seated longing for territorial unity

that corresponds, in their opinion, to cultural unity. This appeal for unity drove movements as ideologically diverse as pan-Arab nationalism and pan-Islamism and is a reaction to the partition of the Arab-Islamic world into artificial and ungovernable units.[41]

While the Arab nation-states grew deep roots with large segments of society dependent on the state for employment, welfare, and security, the legacy of how those states were created—the original sin—continues to haunt the entire system. On the whole, most people reluctantly came to terms with the new territorial map. But with one key condition: as long as their rulers respected an implicit social contract of delivering public goods and protecting the homeland.[42] In light of this, the existential crisis currently facing the Arab state structure has more to do with failed governance and lost legitimacy than with borders and frontiers. The state system is in tatters because the postcolonial, postindependence Arab state did *not* develop formal, transparent, and functioning institutions. It has also failed to deliver the social public goods. As a result, it has gradually, and systemically, lost not only the support of the masses but also its very raison d'être. With nothing else left, it has relied on nepotism, coercion, and domination ever since.

The fraying legitimacy and hegemony of the Arab state system can also be explained by a crisis of identity that has plagued it since its foundation. Pressed from the beginning between the conflicting pressures of *al-wataniyya* (territorial or local nationalism) and *al-qawmiyya* (pan- or supranationalism), the state system has vacillated between the two rival ideologies like a pendulum. The clash between these two ideologies or what scholars called the "raison de la nation" (Arabism or pan-nationalism) and the "raison d'etat" (separate state interests) turned into a fierce cold war that has played out in bitter and costly rivalries within and between states.[43]

The role played by the colonial powers in creating the Middle East we know today—the one collapsing at such huge human cost in front of us— still matters because Britain and France built so many flaws into the system at the start, it was never likely to function properly. They drew borders in the wrong places. They left the Kurds and the Palestinians without a home. They spoke of a new era but kept the old guard in power.

They talked of democracy and open government but denied its expression at every turn.

It would fall to a new elite of young radicals, men like Nasser of Egypt, to overthrow the old order, bring down the colonial state and build a new system. And because the only institution the colonial powers built up was the military, most of these young men came from the army. They came to power with the means of coercion at their disposal: an ominous state of affairs that was largely ignored in the euphoria of revolution.

These new postindependence, postcolonial leaders of the Middle East promised deliverance from the bondage of colonialism. They promised national unity and Arab brotherhood. They promised dignity and development. They promised a new bond, between Arab governments and the people.

It was a tall order. What remained to be seen was whether that bond would respect the people's agency by including them in government power-sharing or whether the new regime would continue the colonial pattern of outright elite rule.

4

Life after Independence

THE SEARCH
FOR A FOUNDATIONAL MYTH

THE END OF THE COLONIAL ERA was a moment of great hope in the Middle East.

Across the region, people were eager to cast off the shackles of imperialism, wipe the slate clean, and start making their own rules. This was the long dreamed of moment when people could take charge of their destiny, build state institutions that reflected their aspirations, and rid themselves of dependency on their former foreign masters. Their new leaders had a once-in-a-lifetime opportunity to create a fairer society, bring about real, transformative political change, and end the tyranny of authoritarian rule once and for all.

The optimism of the moment rested on firm foundations. The Arab world brimmed with untapped promises and potentials. Rich in natural resources, the region literally sat on top of a lake of oil and gas. The oil wealth of the Arabian Gulf was already on its way to becoming the stuff of legend, but it wasn't the only part of the Arab world so blessed. Iraq's oil revenues and wealth increased by a massive 50 percent between 1950 and 1956 and kept on rising for the next three decades.[1] By 1978 Iraq was richer than Portugal or Malaysia.[2] Syria was similarly rich. The country possessed the largest proven reserves of crude oil in the eastern Mediterranean and up to 50 billion tons of oil shale resources.[3]

It was the same story in North Africa. Libya had the highest oil reserves on the continent and the ninth-highest in the world.[4] With a
population of only 1.4 million, it could easily have become the Norway
of the Middle East. Nearby Algeria, with 160 trillion feet of proven natural gas reserves (among the ten highest in the world) had the opportunity
to become a regional economic superpower.[5] Further south, Sudan had
the capacity to produce 50,000 tons of chrome a year at the Ingessana
Hills near Roseires on the Blue Nile. The country is rich in other resources: natural gas, copper reserves, and iron, to name only a few.[6] In
addition, Sudan enjoys the climate and geography to become the region's
breadbasket and to benefit from the wealth generated by an industrial-
scale agricultural sector.

For countries not so blessed with natural resources, other opportunities existed. It might be cliché to call Lebanon the Switzerland (or the
Paris) of the Middle East but clichés sometimes have a ring of truth and
the dynamic. Lebanese knew how to make the most of the hand they had
been dealt. They used their position as a pivot between East and West to
promote prosperity and showcase their tolerance and cultural diversity.
Beirut's service sector thrived and the cosmopolitan city on the coast
became a regional center for publishing and banking and a hub of the
international jet set.

To make a success of the new era, the peoples of the Middle East and
North Africa were going to need all the resources—and resourcefulness—
they possessed. The challenges they faced were immense. The imperial
powers might have left but their influence lingered. During their decades
of dominance, Britain and France had integrated the countries under their
control into the global economy on terms beneficial to themselves but not
at all beneficial to the local people. The knock-on effects of this structural
imbalance were profound and long-lasting. As a result, the newly
independent Middle Eastern states were fragile on many fronts: politically,
economically, socially, and institutionally.

In this, they were not unique. Across the world, other regions were just
as disadvantaged, if not more so. From Asia to Africa to Latin America,
newly independent countries entered the postcolonial era burdened by

the massive structural deficits left behind by their former rulers. While the previous chapters explained in detail the dynamic of colonialism and foreign intervention, this chapter will focus on the domestic developments of the newly independent Middle Eastern states. As outlined in the Introduction, the role of foreign powers cannot be the only lens through which we understand Middle Eastern history and politics. It should be examined in tandem with the political, institutional, and ideological development within each country.

In the Middle East, Egypt—the Arab world's most populous country—demonstrates how the promise of a new social contract between the people and their government ultimately faltered. The ideology of Arab nationalism would at first prove to be a powerful rallying cry for those seeking to escape colonialism, inspiring similar military coups in other Middle Eastern states. But in the fractious aftermath of independence, Nasser's military, like those in other states, would choose to secure its own self-interest in lieu of an expansive and inclusive vision of Arab unity and prosperity.

The Legacy of Colonialism: The Freedom Deficit and the Failure of Liberal Politics

It is one of the contradictions of colonialism that on the face of it, Egypt's political culture appeared to fare well under British rule. From the 1920s to the early 1950s, Egypt had an active political scene with competitive parties; a host of formal institutions, including an elected parliament; a functioning judiciary system; and a flourishing press. But behind the façade of liberalism and parliamentary politics, the British remained firmly in control of Egypt's economic and political affairs. Sir John Eldon Gorst, who replaced Lord Cromer as consul-general in 1907, did not hesitate to use the Exceptional Laws and other penal measures to suppress the nationalists.[7] Legal restrictions impeding the development of an open press remained in place throughout British rule.[8]

The superficial development of a liberal political system in Egypt is perhaps best illustrated by the constitution that took effect when the country was granted limited independence on February 28, 1922. On the one

hand, the constitution inscribed liberal values like freedom of belief, religion, and speech.[9] But on the other hand, it expanded the king's power
at the expense of the parliament.[10] The constant interference behind the
scenes by the British and the Palace greatly hindered the development of
liberal politics in Egypt. The pragmatic attitude of the nationalist Wafd
Party and its unwillingness to challenge the dominance of the Palace and
the British played a major role in the growing sense of disillusionment
many Egyptians felt with the quasi-liberal order.

By 1950, Egyptians were ready for change. They voted in the Wafd Party
whose platform was complete independence from Britain, constitutional
government, the protection of civil rights, and Egyptian sovereignty over
the Sudan and the Suez Canal.[11] But the nineteen months of talks with the
British went nowhere, and Egyptians became increasingly frustrated with
the lack of progress.

A period of violence and instability followed that culminated in the
events of Black Saturday in January 1952,[12] when angry demonstrations
on the streets of Cairo escalated into violent riots. The Wafd paid the price.
King Farouq moved swiftly to remove the Wafdist prime minister from
power. But his actions did little to restore public confidence in the political
elite. If anything, the unpopular king made things worse. Black Saturday
and its aftermath paved the way for the military takeover by Nasser's Free
Officers Movement.

On the eve of the coup in July 1952, there was a general feeling among
the public that parliamentary politics were a sham, nothing but a cover
for the rich to get richer and for the British to preserve the status quo. All
of which meant that when the new era finally dawned, Egypt's new leaders would not look to the parliamentary politics of the past. They would
look to themselves, to their own culture and their own history, for answers.
They found what they were looking for in Arab nationalism.

A New Politics for a New Future: Arab Nationalism

Arab nationalism can be neatly summarized as "the idea that the Arabs
are a people linked by special bonds of language and history, and that their
political organization should somehow reflect this reality."[13] The Arabic

language is central to this concept. As the Arab nationalist thinker and theoretician Sati' al-Husri stated, "People who spoke a unitary language have one head and a common soul. As such they constitute one nation, and so they have a unified state."[14]

The precise historical origins of Arab nationalism are less clear and the subject continues to generate debate. It is argued, for instance, that Arab nationalism only took root at the end of World War I and gradually flourished, reaching its apogee in the 1950s and 1960s under Nasser.[15] Others argue it started earlier and cite 1909 as a pivotal year. Before then, Arabs living in the Ottoman Empire had a sense of "Arab" identity and even though they had grievances against the sultan, they did not entertain notions of separation. Instead, they called for reform and "even when they severely criticized the Sultanate, they remained loyal to the Caliphate."[16]

This attitude changed drastically after the Young Turks came to power in 1909 and started a process of Turkification of the empire. However, this process was more nuanced than questions of race or language or nation. Turkification was the first of several waves of administrative changes that took place as the Committee of Union and Progress solidified its hold over the day-to-day running of government. Many of the Arab notables who lost out under the changes had wielded power for generations and saw the territories under their control as personal fiefdoms. Not surprisingly, they did not welcome the sudden loss of power and status and, as a result, they called for urgent political reform. Their demands for decentralization and reform were not so much a response to "Turkification" but to the new type of centralized government that left the old guard out in the cold.[17]

Furthermore, for significant numbers of Arabs living on the edge of the empire, Turkification was neither a threat nor a motivation for separation. Arab populations in areas vulnerable to European ambition were more concerned by this external threat than by the rising numbers of Turks in the imperial administration. For people in these frontier provinces, "the Ottoman Empire was seen as a vital shield against external powers and there was thus little growth of Arabization before 1914."[18]

As long as the empire lasted, Arabism did not develop into full-fledged nationalism. Its supporters pleaded for administrative decentralization rather than Arab independence. They developed no vision of a post-Ottoman order.

On the eve of World War I, Arabism was mainly articulated in Syria and Iraq, Jordan, Lebanon, and Palestine in intellectual circles and journals.[19] Although it gained political traction during the war, Arabism or Arab nationalism had yet to evolve from a top-down elite-based intellectual idea to a mass movement enjoying popular support.[20]

It was not till the late 1920s and 1930s that Arab nationalism gained momentum at the popular level. In particular, it developed as an anti-hegemonic tool of resistance against the colonial powers as they partitioned the region between themselves after the end of the First World War.[21] The construction of national identities differed from country to country because the colonial experience varied in each case. Each colonial intrusion produced a certain response. In some cases, the responses were in some way nationalist; in others they took a religious form or a secular form, or a combination of both.[22]

In the 1940s, "liberation from colonial rule was the common wish of all Arab peoples ... they wanted to dissolve the frontiers drafted by imperial powers to divide the Arabs and build a new commonwealth based on the deep historic and cultural ties that bound the Arabs."[23] But for all its popularity, the ideology was not without its critics. It proved problematic in North African countries, and in Iraq and Syria, where important ethnic minorities, such as Kurds and Berbers, saw the ideology as a danger to their own cultural heritage. Moreover, across the region, Arab nationalism faced two popular alternative forms of collective identity: religious nationalism and territorial nationalism.[24] Territorial nationalism refers to a leader's calling specifically upon his own nation to see themselves as a singular state with shared Arab identity, while religious nationalism means combining religious and nationalist sentiments in a nation-state's identity. These categories of nationalism are not mutually exclusive, and they often overlapped.

In Egypt, for example, while Arab nationalism had been used by governments as a tool of regional and foreign policy, the "separate historical development in Egypt and the distinctive culture which had grown up in the Nile valley had kept it somewhat distant in feeling from its [Arab] neighbors."[25] Egypt had long enjoyed a stable and well-defined identity as one of the oldest nation-states in the world. Because of this, Egyptians had not felt the need for new self-definition or amalgamation with neighboring entities. The same was true for religion: even though the idea of pan-Islamism gained ground in Egypt after the founding of the Muslim Brotherhood in 1928, territorial nationalism was too potent a force. Yet, in spite of these challenges, the emotional pull of Arabism was strong and Arab nationalism took hold, especially in newly independent states with a recent memory of European betrayal. In contrast to territorial nationalism, Arab nationalism was the rallying cry and coalition-building rhetoric asserting shared Arab identity. In Egypt, Arab nationalism meant solidarity of ranks and inter-Arab coordination, not the establishment of a unitary pan-Arab state.

The promises of Arab nationalism were steep. Its appeal included a more ambitious principle of Arab unity, or a unitary pan-Arab state (the United States of the Arab world), which held resonance for people recently liberated from colonial rule. In this sense, Arab nationalism was initially presented to the public through the narrative of independence, anti-imperialism, and empowerment. It soon became a rallying cry for modernist voices seeking to rid the Arab world of "backwardness," sectarianism, and tribalism. The language of progress, cultural renewal, and development came to dominate the public debate. Arguing that they were on the right side of history, Arab nationalists dismissed their opponents as "reactionary" and out of touch with the aspirations of the people.

After independence, the psychology and mood of the public experienced a dramatic transformation. Expectations were high about the establishment of a pan-Arab front, perhaps even a unitary pan-Arab government: a genuinely independent state that would serve the common public good.

Over the past three decades, Arab public intellectuals, activists, and citizens have repeatedly emphasized to me the importance of that unique moment in the modern history of the Middle East. They felt the region was on the cusp of a titanic shift and they were witnesses to transformative change: "We Arabs might have been materially poor with young independent states; but our aspirations and goals were great and mighty,"

Sayyed Yassin, a distinguished elderly Egyptian public intellectual, confided to me in the calm of his book-lined study in Cairo. "For the first time we felt we were in charge of our destiny and that we would pen our chapter in world history."

With hopes so high and confidence so strong, little wonder that Colonel Gamal Abdel Nasser, the new leader of the newly independent Egypt, chose to speak to his people in the Arab nationalist rhetoric.

From Nationalism to Nasserism:
The Man and His Mission

Nasser embraced Arab nationalism, a vehicle of coalition-building and inter-Arab coordination, as the mantra of his leadership in the mid-1950s. Enormously charismatic, Nasser emerged as the ideological leader and champion of Arab nationalism and promoted a pan-Arab vision that would make "the Arab states stronger through their cooperation in the economic military and cultural fields, and in the sphere of foreign policy."[26] Nasser's pan-Arab worldview did not envision a unitary state of the Arab world.

In his autobiography, *Falsafat al-Thawra* (The philosophy of the revolution), Nasser encapsulates this belief eloquently. Reminiscing on the eve of the outbreak of the war in Palestine in 1948 and its aftermath, he writes: "When the Palestine crisis loomed on the horizon I was firmly convinced that the fighting there was not fighting on foreign territory. Nor was it inspired by sentiment. It was duty imposed by self-defense. After the siege and the battles in Palestine I came home with the whole region in my mind one complete whole. The events that followed confirmed this belief in me. . . . An event may happen in Cairo today; it is repeated in Damascus, Beirut, Amman or any other place tomorrow."[27] Nasser came to identify more and more with Arab nationalist symbols of language and belonging than with religious rituals and forms of identity. As he later stressed in his memoirs, the Arab nation, not the Islamic community (*umma*), "is the most important and the most closely connected with us."[28]

But there was more to it than that. While Nasser may have felt the strong emotional pull of Arabism, he was also a shrewd political operator.

Nasser's vision was not an idealist, political project but a set of realistic calculations he made in the particular set of circumstances he found himself in during the late 1940s and early 1950s.

A closer look at Nasser's use of pan-Arab nationalist ideology in my book *Making the Arab World* shows that three crises played an important role in his shift toward nationalism: the 1948 Palestine war and the crushing defeat of the Arab armies, the Arab-Israeli conflict, and the Suez Canal crisis in 1956.[29]

Nasser's generation in Egypt and neighboring Arab states believed the corrupt and cowardly political establishment they grew up under sacrificed everything from national security to the fight against Zionism on the altar of their own narrow interests. Proud, patriotic army officers like Nasser returned home from the war in Palestine in 1948 changed men. In their eyes, it was no longer enough to expel the British and French from Arab lands and claim independence. They had to overthrow the entire quasi-liberal political order that had acquiesced to, and profited from, foreign rule. For Nasser and his comrades, to "save the homeland" from the grip of "wolves" was now a personal mission and a strategic priority.[30] They wanted nothing less than revolution.

In this shift toward revolutionary change, the impact of the Palestine defeat on the Free Officers Movement cannot be overstated. The war convinced him that the "near enemy" (the king and the British occupier) had to take priority over the "far enemy" (Israel) because prevailing over the former could ultimately lead to victory over the latter.

The Palestine war reminded Egyptian officers, as well as officers from other Arab countries, of the ties that bind Arab countries together strategically and culturally. The Free Officers saw the occupation of Palestine as a reflection of the catastrophe that had affected the rest of the Arab nations.[31] Thus, Palestine figured prominently in the imagination and discourse of postindependence leaders, wherever they ruled. From Nasser in Egypt to Saddam Hussein in Iraq to Ayatollah Khomeini in the Islamic Republic of Iran, all paid homage to Palestine and promised deliverance and liberation.[32]

Immediately after the coup in 1952, Nasser had taken initiatives to address the severe socioeconomic crisis in Egypt. Medical care, education, and employment were key priorities. His progressive radical social agenda "prioritized bread and butter"[33] over the liberal economy of the old regime. Nasser's policies were radical and refreshing when initially introduced and enjoyed widespread support among the masses.

Nasser tapped into their worries and aspirations as he set about reconfiguring society to create a constituency and a technocratic elite that owed loyalty to the Free Officers' regime. He offered a program anchored in social justice, expansion of the education system,[34] land reforms, nationalization of the private sector, and disinheriting the old urban and rural elite.[35]

The social agenda of Nasser, and Arab nationalists in neighboring countries, resonated with a majority of the population, particularly the poor and the working and middle classes overlooked by the old regime. In the Egyptian Constitution of 1956, six principles defining the regime's goals and revolutionary social agenda were listed: "The eradication of all aspects of imperialism; the extinction of feudalism; the eradication of monopolies, and the control of capitalistic influence over the system of Government; the establishment of a strong national army; the establishment of social justice; and the establishment of a sound democratic society."[36]

And none was more popular—or more radical—than land reform, perhaps the *most* significant pillar of Nasser's social agenda. Before the 1952 revolution, the majority of landowners in Egypt were not Egyptian.[37] They were largely Turco-Circassian like the Mamluks who had ruled Egypt for centuries. This sense of Egyptian land not being in the hands of Egyptians helped Nasser isolate the landowning elite, label them as closet colonialists, and garner popular support for the sequestration of their lands. The situation of the peasants was so dire that an Egyptian social critic, Anouar Abdel Malek, described them as "an exploited mass surrounded by hunger, disease and death."[38]

One of the first initiatives by the Free Officers was therefore to pass Law 178 on September 11, 1952. Under this law, landowners were banned from owning more than 200 feddans of land. The old landowning class was destroyed almost overnight.[39] For peasants who owned less than five feddans, the government set up cooperatives to help them obtain fertilizers, pesticides, seeds, and transport for their products to the market. A minimum wage for agricultural workers was also set. As one writer points out, "The footage of Nasser distributing landownership titles to the poor peasants in drab jalabeyas is still a powerful and moving symbol of the rise of poor classes [al-Tabaqat al-Faqeera]."[40] The reform was subsequently revised in 1958 and again in 1961 and 1969. By 1969 the maximum land holding was set to 50 feddans.[41] Or, at least, it was supposed to be. Despite the vast enthusiasm of both the regime and the people for the land reform, it had mixed results. Only part of the land was redistributed, and some large landowners retained larger land holdings than those officially allowed.[42]

For Nasser, however, the land reform program was a huge success. By depriving major players in the rich landowning class of their land, he destroyed their economic and political power in one fell swoop. And by reallocating the confiscated land to small peasants and—even if to a lesser extent—the rural poor, he secured a loyalty that lasted.

Nasser set his sights on winning the support of the urban poor and the squeezed middle classes too. To do this, he nationalized industries and set out to improve working conditions. The nationalization program included a wide range of industries: shipping companies, cotton-ginning factories, cotton-exporting companies, pharmaceutical producers, glass factories, the country's largest book publishing company, and the film industry.

Elsewhere, Nasser's social vision focused on developing mass education. Following the socialist turn in Nasser's worldview in the 1960s, he signed a decree that provided universal and free public education to all Egyptians. To bolster greater enrollment in schools, Nasser also guaranteed employment for all graduates of secondary and postsecondary institutions.[43]

The impact of Nasser's socioeconomic policies quickly spread to other countries in the region and gained popularity with the people of Syria, Iraq, and elsewhere. Nasser's advancement of women's education and literacy in the 1950s arguably influenced the advancement of women's education in places like Iraq, Tunisia, and beyond.[44]

Throughout his rule, Nasser's reforms were motivated by a desire to better the plight of everyday Egyptians and undo the legacy of colonialism.

And his progressive agenda at home won him the hearts and minds of millions of Egyptians. But this new society came at a price. A staunch anti-colonialist, Nasser directly correlated the destruction of the colonial-capitalist framework with the improvement of the socioeconomic conditions of Egypt's impoverished masses. There was no middle ground. His social vision included the nationalization of big businesses, land reforms, and the eradication of monopolies.[45] As Mohammad Fayek, one member of Nasser's inner circle put it: "Nasser's priorities were those of the Egyptian [and Arab] nationalist movement which earned him massive public support and turned him into a hero. But his style of governance was authoritarian, [he was] a strongman."[46] Or, as one historian puts it: "Thanks to the Free Officers, Egypt was independent. But it was not free."[47]

What does the shift toward authoritarianism tell us about the postindependence politics of the Middle East? Nasser was increasingly able to personalize power because of what had taken place during the old regime. By the time of the coup in 1952, the Egyptian masses had lost confidence in the Western system of parliamentary democracy. Disillusioned with a corrupt elite who governed in their own interests, Egyptians felt that liberal capitalism had nothing to offer them. Nasser recognized this but instead of trying to build popular support for a different style of system, one that was more inclusive and open, he used the resentment of the Egyptian masses to his advantage. He knew only too well that a parliamentary system would limit his ability to rule. From the outset, therefore, he was a strong opponent of democracy and repeatedly stated that liberal democracy was a luxury his countrymen could not afford.[48] He accused political parties of having been vehicles of corruption in prerevolutionary Egypt and promptly set about dissolving all of them.[49] He justified his decision by claiming the parties were creating dissent, collaborating with foreign governments, and misusing freedom by fomenting chaos and partisan politics.[50]

After the coup in July 1952, Nasser famously uttered the following antidemocratic words: "I want to press a button so that Egypt moves forward and another so that Egypt moves backward." His interpretation of popular democracy can perhaps be boiled down to a simple dictum: he is the voice of the people. And because he knows what they want, he alone can deliver for them.

The overthrow of the British helped bring him to power, but it would be another run-in with the old colonial power that cemented his standing across the Arab world and catapulted him onto the international stage as an icon of anti-imperialism. The nationalization of the Suez Canal in 1956 was one of the most significant events in Nasser's career and one of the most powerful drivers in his shift toward Arab nationalism.

An act of defiance against the former colonial powers by a newly decolonized state, Nasser's nationalization of the Suez Canal challenged the postwar international order and the role of Britain and France in that order. A secret agreement reached between France, Britain, and Israel on October 24, 1956, stipulated that Israel would invade Egypt; Britain and France would insist on a cessation of hostilities (which was to be ignored); then an Anglo-French force would intervene and occupy the Suez Canal.[51]

As a young, newly independent state, Egypt was neither equipped nor prepared to fight a large-scale war. The Suez invasion did not end until November 7, 1956, when under great pressure from the United States, a ceasefire was agreed, which led to the withdrawal of French and British troops in December 1956 and Israeli troops in March 1957.

The Suez Crisis made a hero of Gamal Abdel Nasser across the Arab world and cemented Egypt's role as the leader of the Arab nations. It was "the classic example of a military defeat turned into a political victory"[52] in which the very act of defiance and survival against three powerful armies, two of which belonged to European colonial powers, was seen as a major political victory. Aided by the increasing popularity of the radio at the time, Nasser's messages and powerful rhetoric through the Sawt al-Arab (Voice of the Arabs) radio station gained enormous traction and support across the Arab world. In Syria, nationalists began to pay attention to Nasser and the potential of Arab unity.[53] The Syrian nationalists, however, advocated for the establishment of an Arab unitary state that encompassed all the Arab people.

After Suez, Nasser became more than a president. He was the man of the moment. People across the region looked to him to answer their problems, to build a fairer society, to make their lives better.

Across the Arab world, however, his wasn't the only view of Arab unity, even if it was becoming the most popular. Like Cairo, the cities of Baghdad and Damascus had once ruled the Arab world. And in the twentieth century, they were hothouses of ideas about the future of the emerging Arab nation. Syria was home to the men who launched the Baath Party: one of the principal vehicles for the spread of Arab nationalism. The postindependence regimes in Iraq and Syria, therefore, had their own views about where next to take the Arab nation.

From Cairo to Damascus and Baghdad: Competing Views of Arab Nationalism

The Baath Party was founded by Michel Aflaq and Salah al-Din al-Bitar in the early 1940s. The party espoused the principles of secular Arab nationalism with the motto: "One Arab nation with an eternal mission."[54] In contrast to Nasser's statist and utilitarian vision of Arab nationalism, the Syrian and Iraqi Baathists aimed at dissolving physical borders and creating a unified Arab nation. At the start, the Baath Party in Syria was rooted in an intellectual debate about the national identity of Syrians in the postcolonial state era and their relationship with other Arabic-speaking communities.[55] This debate was more pressing in Syria than in other Arab states because "the [Syrian] frontiers drawn by Britain and France in their own interests corresponded less than in most Middle Eastern countries to natural and historical divisions."[56]

The answer to the question "What is Syrian national identity?" was increasingly defined in nationalistic terms that focused on Syria's Arab identity. Michel Aflaq highlighted three objectives for the Baath movement: Arab unity, freedom, and socialism. He theorized that unity referred to the elimination of political or physical boundaries between Arab states and also to a regeneration process that would lead to the reform of Arab character and society.[57]

Understanding this Baath doctrine helps explain the appeal and magnetic attraction that Nasser's rhetoric would have on the Baathists and nationalists in Syria and beyond. And with Nasser's star rising, it was only a matter of time before someone, somewhere, called for the idea of Arab unity to become a political reality.

Initially, it was the Baath Party and the Syrian Communist Party that approached Nasser with proposals to unite Syria and Egypt. The two parties differed in their interpretation of this potential merger. For the Baathists, the proposal was merely a federal union while the Communists suggested merging the two countries into one new state. Both parties were essentially interested in bolstering their own popularity at home by capitalizing on Nasser's rising stardom throughout the Arab arena. The Baathists, for example, would not have been able to gain power at the polls by themselves as they won only 15 out of 142 parliamentary seats at the height of their electoral success in 1955.[58]

At first, the proposals for union were not taken seriously in either Syria or Egypt. But then, in January 1958, the Syrian army got involved and the course of history changed. Army officers, mostly Baathists, were drawn to Nasser's military-led government and believed a union with Egypt would lead to the military becoming the dominant power in Syrian politics.[59]

Nasser himself had not been interested in either a union or a merger with Syria or any other Arab state. Arab unity for him "meant, above all ... *the unification of the Arab struggle* ... when he preached Arab unity before the union with Syria, he meant Arab solidarity on foreign policy issues under Egyptian direction and not unity in any territorial or constitutional sense."[60]

Nasser was nevertheless tempted by the proposals set out by the Baathists and the Syrian ruling elite, not least because they offered him the chance to reinforce his standing as the undisputed leader of the Arab world. Nasser also viewed the potential union with Syria as a bargaining card with the superpowers as such a union would prove that Egypt was shaping the new political order in the Middle East. A close friend of Nasser once told me: "Nasser was an Egyptian patriot and nationalist, but he also adopted Arab nationalism as a strategic choice to counterbalance Western hegemonic designs in the Arab world and committed himself and the nation to pursuing it."[61]

From the beginning, the odds were against the Egyptian-Syrian merger. For Nasser, the conditions of the union were clear: Egypt would extend its control over Syria and Egyptian officers would be put in charge of the new province. The Syrian army would come under Egyptian central command, and all political parties would be disbanded and replaced by a single state party, the National Union Party. In other words, Nasser saw the union not as a merger between equals but as a takeover.

Syria's Baathists were initially shocked at the extent of Egyptian domination and disturbed by the idea of dismantling their own party. But the debate on the merger was swiftly silenced when the Syrian army weighed in on Nasser's side and the army's chief of staff warned wavering Syrian politicians: "There are two roads open to you . . . one leads to Mezze [the notorious political prison outside Damascus], the other to Cairo."[62] Faced with this option, they acquiesced. The new state was called the United Arab Republic and was proclaimed on February 1, 1958.

For Syria's military, the union was a Trojan horse. There was a belief among many Syrian army officers that a union with Egypt would empower them against civilian politicians.[63] Yet it is one of the many contradictions of the union that the manner in which the Syrian army imposed it ultimately led to its collapse.

Politics and improvisation soon triumphed over good management and planning and institutionalization. Michel Aflaq, the founder of the Baath Party, subsequently conceded the contradictory Egyptian and Syrian goals behind the unitary project: "We wanted two things which may seem contradictory. On the one hand we wanted a federal state strong enough and centralized enough to stand firm against the maneuvers of opponents at home and foreign governments abroad. . . . But our wish for a strong central Government was tempered by a second consideration. We wanted a federation to make allowances for the different political histories of the two countries. . . . But events moved too fast for our project to be given serious considerations."[64] The failure to resolve these differences sowed the seeds of suspicion and rivalry between the two countries' ruling elites eventually causing the breakup of the United Arab Republic and shattering the "myth" of unitary pan-Arab nationalism.

But for Nasser, 1958, the year the merger was finalized, marked a watershed in his worldview and conduct. It caused him to think the unthinkable: a pan-Arab unitary nation was no longer a dream but a reality. His coronation by the Syrian masses on his first visit there after the establishment of the United Arab Republic was inspirational and, according to Nasser's close aides, had a colossal psychological effect on his character.

The mass popular support shown by the people during his first visit to Damascus sent a shiver down the spines of other Arab leaders in the region. The visit made it clear to them that Nasser's vision of Arab unity had the potential to garner support across the Arab world and threaten the region's conservative order. During his speech in Damascus on February 27, 1958, Nasser directly attacked some of the region's conservative governments and monarchies by warning the assembled masses to watch him speak of "agents of imperialism."[65]

It was the shape of things to come. From 1958 until 1961, Nasser inscribed pan-Arab unity as an important goal of his political discourse and pressured other Arab leaders to join the United Arab Republic. Revisiting this period, it often looks as if pan-Arab nationalism led by Nasser was unstoppable and bound to prevail over the fragile old regimes. Nasserism had shaken the foundation of the entire region.

The Iraqi Revolution of 1958

The Iraqi Hashemite monarchy was ill-equipped to withstand the storm. Around 8:00 a.m. on July 14, 1958, a coup was launched in Baghdad. It was a scorching hot day. But the punishing heat did not deter the plotters. Like the coup in Egypt six years earlier, the Baghdad coup was the brainchild of a clandestine group of military officers. Led by Brigadier Abdel Karim Qasim and his associate Colonel Abdel Salam Arif, these men modeled themselves on their Egyptian counterparts and called themselves the Free Officers. And like the coup in Egypt, these officers wanted revolution. They had had enough of Prime Minister Nuri al-Said. His rampant corruption, his unquestioning subservience to the West, his repeated refusals to listen to the Iraqi people: the prime minister and the regime he served were at odds with Iraqi society. The Free Officers were aiming for nothing less than the overthrow of the Hashemite monarchy established by King Faisal I under British patronage in 1921.

In pursuit of their goals, they were utterly merciless. They executed the entire Iraqi royal family in cold blood in the palace courtyard. No one was spared. From young King Feisal II to his uncle Crown Prince Abd al-Ilah, no one was left who could carry the dynasty forward.[66] Nuri al-Said was caught the morning after and killed.[67]

The Iraqi junta, unlike their Egyptian counterparts, failed to unify the country or stop the bloodletting that scarred both state and society. The Iraqi Free Officers were ideologically splintered along radical, communist, and nationalist lines, and it was not long before they turned on each other. Throughout the 1960s, Iraq was ravaged by successive and bloody coup d'états perpetrated by different factions of Arab nationalists and Baathists.[68]

The sources of Iraq's blood-soaked history are varied and complex, but they stem mainly from the colonial inheritance. Iraq was a state created by the British to serve British interests. The Iraqi people were locked out of the decision-making process from the beginning. Their resentment and sense of alienation were acute. But the bloodletting of the revolution in 1958 and its subsequent aftershocks stoked the flames of political violence in Iraq and institutionalized it as a means to achieve political change.[69] In a way, the savagery of President Saddam Hussein and Abu Bakr al-Baghdadi, the leader of the Islamic State, can be traced back to this formative stage in the country's history.

What happened in Iraq sent shockwaves across the region and the new revolutionary regime's first acts were unequivocal statements of intent: they withdrew from the US-sponsored Baghdad Pact and demanded changes in the oil concessions with foreign companies.[70] Washington, unsurprisingly, saw the new regime as a threat to American interests. Before long, a full-on geostrategic crisis was in motion that threatened to engulf fragile pro-Western states like Jordan and Lebanon. King Hussein of Jordan and President Camille Chamoun in Lebanon feared the Iraqi fire would soon consume them. Playing the Cold War card, they called for urgent Western military intervention to prevent communist and radical pan-Arab nationalists toppling their regimes. Inter-Arab rivalries, which had already become embroiled in the global Cold War, heated up further.

Although the Iraqi revolution was inspired by the Nasserist revolution, it was an internal affair fueled by opposition to Nuri al-Said's subservience to the Western agenda. There is no evidence Nasser provided any material support to the Iraqi Free Officers. On the contrary, Nasser was as surprised as the Americans and the British were by the turn of events in Baghdad. At the time, the world's attention was focused elsewhere: on Jordan and Lebanon. Even so, cold warriors in Washington, particularly CIA director Allen Dulles, saw what they wanted to see and filtered what they saw through the prism of their strategic and economic interests. They believed Nasser was the instigator. Since 1955 the cold warriors tried to cut Nasser's wings and weaken his regime.

Nasser might have expected the Iraqi revolution to strengthen his vision of pan-Arab nationalism. He might also have expected Iraq to join the United Arab Republic. But instead, the Iraqi Free Officers brutally fought each other and resisted Nasser's leadership of the Arab world.

As time passed, Nasser's ideological cohorts would ultimately oppose his Arab nationalist project and offer a sectarian vision of their own. Nasser's vision was thus faced with a two-pronged challenge from conationalists on one side and conservatives on the other. On their own, Nasser's regional and international foes like the Saudis, the Jordanians, and the Americans could not have taken the wind out of his sails. US policy was deeply opposed to Nasser's Arab nationalism, fearing Egyptian imperial ambitions would hurt Washington's conservative clients and vital national interests in the greater Middle East. American opposition converged with local resistance and thwarted Nasser's inter-Arab political aspirations.

The resistance to Nasser by like-minded nationalists particularly softened his defenses, making him an easy target for the "reactionary" camp. This internal challenge not only weakened Nasser's leadership of the Arab world but also exposed the fragmentation of the nationalist camp. Lacking a unified vision and a uniform plan of action, Arab nationalists bickered with each other and constantly tried to outdo one another.

Power and self-aggrandizement trumped the pan-Arab ideal. Revolutionary Iraq was a perfect example of this. Despite singing the praise of Nasser and modeling themselves on his movement, the Iraqi Free Officers refused to join the United Arab Republic, an act that could only be seen as a stinging rebuke to the Egyptian leader they claimed to revere. Brigadier Qasim, the coup strongman, was jealous of Nasser's authority and refused to show him any deference. The rivalry between the two nationalists, Nasser and Qasim, was as bitter as that between Nasser and Nuri al-Said of the old regime, if not more so.

The situation was no more united within the Union. Syrian Baathists turned against Nasser when their power ambitions were not fulfilled. The Baathists' pan-Arabist vision was more expansive, ambitious, and urgent than Nasser's, encompassing a single unitary Arab state from the Atlantic Ocean to the Gulf. The Baathists dreamed of a United States of the Arab World, and they wanted it now, while Nasser was a gradualist who believed the Arab states must reach an advanced stage of social development before they considered union. Far from coherent and unified, the Arab nationalist camp was thus deeply divided along personality and ideological lines. While Nasser and his conationalists professed belief in the pan-Arab ideal, they fundamentally disagreed on how to turn it into a political reality and institutionalize it. Nasserists, Baathists, and other pan-Arabists differed on the design and character of the pan-Arab ideal and the lead architect to carry out the project.

Worse, there was no serious attempt to institutionalize Arab nationalism and to build social networks across states.[71] Those social networks would have deepened the ties that bind among the Arab elite and would have invested the ideology of Arab nationalism with institutional content and material durability. Instead, the pan-Arab ideal became a rhetorical device employed by authoritarian leaders against one other in the struggle for political survival and domination.

All these differences had profound consequences. The current crisis in the region has its roots in the failure of the Nasserist state and the Nasserist order. What is often overlooked in the debate on Arab nationalism is the extent to which the contending and contentious visions of Arab nationalists fundamentally undermined the foundational myth (that the Arab people are an imagined community and are entitled to a physical state) at the heart of the state system. The purpose of the foundational myth was to provide the postindependent states with a new underlying logic and a mobilizational appeal to replace their original colonialist purpose. The pan-Arab vision was subverted from within, sacrificed at the altar of separate state nationalisms and subjected to the whims and predilections of military strongmen. The United Arab Republic was a case in point.

As shown in the previous pages, colonialism left undeletable marks on the trajectories of Middle Eastern states. However, the region's descent toward political authoritarianism was not merely the design of malicious foreign intervention. Middle Eastern leaders' blind political ambition, greed, and petty geopolitical rivalries, including those well-intentioned and revolutionary leaders, helps partially explain the region's current predicament.

5

The Collapse
of the Foundational Myth

WHERE IT ALL WENT WRONG

EGYPT'S POLITICAL UNION with Syria was a risky gamble. The authority on Syrian affairs, Patrick Seale, labeled it a "leap in the dark" and noted that "Nasser agreed to bind Egypt to a country he had never seen."[1] Seale put Nasser's momentous decision down to overambitiousness and suggested the Egyptian leader was "seduced by the boldness and magnitude" of the project and "trapped by his role as a champion of Arab rights and arbiter of its destiny."[2]

Others, including Nasser's close friend and confidante Mohamed Heikal, took a different view. Heikal believed Nasser's consent to the merger was more strategic than personal. The union would safeguard Syria and the rest of the Arab world from external threats such as communism and US intervention.[3] In the Arab world, the need for solidarity in the face of outside interference became particularly acute after Washington's declaration of the Eisenhower Doctrine in 1958. It promised US military aid to any country threatened by "international communism."[4] To many Arab nationalists, the Eisenhower Doctrine was a veiled threat to "overthrow progressive nationalist rule in Syria and contain and roll back the Arab nationalist role of Egypt."[5]

The late 1950s were a time of great hope and greater uncertainty in the Middle East. These years would prove whether the patterns and abuses of colonialism would be overcome or revived in a new form. This chapter will detail how the new, revolutionary postcolonial governments slid deeper into authoritarianism, enabling the mutual interdependence between domestic strongmen and foreign intervention that continues to this day. Critically, even from the beginning the revolutionary governments would fail to respect the agency of the people, ruling through military dictate and leaving no room for power-sharing.

Nasser's Egypt promised a government built on Arab nationalism, a promise that would become bound up with the fate of the United Arab Republic (UAR). But the UAR and Arab nationalism could not survive the botched union, which was marked by a distinct lack of awareness of the Syrian situation and disregard for its people's particular experience and temperament. Following the UAR's dissolution, no ideology would reverse the centripetal forces driving Middle Eastern states apart and continuing the legacy of prolonged violent conflict, all of which benefited foreign powers and domestic authoritarians.

The Socioeconomic Reasons for the Collapse of the UAR

Was the union of Egypt and Syria doomed from the start? A look at the different economic trajectories the two countries had been on prior to the merger helps explain why it went so wrong so quickly.

Statistics show that from the outset this was a political marriage of two very unequal economic partners. In Syria before 1958, half the land under cultivation was concentrated in the hands of large landowners while nearly 70 to 80 percent of the rural population was landless.[6] Before Nasser carried out his famous land reforms in Egypt, the situation of the rural population was similar but, in contrast to Syria where the majority of landowners were Syrian, the majority of landowners in Egypt were not Egyptian. They were largely Turco-Circassian like the Mamluks who had ruled Egypt for centuries. This sense of Egyptian land not being in the hands of Egyptians helped Nasser isolate the landowning elite, label them as closet colonialists, and garner popular support for the sequestration of their lands. The Syrian landowning elite, on the other hand, was embedded in the fabric of Syrian political and economic life. A move against them would have been much harder to accomplish. That Egypt attempted to do this in Syria only highlights the government's failure to include the people, passing down ill-informed legislation from on high.

It was not only in agriculture where the two economies diverged sharply. Before the merger, Syria was dominated by private enterprise. The role of the state was very limited in the industrial sector. Syria had not used the state to instigate an industrial manufacturing strategy aimed at commercialization. Instead, a strong class of urban merchants had developed.[7] The union was meant to iron out such differences. But it quickly became clear who was calling the shots.[8] In 1958, the Syrian economy began to change in Egypt's image when land reforms like those Nasser carried out in Egypt were passed.[9] Before long, a problem arose. The reform program in Syria did not take into account differences in the value of agricultural land: large swathes of the Syrian countryside are arid whereas others are fertile and profitable.[10]

This oversight led to great inequality among peasants who were supposed to benefit from the redistribution program. To make matters worse, the system of repayments imposed on them only complicated the situation. In exchange for their new land, farmers were required to make forty annual payments. But many were unable to do so because they had already invested all their available resources in cultivating the land. Consequently, many farmers sold their lots to the former landowners who then leased the plots back to them.[11] The reforms in Syria did not resolve the issue of landless peasants, many of whom ended up working as sharecroppers.[12]

Other sectors of the Syrian economy also began to change in Egypt's image, as more decrees passed by Nasser after the merger impacted Syria's industrial sector and the urban merchant economy. Banks, insurance companies, and three industrial firms were fully nationalized and twenty-four industrial companies were partially nationalized, with the state retaining at least 50 percent of the shares.[13] The number of people on the boards of directors of all companies was limited to seven with just one workers' representative and one staff representative.[14] The state also fixed the salaries and allowances of directors and imposed a tax of up to 90 percent on incomes over 100,000 Egyptian pounds.[15] Meanwhile, workers and staff were allowed 25 percent of the annual profits of all companies: 10 percent in cash, 15 percent in housing and other benefits. In 1961, the free currency market was abolished with the result that all imports were conditional upon licensing and the availability of foreign exchange.[16]

All these measures ensured the control of the industrial sector by the state. In doing so, they created massive resentment and opposition among Syria's business and merchant class who were more cohesive as a group than their Egyptian counterparts had been. Most of the newly national-ized firms had not belonged to foreigners but to indigenous Syrians who did not like what was happening in their country. Moreover, the nation-alization policies meant that military officers who had little or no knowl-edge of industrial and commercial management were given top positions in the companies' boards of directors. Economic mismanagement and corruption became rife.

Syria, like Egypt, was a crossroads civilization with a long and proud history. Damascus had once ruled the Arab world: it was from Syria in the seventh and eighth centuries that Arab Muslim armies set out to con-quer much of the known world. Syrians were aware of the greatness of their past. They had not joined the union with Egypt to lose their iden-tity and give way to Nasser at every turn. For the locally born elite with wealth and status to lose, the complete redrawing of the Syrian economic map was the final straw.

This discrepancy between Egyptian and Syrian nationalization lies at the heart of the failure of the UAR project. Even though both sides had enthusiastically signed up to Arab nationalism, that enthusiasm by itself was not enough to make the dream of union real. The honeymoon be-tween the Egyptian and Syrian regimes was therefore short-lived. Nasser and the Syrian leaders soon came to blows over everything from ideologi-cal differences to questions of governance to the structure of the union itself. Syrians criticized Nasser for failing to respond to Israeli provoca-tions against their country and for attempting to "Egyptianize" the coun-try. For his part, Nasser suspected the Baathists of trying to sabotage the union and seize power.

Riven by internal tensions, the UAR project proved disastrous and survived for only three tumultuous years before it was dissolved in 1961.
Arab nationalism never recovered from the union's collapse, and no other
unifying ideology came forth to take its place. In 1958, the union between
Egypt and Syria had been widely celebrated by the Arab masses as a new
dawn. In 1961, Arab nationalists mourned its demise as nothing short of
catastrophic. People came face-to-face with the reality that the interests
of ruling elites were so deeply entrenched they would supersede any
supranationalist vision. In the years that followed, the region would not
manage to put aside the colonial legacies of division and conflict. The
dream had died.

The Death of a Dream: The Consequences
of the Collapse of the UAR

The consequences of the collapse of the UAR in 1961 were profound.
Over the course of the next decade, they rippled across the Arab world
and left no aspect of public life untouched. As a unifying ideology,
Arab nationalism had failed to deliver, and that failure led to a permanent rift in the ranks of its followers. That rift would, in turn, seriously
impact the politics of war and peace and lead to even greater disappointment and disillusion when Arab armies saw combat in two very
different theaters against two very different opponents: Egyptian army
in Yemen against Saudi-backed royalists and Egyptian-Jordanian-
Syrian armies defending UAR lands against the state of Israel. The
outcome of these wars reshaped the political landscape, deepened
the fractures in the Arab world, and intensified an Arab cold war that
rages to this day. The ultimate victors in both conflicts would be the
foreign powers who benefited from a weak and divided Middle East
and the domestic authoritarians who would use the continuing conflicts and sectarianism to justify and consolidate their rule. To understand this process and its repercussions, we need to look at the fallout
from the breakup of the UAR.

Disunity and Disillusion:
The Rift within the Arab Nationalist Camp

Egypt's short-lived union with Syria had two immediate consequences. First, the failure of the project reinforced Nasser's initial reluctance toward any form of unity between Egypt and other Arab countries. This aversion put him at odds with pan-Arab nationalists in the Mashreq or the Arab east, particularly Iraq and Syria, who still aimed to establish a single unitary pan-Arab state and who had previously looked to Nasser as their champion. Second, it weakened Nasser's standing because various strands of pan-Arab nationalism were now directly challenging his vision. What had been an ideology of unity now became another site for discord.

Following Nasser's explicit shift from the idea of pan-Arab unity toward a policy of Arab solidarity and cooperation, pan-Arab nationalists in Syria, Iraq, Lebanon, Palestine, and beyond, questioned his revolutionary credentials and accused him of forfeiting the struggle to liberate Palestine. He was more interested, they claimed, in prioritizing Egyptian interests over those of the Arab nation. From then on, the fight between Arab nationalists became as bitter as the clash between nationalists and their conservative rivals. The growing rift within the nationalist camp destabilized the entire state system by shifting focus from cooperation and development to geostrategic rivalries and led Nasser to take risky decisions that proved disastrous.

Meanwhile, public quarrels and rivalry between Nasser and the Baath in Syria heated up after the breakdown of the UAR. The two sides embarked on an unedifying public battle over the future of Arab nationalism in which each side repeatedly questioned the other's credibility and belittled the other's interpretation of Arab nationalism and unity. Tension between the two regimes reached unprecedented heights in 1963 following the failure of the Cairo Unity Talks held between Egypt, Iraq, and Syria.

The Unity Talks took place between March and June 1963 and collapsed due to the mistrust that had developed between Nasser and the Baath Party. But how seriously committed to the process Nasser ever was remains open to question. The weight of evidence suggests that he used the talks to discredit the Baathists.[17]

The Syrians responded to Nasser's attacks by challenging his version of events and presenting their own.[18]

As a result of the failure of the 1963 Cairo Unity Talks, Nasser began to question the very concept of Arab unity as it had been understood thus far. According to him:

> A natural, legitimate union is assured and inevitable, but this also re-quired that we analyse its rationale.... In the past we stated that we would co-operate with all nationalist groups and organizations. But we have now been proved wrong. This kind of multiplicity of nationalist activities seems to lead us to clashes.... We must therefore begin to look ahead into the future and draw the proper lesson from these events.... While every Arab country boasts a party, union seems utterly impos-sible. True political opposition would degenerate into regionalism, with Syria at odds with Egypt, Iraq at odds with Syria, and so forth. For union to emerge, and for all immoral opportunist obstacles to be over-come, we must launch a unified Arab Nationalist movement which would incorporate all the nationalist movements of the Arab world.[19]

The Baathists then proceeded to hit Nasser where it hurt most. The party's ideology focused on the establishment of a unitary pan-Arab state. By drawing attention to their commitment to *all* Arabs, the Baathists ques-tioned Nasser's revolutionary mantle and his genuine commitment to pan-Arab causes, particularly Palestine. No Arab leader could afford to ignore this issue.

This was just one example of the ferocious infighting going on in the nationalist camp at the time. Ironically, the intranationalist dispute played a greater role in undermining Nasser's regional ambitions than the rivalry with the so-called reactionary monarchies. As a self-styled Arab revolu-tionary, Nasser could not afford such a blow to his hegemony and his claims to leadership of the "Arab cause."[20] This was one of the reasons he became involved in the disastrous war in Yemen. Infighting among the Arab nationalists thus stoked violence on the field, furthering the divi-sions that had only been growing from the collapse of the UAR.

A Military Miscalculation: The Yemen War

Egypt's costly military intervention in Yemen in the early 1960s was directly related to the breakup of the UAR and Nasser's increasing feelings of insecurity. More and more often, he felt himself to be under siege. From 1961 to his death of a heart attack in 1970, Nasser no longer entertained the ambitious pan-Arab unity proposals put forward by his Arab counterparts. Instead, he insisted on coordination and collaboration or what he called "Arab solidarity."

But there was little evidence of any solidarity in the corridors of power. Quite the opposite: inter-Arab rivalries intensified following the breakdown of the UAR and led Nasser, still stinging from the union's failure, to lash out against what he labeled "reactionary" Arab regimes like the Kingdom of Saudi Arabia. This sense of being caught between two competing camps led Nasser to send Egyptian troops to Yemen, which shares a long border with Saudi Arabia, in support of a military coup modeled on Egypt's Free Officers' coup in 1952.

The deployment was a disaster. Egyptian troops became bogged down in a tribal and ideological conflict that turned into an Arab civil war: a bloodbath where Arab killed Arab. It was a forerunner of the wars we now see raging across the region as well as an echo of the sectarian violence that had enabled colonial rule. But unlike the colonial powers, the young independent nation lacked the resources and institutional strength to handle such a commitment. The Yemen debacle exacted a heavy toll on the Egyptian state, overextended its military, and undermined Nasser's credibility across the region. Often referred to as "Nasser's Vietnam,"[21] the conflict became a quagmire Egypt could not leave without serious loss of prestige.

But loss of prestige was not all Nasser had to worry about in Yemen. His intervention in the country was a significant factor in his army's defeat in the June 1967 Six-Day War against Israel, as some of Egypt's elite forces were deployed hundreds of miles from the new theater of war. Egypt's war in Yemen thus showed the limits of Egyptian power and, in doing so, undermined the Egyptian state and the man who led it. As Arabs brutally fought fellow Arabs, the war also exposed the painful truth that pan-Arab nationalism was unable to survive the transition from idea to reality. The legacies of colonial division proved more durable than the project of developing a collective political identity, at least as it was formulated and deployed by Nasser and his allies.

Foreign intervention in internal Arab affairs would play a role in this struggle as well. Egypt's engagement in Yemen exacerbated tensions between Nasser and the Western powers, particularly Britain who still ruled the Aden Protectorate.[22] Yemen now offered Britain a chance to exact vengeance on Nasser after its humiliation during the Suez crisis a decade earlier. Britain provided covert military support to the Yemeni royalists and, perhaps more crucially, allowed Israel to operate clandestinely in the war-torn country. Israel used this access to gain valuable intelligence on Egypt's armed forces and its vulnerable position in Yemen during the years leading up to the 1967 conflict.[23]

Falling into Israel's Trap: The Six-Day Disaster

Unfortunately for Nasser, Yemen was not the only military miscalculation he made. Nor was it the worst. Just as his rivalry with Syrian and Iraqi Baathists and other nationalists caused him to overreach in Yemen, he repeated the mistake with a much more determined and dangerous foe: Israel.

In May 1967, in an attempt to outbid the militant Baathists in Syria and Iraq and counter their accusation of cowardice toward Israel, Nasser monstrously miscalculated by upping the ante with Tel Aviv. In doing so, he provided the rationale for Israeli leaders to preempt the Egyptian military and vanquish it on June 5, 1967. The crisis ultimately brought ruin to Nasser's army, to his entire political project, and to him personally.

Tensions between the Arab world and Israel reached boiling point in the spring of 1967 when the Israeli air force downed six Syrian MiG fighters as retaliation for Syria allowing Palestinian fighters to cross into Israel.[24] At this moment, the Soviet Union, an ally of Egypt, leaked a false intelligence report to Nasser that alleged Israel had mobilized troops on the Syrian border. An Israeli invasion of Syria looked imminent. No one knows for sure if the Russians intentionally misled Nasser or if Nasser used the incident to flex his military muscle in a bid to reassert his leadership of the Arab arena. The point here is not to reconstruct Nasser's opaque decision-making, but to show how intranationalist rivalries impacted regional politics in decisive ways.

On May 22, Nasser closed the Straits of Tiran to all shipping headed for Israel, providing Israel with the casus belli, the legal justification, to attack Egypt in June 1967.[25] Nasser's decision to close the Straits of Tiran was as an act of political defiance not only against Israel but also his Arab critics. The passage of Israeli shipping through the Red Sea port of Aqaba had long been used by conservative Arab states, such as Saudi Arabia and Jordan, as a political weapon against Nasser. By failing to impose a blockade on Israeli ships in the past, the Saudis and Jordanians had accused Nasser of cowardice toward Israel. Nasser seized the moment in May 1967 to prove his critics wrong, though he did not want war with Israel. Nor had he mobilized or organized his army in any effective way to prepare for such an eventuality.[26]

It is often argued that the only thing that unites Arabs is opposition to Israel. And that if the Zionist enemy had not existed, they would have had to invent it in order to unite. But that is not true. Israel was, and continues to be, a divisive issue in Arab politics. Nasser and his fellow Arab nationalists fundamentally disagreed on how to deal with the Jewish state. While Nasser counseled restraint and calm, the Baathists agitated for confrontation. This Arab disunity and lack of inter-Arab coordination would prove detrimental in the efforts against Israel in June 1967.

Nasser's approach to war in 1967 was completely different from the path he had previously taken in dealing with Israel. He was traumatized by the Arabs' defeat in 1948, but this trauma led him to turn inward and not challenge Israel directly. From the beginning of his rule, his strategic priorities had focused more on achieving real independence, along with social and economic development at home, and less on the Israel-Palestine problem. He therefore sought to avoid military confrontation with Israel and had even gone as far as to state a preference for a political settlement.[27] This approach is markedly different from that taken by the Syrian regime in the 1960s whose enmity against Israel led them to confront the enemy head on.

Yet in May 1967, with his leadership of the Arab world called into question, and the failure of the UAR and the disaster in Yemen weighing heavily on his mind, Nasser threw his earlier caution to the wind. Faced with a potential military confrontation between Israel and Syria in May 1967, he felt the need to act. His aides insist his actions were defensive and he had no intention or immediate plans to go on the offensive. But if the worse did come to worst and Israel *did* strike, Nasser believed his forces would be able to hold their ground. His chief of staff, Abdel Hakim Amer, had assured him so.[28]

It was a fatal mistake. Neither Nasser nor Amer recognized the disarray within the Egyptian army, the lack of leadership, the poor organization, and the woefully ineffective chain of command and control. Amer had presided over the army as if it were his own personal fiefdom. He had put men loyal to him in key posts and strengthened his hold on this pivotal institution. And with good reason: in a military state, control of the armed forces opened up a vast range of opportunities for anyone with ambition.

As the commander in chief, Nasser was ultimately responsible for Amer's catastrophic mistakes. Yet he refrained from releasing him because the two were close friends and he was wary of Amer's control of the army. Nasser's fateful decision to keep him at the head of it illustrates how cronyism and a lack of public accountability sabotage the decision-making processes of authoritarian states.

Contrast this with Israel. As a conscript army, the leaders of Israel's army were—and still are—publicly accountable in a way that Egypt's military has never been. The different structure of both armies radically alters the outcome of the battle because it radically alters the chain of command. Take, for example, what happened to Israel's chief of staff (and future prime minister) Yitzhak Rabin in the run-up to the Six-Day War. Rabin had worked himself to the point of exhaustion, becoming so overwrought on the eve of war that he came close to a nervous breakdown. He had to be sedated and ordered to rest before he could return to duty. In similar circumstances, it is unlikely such an order could have been given to Nasser's chief of staff, Amer, surrounded as he was by handpicked loyalists.[29]

This lack of accountability at the highest levels of the Egyptian military was a critical factor in Nasser's mishandling of the May 1967 crisis. Perhaps surprisingly for a man of his military experience, Nasser dangerously underestimated the extent to which the Egyptian army was, at the time, overextended in Yemen. Field Marshal Mohamed Abdel Ghani el-Gamasy, a highly respected commander, argues that the Yemen war played a major role in Egypt's 1967 defeat: "Nearly a third of our land forces, supported by our air force and navy, were engaged in an operation approximately two thousand kilometers away from Egypt, with no prospects for either a political or a military settlement.... We incurred heavy losses in manpower, our military budget was drained, discipline and training suffered, weapons and equipment deteriorated, and fighting capability was seriously affected ... levels of training consequently declined. Planes and technical equipment belonging to the air force were subjected to heavy wear."[30]

The lack of strategic coordination between Arab states, together with ignorance of Egypt's compromised military position, also contributed to the Arab defeat in 1967. Even though they signed a mutual defense pact under Soviet auspices in 1966,[31] there was shockingly little consultation between Cairo and Damascus in the run-up to and during the May–June 1967 crisis.[32] For example, Egyptian propaganda led Syrian leaders to believe "they needed to join the fight because the Arab side was winning."[33] Hearing this, Hafez al-Assad, an air force commander at the time, sent his small contingent of fighter jets into the air. The Israelis shot them down on June 5.[34]

Moreover, Nasser faced serious economic difficulties at home. CIA figures at the time indicate Egypt's domestic debt amounted to more than $1.5 billion with its foreign debt likely topping $2.5 billion.[35] Egypt's costly commitments abroad only worsened its economic situation. The war in Yemen cost $60 million annually.[36] Nasser was on the defensive. He yearned for a comeback and a boost to his reputation and brand of Arab nationalism.

In his fiery speeches, Nasser appeared utterly oblivious to the consequences of his rhetoric, especially as the Egyptian army was woefully unprepared for war with Israel. There was another problem: he was not saying what he really meant. For all his provocative language, Nasser did not want a war. He believed superpower intervention, as had occurred in the past, would prevent the breakout of war. Of course, when the hoped-for foreign intervention could have advanced peace and unity in the region, no one came running. What Nasser failed to appreciate was that by 1967 the United States was preoccupied in Vietnam and the Soviet Union had lost much of its leverage to influence local players.[37] Worse still, Nasser failed to foresee the potential alignment between the United States and Israel that would solidify in the aftermath of the 1967 conflict and transform into a special strategic relationship, the like of which the United States does not enjoy with any other country in the region.[38]

Nasser's words and actions were designed for public consumption at home and in the Arab neighborhood. But they were a colossal miscalculation. He projected power he did not have and, in the process, dangerously raised the public's expectations. Added to that, he underestimated the strength of Israel's armed forces and more importantly, Israel's eagerness to demonstrate its power and to humiliate the most popular leader of the Arab world.

Israel launched a multipronged attack on June 5 and delivered a crippling blow to the Egyptian, Syrian, and Jordanian armies in less than a week. It destroyed the Egyptian air force and occupied the Sinai "as far as the Suez Canal, Jerusalem and the Palestinian part of Jordan and part of southern Jordan [and Syria's] (the Jawlan or 'Golan Heights')."[39] The fighting did not stop until the United Nations stepped in and brokered a ceasefire on June 10, 1967.

The defeat left deep scars on the Arab imagination. For more than a decade, Egyptians in particular, and Arabs in general, were repeatedly told that Egypt had the most powerful army in the Middle East and that Israel would be utterly destroyed if it dared to attack. Nasser seems to have hypnotized the Arabs: as long as their lion roared, Arab lands were safe and secure. In June 1967, all this was shown to be empty talk. As the dust settled on the battlefields in Sinai, the Golan Heights, and Jerusalem on June 10, 1967, Arabs confronted the grim reality of loss and humiliation. "Defeat goes deeper into the human soul than victory," wrote the prominent historian of the Middle East, Albert Hourani, in his classic work

History of the Arab Peoples: "To be in someone else's power is a conscious experience which induces doubts about the ordering of the universe."[40] Israel's crushing victory over the Arabs in 1967 was widely regarded as a kind of "moral judgment."[41]

More than the defeat in the Palestine War in 1948, the Arab defeat in June 1967 dealt a devastating blow to the Egyptian-led Arab bloc. As the pivot of the Arab order, Nasser's Egypt was no longer capable of promoting the foundational myth at the heart of what little regional unity remained. Time and again, people who knew Nasser have told me his legacy was buried beneath the rubble of his army in the Sinai in June 1967.

But no matter how much the defeat hurt Nasser, it hurt the Palestinians more. For nearly two decades, they had endured the pain of exile by holding onto the hope their situation was temporary. That they would, one day very soon, return home. But if the most powerful man in the Arab world could not make their dream of return real, who could help them now? And they now faced a new problem: Israel was not fighting alone. Standing shoulder to shoulder with Israel was the world's greatest superpower: the United States.

One of the most enduring legacies of Nasser's miscalculation in 1967 and the subsequent rise of Israel as a regional power has been the revival of American role in the Middle East. Finally, the cold warriors in Washington succeeded in cutting Nasser's wings. The United States viewed Israel's victory as an exceptional opportunity to "destroy or gravely weaken Nasser, strengthen conservative states, force Arab acceptance of Israel, and resurrect US influence in the region."[42] It was at this junction in history that America's Middle East strategy would be defined for the next half century. The new American approach to the region was summarized by Walt Rostow, assistant to President Lyndon B. Johnson, on June 8, 1967, as opposition to any United Nations resolution that required Israel to concede war gains unless it involved a conclusive Arab-Israeli settlement.[43] The United States now began to supply Israel with the advanced offensive weaponry that would allow it to maintain its military edge and keep control of the occupied Arab territories.[44]

Even though Israel became the biggest recipient of American aid, the United States did not limit its support in the Middle East to Israel alone. Key to Washington's strategy in the region were Nasser's old foes: the conservative kings he had taken on in the proxy war in Yemen. This preexisting division of the Arab world into two camps—conservative kings on the one hand, radical presidents on the other—which the United States had already been exploiting, undermined the idea of secular Arab nationalism and unity. With US backing, Saudi Arabia promoted pan-Islamism as a counterweight to Nasser's pan-Arab nationalism. Both camps used rival ideologies to gain geostrategic advantage. This was only the newest round of the old colonial strategy of divide and rule. The United States effectively revived the roles Britain and France had played decades earlier, ensuring an instability that would make the region more vulnerable to foreign intervention. This hugely divisive Arab fault line between presidents and kings persists to this day.

Arab against Arab: The Arab Cold War

From independence, the Arab world was divided ideologically between the military-led regimes in the newly independent states and the ruling families who had held power for decades, sometimes centuries. The identity of Arab nationalism was thus constructed in opposition to the more traditional forms of Arab governance espoused by the monarchies. After 1958, the republican regimes in Egypt, Syria, and Iraq used Arab nationalism and pan-Arabism as weapons in this rivalry with the region's ruling families. The monarchies were not themselves immune to the appeal of Arab unity—they were keen to project an Arab image in which Palestine was an integral part—but their vision of Arabism was more limited than that of their republican counterparts. They preferred to concentrate on cooperation and solidarity among sovereign Arab states in line with the Arab League's mandate.[45]

The term "Arab Cold War" was coined by the late American historian Malcolm H. Kerr and symbolized the inter-Arab rivalries that developed in the 1950s and 1960s. On one side stood radical Arab nationalists and pan-Arabists led by Nasser and the Arab republics. On the opposing side were the forces of religious conservatism led by the Arab monarchies of the Gulf, first by Iraq till 1958 and then by Saudi Arabia, which used pan-Islamism as a counterweight to pan-Arab nationalism.[46]

For the monarchies, political Arabism first and foremost upheld the sovereignty of the state. But for the radical regimes in Egypt, Syria, and Iraq, the vision was much broader. In their eyes, the interests of the common Arab nation (or supranationalism) took precedence over those of individual states (or territorial nationalism).[47] When they seized power, the radical republican military regimes in Egypt, Iraq, and Syria were quick to bolster their legitimacy and present themselves as the gateway to the future. They did this by opposing the conservative monarchies they labeled "backward" and "reactionary." By way of contrast, they portrayed themselves as standing on the right side of history and the republican model as more viable, progressive, and forward-looking. In spite of their radical rhetoric, the presidents nonetheless shared one area of common ground with the kings and emirs: the radical regimes developed a strong social agenda but did not foster a more balanced, inclusive contract with the people. This lack of power-sharing would gradually descend into an authoritarianism to rival that of any hereditary ruler.

The ongoing Arab cold war was marked by a complex interplay between domestic and regional agendas with each impacting the other. The framing of politics around Arabism contributed to this interconnectedness. Moreover, the permeability of the long, porous borders across the region allowed for greater meddling by Arab states in each other's domestic and foreign policy. Before long, this meddling reached a level never seen in the Middle East or indeed in other regions of the postcolonial world.[48] Arab rulers constantly intervened in the internal affairs of one another and paid little or no attention to sovereignty.

Nasser's recurrent speeches on the Sawt al-Arab (Voice of the Arabs) radio station were an illustration of the "low salience of sovereignty" in the region. Nasser symbolized the radiant possibility of an Arab identity that transcended sectarian squabbles. His radio broadcasts were eagerly anticipated events. In cafés and living rooms from Algeria to Syria, people from all walks of life stopped what they were doing to huddle round the radio and listen. In these speeches, Nasser gave his opinions on developments across the region, going over the heads of local leaders and, at times, even vehemently criticizing their conduct.

His unreserved support for Algerian independence and African liberation movements helped extend his power base far beyond Egypt and the Arab east. But other Arab rulers feared Nasser's popularity and the extent of his outreach more than they feared his military might. In June 1967, for example, King Hussein of Jordan felt he had little choice but to side with Egypt in the war against Israel. Failure to do so, the king feared, would have provoked a popular revolt at home.[49]

Egypt's defeat in the Six-Day War showed that Nasser had miscalculated strategically in thinking Egypt's military prowess could match its ideological reach. His decision to stand up to Israel was driven by inter-Arab competition over the Palestine cause as Egypt, Iraq, and Syria tried to outbid each other as the true defender of all Arabs.[50] Similarly, Egypt's disastrous military campaign in Yemen was a direct result of rivalry with another Arab state—Saudi Arabia—over regional influence and hegemony. Positioning and rhetoric thus trapped Arab leaders in a downward spiral of internecine rivalry. Ironically, their very insistence of Arab brotherhood had become a source of conflict as each regime jockeyed to be the first among ostensible equals. In this context, the institutionalization of pan-Arab nationalism did not stand a chance as the Arab cold war tainted regional politics throughout the 1950s and the 1960s. And the failure of the ideology meant the fall of those who espoused it.

The Death of Nasser and the Waning of Arab Nationalism

The failure of Arab nationalism as a foundational myth and the humiliation of its custodian, Nasser, fundamentally undermined the Arab state system and deepened its legitimacy deficit. The rosy promises of the late 1950s had shattered beyond repair. For years, people had been fed a diet of cultural glory, empowerment, and unity. Arabs had, at last, awakened from their long political slumber to become a power to be reckoned with—or so Nasser and other nationalist leaders told their people. But when this was shown to be nothing but wishful thinking, it led to a crisis of self-confidence that Arabs have yet to overcome.

Division and violent discord drove states further apart, isolating their rulers, who turned their attention to consolidating authoritarian control. As Arab rulers bickered over influence and personal fiefdoms, the postindependent Arab states gradually morphed into a variety of overbearing, tyrannical police states. Arab nationalism and pan-Arab issues were stripped of their substance and reduced to little more than justification and rationalization for the actions of the ruling elite.

As a result, the grand narrative of the radical postindependence elites suffered a serious setback. Prosperity and a social contract that recognized the agency of the people remained a distant dream. The new order was more equitable and less socially hierarchal than the old had been—the gulf between the haves and have-nots diminished—but social justice came at the expense of the declining wealth of these young nations. Deficits soared as public spending far outstripped state resources. State control begat failures that only justified further state control.

In Egypt, Nasser tackled urgent social problems, including abject poverty and access to education and medical services, but he sacrificed sound economic planning and management to populism and cronyism. A small inner circle of his most trusted aides formulated domestic and foreign policies behind closed doors, all of which led to widespread inefficiency, mismanagement, and corruption as state capitalism replaced liberal capitalism without the ironclad checks and balances in place to ensure transparency, inclusive development, productivity, and growth.[51]

In particular, the absorption of private assets into the public sector proved problematic. If the goal had been to transfer power from the small capitalist class to the people, the plan did not work. The main beneficiary turned out to be the army. The Nasserist state aimed to maintain firm command of all key institutions so military officers were put in charge of most company boards. The consequences for the economy were disastrous.[52] Between 1960 and 1965, government economic policies had seemed to work as the economy grew, but after 1965 the trend reversed and yields started to decline.[53] This was the beginning of a serious economic crisis the government desperately tried to resolve by expanding external borrowing even more.[54]

This top-down authoritarian system of governance caused massive economic mismanagement and flawed decision-making. It exacted a heavy toll on state and society, and reproduced the worst aspects of the colonial era, while dismantling its thin institutional legacy. And because Nasser was the most popular leader in the most populous state in the region, his top-down authoritarianism influenced the conduct of his contemporaries. All across the Middle East, Nasser's generation of young radicals who, like him, came from the military and who, like him, seized power in coups, followed where he led.

The failure to engender a real industrial revolution through the development of a competitive private sector had long-lasting consequences and led to the establishment of a corporatist state system with an "exaggerated role of the state" in the economy.[55] Corporatism emerges in countries where class structure is weak. It allows the state to pit different sections of the population against each other to prevent the emergence of a hegemonic class beyond the control of the state.[56] To fill this hegemonic vacuum, the state develops strategies of inclusion and exclusion with social groups.[57] Those included are provided with public goods in return for a "tacit political pact" of compliance with the regime.[58] The development of the state along these lines led to the rise of informal patronage networks in state institutions and to the dependency of certain social groups on the state.[59] The development of the Nasserist state structure along corporatist lines proved remarkably durable and set the foundation for the following decades. Anwar al-Sadat, Hosni Mubarak, and Abdel Fattah al-Sisi, Nasser's successors, broke away from his economic policies but continued to develop the state along corporatist lines.

But the corporatist system, like the colonial system before it, only works for those at the top. It is politically, economically, and socially disastrous for everyone else. By the end of the 1960s, a sentiment spread among Arabs that their nations and leaders were infested with moral hypocrisy, self-aggrandizement, and hubris. The brutal proxy war in Yemen between Egypt and Saudi Arabia proved Arab disunion was more a reality than Arab union. Worse still, inter-Arab rivalries were escalating into assassinations and bloodletting on Arab streets. Creeping cynicism and disillusion about the prospects of Arab cooperation and unity replaced hope and optimism.

This bleak new reality was clear at the Arab Summit in Khartoum, Sudan, on August 29, 1967, just a few weeks after the Arab defeat. This summit of Arab heads of state in Khartoum formalized Nasser's withdrawal from leadership of the Arab arena and marked the ascendancy of territorial nationalism over pan-Arabism. Territorial nationalism could have developed a foundational myth of its own had it pursued a new social contract between rulers and citizens and an open society governed by the rule of law. Nothing of the sort was ever attempted. In fact, the post-1967 era witnessed the deepening and consolidation of the police state in most Arab rulers. In Khartoum, an agreement was reached that saw Egypt focus on rebuilding its army and putting its own house in order. Ironically, it was Nasser's old foe Saudi Arabia who came to the country's financial rescue. After a meeting with King Faisal, Nasser agreed to withdraw Egyptian troops from Yemen while Faisal promised to cease military aid to the royalists.[60] It was another humiliating defeat for Nasser.

As Ahmed al-Shuqari, the first leader of the Palestine Liberation Organization (PLO), noted: "The Arabs' oil defeated the Arabs." In other words, the outcome of the Yemen war proved that power in the Middle East rested not on ideology but on money and religious capital. Nasser's surrender in the rivalry between Egypt and Saudi Arabia and his acceptance of financial dependency on Saudi came down to numbers: thanks to oil, the Saudis had resources Egypt lacked.[61] The Khartoum summit was an explicit acknowledgment of the decline of Arab nationalism, as spearheaded by Nasser, and the rise of Saudi Arabia and petrodollar politics and pan-Islamist ideology.

This power shift from an Egyptian-dominated pole to a Saudi one went hand-in-hand with a systemic campaign to discredit secular-leaning Arab nationalism and Arab socialism as practiced by Nasser. When his successor, Anwar Sadat, consolidated his grip on power following Nasser's death in 1970, he joined forces with the Gulf states and launched a multipronged assault against his predecessor's ideological inheritance. Seeking to build his own legacy, Sadat used piety and Islamic references as an alternative to Nasser's secular-leaning Arab nationalism. The holy alliance between Sadat and the petro-dollar and pan-Islamism continued the project of discrediting Arab nationalism that had reached its apogee following the Six-Day War.[62]

With Nasser gone, Arab nationalists felt orphaned and besieged by petro-dollar Gulf leaders and their allies like Sadat. These new leaders sought to build their own legacy and lay Arab nationalism to rest once and for all. But the new elite failed to offer an alternative foundational myth or a new ideology. Far from remedying the democratic and developmental deficits in the region, the second and third generation of postindependence ruling elites, such as Sadat, Bashar al-Assad, Hafez al-Assad, Saddam Hussein, and Hosni Mubarak, consolidated the deep state and pursued neoliberal economic policies that led to the pauperization of the Arab people. In the process, the entire state system lost its equilibrium, making it easier for authoritarians to capitalize on the violence and mistrust.

The Syrian poet Nizar Qabbani encapsulated this sense of Arab loss and bereavement. Qabbani's powerful and widely read poem "When Will They Announce the Death of the Arabs" reflected his disillusionment with Arab leaders. Here the hugely popular poet laments the tragic predicament of the Arabs:

> For fifty years,
> I have watched the state of the Arabs,
> As they thunder, without rain,
> As they go into wars and never come out,
> As they chew the hide of rhetoric,
> But never digest it. . . .
>
> . . . After fifty years
> Of trying to keep record of what I have seen,
> I can say that I have seen nations who believe that men from
> the security services
> Are decreed by God, just like a headache, or the flu
> Or leprosy, or scabies;
> I have seen Arabism on display in antique shops.
> But I have not seen the Arabs![63]

Arab nationalism has never recovered. It has since been superseded by the many shades or incarnations of political Islam, including pan-Islamism and Salafi-jihadism. Yet despite the intensity and popularity of political Islam, Islamists have never offered a political vision or a blueprint for governance.

In an ironic twist, following the failure of Arabism, Arab monarchies led by Saudi Arabia attempted to fill the ideological vacuum with pan-Islamism. The rise of 'ulema as an ideational force among the poor Arab masses is a case in point. Moreover, the humiliating defeat of Nasser in 1967 was portrayed in Islamic circles as a godly retribution for his turn toward a more modernist and "Westernized" Islam. In contrast, supporters of the petro-dollar monarchies depicted the rising influence of these monarchies after 1967 as a godly reward for those who never turned away from the authentic power of Islam.

As an ideology, Arab nationalism emphasized the glories of past Arab civilization, colored by a longing for Arab solidarity and the articulation of a common identity based on opposition to Western domination and colonialism.[64] It promised an end to the corruption and division of the past. Arab nationalism could have provided the political logic for better governance in the Middle East (as the moral backbone of a contract between the people and their governments) as well as the foundation for Arab cooperation across state lines. Yet under the combined pressures of the global Cold War, external threats, political authoritarianism, intra-Arab rivalries, and a fraying social contract at home, it fell prey to the very corruption and division it sought to avoid. In its place, conservative movements such as political Islam and pan-Islamism began to fill the vacuum, promising to deliver welfare where existing states had failed to do, but the reality turned out to be different. With the failure of nationalism and the inability of pan-Islamism to put forward an alternative that enjoys similar broad appeal, there appears to be no viable ideology that could unlock the potential of the region by establishing the cause of Arab cooperation as a balm for sectarian violence. The Middle East state system has been running on empty (ideationally) for decades.

The Road to Where We Are Now

Abandoned by the state and courted by religiously infused nonstate actors, the people of the Middle East have gradually retreated into their parochial, ethnic, communal, and tribal affiliations for sustenance and security. The result is the breakdown of institutional Middle Eastern politics and the fracturing of the regional order. The Lebanese civil war, which lasted from 1975 to 1990, was a brutal example.

A diverse and open society, Lebanon all but collapsed as it descended into an internecine civil war that made Beirut a global byword for sectarian slaughter. For fifteen years, Lebanon became a battlefield for regional and global proxy wars.[65]

Like Lebanon, the eight-year conflict between Iraq and Iran (1980–1988) was costly in blood and treasure and it, too, drew in actors from the wider region.[66] It also showed that time had done nothing to lessen intra-Arab rivalries. Because of Syria's long-running rivalry with Iraq, Syria chose to ally with Persian Iran. Most other Arab states supported Iraq, albeit with varying degrees of enthusiasm.[67] Before the dust had settled on the Iraqi-Iranian killing fields, Saddam Hussein invaded and occupied neighboring Kuwait, hammering a final nail in the coffin of Arab nationalism and inter-Arab institutions like the League of the Arab States. Many Arab states, including Egypt, joined forces with their past enemy—the United States—in an effort to expel Iraqi troops from Kuwait.

It is precisely this rivalry and the adoption of what is essentially realpolitik, which contributed to the fall of Arab nationalism. This tendency was predicted by Sati' al-Husri, the leading theoretician of Arab nationalism, following the Palestine War of 1947–1948, when he repeatedly pondered how the Arabs could have lost the war when they were seven states against one. His answer was that "the Arabs lost the war *precisely because they were seven states.*"[68] For Husri, the solution to the divisions between the seven states was obvious: "to avoid losing future wars, the Arabs had to unite into one Arab state."[69] By doing so, they could redraw the map of the Middle East to suit *their* aspirations rather than those of the colonial powers that had created the current state system.

From the 1950s, multiple cleavages existed that had the potential to tear the system of the Arab states. Arab rulers, whether nationalist or conservative, were more concerned about scoring political points against each other than with defending an imagined Arab ideal or genuinely forging a defense pact against foreign foes. The Six-Day War put to rest the rhetoric of Arab unity and common destiny that Arab rulers had repeatedly used and abused over the years. When Egypt, Syria, and Jordan faced the brunt of the Israeli assault on June 5, 1967, other Arab rulers sat on their hands and did nothing, their inaction a stark contrast with the loftiness of their rhetoric. It was also an indication that they were happier to see their Arab rivals fall than to intervene and help the Palestinians.

Broken promises repeatedly exposed the weakness of Arab rulers when it came to alleviating the plight of the Palestinians. In fact, Israel won every military confrontation with the Arab state system, individually and collectively. Only Hezbollah (and Hamas to a lesser extent), a nonstate actor, stymied Israel's war effort in 2006 in Lebanon. Furthermore, the internationalization of the Arab-Israeli conflict during the Cold War turned the Middle East into a dangerous theater of a US-Soviet proxy war, thus militarizing regional politics and consolidating the security-based state. In this sense, the Six-Day War undermined the foundational myth of the state system and dealt a fatal blow to the authority and legitimacy of the ruling elite. As people digested the gravity of the loss, they felt embittered and deceived by the strongmen who had promised them victory and dignity but delivered defeat and humiliation. A rupture opened up between the people and their rulers, which only led the rulers to crack down with greater urgency

As the ruling elites became increasingly preoccupied with survival and with fighting foreign rivals and domestic opponents, state-society relations fractured further. Institutions were steadily gutted and replaced by a vast security apparatus and bureaucracy. An independent judiciary that could uphold the rule of law and mediate conflict in society was systematically dismantled. The expanding securitization of the state in many Arab countries was directly proportionate to the growing sense of insecurity of the ruling elites. Increasingly uneasy about dealing with the populace, Middle

Eastern strongmen prioritized political survival over sound economic policies and giving citizens a voice in the political process. The declining legitimacy of ruling elites then mixed with growing security fears that originated in other states in the region and beyond. This created a vicious circle where the ruling elites framed both domestic and foreign policy in zero-sum terms, thus preventing the emergence of more inclusive and cooperative relations within states and between them.

Moreover, the emphasis on regional politics and foreign affairs has been used by authoritarian regimes to divert attention from pressing domestic problems that have been accumulating for decades. Fifty years after the waning of Arab nationalism, Arab rulers still use anti-imperialist, anti-Western, and anti-Zionist rhetoric to deflect blame for their own incompetence and bad governance. From Saddam Hussein and Muammar Gaddafi to Bashar al-Assad and Hosni Mubarak, autocratic rulers and their apologists accuse foreign powers of conspiring against the Arab homeland. Burying their heads in the sand, they are their own worst enemies.

It is critical not to forget that the cumulative effect of prolonged conflicts in the region only grows as those conflicts continue. Wars great and small take greater tolls on the people the longer they drag on, and taken collectively the last century in the Middle East provides a nearly continuous backdrop of crippling, violent conflict. These conflicts have had a devastating impact on the state, society, and economy in the region. Once again, the history of the Arab world shows how these factors are organically linked and interact with each other. The Arab-Israeli wars, the fierce rivalries between nationalist and conservative regimes and among nationalists themselves and other conflicts left an indelible mark on the development of Arab institutions. These prolonged conflicts fed political authoritarianism and created a huge gap between the ruling elite and the people. The Arab Spring uprisings that erupted in 2010–2012 should be seen as more than an explosion of anger and frustration fueled by decades of economic mismanagement and deepening political authoritarianism. The first wave of the Arab uprisings and then the second wave in 2018–2019 are a message from the Arab people to their leaders, telling them to stop blaming everybody but themselves for the continuation of colonial practices in the postcolonial state.

6

From Colonialism
to the Cold War

THE SUBVERSION OF THE
POSTCOLONIAL STATE
FROM THE OUTSIDE

THE REPUBLIC OF AZERBAIJAN isn't in the Middle East. But what happened there in the spring of 1946 would have profound consequences for the Middle East and shape its destiny for decades to come. It was in Azerbaijan that many historians believe the Cold War started.

Azerbaijan sits on the western shores of the Caspian Sea. Sandwiched between Russia to the north and Iran to the south, Armenia to the west and Georgia (birthplace of Joseph Stalin) to the northwest, the country's strategic position long attracted the eyes of empires. For centuries, Azerbaijan's fate was determined by a succession of tsars and shahs who carved it up to suit their imperial interests and territorial ambitions. Russia claimed the north, Iran the south.

The collapse of tsarist power in the Russian Revolution in 1917 changed this dynamic, and Azerbaijan seized the moment. On May 27, 1918, it became the first Muslim country in the world to declare itself an independent democracy. The Azerbaijan Democratic Republic was born. It wasn't to last. The tsars might have gone, but Russia's need for fuel had not. Vladimir Lenin took one look at Azerbaijan's vast reserves of oil and calculated that the nascent Soviet Union needed them more than

Azerbaijan needed independence. Or democracy. The Azerbaijan Democratic Republic became the Soviet Socialist Republic on April 28, 1920.

As it began, so it continued. The role of oil remained critical. Azerbaijan's reserves were so vital for the Soviet system that in World War II (or the Great Patriotic War, as Russians call it), the region supplied over three-quarters of all oil needed by the Red Army on the Eastern Front. And the strategic importance of the region and its oil was not lost on the German invaders. Fighting over Azerbaijan was so ferocious, Stalin stopped at nothing to win. The families of generals waging the war were often held hostage in Moscow to remind the men in charge at the front what was at stake for them personally if the battle did not go Moscow's way.

The end of the war brought little change. Just as Azerbaijan had in the past been fought over by tsars and shahs, Soviet socialists, and German Nazis, a new tug-of-war now began. As the eminent scholar Fred Halliday explains, "The crisis over the Soviet refusal to withdraw forces from Iranian territories in Azerbaijan in March 1946 was the first major crisis of the Soviet-American alliance after the end of the Second World War."[1] The incident revealed the cracks in the wartime marriage of convenience between Moscow and Washington, DC, and is seen by many as the spark that ignited the global Cold War.

It was followed a year later by the Truman Doctrine, the first of many such US security doctrines aimed at bringing huge swathes of the postcolonial world under the American defense umbrella and, in reality, into its "informal empire."[2] The new informal empire that the United States built during the Cold War differed in name but only partly in substance from the old European colonial empires. Rather than planting the Stars and Stripes and conquering lands all over the world, this new form of imperialism was based on more subtle forms of coercion, such as military networks, arms sales, economic sanctions and rewards, and intelligence operations. Most often, America's control and hegemony depended on the consent of the local elite, a mutually convenient partnership between the neoimperial power and the oligarchies in power in the world's peripheries.[3]

The postwar division of the world was now underway. Regardless of whether they wanted to, nations and peoples across the world had to take sides. For the next half a century, the world would be divided into two warring blocs as the United States and the Soviet Union actively sought to export their model of liberal capitalism and communism, respectively. The horrors of World War II had created a vacuum of legitimacy in international politics that the new emerging superpowers were determined to fill. They each appropriated Europe's claim to the universality of the enlightenment project but rejected the European colonial approach. Instead, they asserted that the dissemination of their values would enable the establishment of a modernity in which *everyone* could be free and independent.[4]

The reality turned out to be very different. What happened in Azerbaijan in the spring of 1946 was a harbinger of what was to come in the Middle East. Like Azerbaijan, the countries of the Arab world are strategic hot spots. Gateways between east and west, north and south, many have sovereignty over shipping routes vital to global trade and essential for the passage of naval fleets. And like Azerbaijan, many are resource-rich: their lands are full of the black gold without which the superpower militaries and the global economy cannot function.

For the Middle East, the timing of this new alignment in global politics could not have been worse. At the very time the old formal empires of Britain and France were drawing down and their colonies were daring to dream of independence, those same colonies were about to become deeply enmeshed in a fierce global power struggle between the United States and the Soviet Union. The Azerbaijan conflict took place six years before Egypt won independence from Britain and sixteen years before Algerians won theirs from France. Iran had also been slowly progressing toward representative democracy with the establishment of a deliberative parliament and an opposition. These countries had not even begun to function as autonomous entities and the ground had already shifted beneath them.

As the rules of global power changed, a new Great Game began—one that few, if any, of the new rulers of the Middle East had seen coming. Formal independence was of little value as the international system developed along bipolar lines and transformed the Middle East into a theater for proxy wars and superpower rivalry. Decolonization did not usher in freedom from foreign intervention. If anything, the situation became worse. Although no longer technically colonized, foreign influence was no less insidious for being indirect. Arab and Iranian independence, so long dreamed of, risked being in name only. One of the most urgent challenges facing the leaders of the newly independent states of the Middle East was how to negotiate their country's place in this new world order. The side they chose, the alliances they built, and the policies they pursued would all have lasting consequences. Not only would they affect the day-to-day lives of millions of people, they would determine the very viability of the postcolonial state. Sadly, many of the new rulers chose a similar path to their predecessors, echoing the arrangements of the colonial era where local elites served the interests of foreign powers at the expense of the people.

As I have noted in my latest book, the decades of the Cold War were consequential in changing the political and economic trajectory of the contemporary Middle East.[5] The global confrontation between the United States and the Soviet Union played out on Middle Eastern streets from Tehran to Cairo. While the Soviet adventures in the region proved ephemeral, the Cold War allowed the United States to replace the former European colonial powers and to add the Middle East to its nascent "informal empire."

Us or Them: The Problems of Bipolarity and How the Cold War Affected the Region

Barely had they cast off the shackles of colonialism when the young, fragile states of the Middle East faced a stark choice: told there could be no neutrality between good and evil, newly decolonized Egypt, Iran (not formally colonized), Iraq, Syria, Jordan, Lebanon, and others were caught in the dragnet of the bipolar Cold War. They had to take sides or pay the consequences of going it alone.

Neither option was without risks. Taking a side meant a loss of independence and sovereignty. But not taking a side meant the loss of desperately needed aid and incurring US wrath. The United States exerted particularly heavy pressure on local actors to join defense pacts designed to encircle Russia and limit Moscow's influence in the region and beyond. Middle Eastern rulers who refused to side against the Soviet Union were ostracized, penalized, denied financial aid, and even removed from power. The United States and Britain made an example of Iran's democratically elected prime minister, Mohammad Mossadegh, by orchestrating a coup that removed him from power in August 1953. Egyptian president Gamal Abdel Nasser almost suffered a similar fate to Mossadegh during the Suez crisis in 1956. Right from the outset, the Cold War weighed heavily on the newly independent states and stunted their institutional and societal growth. Independence quickly turned into an opportunity lost.

Life after independence did not therefore mark a dramatic departure in the international relations of the Middle East. The ability of the new ruling elite to act independently was extremely limited. Postindependence leaders had to navigate the minefield of East-West rivalry and avoid a trip-wire. It was no easy task. The initial response of many Middle Eastern leaders to the bipolarity of the new world order was to try and make the best of a bad situation. If you had to choose sides, why not play both sides off against each other and gain leverage? Throughout the Cold War period, we observe similar dynamics in the relations between foreign powers and local elite that we saw during the colonial moment. Postindependence Middle Eastern countries were as dependent on their superpower patrons as their predecessors were on their colonial masters, though informally.

From the mid-1950s to the end of the Cold War in 1989, the likes of Egypt, Iran, and Syria successfully extracted billions of dollars in military and technical aid from Washington and Moscow. Between 1954 and 1970, Nasser obtained almost $2 billion in aid: $1 billion from the United States and another $1 billion from the Soviet Union. Israel also mastered the art of milking the Cold War to its advantage, procuring tens of billions of dollars from the United States and Europe. For example, Israel's victory in the Palestine War of 1947–1948 owed in part to a first major arms deal from Soviet Czechoslovakia in 1948.

There was a downside, however. The leaders of the region paid dearly for peddling in this Cold War bazaar. The newly decolonized Middle

Eastern states became too dependent too quickly on their superpower patrons for military and financial assistance. Instead of putting their own houses in order and avoiding involvement in the East-West quagmire, local actors plunged in feet first. Seduced by the lure of readily available money and seemingly effortless power, the new rulers abandoned their earlier reluctance and recklessly played the superpower game, heedless of the consequences that foreign loans came with punishing rates of interest and military aid came with punitive contracts for technical training and spare parts. At the height of the Cold War, the game was so intense that it was often difficult to distinguish who was wooing whom: the superpowers, the local actors, or vice versa.

In this asymmetric relationship, the latter were at a disadvantage from the start. They had limited room for maneuver and fewer options to choose from. And this led to fatal miscalculations. At times, even pivotal regional players like Nasser in the late 1960s and the shah of Iran in the late 1970s misjudged the degree to which America or Russia would come to their rescue. Neither Nasser nor the shah recognized they were expendable and that their superpower patrons would not hesitate to sacrifice them on the altar of their own national interests.

The global East-West rivalry distorted the internal politics and economies of the decolonized states and diverted precious resources from building institutions of governance. The material temptations were just too attractive for the new elite to resist. But while foreign aid was available from one or the other superpower, it came with strings attached. It was a scenario deliberately designed (like the colonial debt financing of old) to draw Arab and Middle Eastern elites deeper and deeper into bipolar Cold War alignments from which they could not easily escape. This dependence weakened their legitimacy at home. It made a mockery of their claims to be independent. This, in turn, led to increased authoritarianism and violent repression against people demanding inclusive governance. Rather than aiding development, securing independence, and making the lives of local people better, foreign funds instead became a tool to consolidate authoritarian rule. In a cruel twist of fate, the new postcolonial reality was not as different from the colonial era as the new rulers of the Middle East would have liked to believe.

This paradox fed into a deeper problem. The postindependence state in the Middle East was characterized by an increasing deterioration of state-society relations. Many of the societal struggles that started during the colonial period had not yet been resolved. At the same time, the cracks in the heroic narratives of nationalist leaders had widened because it was clear they were not living up to their promises. But the more often opposition activists exposed the weaknesses and failures of those in power, the more often authoritarian leaders resorted to violence to preserve the status quo and cement their grip on power. This resort to violence undermined public acceptance of state institutions and fueled polarizing tendencies within societies—a state of affairs from which the region has still not recovered.

A second, and equally pressing, problem of bipolarity was the impact it had on the region's conflicts: the Cold War internationalized local and regional conflicts. Everything from the Arab-Israeli conflict to inter-Arab rivalries to the war between Iran and Iraq and the Lebanese Civil War: all became entangled in the dynamics of the global Cold War, which aggravated tensions and made their resolution more difficult to achieve. In particular, the internationalization of the Arab-Israeli conflict profoundly changed attitudes and affected relations between the Middle East and the United States.

More than any other issue, Washington's unequivocal backing of Israel alienated Arab and Muslim opinion. Early in the twentieth century, Arabs had high expectations of the United States. The country had never ruled Arab and Muslim lands and, unlike Britain or France, was seen as an honest broker. But in Middle Eastern eyes, America's neocolonialism became every bit as insidious as Anglo-French colonialism had ever been, and its imperialism became very real, even if it was informal.[6]

As was the case with foreign financial assistance, the internationalization of regional conflicts was a scenario that local actors initially embraced willingly. To gain strategic advantage, both Arabs and Israelis vied for the support of the Soviet Union and the United States, respectively, and welcomed their intervention. The result was that from 1956 onward, the Arab-Israeli fault line, which is basically a local problem, escalated into a superpower proxy war and more than once risked a direct nuclear confrontation between Russia and the United States. In fact, "in the twenty cases in which the US forces were put on nuclear alert, and in the one known case where Soviet forces were," seven were as a direct result of events in the Middle East.[7]

Given the intensity of superpower rivalry in the region, it is nothing short of miraculous that no nuclear confrontation ever took place in the Middle East. The United States and the Soviet Union succeeded in exercising great restraint and did not allow their competition to spiral out of control. As nuclear powers, they had an implicit understanding to avoid a direct clash, both in the region and throughout the world. During the highly charged Arab-Israeli wars of 1956, 1967, 1973, and 1982, they worked through the United Nations Security Council to limit the scope of the conflict and prevent it from further escalation.[8]

In their pursuit of modernization and the consolidation of their regimes, leaders of postindependence states in the Middle East were confronted with two models of development. The capitalist and communist systems shared some characteristics, relating primarily to the need for a strong central authority capable of implementing top-down reforms in the economic, social, and political domains, but their outlook on international relations was vastly different. After a brief period of flirtation with Soviet and socialist ideals, it was the Western US-led model that came to have the greatest implications for the region. Embedded in this model were a number of approaches (generally summarized as modernization theory) supposed to dictate the phases of state-centric reform needed to catapult a state into modernity. Yet these prescriptions were based on the Western experience of state-led development. In this respect, the road map for modernization was much closer to a prescription for "Westernization."

Furthermore, Washington's use of modernization theory in the Middle East, particularly in the realms of industrializing, mechanizing, and modernizing the armed forces, was to have devastating effects on local modes of production. It increased socioeconomic grievances and, in so doing, significantly weakened the legitimacy of postindependence ruling elites. Thus, while the two superpowers, particularly the United States, abandoned the old colonial modes of operation and control, they replaced them with a more nuanced and indirect neoimperialism, which maintained many of the same characteristics and carried the same political consequences for the local elites who adopted them. The domestic authoritarians prioritized their own self-interest over that of the people, sacrificing the opportunity to build local economic production and the institutions that go with it.

In the former colonies, the economy was one of the top priorities. Nationalist elites had to consolidate political and economic sovereignty as well as independence. To achieve this, they needed assistance from financial institutions beyond their borders. But they saw the post-postwar financial institutions, the IMF and the World Bank, as forms of neocolonialism because of the role played by their former colonial masters in setting up and managing these entities. Headquartered in Washington, these organizations were charged with overseeing macroeconomic policies and the provision of technical assistance, including loans, for third countries involved in implementing free-market reforms. The role of the IMF and the World Bank in the Middle East and North Africa, especially since the mid-1980s, has turned out to be highly contentious. These organizations have deepened dependence on foreign powers and called for economic reforms that have weakened local economies and production capacity to the benefit of Western interests.[9]

Because of the problems associated with bipolarity, a number of regional actors, along with their counterparts across the developing world, sought to counter the pressure and legitimize their status as leaders of the postcolonial world by establishing a "third way." Nationalist elites formed the Non-Aligned Movement, an organization that allowed them to have an independent voice in international affairs. Although the Non-Aligned Movement is often described as a "third bloc," its founders were against the very concept of blocs and sought to avoid taking sides between the two superpowers. Organized in April 1955, the Bandung Conference laid out the principles of the Non-Aligned Movement. These included mutual respect for each other's territorial integrity and sovereignty, nonaggression, noninterference in each other's domestic affairs, equality and mutual benefit and peaceful coexistence.[10]

The main outcome of the Bandung Conference was a call for greater cooperation between the members in the fields of economy, education, science, technical training, and the setting up of multilateral trade and financial arrangements.[11] The conference also called for the establishment of national and regional banks and insurance companies.[12] One of the principles on which the participants in Bandung never reached a consensus, however, was involvement in superpower-sponsored military pacts. They were unable to do so because some members had already joined them.

The Non-Aligned Movement was led by prominent figures such as Nasser of Egypt, Jawaharlal Nehru of India, Kwame Nkrumah of Ghana, Sukarno of Indonesia, and Josip Tito of Yugoslavia. Its focus, unlike that of the superpowers, was not on economic and military power. Rather, it aimed to shape postcolonial debates about the identity and place of the newly independent states in world politics. As well as this empowering narrative, it also helped increase the legitimacy of nationalist leaders in their own countries and regions. Thus, when Nasser suffered a humiliating defeat by Israel in 1967 and passed away three years later, the effects were felt far beyond his native Egypt. Like the Arab world, the Non-Aligned Movement had claimed him as a champion of their interests.

This attempt to navigate a "third way" through the bipolarity of Cold War politics faced constant pressure, from Washington in particular. The superpowers each had their own views about the way ahead for the Middle East, and they had the means—and the motivation—to try to impose those views. To understand what the superpowers hoped to achieve in the region, we need to take a closer look at the view from Washington and Moscow.

The View from Washington: America's Cold War Syndrome

Nasser was enamored with American culture. In the first year after the coup, he and other senior officers were often at the US embassy socializing and networking. These were not purely social occasions. Americans and Egyptians alike had good reasons to want to build a solid working relationship. Washington recognized Cairo's strategic, and growing, importance in the region. Egypt was the focal point of Arab international relations in the 1950s: Cairo was the capital of the revolutionary Arab bloc and Nasser the disruptor president set to overthrow the status quo and lead the Arab world out of the shadow of colonialism. US diplomats in the early 1950s regarded Egypt as nothing less than "the key to the establishment of a Middle East Defense Organization and to a new relationship between the West and the Arab states."[13]

Cairo, in turn, recognized Washington's strategic, and growing, influence in the world. Nasser and the Free Officers initially saw America as a natural ally and a bulwark against colonial Britain. Egypt's new rulers went out of their way to build bridges with the rising Western superpower. Of all outside powers, Nasser and his comrades gave only the US embassy in Cairo advance notice of their coup in the summer of 1952 in the hope that the Americans would stop Britain intervening to prop up the monarchy.[14] In the early days after the coup, the relationship between the Free Officers and the United States looked like it might blossom into a new, strategic alignment between the two countries.

But the honeymoon was short-lived. An ideological chasm soon opened up between policymakers in Washington and US diplomats on the ground in Cairo. Cold warriors like Secretary of State John Foster Dulles (1953–1959) and his brother Allen, director of the Central Intelligence Agency (1953–1961), were obsessed by Soviet communism and the free flow of cheap Middle Eastern oil to the West. The global Cold War and global finance were the lenses through which they saw the world. Every aspect of foreign policy, no matter how large or small, had to be filtered through these two lenses. Regional developments were not viewed in their local context, but for how they fit into the American Cold War perspective.[15]

The result was that Cold War hawks like the Dulles brothers dismissed reports from US diplomats in Cairo who were sympathetic to the Free Officers and who recommended that their superiors should co-opt Egypt's young officers by granting them aid. These diplomats in the field were more attuned to local circumstances than their superiors at home and had a greater grasp of the facts on the ground. But their calls fell on deaf ears in Washington. The issue would soon come to a calamitous climax over arms and aid and Washington would lose Cairo as an ally.

Washington's determination to build an informal empire at all costs distorted the vision of US policymakers and blinded them to the complex realties of local politics. This ideologically charged and culturally insensitive approach alienated people in the region who, until the end of World War II, had been positively disposed toward the United States. Arab and Muslim perceptions of America now started to shift. No longer did they see the country in the Woodrow Wilson mold of a noninterventionist anticolonial power. Now they saw it as an aggressive, interventionist neocolonial superpower intent on remaking the Middle East to serve its own interests. But for key players in Washington, all that mattered was the need to contain the Soviet Union and extract oil and no effort would be spared to prevent Moscow securing a foothold in the Middle East.

America's imperial position was supported by its allies in Europe, particularly the former colonial powers, Britain and France. The Cold War offered these Western powers the perfect cover to maintain their interests in the region following decolonization. That they should wish to do so is hardly surprising given the extraordinary concentration of vital Western interests in the Middle East: access to inexpensive oil and gas, transit routes and waterways, military bases located in close vicinity to the Soviet Union's underbelly not as well defended as its borders with Europe, and support for the state of Israel. Ultimately these Western interests of oil, support for Israel, and the need to contain soviet communism "were intimately linked: the Soviets had to be denied control of Middle East oil through which they could strangle Western Europe but Western support of Israel inflamed pro-Soviet sentiment in the region and increased the threat to oil."[16] Consequently, the hegemonic presence of Western influence in the region became a priority for policymakers in both America and Europe.

From Harry S. Truman and Dwight D. Eisenhower through to John F. Kennedy, Lyndon B. Johnson, Richard Nixon, Jimmy Carter, and Ronald Reagan, the United States justified its role in the Third World and its determination to impose its will through these security doctrines.[17] The Eisenhower administration weaponized the Cold War against assertive nationalist leaders who dared to pursue a nonaligned foreign policy as well as nationalize oil in order to improve the plight of their citizens. The Dulles

brothers dealt Iran's Mossadegh a fatal blow in 1953 because of his nationalization of oil and his tolerance of the country's socialists and
communists.[18]

Joining a US-led defense pact and opening the economy for global finance became the way to demonstrate loyalty to Washington. And as the
most populous Arab state with ambitions to lead the Arab world, it was
Nasser's Egypt that bore the brunt of American pressure to join such a
pact. Nasser, however, objected to what he saw as heavy-handed and the
attempt to force Arabs into an anti-Soviet bloc. He was particularly in-
censed that the United States in conjunction with his old rivals in Britain
bypassed him by lining up Iraq, Iran, and Turkey in a pact and then
presented it to him as a fait accompli. But his refusal to sign up to US
defense schemes was exceedingly costly. In a humiliating slap in the face
to Nasser, John Foster Dulles overlooked the advice of his diplomats in
Cairo and publicly withdrew an offer to help finance the Aswan Dam, a
key developmental project for the Free Officers. The United States also
refused to sell arms to the new regime in Cairo, which was anxious about
the state of preparedness of its military, not least in light of the rising
number of military clashes along its borders with Israel.

Nasser responded by trying to play the game of bipolar politics to his
own advantage. He turned to the Russian-led camp for arms and financial and technical aid, thus signaling an end to the brief honeymoon between the Free Officers and America. In one stroke, the United States
turned Egypt from a potential friend into a reluctant antagonist and
opened a window of opportunity for the Soviet Union to establish a foothold in the Middle East. The result was that in the 1950s and 1960s the
global Cold War fed into what has been termed the "Arab Cold War."

Driven by what were essentially local and regional disputes, the deepening rivalries between Arab states were exploited by foreign powers,
and also by Israel, to further entrench their influence in the region. In the
process, Cold War dynamics added another layer of complexity to regional
realities in the greater Middle East.[19]

In their dealings with Nasser, Western powers showed how much
they misunderstood the complexity of local conditions. The American
obsession with Communist Russia and its military networks and alliances

meant that nationalist and anti-colonial currents in the Middle East were often misinterpreted as communist leanings.[20] Cold warriors grouped all these ideologies together as a threat to US national interests. This narrowly focused view of the Cold War in the Middle East was especially dangerous because it led local people to feel their legitimate grievances were not being heard and their values were being dismissed.[21] Nevertheless, Western policymakers like John Foster Dulles and UK prime minister Anthony Eden continued to see what they wanted to see and obsessively focused on Nasser as the single most influential leader in the Arab world.

As a result, they ignored significant trends such as nationalism, non-alignment, and independence—all of which were important in the region at the time. Fixated with the Soviet Union and access to cheap oil, the United States and the United Kingdom misread the facts on the ground and failed to understand that Nasser's popularity and influence in Arab politics were precisely because he appealed to "higher" normative values. Encapsulated in the ideas of populism, Arab nationalism, political independence, territorial sovereignty, Third World solidarity, nonalignment, and socialism, these norms resonated with many Arabs because they symbolized a revolt against the colonial West.[22] Nasser earned his status as the undisputed leader of the Arab world because he stood up to Britain, France, and the United States and challenged their hegemony in the region.[23] By tapping into the politics of identity and the anti-colonial struggle, Nasser became the voice of millions in the region and the Global South as well.

To neutralize Nasser's popularity and the lure of Arab nationalism, the Americans decided to create an opposing ideological coalition. In a region where religion rules supreme, they found their answer in Islam. President Dwight Eisenhower believed Islam was the counterweight to radical Arab nationalism, socialism, and communism.[24] All efforts to co-opt Nasser, or any other Arab nationalist, now ceased and the United States moved to support the conservative religious-based Arab monarchies (and Israel) as a counterweight. In doing so, they significantly assisted the development and enrichment of the American arms industry. America's conservative allies needed arms to defend their kingdoms and oil gave them the means to buy them, especially after the 1973 oil crisis sent prices through the roof: "The explosive growth of OPEC's revenues made the cartel's members ideal clients for weaponry, and in 1974, after the US exit from Vietnam, the Middle East became the world's largest importer of armaments."[25]

From the perspective of Middle East societies, as political economists point out, the massive import of weapons and the availability of the re-sources to pay for them substantially shaped political authoritarianism in the region and continues to do so today.

The year 1958 thus marked the beginning of a holy alliance between US foreign policy and Islamic-based states and groups in the Middle East, most notably conservative Saudi Arabia, on whom the flow of oil depended. It was an alliance that sought stability yet increased US coop-eration with the ultraconservative Salafism of the Arabian Peninsula and deepened Nasser's mistrust of American motives, thereby driving him closer to the Russians. It also intensified the interregional rivalries associ-ated with the Arab cold war, particularly in Yemen, and entrenched insta-bility in the region. America's intervention in inter-Arab affairs actively sought to undermine the unity and agency of the people by fracturing the coalition-building power of Arab nationalism. An Arab government with a popular mandate is precisely one that can resist foreign intervention, which was unacceptable to the Cold War hawks in Washington.

The US-Islamist relationship soon became a means to oppose the spread of "godless communism" among Arab societies. By the 1970s and 1980s, this relationship was strengthened and moved from a defensive pos-ture to a more proactive and offensive posture. The turning point was the fateful year of 1979, a time when the United States' strategic posture in the region had received a number of striking setbacks: the loss of the shah of Iran; the Soviet invasion of Afghanistan; and the spread of communist-linked movements in many areas of the developing world, particularly in Southwest Asia, in what President Carter's national secu-rity adviser, Zbigniew Brzezinski, famously termed the "arch of crisis." The ramifications of US support for radical jihadist fighters traveling to battle the Soviets in Afghanistan should have been obvious, but once again America's strategy to roll back Soviet communism led policymakers to ignore the long-term consequences of what was going on right in front of them.

Before 1979 ended, more upheaval befell US allies in the region. In November, just as the Hajj was ending and a new Muslim century was about to start, a group of radicals stormed the Grand Mosque of Mecca in Saudi Arabia, occupied the holy site, and called for the overthrow of the monarchy. The Saudis had to call in outside assistance to deal with this serious threat. With the help of the French, the uprising was violently suppressed after days of intense fighting. The event should have served as a wake-up call about the dangers of encouraging and bankrolling such radical religious ideologies.[26] Yet, these warning signs were missed, and the United States' shortsighted policy of support for such groups continued throughout the 1980s. Al-Qaeda was itself an outgrowth of these processes and shows the important link between 1958 and the slow but steady rise of pan-Islamism throughout the Arab-Islamic world.

The View from Moscow: Russia's "Egyptian Syndrome"

Washington's wholehearted support for Israel and its unwillingness to look beyond the bipolar framework of the Cold War caused more than estrangement with would-be supporters in the region. It ultimately undermined the United States' early attempts to co-opt the rising tide of Arab nationalism and attract Nasser into the West's orbit. This allowed Moscow to gain a foothold in the region and by the mid-1950s Soviet involvement in Middle Eastern affairs began to grow. It is worth emphasizing that the US-USSR rivalry over the Middle East was asymmetrical. The United States was economically and technologically disproportionately much more powerful than the Soviet Union, whose economy and society was brought to the ground by Germany's Adolf Hitler in World War II. Moreover, while the Soviets in the Middle East were starting from scratch, the Americans had gradually inherited the colonial networks, relations, and interests built by Britain and France with local Middle Eastern oligarchies, monarchies, and state institutions.

It was a far from straightforward process, however. From the outset, Russia's positioning in the Middle East was based on shaky foundations.

Soviet leaders were hard-pressed to demonstrate the effectiveness of their aid and military-diplomatic support compared to that of the Americans. While the Soviet model of development and modernization held a degree of attraction for many in the Global South—and in this respect represented a countermodel to the free-market capitalism espoused by the United States—there were a number of important factors limiting the general appeal of Communist ideals in the Muslim world.

For a start, Soviet Communism challenged the belief in God and banished religion from public life. No power was allowed to rival the power of the collective. But in the Middle East, where God is literally greater than everything else, the Soviet atheist model was a tough sell. Added to that, the more general appeal of the American soft power helped to limit the standing of the Soviet Union in the Middle East.

In spite of the ideological and cultural differences separating the Middle East from the Soviet Union, from the mid-1950s, Russia began to acquire a strong following among Arab nationalists. The fact that these groups had a secular approach to politics facilitated the burgeoning alliance with Soviet Russia. For two decades this was to be the main axis of its influence in the Middle East. Aided by the Suez crisis in 1956, Russia then established close ties with Syria, Iraq, Algeria, Sudan, North Yemen, and later South Yemen and Libya. As a counterbalance, the United States developed strategic relations with Israel, Iran, Turkey, Saudi Arabia, and Jordan.[27]

Although the Russian-Egyptian relationship deepened in the late 1950s and 1960s, it was more a marriage of convenience than a love match. To begin with, Nasser was by no means a communist sympathizer. In fact, he brutally suppressed Marxists and socialists at home and imprisoned them en masse, knowing full well that Russian officials were cognizant of his actions.

Then there were the reasons Nasser established closer relations with the Soviet Union in the first place: because of America's refusal to provide him with arms and loans. The Egyptian-Russian relationship was therefore utilitarian and transactional, based more on realpolitik and a temporary convergence of interests than shared ideology and values. From the very beginning, it was clear Moscow was Nasser's second choice.

Nor was the relationship between Cairo and Moscow an easy one. There were a number of tense moments during the Cold War when Nasser pursued Egypt's national interests at the expense of his alliance with the Soviet Union. For example, after Iraq's prime minster, Abd al-Karim Qasim, began to develop a close relationship with Moscow, Nasser was upset the Russians would treat an Arab rival as equal to him and accused them of imperialist meddling in his Arab sphere of influence. In a bid to balance the alliance with Moscow, Nasser did his best to exploit America's eagerness to thwart Soviet ambitions in the region. Even though Washington had refused him arms and aid, Nasser managed to obtain US food aid vital to feed Egypt's burgeoning population.

Egypt was not the only Middle Eastern state to try and pursue an independent foreign policy via the superpowers. From 1954 onward the relationship between Russia and Syria appeared to be as solid as a rock. As Patrick Seale put it, "So close did their relations seem that outsiders often portrayed Damascus as Moscow's principal Arab ally, even as its main Cold War partner in the region, more steadfast than Egypt, less fickle than Libya, less marginal than Algeria, more predictable than South Yemen."[28] Yet like Egypt's relationship with the Soviet Union, the reality was more complex and the relationship between Moscow and Damascus was tarnished with "false expectations, contradictory ambitions, mutual suspicion and plain muddle."[29]

Syria's early ties with the Soviet Union were based on security considerations: protection from potentially hostile neighbors, former colonizers, and Israel. As a newly independent state, memories of European colonization were still fresh in the Syrian psyche. The occupying French troops had only left the country in 1946. For that reason, any outside power that helped Syrians limit Western encroachment was welcomed eagerly. The Russians, for their part, had their own agenda in Syria. Moscow's primary concern was to secure a naval base on the Mediterranean and protect its Black Sea ports from the regional buildup of American power.[30]

In spite of the substantive investment Russia made in the region throughout the Cold War, it could not translate that investment into cultural capital. The Soviet Union simply could not compete with the West's soft power and seductive materialism. While the Arabs sought weapons and training from Communist Russia, they prized Western luxury goods and services and financial institutions, including education and medicine. The new Arab elites might be highly critical of Western foreign policies but that did not stop them sending their children to study in America, Britain, France, and elsewhere. The American University in Beirut (AUB) and the American University in Cairo (AUC) did much to reinforce the appeal of American soft power at a local level. There are no similar examples of Russian colleges in the region. And graduates of Russian and other Communist Eastern European universities were compared unfavorably to those graduates of Western institutions even though many from Syria, Iraq, and Palestine studied in the Soviet Union.

Communism just did not resonate on an emotional level with the majority of Middle Easterners. And even though socialism and communism gained a large following in Afghanistan, Egypt, Iran, Iraq, Lebanon, Palestine, South Yemen, and Syria, communist-led parties remained an elite phenomenon in the region.[31] Despite its proximity to Russia, the Middle East was less affected by communism than other parts of the Global South.[32] In only one country in the Islamic world did a communist party ever come to power, Afghanistan in 1978. But it took a Soviet invasion to keep that government in power, and even that government collapsed after the Soviet troops retreated in 1989.[33]

It is worth mentioning that the United States launched a systematic campaign to discredit "godless" socialism and communism worldwide, including in the Middle East. US officials collaborated with conservative Islamic states like Saudi Arabia and Pakistan and Islamist groups like the Muslim Brothers to counter Soviet influence.[34] Middle Eastern socialists and communists faced great odds and were demonized from all sides. Leading social and political forces—radical Arab nationalists, Islamists, and pro-US allied states—all took aim at them. Socialist and communists were also swimming against the rising ultraconservative cultural and pan-Islamist tide in a region that prizes religion.

Russian officials recognized the limits of their influence in Egypt and the wider region and acted cautiously, avoiding deeper entanglement. This Soviet caution showed in a number of ways. For one, Soviet leaders did not speak up for their fellow Marxists in the region. Perhaps because they could not guarantee their safety, the Soviets turned a blind eye to the ruthless suppression of Marxists in Egypt, Iraq, Syria, and beyond. In doing so, Moscow chose to sacrifice these comrades on the altar of interstate interests, a decision born of necessity and lack of options, but one that showed all too clearly the Soviet Union did not prioritize loyalty and did not stand by its friends in their time of need.

Further evidence of this caution was apparent in 1967, when the Soviets showed themselves to be less militarily aggressive than the United States. During the Six-Day War in June, Russia refrained from active military intervention on behalf of its Arab allies, leading many Arabs and Muslims to conclude the communist superpower was not as committed to their defense as the United States was to Israel's. While the United States backed Israel fully and provided it with state-of-the-art offensive weapons to ensure victory, the Soviet Union supplied only defensive arms to Egypt and Syria and impressed upon them the need for restraint and compromise.

The Six-Day War and its aftermath confronted the Arabs with the reality of their relations with Moscow: the Soviet Union was not going to risk a direct confrontation with the United States. The war was a rude wake-up call for Nasser and other Arab radical nationalist leaders whose wishful thinking about the extent of Soviet support had partially led them to miscalculate.

In the 1950s and early 1960s it appeared as if the Soviet model had found a receptive audience in parts of the Middle East. But it had lost its appeal in the early 1970s. The "crisis of the petty bourgeois regimes" did not lead, as some left analysis had hoped, to a more radicalized and progressive Middle East, but rather to the rise of the right-wing development in Egypt under President Anwar al-Sadat and the petro-dollar and pan-Islamism in the Gulf.[35] Even under Nasser, the Soviet model's replication had been limited, "while the revolutionary officers immediately enacted the agrarian reform law in which large tracts of lands were divided into smaller lots and given to tenant farmers and landless peasants, they also undertook the far from socialist policy of offering liberal incentives for business and industry, enacting laws that encouraged foreign capital, allowed tax exemptions for investment, lowered custom dues on imports, etc."[36]

The shallowness of Egyptian-Russian ties were exposed in 1972 when Sadat expelled 20,000 Russian defense advisers after Moscow refused to provide Egypt with more advanced weaponry. Almost overnight, Moscow saw its massive strategic investment wiped out in the heart of the Middle East. It was a hard blow and a lasting lesson. As a keen observer noted, "If the Americans suffered from a 'Vietnam Syndrome,' the Russians were affected by an 'Egyptian Syndrome,' a reluctance to trust and subsidize militant nationalist regimes that could all too easily, turn their backs on the USSR."[37] Sadat's decision tilted the balance of power in America's favor in the Cold War rivalry in the Middle East.

The collapse of the Egyptian-Russian relationship also showed how Washington understood the transactional nature of its strategic partnerships in the region better than the Soviet Union ever did. Where Moscow was cautious, fearful of being drawn into conflicts it could not control, Washington did not hesitate. When one of Washington's allies needed weapons to fight a war the United States wanted them to win, Washington delivered.

The retreat of the Soviet Union from the Middle East, however, left only one superpower in town, eroding the little bargaining power that bipolarity had given local rulers. It also exposed in the eyes of public opinion the subservient relationship between the United States and regional autocrats, sowing the seeds of further radicalism and anti-American sentiments throughout the region. This radicalism, which became more religiously dominated in the 1990s, known as pan-Islamism, would turn against the United States, its previous backer with a vengeance.

The rivalry between the United States and the Soviet Union in the newly independent Middle East turned out to be a parenthetical; the most durable historical process of the Cold War was the shift from Anglo-French colonialism to informal American imperialism or Pan Americana over the region.

Winning the War but Losing the Peace: The Legacy of the Cold War in the Middle East and Beyond

Long before the Cold War officially ended in 1989, US officials had proclaimed triumph in the Middle East. Yet it was a pyrrhic victory. The Americans won the war against the Soviets but lost the peace.

US policymakers felt vindicated by their muscular actions and offensive policy in the region and took credit for vanquishing subversive ideologies, such as radical Arab nationalism, socialism, and communism. But there was little or no reflection in Washington about the collateral damage to Middle Eastern states and societies done in the process or any grasp of the depth of popular resentment against US policies.

By waging a scorched-earth campaign against radical nationalists, Washington's cold warriors empowered pan-Islamist groups and reactionary conservatives throughout the region. On a deeper level, the Cold War changed the trajectory of the region, by leading to the further weakening of progressive, liberal voices, who the United States, as leader of the Free World, had rhetorically claimed to champion. The unmistakable appeal of American values, the freedom and choice at the heart of the American way of life, the importance of faith and family to many Americans: all of these factors mean the United States should find an abundance of natural allies among the peoples of the Middle East.[38]

But as is the case across the postcolonial world, so many people who *are* natural allies of the American system are left shocked and confused when they see that system in action. The reality of what they see on the ground is so utterly at odds with what they understood to be true of it, it leads them to conclude there is an inherent double standard at work. American values are not universally applied. While America preaches self-determination and freedom, it acts as an informal empire. From the beginning of the Cold War to the end, the United States tried to tame assertive nationalist leaders like Iranian prime minister Mossadegh and Nasser.

This state of affairs is not helped by the actions of US policymakers who so often undermine their own argument by saying one thing and doing another. They claim to want peace between the Israelis and the Palestinians and to be an honest broker in pursuit of that goal, yet they repeatedly use their veto at the UN Security Council to block any condemnation of Israel. America's blind support for Israel emboldens its politicians who do not feel the need to reconcile with the Palestinians. In this sense, the United States is not only a dishonest broker in the Israel-Palestine conflict but also the most important obstacle to the establishment of a viable and independent Palestinian state.[39] US leaders claim to support democracy yet they entrench the power of dictators and autocrats. They claim to want to de-escalate tensions yet they have turned the region into a massive arms market.[40]

Iraq is a perfect example of these contradictions, lies, and their consequences. With the outbreak of the Iran-Iraq war in 1980, the Reagan administration chose to support Saddam Hussein as the lesser of the two evils against the hostile revolutionary Islamic Republic. As the Iran-Iraq slaughter dragged on for eight bloody years, the United States directly and indirectly provided secret arms to both sides, thus pouring gasoline on an already raging fire. US policy in the Iran-Iraq war was best summarized by Henry Kissinger, at the time acting as an informal adviser to the Reagan White House, when he simply exclaimed that it was a "shame there can only be one loser."

The Iran-Iraq carnage cost the lives of over a million people and hundreds of billions of dollars.[41] It bled Iran and Iraq dry and set their development back years. So determined was the Reagan administration to ensure Iran's mullahs did not prevail, they turned a blind eye to Saddam Hussein's repeated use of chemical weapons against Iran and against his own people.[42] They also doggedly shielded him from calls by their European allies to refer the matter to the United Nations Security Council. America's obscene realism in this war would come back to haunt US foreign policy in the Middle East. Saddam Hussein's use of chemical weapons against Iran, together with the culpability of the international community, convinced the clerics in Tehran to go it alone and try to develop a nuclear program. Saddam's gassing of Halabja, a village in Iraq's Kurdish region, in March 1988, and the subsequent counterinsurgency campaign known as *Anfal* or "The Spoils," in which some 80,000 Kurdish civilians were expelled from their homes, fueled the Kurds' quest for a nation of their own. Equally important, US support for Iraq during the war directly contributed to Saddam Hussein's invasion of Kuwait in 1990, which led to the Gulf War of 1990–1991.

Iraq is only one example. Across the Middle East, in a region that has suffered disproportionately from prolonged conflicts and foreign intervention, everyone has a story to tell. But those stories do not usually make

it through the filter of unipolar political priorities. Intoxicated by trium-
phalism, the US foreign policy establishment neither appreciated the damage the Cold War had inflicted on the region nor cared to remedy the
situation.

As a postgraduate student at the University of Oxford, I vividly remember attending a conference on the United States and the Middle East in
Austin, Texas, in 1990. In a speech, the prominent US academic-diplomat
William Quandt reminded us that the United States had won the Cold
War in the Middle East without incurring major costs in blood and
treasure. Only a few hundred American lives had been lost in the four-
decades-long East-West struggle, according to this well-meaning scholar
and diplomat. There was no mention of the losses suffered by the people
who call the region home or of the other costs to state and society in the
Middle East.

After the Cold War, US policymakers saw no immediate challenges or
threats on the horizon and did not feel the need to rethink their cynical
approach and imperial ambitions toward the Middle East. America's key
goal was to maintain the status quo at all costs, particularly the protection of its loyal allies and its access to petroleum resources and the
maintenance of Israel's military-technological superiority over all of its
neighbors. Human rights and reforms had not figured prominently on
the US agenda in the Middle East during the Cold War or immediately
after. They would not do so now. The American attitude could best be
described as business as usual.

With the Soviet Union out of the picture, the United States emerged
as the world's unrivalled superpower. The bipolar system of the Cold War
was replaced with a unipolar system. As the dominant hegemon, the
United States now faced the wrath of those religiously based forces with
which it had collaborated so successfully during the Cold War. Less than
a decade after the collapse of the communist camp, the bitter inheritance
of the Cold War came home to haunt American policymakers. On September 11, 2001, the United States was targeted on a massive scale. New
York, the nation's financial center, and Washington, its political center,
were hit by a series of attacks that marked a significant shift in how
nonstate actors like Al-Qaeda battle global powers. Nearly 3,000 civilians

were killed, countless more were injured, and even more were left traumatized.

In the shocked aftermath, it was hard for Americans to believe that the man behind the attacks, Osama bin Laden, emir of Al-Qaeda, was a former friend of the United States. A creature of the Cold War, he had played a prominent role in the American-led fight against the Soviet invasion of Afghanistan in December 1979 and the subsequent Soviet occupation of the country. In their efforts to turn Afghanistan into Russia's Vietnam, the Carter and Reagan administrations had funneled money and arms via Pakistani intelligence services into the war-torn country. More than 50,000 radical Islamists traveled from all over the world to Afghanistan to do jihad against the "evil empire." Reagan's men either turned a blind eye to this jihad migration or actively facilitated it by working together with the Egyptian, Pakistani, and Saudi governments, which were only too glad to export their domestic jihadi problem to Afghanistan. It was the US-Soviet proxy war in Afghanistan that gave birth to Al-Qaeda and fueled the ideology of Salafi-jihadism and global jihadism.[43]

The blowback on September 11, 2001, was evidence of the Cold War's enduring legacy for relations between the United States and the Islamic world. An even greater consequence of the rivalry between the superpowers, which is often underestimated, is what is going on within Arab and Muslim politics. Although on 9/11 Osama bin Laden attacked the United States, his primary target was back home in Saudi Arabia. As a nonstate actor, Al-Qaeda's transnationalism masks a very local concern: to topple pro-Western Arab-Muslim regimes in Algeria, Egypt, Iraq, Pakistan, Saudi Arabia, Syria, and beyond. By punishing the Americans on 9/11, bin Laden and his deputy, Ayman al-Zawahiri, sought to force the United States to withdraw from the Middle East, thus leveling the playing field in the jihadis' battle against Muslim rulers. For bin Laden and al-Zawahiri, by colluding with the United States, the Saudi and Egyptian regimes had forfeited their Islamic identity and even sovereignty. In this sense, the United States was the secondary target on 9/11.

It is worth stressing that prior to the US military intervention in the Gulf in 1990–1991, bin Laden was on the US side combating the "evil empire." This Saudi multimillionaire was obsessed with "godless" communism and socialism, and waged a crusade to expel atheism from Muslim lands. However, two developments changed that and soured bin Laden's attitude toward his former Saudi and US patrons: America's military intervention in the first Gulf War and its subsequent decision to station troops permanently in his native home, the birthplace of Islam and its Prophet Mohammed. After Saddam Hussein invaded and occupied Kuwait in 1990, bin Laden implored Saudi royals to refrain from calling on the United States to intervene and expel the Iraqi army. He offered to raise a mujahideen vanguard to force the Iraqis out and protect the Saudi kingdom and its holy lands. Bin Laden's entreaties not only fell on deaf ears, but the Saudi monarchy rubbed salt in the wounds by inviting the Americans to establish military bases in the kingdom after the liberation of Kuwait. This was a turning point for the ambitious and charismatic bin Laden who blamed the Saudi ruling family and the Americans for desecrating Islam's holiest lands.

The year 1991 marked a revolt by bin Laden against both Saudi Arabia, his native homeland, and the US presence in the region. As a nonstate actor, Al-Qaeda anointed itself as the legitimate authority to defend the *umma* (the global Muslim community) from Western imperialism and the subservience and collusion of local rulers. These two goals help explain the proliferation of nonstate actors in the Middle East since the end of the Cold War, including Al-Qaeda and the Islamic State.

On a deeper lever, the resurgence of subnational identities and the emergence of nonstate actors reflect an ideational and institutional vacuum in the region, a vacuum that widened during the Cold War period. Although superficially stable, the Arab state system suffers from an organic crisis that has sapped its strength, its legitimacy, and its capacity to deliver social public goods.[44] Its dependency on the Great Powers exacerbates its crisis of legitimacy and hegemony.

In this sense the Cold War was a major contributing factor in helping tip the balance of social forces in the Middle East in favor of autocrats and ultraconservative religious and pan-Islamist forces. In its attempt to control access to the region's oil and roll back Soviet communism, the United States targeted independent forward-looking nationalist leaders who prioritized sovereignty and state-managed development. It backed reactionary rulers who opened their economy to global capital and joined the US-led anti-communist front. The Cold War allowed authoritarian rulers to consolidate their power by extracting resources from the two rival super-powers and tightening their grip on society. After independence, Middle Eastern states had hoped and planned to challenge long-established West-ern political, economic, and security hegemony in the region. It was an almost impossible task. These states could never truly escape the clutches of neocolonialism or informal imperialism. The East-West rivalry placed massive constraints on the Middle Eastern state system and outside pow-ers, particularly the United States, and repeatedly subverted popular, legitimate leaders and institutions that did not play by their rules and serve their interests.

Observers who downplay the effects of the East-West conflict on Middle Eastern politics overlook a salient truth: the seamless continuity between the colonial moment and the Cold War moment. This led to the revival of the interdependence between foreign powers and domestic authoritar-ians while actively neglecting the will of the people. In all the three con-tinents of the postcolonial world, people discovered that independence did not translate into sovereignty. A new form of colonialism tied them to their old masters. When the old European colonialists were not power-ful enough, America stepped in.

7

The Winter of Discontent

THE PAUPERIZATION
OF THE ARAB PEOPLE

IN THE TUNISIAN CITY of Sidi Bou Zid, Friday, December 17, 2010, began like any other winter day. But just a few hours later, a political earthquake had ripped through the city and a revolution was underway. Within weeks, Sidi Bou Zid would become famous the world over as the birthplace of the Arab Spring.[1]

That fateful Friday, a young man named Mohammed Bouazizi went to work just as he did every day. Mohammed was twenty-six. He had a cart and worked as a street vendor selling fruit and vegetables. It wasn't what he had planned to do with his life. As a young teenager he had studied at Sidi Bou Zid's technical institute, but at age sixteen he was faced with a difficult choice: his own future or his family's. His sister had a chance to go to university but the family could not afford for both of them to pursue their education.[2]

As a good son and brother, Mohammed put his family first, dropped out of school, and went to work. His decision to put his family's interests over his own was something he had been doing his entire life. His father died when Mohammed was just three years old, and although his mother had since remarried, it was a constant struggle for the family to make ends meet. As a result, Mohammed had been working to help feed his family since he was ten years old.[3] When he went to work on Friday, December 17, 2010, he did so knowing that his entire family depended on him.

Times were tough. Tunisia was suffering financially. Over the years, the country had built up a reputation as a popular tourist destination, especially during the winter months when Europeans have to travel farther south for the sun. Yet there is so much more to Tunisia than sun, sand, and sea. With its Roman ruins and mosque masterpieces, Tunisia is a crossroads civilization, where East meets West, where the foreign and the familiar come together and, on the surface, seem to do so quite comfortably. In this secular-leaning country, there is none of the culture shock tourists experience in more conservative parts of the Arab-Islamic world. Tunisia took advantage of its cultural and geographical proximity to Europe and made tourism a vital component of the economy. The sector offered a wide range of employment opportunities and injected much-needed hard foreign currency into the country's coffers. But after the global financial crash in 2008, Europeans tightened their belts. For many, foreign holidays were a luxury they could no longer afford. Lacking the oil or gas of neighboring Algeria and Libya, Tunisia had nothing to cushion the blow.

It was not the only financial problem Tunisians faced.[4] After 2008, investment bankers in the world's financial centers were no longer so keen to speculate on the price of home loans. They turned their attention to, among other things, commodities. The price of food and oil went through the roof. The impact, particularly on the poor, was immediate and it was devastating. By December 2010, food prices were at their highest levels in two decades. The price of a barrel of oil had risen by over 40 percent in just five months. People had to do more with less.

And it wasn't as if people could turn to the local rural economy to make up the shortfall and fill the markets with cheap, homegrown produce. Across the Middle East and North Africa, thanks to years (or rather decades) of political incompetence, corruption, and mismanagement, the rural economy was a mess. Extreme poverty had become the norm. Farmers struggled to eke out an existence and large swathes of the rural community were living in dire circumstances. The statistics speak for themselves and reveal a disturbing reality: the Arab world cannot feed itself. Egypt, once self-sufficient in food production, can no longer feed its own people and is now the biggest importer of grain in the world.

Close to 50 percent of Egypt's rural population live in abject poverty. Yemen, once famous for its role in distributing to the world a drink many of us can't live without—coffee—imports nearly 90 percent of its wheat and is fast running out of water. And Syria, from where the orange first made its way into northern Europe, is no longer so fertile. Over 60 percent of the country's rural population lives well below the poverty line.[5]

For Mohammed Bouazizi, on top of the combined pressures of being his family's main breadwinner and the rising price of food, there was yet another one: the cost of doing business in Tunisia. To tourists from Europe, Tunisia might have looked like a home away from home, but beneath that beguiling surface, Tunisia was a police state where corruption was rampant and ordinary people defied the agents of the state at their peril. Since independence from France in 1956, Tunisia had had only two presidents: Habib Bourguiba, the hero of the independence struggle, and Zine El Abidine Ben Ali, a former police general who ousted his predecessor in a medical coup in 1987 when he had doctors declare Bourguiba senile. Neither man had a democratic mandate. Neither man looked kindly on opposition. And that attitude trickled down. The state did not function in the interests of its people. Often the only way for ordinary people to avoid a run-in with the servants of the state was to pay their way out of it.

This was the situation Mohammed Bouazizi regularly found himself in. Like everyone else who worked as an unofficial street vendor, he could not afford to pay for a permit. This left him vulnerable to local officials who sought bribes in return for turning a blind eye to unlicensed trading. If vendors like Mohammed didn't pay up, these local officials took their goods. On Friday, December 17, that is exactly what happened. Even worse, after they had taken Mohammed's goods, the officials threatened to take the scales he used to weigh the fruit and vegetables he sold. The scales weren't his and the prospect of losing them piled even more pressure on Mohammed.[6] There was worse to come. A female police officer, Fayda Hamdi, allegedly slapped him across the face and overturned his cart. In a patriarchal society where it is forbidden for a woman to slap a man, Hamdi's act was the ultimate public humiliation for a young Arab man. Already in debt, already under pressure to feed his family, already suffering from years of abuse from the police, Mohammed's friends and family say he was driven to the point of ultimate desperation.[7]

He went to the police station, then to the governor's office, to seek the return of his goods. In both places, he was stonewalled. In despair, Mohammed stood in the street outside the governor's office, poured gasoline over his head and body, and set himself on fire. His immolation was neither an accident nor a cry for help. It was a defiant last stand against the silent oppression that millions of Tunisians endure on a daily basis as they try to navigate a broken system that works for the benefit of those at the top while everyone else lives hand to mouth, uncertain of what tomorrow will bring.

After Mohammed was rushed to hospital, his friends met that evening outside the governor's office and, refusing to be silent any longer, they chanted their friend's name over and over again. The following day, trade unions mobilized. Within days, protests against the regime had spread across the country.[8]

By December 28, the crisis facing the ruling elite had become so acute that President Ben Ali, usually so aloof from his people, took the drastic step of visiting the Ben Arous Hospital where Mohammed was being treated in the intensive care unit. Ben Ali offered support for the young man's family and fired Sidi Bou Zid's governor and the chief of police.[9] His gestures came too late. The crisis had passed the tipping point. The fear that kept people silent for so long had gone. Across the country, people were openly calling for the president to go and to take his entire regime with him.

When Mohammed Bouazizi passed away from his injuries on January 4, 2011, there was no going back. The only card the president had left to play was to set the army on his own people—a cynical tactic Bashar al-Assad would later deploy in Syria with such grim consequences—but the Tunisian army's chief of staff, General Rashid Ammar, put his country before his president and defied the order.[10]

Only one option now remained for Ben Ali: exile. On January 14, 2011, exactly four weeks after Mohammed Bouazizi decided to die on his feet rather than live on his knees, Ben Ali, his wife, and his entourage took off in a private jet for exile in the Kingdom of Saudi Arabia. The rumor mill went into overdrive. In her haste to leave, it was claimed that Ben Ali's wife, who was universally hated by the Tunisian people, had hidden gold bars in her underwear. On a more serious note, Tunisian authorities later said Ben Ali had hidden over $11 billion of state funds in foreign bank accounts they could not locate. That money was never returned to the Tunisian people.

Despair

In Tunisia, it took twenty-eight days to bring down a one-party system that had held sway for fifty-four years. And the protesters did it without firing a single shot. They successfully brought down a dictator with nothing more than the size of their crowds and the volume of their chants. One of the reasons for their success was that so many of them looked at Mohammed Bouazizi and saw themselves. Tunisia has a population of just under 11 million people, over half of whom are under twenty-five years of age. This youth bulge is common across the Arab world. Also common are the challenges these young people face in trying to secure their future. Youth unemployment is at record levels: a staggering average rate of 40 percent.

Over the past two decades I have conducted extensive field research with young people in the Middle East, and time and again young men and women of all backgrounds have told me about the lack of opportunities and expressed their frustration that their future prospects are bleak. "Jobs are scarce" is a common refrain. And even if a young graduate or school leaver is lucky enough to get a job, salaries are paltry and do not allow young people to achieve the financial independence necessary to get married and raise a family of their own. For those in middle age who are already supporting a family, there is no letup either: the financial pressure on them is unrelenting. Not surprisingly, there is a widespread belief that the system is rigged against them because special interests and crony capitalists have hijacked the state.

The young people who shared their fears and frustrations with me are not wrong in their analysis of how the state works against them. Mohammed Bouazizi's desperate act of self-immolation testifies to a severe social crisis in Arab societies. Further evidence of this crisis has come in the wave of similar acts. Three weeks after Mohammed's death, another Tunisian, Hosni Kalaya, also set himself on fire following a dispute with the police. Unlike Mohammed Bouazizi, Kalaya survived.[11] On January 18, 2011, in neighboring Egypt, Abdou Abdel-Monaam Hamadah doused himself with gasoline before striking a light. Under severe financial pressure and driven to breaking point, Hamadah, 48, could be heard shouting protests at the security services as he set himself on fire. The incident was followed by another one: this time in Mauritania, where Yavoub Ould Dahoud, 42, set himself on fire in front of the Senate in the country's capital, Nouakchott.

Even Algeria, where the Arab Spring did not take off in 2011, witnessed a wave of self-immolations immediately after Mohammed Bouazizi's death and then a powerful wave of protests starting in 2019, which continues to unfold.[12] In addition to Algeria, this second wave of large-scale social protests engulfed Sudan, Iraq, and Lebanon in 2019 and clearly showed the depth of public discontent, as well as the resilience of agency.

All of this happened because the postcolonial state massively misman-aged the economy and, in the process, caused the pauperization of large segments of the population, especially the young. Across the region, huge numbers of people live on less than US$1 or $2 per day. The extent of the economic mismanagement of many countries became apparent as oil prices fell and remittances slowed in the 1980s and numerous states were faced with the prospect of economic collapse.[13] Responding to pres-sure from the World Bank and IMF to structurally adjust their econo-mies in the 1990s, ruling elites privatized state institutions and social services and turned them into crony businesses.

These enterprises were then handed over to loyal friends and family; people who would never question the ruling elite or the status quo. This Faustian pact between the ruling elite and the business elite contributed to the emergence of a new class of businessmen who effectively owed their fortune and status directly to the state and its leader. This crony capital-ism then led to growing and deep-seated structural poverty, high unem-ployment among young people, waves of migration to the cities, and a spike in population growth. It also widened the gulf between the regime and its supporters and everyone else.

The cumulative effect of these economic policies has been beyond cata-strophic. Andre Gunder Frank famously coined the acutely accurate but depressing phrase "the development of underdevelopment."[14] It aptly ap-plies to the Middle East and North Africa. In the past three decades, the Middle East has experienced underdevelopment.

Not surprisingly, despair is widespread. It is no exaggeration to say that prior to the Arab Spring uprisings many young Arabs were facing noth-ing short of an existential crisis. Faced with an economic system that makes no room for them, and that limits their options to a Hobson's style choice between a bad option and an even worse one, millions of young Arabs have had little choice but to live in the hope of a better tomorrow.

When Mohammed Bouazizi put his own life on hold to help his sister go to university, he was doing what had become the norm for his genera-tion: writing off today and betting on a better tomorrow. But as time passes and that better tomorrow never arrives, the psychological conse-quences are enormous. Such consistent denial of possibility is crushing to the spirit. Across the Arab world, it has led to a crisis of masculinity. It is not often discussed openly but in recent years, sexual impotency has become a phenomenon in parts of the region.[15]

Young men, desperate to take care of their parents and younger siblings, to marry and establish their own families, feel utterly trapped by a system that offers them nothing. In a culture that places a high social premium on respect, many young men are left feeling powerless and worthless. In an open political system, there are numerous options for people who feel left behind by the system. They can blog, protest, or join a political party. No such options are open to anyone living in a military state. So, when Mohammed Bouazizi set himself on fire, he spoke for a generation who, like him, had had enough and wanted their dignity back. Even if they had to die for it.

Days after Ben Ali fled Tunisia, people took to the streets of Egypt to call for the downfall of the regime there. The Arab world's biggest coun-try in terms of population and the region's political bellwether, Egypt is the ideal case that shows how the postcolonial state impoverished its own people. It is a historical exemplar for the entire Arab arena, shedding further light on similar political and social dynamics that exist through-out the region. As a case study, Egypt is a microcosm of the Arab condition that helps us make sense of the partnership that exists between domestic authoritarians and external powers. We left Egyptians mourning Nasser's death in 1970, we turn now to the policies of his successor, Anwar al-Sadat, which have shaped the country's politics, economy, and society in ways that are still recognizable today.

Egypt as a Case Study

The Sadat Era: Power, Peace, and Piety, 1970–1981

When Nasser passed away in 1970, he was only fifty-two. The Six-Day War had broken him and led the country to disaster. Even so, large numbers of Egyptians stayed loyal. Because of his role in the revolution, his land reforms, and his efforts to improve the lot of the forgotten man and woman, they refused to give up on him. But beneath the cheering crowds who lauded Nasser no matter what he did, there was a darker reality. Nasser had built a deep authoritarian state where opposition of any kind was not tolerated. Those who dared disagree with him, most famously the Muslim Brothers and leftists, were carted off to prison camps where conditions were so extreme, they bordered on inhumane. With political, financial, and social tensions on the rise, it would fall to another Free Officer, Anwar Sadat, to resolve the tensions that had been bubbling beneath the surface in Egypt for years but which, thanks to Nasser's firm hold on power and his even firmer hold on the public imagination, had been kept in check.

The new president's background was typical of the Free Officers. He had known poverty as a child. Born in 1918 in a poor village to a poor family in the governorate of Monufia in the Nile Delta, Sadat grew up a world away from that of the rich urban elite. Like Nasser, he joined the military as a way to improve his lot in life. And like Nasser, he rose to the rank of colonel. The two met during Nasser's first military posting, and Sadat became part of his inner circle and was serving as his vice president when Nasser died.[16]

Once president himself, however, Sadat set out to be his own man even though he had earned the title of "yes man" during his fifteen years of service to Nasser. He now believed Nasser's political, economic, and foreign policies had failed and decided to move away from his predecessor's strategy of a war economy, coupled with Arab socialism, in favor of economic liberalization and consumerism. He also radically realigned Egypt's foreign policy, moving it out of the Soviet sphere into the West's. Although Sadat said he wanted to build "a society of dignity, serenity, tranquility, and affluence,"[17] his real aim was to create his own legacy and escape Nasser's shadow. Sadat was a disrupter who was in a hurry to demolish the Nasserist project and replace it with his own.

During the last years of Nasser's life, social tensions had been on the rise. The painful defeat in the 1967 war as well as growing economic problems had fostered discontent across sections of the Egyptian society. Students organized mass protests and workers mounted strikes, all of which were supported by professionals and intellectuals. Sectarian violence reared its ugly head. But rather than calm this situation, Sadat's ascent to power exacerbated it. By 1970, the overall share of wages had started to decline, falling from 50 percent in 1970–1971 to 49.6 percent in 1973. By 1975, it had dropped to 45.6 percent.[18] Employment rates were falling too.[19] Gross domestic product (GDP) growth in 1970–1974 was only 4.2 percent. The recovery was imbalanced because, contrary to what Sadat was calling for, little progress was made in the productive sector of the economy. Growth came mostly from increased public spending on administration and defense and an expansion in the service sector, where it rose to a healthy 8 percent. The rise of this bureaucracy and a new parasitic private sector created an acute crisis of inequality: the richest 4.7 percent of Egyptians received 22 percent of the national income. This fed populist anger and made the need for a new political and economic direction all the more pressing.

In July 1972, Sadat shocked many within Egypt (and many more outside it) when, after a row with Moscow over Russia's failure to supply Egypt with weaponry, Sadat expelled all Soviet military advisers stationed in the country. The move signaled a dramatic shift in Egypt's foreign policy and Sadat started to edge closer to the West. He needed the weapons because he was planning a war against Israel to compensate for the losses of 1967, thus forcing Israel to come to the negotiating table.[20]

That war came the following year when on October 6, 1973, Egyptian forces took the Israelis by surprise, crossed the Suez Canal and breached the Bar Lev Line. Although the Israelis quickly regrouped, the ability to inflict a surprise attack on Israel was a psychological victory for Egypt and earned Sadat the title: "hero of the crossing."[21] The subsequent Camp David Accords and the peace deal with Israel made him the first Muslim recipient of the Nobel Prize for Peace. The deal also made Egypt the second-largest recipient of overall US aid in the Middle East, a position the country still holds.

For most Egyptians, the peace with Israel was a "cold" peace, but regardless of how they felt about it, Sadat was determined to break with the past and move the country into the Western camp. In doing so, he set Egypt at odds with the rest of the Arab world and opened a breach that took years to heal. For Sadat, however, the peace was a win-win outcome. It injected billions of US dollars into Egypt every year and guaranteed that flow of money for years to come. Even more significantly, it lifted the threat of war with Israel and freed up money earmarked as defense spending for other parts of the budget.

Cairo's tilt to the West was evident elsewhere.[22] Consumerism replaced socialism. State capitalism became the new normal.[23] After the 1973 Arab-Israeli War, Sadat introduced a package of reforms aimed at liberalizing the economy.[24] These reforms became collectively known as the "Infitah" or Open Door Policy, and they opened the Egyptian economy up to investment from the United States, the Gulf, and new actors as well. Suddenly, stores were full of previously unattainable consumer goods. BMWs became a common sight on Cairo's streets. To help the "opening-up" process move along, Sadat changed the taxation system and introduced exemptions for the private sector. Throughout the whole of the Infitah period, the state-led, inward-looking economic strategy of the Nasser era gave way to one where the private sector was actively supported by the state, and restrictions on external trade and foreign direct investment (FDI) were reduced. Tourism and the textile industry flourished. Egypt's economy took off. Between 1974 and 1977, average growth reached 8 percent and industrial production sharply increased.

But net returns turned out to be short-lived. From the beginning of the Infitah until the end of 1979, the rhetoric did not match reality. Critics took the policy to task because it was more consumer-orientated than production-based.[25] Investment authorities, for example, approved 766 projects, investing approximately 2,277 million Egyptian pounds, but only a third of these projects ever started production.[26] These projects employed almost 20,000 workers, almost all of whom were Egyptian, and Egyptian firms were the main financial contributors to these projects, followed by Arab countries (16 percent), the United States (7 percent), and other states (12 percent), but they did not lead to any long-term future development or sustainable contribution to the productive economy.[27] Hopes for a tsunami of Western capital investment, large corporations, and petrodollars did not materialize.[28]

More dangerously, the Infitah institutionalized a winner-takes-all economy and entrenched the deep-seated inequality that was a hangover from the colonial era. The consumer goods now so readily available were beyond the reach of the vast majority of people. But everywhere they looked, they could now see what they could not afford to buy. This had ominous consequences for social cohesion. There were consequences for the political economy too. As part of the Infitah, the Sadat regime set up a system of patronage through which government officials benefited directly from the distribution of licenses and other privileges. Corruption became endemic. Massive scandals came to light. The infamous Pyramids Plateau Project was one among many.[29]

Such widespread corruption and nepotism created the perfect climate for the rise of a nouveau riche elite: a new business class with deep political connections and influence over the economy. The state-sponsored capitalism they espoused became known as "crony capitalism" and its chief beneficiaries as "fat cats." President Sadat's half-brother, Esmaat al-Sadat, was a notorious example of this phenomenon. Before his brother gained power, Esmaat had been a bus driver earning a monthly allowance of $60.[30] By 1981, the final year of his brother's presidency, Esmaat owned a fleet of trucks, a fifty-four-room mansion in a southern suburb of Cairo with 100 telephone and telex lines.[31] According to Egyptian authorities,

his assets were valued at around $150 million.[32] Esmaat epitomized every-
thing that was wrong with Egypt under Sadat. In 1983, he and three of
his sons were convicted of having committed acts harmful to the interests of the community. He was charged with twenty-four counts of corruption including illegal acquisition of land, influence peddling, black
racketeering and the import and sale of defective and rotten food.[33]

As parasitic corruption reached new heights, social tensions rose and
conflicts intensified. While the rich grew richer, wealth did not trickle
down. Although the private sector grew during this period, growth was
uneven and, in real terms, wages fell. More and more people started to
look for solutions outside Egypt. This was the period when emigration
to the Gulf to work became a feature of Egyptian life. For those who stayed
behind, state resources had to be used to create a social safety net and soak
up unemployment in the public sector. But this too had negative consequences: there was little regard to the standard of services provided. As
a result, quality became a casualty and two of the most important state
services, education and health care, suffered.

The bread riots of 1977 were a direct consequence of the deepening division between the new rich and the urban proletariat. These riots took
place after the IMF demanded Arab countries end subsidies on a number
of basic commodities, including bread.[34] Consequently, the price of rice
shot up by 16 percent and the price of cooking gas by a massive 46 percent.[35]
The army had to be deployed to restore calm. Rioters were heard shouting, "Hero of the crossing where is our breakfast?" Others simply chanted
"Nasser!"[36] It was a pivotal moment in Sadat's presidency. His unpopularity was now out in the open for all to see.

Sadat blamed the Left. Holding them responsible for Egypt's political
woes became his default position. To balance Nasser's socialist and leftist
legacy, Sadat wanted to cut the Left out of the political debate altogether.
He decided the best way to do it was to co-opt an alternative opposition.
In a culture where religion remained a primary point of identity, he chose
Islamic norms and values and promoted Islamist groups.[37] As part of this
strategy, Sadat cultivated an image of personal piety himself. "The Believer President" as he became known even had a prayer mark on his
forehead as a sign of this piety. Politically, his aim was to open up a small

but heavily controlled space in the public arena in which Islamists could operate. After the brutality they endured under Nasser, Sadat calculated that the Muslim Brotherhood and other Islamist groups would prefer to work with the system rather than face repression and suppression. That, in turn, would make it easier for him to control them. There was the added bonus that they would function as a powerful counterweight to the Left.

The problem for Sadat was that Islamists saw right through it. They recognized his plan for what it was: all shadow and no substance. They knew Sadat was using them to keep all opposition movements off-balance. But political Islamists like the Muslim Brotherhood took a pragmatic, realist approach: they took the advantages on offer—most notably, the ability to operate in the open—and built up an impressive welfare system that ran parallel to the state. This gave them deep roots in the community, particularly in poor areas where the state was failing to deliver and where people depended on the services the Brothers provided. To fund these activities, they did not rely on charity alone but set up businesses to secure income for the long term. In this way, Sadat inadvertently created an Islamist bourgeoisie in the private sector and helped facilitate the development of a state-within-a-state.

Sadat's real aim was not to co-opt but to divide and conquer, and because of that, the policy could change at a moment's notice depending on the political circumstances. Furthermore, it did not extend at all times to all Islamist groups so roundups of "more radical" Islamists became routine. Regardless of whether they were violent or not, these men and women were deemed terrorists, arrested under emergency laws and were then "disappeared" into the system for indefinite detention. It was a policy that made radicals out of moderates and made radicals feel righteous about committing acts of violence.

On October 6, 1981, Sadat reviewed a parade in the company of the country's great and the good. Foreign dignitaries were also in attendance. An armored vehicle suddenly stopped in front of the review stand and four men, armed with grenades and automatic weapons, leapt out.

There was pandemonium. Sadat's bodyguards fled. Sadat was killed, and seven others also died. The carnage would have been greater if the grenades had hit their targets. Nearly all of Egypt's political and military leadership was in the stand, including Vice President Hosni Mubarak.

The reaction to Sadat's death was revealing. In Egypt, there was no mass outpouring of grief. No emotion similar to that shown on Nasser's death. The unpopular president who brought his people a cold peace with Israel received the cold shoulder from his people in death. Khalid al-Islambuli, on the other hand, achieved cult status overnight. His words "I have killed Pharaoh" quickly became part of folklore.[38]

In the corridors of power in the West, it was a different story. Sadat was celebrated as a man of peace and his passing was mourned. His authoritarianism, his unpopularity, and his corruption were ignored. No fewer than three US presidents attended his funeral, a rare honor for the US political establishment to bestow on a foreign head of state. Sadat's partner in peace, Israeli prime minister Menachem Begin, also attended.

But this positive press in the West could not obscure the reality of life in Egypt under Sadat: this was a country on a course seriously at odds with the wishes of its people. Sadat entrenched many of the same tactics the colonial powers used—concentrating economic opportunities and prosperity in an elite caste (through cronyism and corruption), strengthening a repressive and brutal police state, and stoking sectarian division to prevent any united opposition from deposing his regime.

The Mubarak Era: Power, Privilege, and Poverty, 1981–2011

Vice President Hosni Mubarak was sitting next to Anwar Sadat when the latter was assassinated and only narrowly escaped with his life. He became president on Sadat's death. Born in 1928, Mubarak came from the same governorate to the north of Cairo, Monufia, as Sadat. Unlike his presidential predecessors who were a decade older, Mubarak was not one of the Free Officers. He did, however, have a strong military background. Like Nasser and Sadat before him, Mubarak was a graduate of the Royal Military Academy. From there, he joined the air force and became a pilot. Three decades after the revolution, one thing was very clear about politics in Egypt: the presidency belonged to the military.

There was continuity in the economy too. Between 1981 and 2000, Mubarak's economic strategy was a carbon copy of his predecessor's. Like Sadat, Mubarak oversaw an economic policy that overrelied on "rent" from Egyptians working abroad. The result was underinvestment at home and low productivity. On paper, Mubarak's strategy appeared to generate positive growth as FDI and trade increased. But enormous amounts of bureaucratic red tape and high levels of corruption, not to mention the uneven playing field in the private sector, took their toll and had an adverse effect on overall economic productivity. Declining education standards and the dearth of vocational training hindered productivity even further.

Across the globe, the 1980s witnessed a shift toward the market economy and Egypt was no exception. But the Arab oil producing states, together with rent-seeking states like Egypt, lagged behind in terms of development and productivity. As a result, they remained overly dependent on oil. The sharp decline in oil prices in the 1980s therefore hurt the region badly. While Egypt's economy managed to keep on growing, this growth was wildly uneven. It did not foster economic development because of a huge gap in income distribution and the poor quality and diversity of investments.

During Mubarak's early years, productivity continued to slide and fewer jobs were created. But firms with political ties thrived. They flooded the private sector, putting a new pro-regime business elite in control of the economy, and reinforcing the trend that had started during the Sadat era.

This widening gap behind the well-connected rich and the dispossessed poor raised social tensions and piled more pressure on an already fracturing society. Social unrest increased in the mid-1980s following government cuts to the public. From 1984 until 1990 the country was rocked by more than 100 strikes, over two dozen serious riots, and nearly 200 demonstrations. Political assassinations happened more frequently. On October 12, 1990, the speaker of parliament, Rifaat al-Mahgoub, was gunned down as he left a luxury hotel on the Nile.[39] An attempt to assassinate three former ministers failed.

As anger, dissent, and violence against the political establishment continued to grow, so did the government's repression. In April 1989, the interior minister, Zaki Badr (known as "Iron Fist") jailed a thousand supporters of the opposition. But in spite of the protests, nothing changed. The economic inequality, directed from the top, continued. Most people continued to be employed in the unproductive public sector rather than the profitable private sector. The education sector continued to decline and the gap in quality with other emerging market economies continued to widen.

In the 1980s and 1990s, Mubarak's neoliberal economic policies downsized the role of the state in the economy but, in a move that would have horrified Nasser, Mubarak failed to put any safety nets in place to protect the poor. Instead, he adopted a Western model of economic development for a country that did not have Western levels of development. The reverse was, in reality, true: Egypt had a severe development deficit because of the structural imbalances inherited from colonialism. And in a country that was chronically low on water, the food subsidies frowned upon by institutions like the World Bank and the IMF were not only desperately needed, they were also essential for people's survival.

Mubarak was creating a free market economy in a country that was not free. His new policies benefited his cronies in the private sector but hurt small businesses and enterprises, which faced not only tougher competition but also the burden of having to navigate Egypt's byzantine bureaucracy.[40] Mubarak also established a corrupt system to award licenses. His neoliberalism and state-sanctioned corruption led to greater poverty and the rise of an informal economy. Now there was not only a political state-within-a-state, but an economic one too.

The expectation for Mubarak's new policies was that a larger private sector would reduce unemployment. But that did not happen. The problem was that since the 1990s, productivity had slowed down considerably. The public debt, in turn, skyrocketed due to reliance on foreign loans, fiscal mismanagement, and wasteful spending on inefficient subsidies and an overstaffed public sector. Productivity also declined because of de-industrialization. The share of GDP produced by the industrial sector dropped from 21 to 15 percent. From 1993 to 1998, between 50,000 and 100,000 workers were forced out of the labor market by early retirement packages.

Throughout the 1990s, a number of government-business councils were created but they failed to reduce the expanding cleavage between the new elite and the poor. These councils were another example of the chronic and systemic nepotism of the Mubarak regime. For example, the Egyptian-American Businessman Council's spokesperson was none other than Gamal Mubarak, son of the president. Gamal's rising profile led to speculation that his father was intending to break with revolutionary protocol and pass the presidency to his son, as if the governance of Egypt was a family business.[41] Or, as best-selling Egyptian author Alaa al-Aswany put it, the country was nothing more than a "private estate or a poultry farm."[42]

This determination to "keep it in the family" was becoming the norm for the new elite in Mubarak's Egypt. As a result of his neoliberal reforms, the state bourgeoisie that rose under Sadat consolidated and expanded its power base under Mubarak. The crony capitalism of Sadat and Mubarak fostered business dynasties with idealized founding fathers. These men then handed their businesses over to their sons, who in turn maintained their contacts with the powerful and continued to expand the family empire.[43]

Under Sadat and Mubarak, strong links with the ruling elite could secure a direct path to the acquisition of very profitable state-owned companies.[44] Access to capital reinforced this system and denied access to outsiders. These favored companies were able to accumulate a vast amount of wealth and therefore buy up an even greater chunk of the economy, thanks to cut-price loans awarded by state-owned banks.[45] The divestiture of state-owned shares in joint-venture banks is directly linked to the problem of credit concentration.[46]

The statistics speak for themselves. According to the World Bank, 51 percent of credit extended to the private sector in 2006 went to an unbelievable 0.2 percent of the sector's clients.[47] A mere thirty corporations accounted for 40 percent of the total credit supply.[48] Under Mubarak, only two groups of entrepreneurs with big capital could operate: the Infitah bourgeoisie and the new business class connected to Gamal Mubarak, the president's son.[49] As one keen observer of Egyptian affairs noted: "Distribution of political positions in Egypt obeys a precise equation that reflects the relative weight of various groups in the regime."[50] In other words, a small inner-circle group around the regime horded economic and political power.

The difference between the Infitah bourgeoisie of Sadat's era and the new business class of Mubarak's was that the former steered away from politics whereas the latter increasingly embraced them.[51] Institutionally, this shift was enabled by two mechanisms. First, the Ministry of Planning, a key institution during the state's centralized phase, was replaced by the Ministry of Trade and Industry, which was more outward looking and therefore more open to influence peddling.[52] During the Nazi cabinet, for example, key economic decisions were not taken by the cabinet acting as a collective. Instead, the power to make economic decisions was concentrated in the hands of the so-called troika, made up of the ministers of finance, investment, and trade and industry: Youssef Boutros Ghali, Mahmoud Mohieddin, and Rashid Mohammed Rashid, respectively.

Second, businessmen engaged directly in politics in the 1990s. This was a decade characterized by high deficit and low growth, and the ruling party decided to broaden its membership by attracting a new generation of entrepreneurs who had done well in the private sector.[53] Again, it was the president's son, Gamal Mubarak, who was given the pivotal role in co-opting young businessmen in their thirties and forties to join the ruling party, a process that was accelerated from the 2000s onward.[54] The number of businessmen in parliament increased from 37 in 1995, to 77 in 2000, to 100 in 2005.[55] Prime Minister Ahmed Nazif went as far as to appoint six businessmen to his government.[56]

In Mubarak's Egypt, the rich received more subsidies than the poor because of the fixed exchange rate. State-sanctioned corruption made the problem worse. Ultimately, the problem was not that the Mubarak regime "let the private sector do the development job." In principle, the private sector could have generated high growth and reduced income inequality. Rather, the problem was that the regime's core goal was self-preservation and self-enrichment. Those priorities constrained the development of small business. No one was allowed to develop or produce anything that challenged the business interests of the elite. By the end of Mubarak's rule in 2011, the lines between the public and private sectors had become so blurred it was almost impossible to disentangle them.

The Free Officers revolution had come a long way from the days of its founding fathers. Nasser's era had seen the military take control of politics. Mubarak's saw the businessmen take control. State assets were seen as theirs to plunder. The military was still a key part of the power equation, but it was no longer the only one. It had its own stake in the economy: as far back as Nasser's era, parts of the economy had been given over to the military to run as virtual monopoly businesses. That remained the case, and it was one of the reasons the military retained an interest in maintaining the status quo.[57]

And Mubarak needed its support. He could not rule without a strong security apparatus. As the gap between the fat cats and ordinary people grew, as the rich accumulated ever more obscene levels of wealth while the poor saw their income plummet to less than a dollar a day, the president's unpopularity hit record lows. Mubarak now saw only one way to fill the gap between power and the people: to silence it. Torture of the most brutal and dehumanizing kind became routine.

More than his predecessor, Sadat, Mubarak increased Egypt's dependence on the United States. The longer he stayed in power, the worse the situation got for Egyptians. Protected by the West thanks to the peace deal with Israel and his decision to join the US-led Global War on Terror, Mubarak faced no external criticism. Consequently, there were no restraints on his ability to exercise power against his own people. That attitude filtered down to the security forces on the ground. They had the power to make people disappear and they did not hesitate to use it. No longer were political opponents the only target of the repressive state, everyone was. People could be arrested and not even know why. The state did not have to provide answers.

How Did This Happen?

How did the promise and optimism of the anti-colonial and independence era become so subverted? The Middle East was not unique in bearing the burden of colonialism. It was not even unique in succumbing to authoritarianism. Nor was it unique in attracting the eye of the new superpower. Many countries across Africa, Asia, and South America suffered a similar fate and inherited similar structural imbalances in state and society.

In theory, political authoritarianism does not automatically lead to economic failure. The Four Asian Tigers (Hong Kong, Singapore, South Korea, and Taiwan) are a case in point.[58] In contrast to Middle Eastern states, they have achieved unprecedented economic progress and become part of the wealthy high-tech industrialized club.[59]

At the beginning of the 1950s, Egypt, Iraq, Lebanon, and other countries in the Middle East had a similar median income to those of the Four Asian Tigers. Yet while the economies of Arab countries stagnated and then went into reverse, Hong Kong (China), Singapore, South Korea, and Taiwan underwent rapid industrialization and technological innovation and enjoyed over 8 percent growth rates between the mid-1950s and early 1990s.[60] They have used this wealth to create educational centers of excellence, world-class universities, and state-of-the-art infrastructure. While young Arabs lag further and further behind, held back by a system that fails them, young people in the Tiger economies forge ahead. Their results in math and science exams such as the Programme for International Student Assessment (PISA) so consistently outrank the rest of the world, these young Asian students have become synonymous with scientific success.[61]

By contrast, Arab high schools produce semi-illiterate students and Arab universities are overcrowded, underfunded, and understaffed. Very few Arab universities make it into the ranking charts whereas Cairo University was once an institution of excellence.

For the Middle East, the twentieth century and the early part of the twenty-first century have been marked by colossal failures and painful tragedies. It is critical that we understand how the region's political economy went wrong and why postcolonial elites have been unable to establish diverse, competitive, and productive economies like their counterparts in East Asia, even though most Middle Eastern states possess vast natural resources and impressive human capital. Political development has been no less dismal than economic development despite the obvious determination of the people to struggle for their freedom from colonialism.[62]

Is bad governance to blame for the wretched social conditions of Arab societies? Or are structural forces—foreign intervention, chronic conflict, heavy reliance on one source of income, the low salience of FDI—equally to blame?[63]

What explains why Arab states have fallen so far behind? Is there another explanation we need to consider, one that will explain why the Middle East became a place where so many of its young citizens believe dying or migrating is a better option than continuing to live this way at home?

8

How and Why Did the Middle East Fail to Achieve Its Potential?

THE QUEST FOR ANSWERS has to start at the top. The postcolonial elite—the first generation of leaders who expelled the colonialists and who promised their people a new dawn—failed to deliver on their lofty promises.[1] Instead, they built republics of fear and imitated the colonial tactics of divide and rule to consolidate their power. The institutions of the deep state were erected immediately after the end of the colonial era in the late 1940s and early 1950s and they never stopped expanding. Charismatic leaders like Egyptian president Gamal Abdel Nasser set the stage for a new populism that swept the Middle East in the 1950s and 1960s. The sole leader became the voice of the masses. He disinvested citizens of independent human agency and acted as their agent and guardian, going as far as to set himself up as a surrogate father figure. An implicit social pact gained currency in Arab countries among both the wealthy and the poor—whereby the state would provide jobs and bread in return for the population's political acquiescence. This "Arab social contract" allowed the postindependence elites to limit participation in the political space.[2]

Preaching national unity and calling on the people to put their trust in him, the leader-cum-father-figure monopolized power and suppressed all organized opposition. By the end of the 1950s, postindependence elites across the newly decolonized Arab republics had succeeded in dismantling the fragile multiparty system put in place after World War I and replaced it with one-party rule. Even more ominously, this one-party rule became a fig leaf for a cult of personality where a strong man surrounded himself with a small inner circle of cronies who did his bidding. A top-down authoritarian system thus took hold in the Arab Middle East and Iran as well: a political system controlled by a military-security apparatus (commonly known as *Dawlat al-Mukhabarat*, intelligence-dominated state). Aside from its repression and brutality, this political system was insular. It lacked transparency, accountability, and rationality. And it proved to be catastrophic.

Bunker mentalities produced disastrous results including the May crisis that provided Israel with the rationale to bloody the Arab armies in the Six-Day War in June 1967 and Saddam Hussein's calamitous invasions of Iran in 1980 and Kuwait in 1990. A closed top-down process of decision-making invited neither open debate nor input from civil society for fear of contradicting the views of the head of state. There was safety in silence. No subordinate would have dared challenge the viewpoint of Hafez al-Assad in Syria or Saddam Hussein in Iraq and offer a different narrative. The leader was surrounded by yes men.

By steering clear of internal debate and showing absolute deference to the sole leader, the authoritarian political system was inherently error-prone and ineffective. The durability of political authoritarianism in the Arab world should not obscure its colossal failure to deliver on its promises or its propensity for miscalculation. An overview of systemic factors and economic decisions taken by the postcolonial elite provides a balance sheet of how the Arab republics mismanaged the economy and caused development failure. My conclusion is that bad governance combined with structural reasons led to the pauperization of huge sectors of the population. I believe human agency is just as important as structural variables, if not more so. Leadership is a precious commodity that is in woefully short supply in the Arab Middle East. Leaders like Hafez al-Assad and his son Bashar, Zine El Abidine Ben Ali, Muammar Gaddafi, Saddam Hussein, Hosni Mubarak, Anwar al-Sadat, Ali Abdullah Saleh, and others let their people down when they consciously made economic choices that proved catastrophic. It is misleading and disingenuous to blame only systemic and intervening variables for their strategic blunders.

Assigning responsibility to inept leadership, however, neither negates nor minimizes the links between the region and the world economy that go back more than three centuries. Nor does it dismiss the negative structural imbalances that resulted from those links and the impact they continue to have on Arab and Middle Eastern economies. Long before European governments colonized the region after World War I, they set out to dominate the economies of the Ottoman Empire and those of semi-independent states like Algeria, Egypt, and Iran. From the eighteenth century, Europe's Great Powers battled for strategic advantage in the Middle East and North Africa. The area was a hugely important theater for cheap raw materials, markets, waterways, and a strategic gateway to Europe's imperial territories in India and the Far East.

The end of formal colonialism after World War II did not mark the end of Great Power intervention in the Middle East. The flow of inexpensive petroleum from the region was crucial to the recovery of the postwar global economy, particularly those of the Western powers that were becoming addicted to oil and gas. While Cold War rivalry in the Middle East between the United States and the Soviet Union was superficially about power politics, the region's huge reserves of black gold were the real driving force. As the guardian of the postwar international order, American policymakers were determined to protect the flow of Middle Eastern petroleum to the Western economy at all costs.

The global economy runs on inexpensive oil and gas from the Gulf. More than any other region in the world, the Middle East's precious raw resources, along with its location on key East-West trade routes, make it indispensable to established superpowers and potential future rivals. An umbilical cord thus links the Middle East to the international system. Black gold and billions of US dollars of Arab investment in Western financial institutions as well as an unquenchable arms market: these are the ties that bind the United States (and less so European powers) to Middle Eastern authoritarian rulers, not the promotion of democracy, human rights, and the rule of law. As long as regional actors deliver, they are assured of US patronage and protection regardless of how they behave at home.

This compliant international environment gave ruling elites in the region a free hand to crack down on opposition at home and pursue policies that serve the interests of the few at the expense of the many. As long as Arab and Middle Eastern regimes face no accountability for their decisions, their inept leadership will continue and the consequences will keep leaking into every aspect of life.

Within this context, the durability of the authoritarian political system, and the bad decision-making that results from it, has done little to address the structural reasons causing development failure in the region. On the contrary, they have made them worse. Previous chapters have often highlighted the continuities with the colonial era by focusing on the role played by foreign intervention in the Middle East, an outside-in approach. This chapter will provide a complement to those investigations by beginning from within the Middle East, considering the structural aspects of the region and their impact on domestic governance, paying particular attention to how authoritarianism perpetuates itself in this context, making it more difficult for the people to exercise their collective agency.

Collapsing from Within: The Structural Reasons for Development Failure

There are a number of structural reasons for the failure of development in the Middle East and North Africa. In what follows, we will take a closer look at four of the most important: the prevalence of armed conflicts, the volatility of the oil market, the low salience of foreign direct investment (FDI), and water security.

The Prevalence of Armed Conflicts

As analysts point out, political and military conflicts constitute an important cause of development failure.[3] The costs of war exact a heavy toll on state, society, and economy. The Middle East and North Africa has witnessed wave after wave of interstate conflicts, civil wars, and terrorism since the decolonization period. In Algeria, for example, political violence did not stop after the long war of independence against colonial France (1954–1962), which killed roughly a million people. Thirty years after independence in the 1960s, Algeria was torn apart by an eleven-year civil war known as the "black decade" in which at least another 200,000 Algerians lost their lives.

Algeria was not alone. Across the region, war is rampant. From 1962 to 1968, Yemen, the poorest Arab state, was the theater of a bloody civil conflict where two key regional actors, Egypt and Saudi Arabia, fought a proxy war. In 1975, a prolonged civil war started in Lebanon that lasted fifteen years. Between 150,000 and 200,000 people were killed and 1.25 million were displaced. Lebanon came close to the brink of collapse. The Iran-Iraq war, which broke out in 1980 and ended in 1988, killed nearly one million Iranians and Iraqis, cost hundreds of billions of US dollars, and nearly ruined the economies of both countries. While these devastating conflicts could have provided an opportunity for Middle Eastern rulers to rethink their failed policies, leaders chose instead to use national security as a way to maintain the status quo.[4] Saddam Hussein and other regional strongmen saw security more in terms of regime survival than human security and political development. The Israeli-Palestinian conflict is a case in point. Time and again, Arab rulers pointed to Israel as the reason they had to set up a massive security apparatus, the cost of which was used as an excuse to explain the lack of resources available for development.

Although these interstate conflicts and civil wars have bled Middle Eastern societies dry, authoritarian regimes managed to gain financial relief from their superpower patrons. During the Cold War, regional actors manipulated the global rivalry between the United States and the Soviet Union to obtain foreign aid and arms. Some sided with America, while others sided with Russia, and a third group joined the Non-Aligned Movement. For example, after Anwar Sadat made peace with Israel in 1978, the United States provided Egypt with $2 billion annually in economic and military aid. Known as "the peace dividend," the US aid package was meant to stimulate Egypt's economy, though academics and economists argue that, at best, it had mixed or even meager results.[5] After Egypt's participation in the US-led Gulf War in 1990–1991, President George H. W.

Bush granted the country partial relief of its foreign debt with both the United States and creditors of the Paris Club.[6] Unlike Nasser, Anwar Sadat and Hosni Mubarak aligned Egypt closely with the United States in return for "rent" or financial aid and arms. Unfortunately, neither Sadat nor Mubarak invested this rent in developing the economy or alleviating poverty.

As Iraq's invasion of Kuwait in 1990 and the subsequent US intervention show, the end of the Cold War did not lead to a decrease of violence in the Middle East. The reverse is true. Interstate and civil conflicts continue to tear the region apart. The statistics are shocking. Between 2000–2003 and 2010–2015, armed conflicts in the Arab world have risen from four to eleven.[7] Since the beginning of the Arab Spring uprisings, Iraq, Libya, Syria, and Yemen had witnessed social and political upheaval and turmoil, with some of these countries descending into prolonged civil wars that destroyed some of these states' institutions and created tens of millions of refugees. In Spring 2023, Sudan was added to the gruesome list of active civil conflicts (pitting one faction in the military against another) in the region.[8]

Politically driven violence is also on the rise.[9] Since the US-led invasions of Afghanistan in 2001 and Iraq in 2003, terrorist attacks have skyrocketed across the Islamic world, particularly in Afghanistan, Iraq, Libya, Pakistan, Syria, and Yemen. Between 2000 and 2014, there have been more than 26,000 terrorist attacks in various Arab countries. These attacks have killed over 74,000 people and wounded more than 127,000.[10] This politically driven violence[11] has also had a direct impact on these states' economies and financial stability, including the tourist sector and foreign investments. Egypt's economy, for instance, has suffered a persistent decline since the uprising in 2011 and the coup in 2013. Estimates by the United Nations Economic and Social Commission for Western Asia (ESCWA) indicate that conflict and turmoil in the region between 2011 and 2015 have led to a net loss of $613.8 billion in economic activity, and an aggregate fiscal deficit of $243.1 billion for Middle East and North Africa (MENA) states. Since the rise of the Islamic State from 2014 till 2019, a new wave of terrorist attacks have shaken the region and undermined the revival of the tourism sector. The COVID-19 pandemic in 2020 and Russia's invasion of Ukraine in February 2022 had devastating effects on Middle Eastern economies, exacerbating poverty, food insecurity, youth unemployment, and indebtedness.[12] The unfolding Israeli war in Gaza in 2023–2024 has destroyed the Palestinian economy and made large swaths of the Gaza Strip uninhabitable as well as exacting a heavy toll on Israel's economy and society.

On a per capita basis, Middle Eastern governments outspend the rest of the world on defense, with Saudi Arabia being one of the world's biggest spenders, the eighth in 2022 and the fifth in 2023. On average, defense budgets in the region are equivalent to more than 5 percent of GDP.[13]

Since independence, the postcolonial state in the Arab world has been weighed down by interregional rivalries and armed conflicts that have come at the expense of meaningful human development. The toll on society has been enormous. The militarization of the region has had a discernible and direct impact on the economic welfare and wellbeing of the population with billions of US dollars redirected to security and defense spending. That gap could have been filled with investment from oil revenues, but with leaders' priorities elsewhere that has not been the case.

Oil, Growth, and Volatility

Oil, which should have been a blessing, is now seen as a curse that bewitched development in the region, creating dependency on a single resource and providing the financial means that allowed ruling elites to maintain the status quo. It is often argued that petroleum served more as a mechanism for system maintenance than system transformation. Because of this, oil has acquired a negative reputation and become known as the "resource curse" in development literature. Instead of using the massive flow of cash from the sale of oil to create a diversified economy, with few exceptions Middle Eastern regimes were complacent and chose to act as if oil would last forever and the price would never fall.

Moreover, oil revenues sustained political authoritarianism by providing republican strongmen and kings with the resources to keep their populations under control. Oil revenue also freed them from the need to generate taxation. That placed them beyond obligation to make political pacts with their citizens. Doing so would have forced them to be accountable and transparent and, more importantly, to accept constitutional checks and balances. In this way, the revenues from oil and gas have acted as a powerful disincentive to political liberalization and have deepened authoritarianism.

From the 1970s to the early 1980s, the spectacular increase in the price of oil benefited oil producers and exporters immensely. In the late 1970s, the Kingdom of Saudi Arabia was one of the richest countries on the planet. And the oil producers believed this good fortune would continue indefinitely. They calculated oil would provide them with a comfortable "rent" that they could rely on for decades to come.[14] That complacent dependency drew in the rest of the Arab and Islamic world. In constant demand for labor, Gulf monarchies welcomed immigrants from these parts of the world. Workers sent their remittances home and so helped their own countries' economy develop. But this development came at the cost of establishing dependency on foreign rent.[15]

As most Middle Eastern states were "rentier" states, they were able for a time to support bloated bureaucracies and offer a complex system of payoffs. These trade-offs sustained the regimes in the short term but did so at the expense of growing inefficiency and massive corruption. Countries lacking such resources, like Egypt, Jordan, and Syria, were forced instead to rely on foreign aid from one of the two opposing superpowers, which in turn entangled them in Cold War rivalries and furthered their loss of legitimacy in the eyes of their people.

The oil boom of the 1970s sustained this state of affairs as rising energy costs ensured the state coffers of oil producers were well-stocked and loans from abroad were easily found. Yet even high oil prices could not hide the gross mismanagement, authoritarianism, and corruption that had become endemic across the region. The popular revolution that overthrew the shah of Iran in 1979, the internal revolts against the Syrian regime of Hafez al-Assad in the early 1980s, and the repeated bread protests in Egypt were proof of rising discontent.

The 1980s, however, saw a steep drop in revenue that strongly affected oil producers and neighboring countries whose economies were dependent on remittances from the Gulf. Saudi Arabia's GDP, for example, halved between 1981 and 1987.[16] In the 1990s, oil prices stagnated but the 2000s witnessed a new hike that was then followed by another slump. These ups and downs of the price of oil since the 1970s show the volatility of the oil market and how prone it is to fluctuations in the global economy. Anything from a terrorist attack to a hurricane in the Gulf of Mexico can cause jitters in the market. Consequently, oil producers face a serious problem when it comes to managing their future economic planning: they cannot factor the full impact of this unpredictable variable into their GDP.[17]

But the truth is they have felt no real pressure to adapt. Complacency crept in because the huge revenues gained during the years of price hikes allowed big producers to repay their foreign debts and accumulate substantial reserves of foreign currency. Those fat years reinforced the complacency and postponed the inevitable: the need to diversify the economy and make it less dependent on petroleum. Saudi Arabia is a good example of this (Algeria also remains over 90 percent dependent on hydrocarbon exports). The Gulf kingdom has undergone an impressive economic development since the 1970s due to massive oil income, investment projects, and financial reserves.[18] Huge investments were made in infrastructure and industry. At the same time, however, "imports also increased sharply as the country could supply neither the investment goods needed for development nor the demand for consumer goods that higher incomes made possible."[19]

As the price of oil declined in the early 1980s, Saudi Arabia faced a serious economic crisis and, by 1988, it was running a budget deficit of $13.7 billion. This deficit skyrocketed during the Iran-Iraq War in the 1980s and the first Gulf War in 1990–1991.[20] The ruling family subsidized both conflicts by providing Saddam Hussein with billions of US dollars for his war with Iran and then shouldered the financial costs of US intervention against the Iraqi ruler when he invaded Kuwait in 1990. The Saudis also provided generous subsidies to their own citizens and regional allies who joined the fight against Saddam Hussein.[21]

The Saudi case is revealing because the country produces more than nine million barrels of oil, making it the biggest exporter in the world and, in a crisis, it acts as the swing producer that makes up shortfalls elsewhere in the system. Yet, even with this huge source of income on tap, it has still been unable to escape the trappings of the resource curse and develop a dynamic and diverse economy. Despite the rapid transformation of the Saudi economy since the mid-1970s, economic growth has nevertheless been uneven and unbalanced. Today the country suffers from a high unemployment rate, especially among the young, and it remains overwhelmingly dependent on a single source of income.[22] One of the key challenges facing the young leadership of Crown Prince Muhammad bin Salman (also known as MBS) is to transform the economy and make it more diverse and productive. The future of Saudi Arabia will depend on MBS's declared efforts to diversify the economy and to co-opt aspiring young men and women to his vision. The jury is still out.

In general, since the 1970s, the GDP of Arab countries has often been closely linked to fluctuation in the price of petroleum. In 2006, for example, fuel exports constituted, respectively, 75.0, 72.6, and 81.4 percent of the total exports of high-income, middle-income, and low-income Arab countries. In Kuwait, when GDP declined by 18 percent in 1981 and 1982, the oil shock had social repercussions on neighboring countries like Jordan and Yemen, which, although not oil producers themselves, relied on remittances from their nationals working in the Gulf. Between 1973 and 1989, financial aid from Saudi Arabia in the form of public or private investment, as well as workers' remittances, provided $140 billion dollars to other Arab countries. Of this, only $50 billion came from official assistance; the rest was from workers sending money home.[23] This heavy reliance on financial assistance or rent provided a strong disincentive for Arab rulers to restructure their economies and carry out the reforms necessary to make a more market-orientated, globally competitive economy.[24]

Because the primary focus of regimes is to stay in power, they filter every decision through that lens. The result is that the structural problems facing the region, whether the prevalence of wars or the overreliance on oil, negatively reinforce each other and create a spiral of downward development. This, in turn, further hinders the development of the region's economy as it creates an adverse environment for foreign investors and lowers rates of FDI.

The Low Salience of Foreign Direct Investment

The low salience of FDI is another key problem in the economic development of the region. Contrary to other emerging economies, states in the MENA have failed to significantly attract large sums of FDI. Between 2002 and 2007, the Middle East seemed to follow the increasing trends of growth of the rest of the developing world. The increase in FDI, however, was largely concentrated in the extractive rather than the productive sector. According to World Bank data, after a peak of $126 billion of net inflows in 2007, FDI to the region dropped following the global financial crisis in 2008, reaching a low of $37 billion in 2014. This steep drop in FDI flow to the region occurred in the midst of the post–Arab Spring uprisings instability.[25] Inflows have partially recovered since, yet never to the level of 2007. Moreover, the same World Bank data, when broken up country-by-country, show huge disparities between the rich countries of the Gulf and the war-ravaged states of the Mashreq, or Arab East.[26]

Iraq was, for a brief period, a rare example of a country bucking this trend. In 2012, Iraq experienced the greatest increase in FDI in the MENA: a quite staggering rise from $960 million in 2012 (1.2 percent of the regional total) to $14.96 billion a year later (15 percent of the regional total). As a result of this phenomenal increase, Baghdad became the top regional beneficiary of FDI. Reconstruction was the motivating factor. In 2012, the Iraqi government invited Middle Eastern companies to invest in rebuilding the war-torn country. By 2013, it had signed deals with seven developers to build affordable and luxury housing complexes, including with two United Arab Emirates (UAE)-based companies, Emaar Properties and Bloom. A year later, the UAE was the leading source of investment in the entire MENA, responsible for $14.8 billion outward investment, a figure that works out at nearly one-third of all investment in the region. After the peak of growth in 2012, however, political instability spilling over from the Syrian Civil War and the rise of the Islamic State led to a massive capital flight, reversing any progress made in the previous decade.[27]

During the brief boom, Emaar Properties' plan to finance a $3 billion tourist project in the Kurdish city of Erbil contributed to this rise of investment. The projects, which were supposed to create more than 45,000 jobs, aimed to build 15,000 houses and hotels and renovate the citadel.[28] Other projects in Iraq included plans by Bloom, a subsidiary of Abu Dhabi's National Holding, to build 40,000 houses in the city of Karbala as well as hotels, offices, markets, clinics, schools, and mosques.[29] But as Iraq descended into all-out war with the Islamic State in 2014–2015, these projects were put on hold. And the longer the delays last, the costlier the projects become.

After Iraq, Jordan was the second-largest beneficiary of FDI in the MENA, with 11 percent in 2013. But these statistics mask a less positive underlying trend: the number of new projects has actually declined, even though Jordan has aggressively pursued FDIs since the 1990s. As part of this process, the country passed a series of regulations over the past few years to attract foreign capital and shore up its declining economy. The results, however, have been mixed. Critics suggest the focus on FDI has come at the expense of the small and medium enterprises (SMEs) that form the backbone of the Jordanian economy. SMEs represent 96 percent of businesses and generate more than 50 percent of the country's GDP, but they pay high taxes and face overwhelming regulations.[30] Some commentators consider Jordan's interest in FDI as nothing less than subordination of the national interest to foreign capital.[31] The purchase by Kuwait's telecommunication company Zain of the Jordanian Fastlink in 1994 (now called Zain Jordan) was extremely unpopular. Despite these aggressive policies designed to attract foreign investors and despite its relatively stable political situation and pro-Western stance, flow of FDI to Jordan followed the same poor pattern as that of the region. After a peak of $3.54 billion in 2016, foreign investments dropped to just 622 million in 2021, confirming the general trend of capital moving out of the poorer and more fragile countries of the region.[32]

The more populous Arab states, like Algeria and Egypt, where investment is desperately needed to absorb huge growth in population, have struggled to attract any new FDI. In recent years, both countries have hit record lows of both inward and outward investment due to political instability, lack of transparency, and rising levels of corruption.

Another trend of FDI in the region is the relatively low level of intra-multinational trading among MENA states, even though a third of trade is conducted between affiliates of multinational firms.[33] Moreover, Arab regimes often restrict the flow of information, including economic news, which creates an inhospitable environment for potential investors.[34] State-controlled banking systems also limit information.[35] As Henry and Springborg note: "The German or French state capitalism prevailing in much of the region is inimical to the development of stock markets, yet portfolio equity is one of the principal sources of capital in the integrated financial markets of the new world order."[36]

In the digital age, information is a vital commodity. It is the very basis of free trade. But in the Middle East, it is not the only vital commodity that does not flow freely. Water, the very basis of life itself, is in increasingly short supply.

Water Security

Without water, there is no trade, no society, no life. From all human life to all of the economy, from transportation to agriculture to industry, nothing can function without it.[37] Water security is an ongoing problem in the region. All Arab countries suffer from chronic water scarcity. The region has an estimated 300 billion cubic meters of water, roughly 1 percent of the world's total, but is home to 5 percent of the world's population.[38]

Yemen, in particular, is facing a full-on crisis. The country is rapidly running out of water.[39] Even in countries with major rivers, such as Iraq and Syria, the situation is far from straightforward. Turkey shares the Tigris and Euphrates basins with Iraq and Syria and controls the runoffs of the two rivers. To date, Turkey has refused to subject the Euphrates and Tigris to international law and has yet to reach an agreement with its neighbors to share the waters.

The tensions between Egypt and Sudan, on the one hand, and Ethiopia, on the other, the Nile basin countries, is another example. Egypt and Sudan fear for their future water supplies as Ethiopia has completed the construction of the colossal Grand Ethiopian Renaissance Dam on the Nile. Nearly 90 percent of Egypt's fresh water comes from the Nile, making the Ethiopian dam, in the eyes of Egyptians, the most fundamental of threats.[40] This level of vulnerability is widespread. Most Arab states have large areas of arid or semiarid land, so over two-thirds of their water has to come from outside the region: a situation that leaves them vulnerable to fluctuations in the commodities market.

The ongoing process of desertification afflicting most Arab countries makes a difficult situation even worse.[41] Because water is in such scant supply, agriculture has become heavily dependent on rainwater and underwater aquifers. But this, too, is problematic. In a part of the world where temperatures can easily reach 50 degrees Celsius in the summer, water evaporates at a startlingly high rate. Rainfall cannot therefore meet the needs of agriculture. All of which means the Middle East is in the highly precarious position of not being able to independently feed itself.

The problem of water scarcity in the MENA is exacerbated further by the lack of qualified human resources, adequate funding, and modern methods in the agricultural sector. Because of the aridity of Arab lands and the lack of advanced technical capabilities, investors are more interested in sectors that bring easy profits. The subsequent low level of investment and development in agriculture is problematic as the region faces a serious nutrition challenge, made all the more acute by rapid increases in population growth. With growing populations, Arab countries are struggling to cope with the rising demand for food products.[42]

The high costs of importing food affect economic development, forcing some states to try to improve the agriculture sector. The problem, however, is that in most cases, agricultural development requires a disproportionately high share of available freshwater.[43] Between 1996 and 2006 Arab countries used just over 70 percent of their available water resources in contrast with a global rate of just over 6 percent.[44] Another problem linked to water scarcity is the poor management and inefficient use of irrigated water. This, in turn, has led to alkalinization, waterlogging, and nutrient depletion.[45]

Syria and Iraq, on top of war and instability, are also suffering from the dramatic reduction of the water level of the Euphrates and Tigris Rivers because of the construction of dams along their upper course in Turkey.[46] The Euphrates is essential for human survival and economic activities of central and western Syria. The situation is even more dire for Iraq, which completely relies on the two rivers for its water supply. In addition to those built upstream in Turkey, Iraq is affected by the dams built by Iran on the many tributaries that feed the Tigris from the east.[47]

Jordan and Palestine, in particular, face an acute water shortage, a situation complicated by the conflict with Israel. As their primary source of water, both Palestinians and Israelis depend on the Jordan River, which runs through Israel, Syria, the West Bank, and Jordan, before flowing into the Dead Sea. Soon after its creation in 1948, Israel blocked the construction of wells and water springs and exploited existing water resources for its own settlements. Israel also launched major agricultural projects such as the one in the Haula Valley in 1951. The move had catastrophic ecological consequences as it led to the drainage of the Haula Lake and the wider wetlands system. But Israel has continued undeterred. From the mid-1960s, Israel diverted the water of the Jordan to private settlements in the Negev desert area through the National Water Carrier. Following the Six-Day War in June 1967 and Israel's occupation of the remaining Palestinian territories, Israel now has control of 90 percent of Palestinian water resources. In the Oslo Accords, the water question was referred to as a final-status issue, along with Jerusalem, refugees, borders, security, and settlements, which means Israel remains in charge and faces no pressure to change course.

Vicious Cycles of Ever-Decreasing Prosperity: The Causes and Forms of Pauperization

Wars and water, oil and investment: in the previous section we looked at the structural reasons for development failure in the Middle East and North Africa and how a broken political system has done nothing to fix the gaps in the system. How, then, have these failures affected people in their daily lives? In what follows, we will look at how these structural imbalances translated into vicious cycles of ever-decreasing prosperity across the region. From population booms to gender inequality, from youth employment to poor education, we will see that poor political leadership has influenced every aspect of society and kept people trapped in cycles of despair with little or no hope of ever escaping or building a better life.

Population Increase and Poverty

Birth rates in the region are consistently higher than the world average. In a part of the world where water, land, and food are scarce, high population levels are not mere statistics. They have the potential to cause real social upheaval. Complicating the picture further is the rise in urbanization. Since independence, more and more people have moved from the country to the city in search of a better life. Between 1970 and 2005, the urban population in the Arab world grew from 38 percent to 55 percent.[48] The trend has since partially stabilized, with 57.9 percent in 2020 and a peak of 59.5 predicted for 2030.[49]

This rapid growth in the urban population exerts pressure on infrastructure and creates huge poverty belts and overcrowded areas where living conditions are unhealthy, insecure, and, in some places, hellish. Anyone who has ever visited Cairo will have seen the uncomfortable extremes of wealth where slums, in which people have little choice but to scavenge rubbish dumps for food, sit uneasily alongside luxury gated communities that are home to the mega-rich.

In the last decade, Arab states have witnessed a noticeable rise in the ratio of undernourished people, with roughly one-third of Arab households suffering from hunger according to the United Nations.[50] Across the region, the situation is grim. The wars in Gaza, Sudan, Syria, and Yemen have caused the greatest humanitarian crisis since the end of World War II. As Yemen descended into all-out war, the whole population is on the verge of starvation and famine. Israel's war in Gaza in 2023–2024 displaced 90 percent of the 2.3 million population and destroyed the economy and society, making the tiny strip uninhabitable. The United Nations repeatedly warned that more than a quarter of Gaza's 2.3 million population faces starvation, while the entire population suffers from food shortages. As Israel's onslaught entered its sixth month, humanitarian organizations say that Gaza had the highest proportion of people living with food deprivation anywhere in the world, particularly children.[51]

The average household income in the poorest areas of the region is also in decline, from $4,600 per year in 2008 to $4,200 per year in 2012.[52] By 2009, more than 60 percent of the population in Mauritania, 45 percent in Yemen, and 40 percent in Egypt were living on less than two dollars a day. In the same year, 34 percent of the population in Morocco was living on less than one dollar a day, while in Egypt this number had reached 20 percent.[53] Conversely, the richest households are getting richer, with their average income growing from $29,000 to $33,600 in the same period.[54] In the Arab region, the richest families earn up to 25 percent more than their counterparts in middle-income countries in the rest of the world.[55] At the time of writing, the division between rich and poor has gotten worse. As these figures make clear, inequality is growing rapidly and the region now has one of the highest income gaps in the world.[56]

Gender Inequality

The first UN *Arab Human Development Report* in 2002 listed gender inequality as a key problem in the Arab world. Most of the constitutions in the Arab world acknowledge the equality of their citizens before the law and have ratified the UN Convention on the Elimination of All Forms of Discrimination against Women. But the reality is different. On the whole, women in the region face discrimination that starts in early childhood. Personal status laws, including those relating to marriage, divorce, child custody, freedom of movement, and property ownership, discriminate against women.[57]

In Algeria, Jordan, Palestine, Sudan, Syria, and Yemen, a woman cannot get married without the approval or nonobjection of her male guardian.[58] In Saudi Arabia, a woman must obtain the written consent of her male guardian to travel, enter the labor market, and access secondary education and medical services.[59] Limited reforms have been implemented after the rise to power of MBS and, in 2018, for the first time Saudi women were allowed to drive. Despite domestic backlash from the ultraconservative religious establishment, MBS, as he is called, implemented more reforms, allowing women to participate in the public space. Although there is no certainty that progress will not be reversed, women in Saudi Arabia have made limited progress under MBS's rule.[60]

In many of these countries, women do not enjoy the same status as men when they testify in court. One of the most discriminatory examples in criminal laws is the so-called honor killing. The criminal codes of Palestine, Syria, and Yemen still call for lenient sentences in these cases.[61] In Iraqi Kurdistan, honor killings are often judged to be manslaughter, allowing the perpetrator to benefit from a more lenient sentence.[62]

Jordan and Lebanon have passed tougher regulations regarding the sentencing of male perpetrators and some countries have taken steps to curb domestic violence.[63] In Algeria, Bahrain, Jordan, Lebanon, and Saudi Arabia, domestic violence is now an offense punishable by the law.[64] Similarly, Egypt, Morocco, Palestine, and Tunisia plan to criminalize violence against women, a decision hailed as a "landmark" of progress by human rights groups.[65]

That the Middle East remains a man's world becomes even clearer when you look at the labor market. Although labor laws generally guarantee equal access to work for men and women, female labor force participation in 2012 was below 24 percent.[66] At 48 percent, the rate of female unemployment is the highest in the world.[67] And those women who are lucky enough to be allowed to work and who manage to find a job soon encounter another problem: the gender pay gap. The male-female wage gap is extremely high: 20 percent in Jordan, 25 percent in Palestine, and 35 percent in Egypt's private sector.[68]

Employment is not the only area of discrimination. Women are also seriously disadvantaged in their access to health services. In the region's least developed countries, skilled medical personnel are only present at 34 percent of the births.[69] This gap is reflected in class dynamics. In Egypt's poorest households, only 55 percent of births have medical personnel in attendance. Compare this with 97 percent for the richest families. In Sudan and Yemen, the gap is even wider with 27 percent and 17 percent for the poorest families in comparison with 88 percent and 74 percent for the richest, respectively.[70]

Since this data was released, civil strife and conflict in the region has exacerbated the humanitarian crisis, often wiping out most progress previously made. According to a UN report in 2023, countries in conflict like Palestine, Sudan, Syria, and Yemen have seen disruptions in humanitarian aid, a major concern for millions of refugees and internally displaced persons.[71] One area where young girls and women are making progress is education. Throughout the Middle East female students out-number male students in professional fields like pharmacy, medicine, and law, a development that promises future employment gains for women and economic empowerment.

Youth Unemployment

The youth population has rapidly increased across the region, and unem-ployment among the young is the highest in the world. For a region disproportionally blessed with resources that the rest of the world cannot live without, the figures are nothing short of shocking. Bear in mind when reading these numbers that Qatar is home to a quarter of the world's gas and Saudi Arabia is the world's biggest oil producer.

In 2005, 40 percent of the population in the Middle East and North Africa was fourteen years old or younger and 56 percent was twenty-four years old or younger.[72] In 2013, youth unemployment stood at an average of 29 percent. That figure is more than twice the global average of 13 percent.[73] But unofficial figures are much higher. The region is full of young men like Mohammed Bouazizi who work but still face a daily struggle to make ends meet.[74] In the following two decades, the region was ravaged by instability, conflict and war, and COVID-19 pandemic and Israel's war in Gaza, making the social and economic situation worse. By 2021, according to data from the International Labor Organization, youth unemployment in the Arab world has reached 25.9 percent.[75]

In the MENA, people aged fifteen to twenty-nine make up 30 percent of the population, a total of 105 million.[76] It is the first time the region has had such a large proportion of young people.[77] In Saudi Arabia, popula-tion growth has been one of the highest in the world for some time. In 1960, the kingdom's population was about 4 million. By 2016, it had reached 31.7 million. In the desert kingdom, nearly 79 percent of the youth population is urban. According to the United Nations Development Programme's (UNDP) *Arab Human Development Report 2016*, this is a pattern repeated across the region. Most young people live in urban areas: 82 percent of the youth in Jordan, 67 percent in Tunisia, and 42 percent in Egypt.[78] Alarmingly, the highest number of young people in urban areas is concentrated in slums, poverty belts, or informal settlements.[79] Even more alarmingly, by 2016, youth unemployment had reached a rate close to 30 percent across the region and is expected to remain high.[80]

Due to the predominance of public sector employment, many young men spend years in idleness waiting to secure a safe job working for the state.[81] But as Arab rulers fail to maintain their bloated bureaucracies, the social contract between the youth and the state is breaking down.[82] And the private sector is in no position to pick up the slack. The problem is that Arab states invest in private sector industries with low potential for employment growth.[83] Consequently, a large segment of the youth is forced to rely on family connections to obtain a job.

Education

The poor quality of education in the MENA is one of the most important challenges for pursuing development. On the plus side, net enrollment rates in primary and secondary education have increased in most Arab states but the downside is that overall quality is poor.[84] Arab countries still lag behind in standardized international tests. This, in turn, means the workforce has limited skills and is not able to meet the demand for highly specialized jobs. The focus in many Arab states on tourism and the service sector reduces the need for skilled labor and for high-quality, competitive educational institutions. In contrast with Israel, which has developed a cutting-edge high-tech sector that brings in billions, information technology is one of the areas where the Middle East performs worst.

The *Arab Human Development Report 2016* shows that in most countries of the region, access to primary and secondary education largely depends on the income of the family. In Egypt for example, only 54 percent of boys and 43 percent of girls from the lowest-income families go on to secondary education while 100 percent of boys and 99 percent of girls from wealthier homes do so.

In Iraq, the figures are even more shocking. Only 38 percent of poor boys and 24 percent of poor girls have access to primary education compared with 100 percent of their richer peers. That means that over half the boys and over three-quarters of the girls from underprivileged backgrounds do not go to school. No country can hope to develop its full potential when it leaves so many people behind. For secondary education, the figures are even worse. Only 8 percent of boys and only 3 percent of girls from the most vulnerable classes have access to secondary education compared to 94 percent of boys and 96 percent of girls with a privileged background.

In Yemen, the situation is aggravated by the gender gap: 40 percent of boys and only 6 percent of girls from poor families access primary education. When it comes to secondary education, boys and girls from the same demographics attend at the rates of 27 percent and 4 percent, respectively. In contrast, the attendance rate for primary and secondary education of upper-class children is between 99 percent and 100 percent.

As the UNDP report shows, members of the privileged class receive the best education and the best medical care, while the poor are excluded. The working classes must rely on public schooling, the quality of which has greatly declined in the past decades.[85]

From the mid-1950s until the early 1970s, a solid middle class steadily evolved along with an upper-middle class. But the fortunes of the middle class began to deteriorate in the early 1990s. What the data on education reveals is that the only thing steadily increasing in the Arab region in the past three decades is inequality: while the richest become richer, the poorest become poorer.

Climate Change

Climate change, which includes increasingly volatile weather and rising sea levels, exacerbates the social and economic problems facing Middle Eastern countries. The desert is creeping in almost everywhere in the Middle East, consuming huge chunks of the landscape in Iran, Saudi Arabia, the Gulf in general, Egypt, and beyond. Environmental degradation coupled with population growth increase pressure on governments, which already face a severe socioeconomic crisis. There is an urgent need to address environmental degradation because it might be a significant cause for instability in the coming decade.[86]

According to a 2016 study by scientists from the German Max Planck Institute, temperatures in the Middle East are rising twice as fast as the global average and significant parts of the region might become uninhabit-able in the next decades, triggering waves of climate refugees.[87] The effect of these trends on food and water scarcity are already felt in many coun-tries in the Middle East, contributing to the crisis of the provision of basic services. The Arab Spring uprisings and the most recent waves of protests in Iraq, Sudan, Algeria, and beyond have been triggered by conditions that are continuously exacerbated by climate change and the ecological crisis driving a vicious spiral of instability and suffering.

Development Failure and the Pauperization of the People

Injustice, Violence, and Exclusion

The Arab world has witnessed a series of genocides and state-sanctioned war crimes and crimes against humanity. Saddam Hussein's gassing of the Kurds was deemed genocidal by Human Rights Watch. Human rights groups and the United Nations view the Islamic State policy toward Yazidis as genocide. Sudan's actions in Darfur are also considered geno-cide. The situation in Syria under Assad was so grim it is considered a mass "politicide." This politicide has produced so much documenta-tion that international law experts believe it to be the easiest case to pros-ecute since the Nuremberg trials in Germany after World War II. Israel's genocide in Gaza is being abjugated by the International Court of Justice in the Hague.

Political assassinations are common practice in the Middle East and are regularly used by authoritarian regimes against the civilian opposi-tion. According to a report on injustice in the Arab region, the phenom-enon known as "politicide" or "political extermination" has been on the rise across the region since 1970s.[88] Although violence against civilians can be extreme during any conflict, in the Arab world violence is used as a means to silence or co-opt the entire population. Politically based violence has been normalized for decades. In Egypt, President Anwar Sadat's secret police terrorized the public, and many people arrested by the Mukhabarat (the intelligence services) disappeared into the prison sys-tem for years. The lucky ones who make it out alive bear the physical and psychological marks of torture for the rest of their lives. In Iran, the shah weaponized the Savak police, with US training and advice, to terrorize dissidents and critics of his rule in the 1960s and 1970s.

Political killings have become such a key instrument of policy they are actually inscribed in the law of the state. In Syria under the Assads (father and son), membership of the Muslim Brotherhood was a crime punishable by the death sentence.[89] In Baathist Iraq, the same penalty applied to members of the Shia Dawa Party.[90] These laws represent one of the most potent forms of injustice. Civilians can be summarily detained and put on trial in military courts. States that do not have such laws in their constitution often use emergency regulations to repress the opposition. Across the region, state repression and political violence have been on the rise since the US-led invasion of Iraq in 2003.

In the Middle East, minorities continue to suffer discrimination and persecution, in particular the Shia, Yazidis, Kurds, Assyrians, and now the Sunnis in Syria and Iraq.[91] In addition to the catastrophic human cost, this policy has had disastrous political consequences. State repression of minorities has played a key role in the resurgence of subnational identities and loyalties. To marginalize minority and vulnerable groups, Arab states have often resorted to punitive measures like stripping them of their citizenship. Article 15 of the Universal Declaration of Human Rights and Article 29 of the Arab Charter on Human Rights state that "everyone has the right to a nationality" and that "no one shall arbitrarily or unlawfully be deprived of their nationality."[92] Despite the clarity of these declarations, many inhabitants of the Arab world are in fact stateless. People are regularly stripped of their nationality for no other reason than because of who they are or what they think. Israel's settler colonialism has left millions of Palestinians stateless, living under military occupation.

In Syria in early 2011 there were more than 200,000 stateless ethnic Kurds. They are considered *maktoumi al-qayd*, a phrase used to refer to people not recorded in the civil register even though they were born and raised in Syria.[93] Even though their stateless status deprives them of the rights of citizenship, they are not excused its responsibilities and must enlist in compulsory military service. Children inherit their parents' stateless condition and are not entitled to education and health care. The Syrian authorities were forced to pass a decree granting citizenship to foreigners in 2011 after the uprising but they did nothing to change the status of the *maktoumi al-qayd*. However, Syria under the Assads still used the practice of stripping citizenship to antiregime supporters via introduction of mandatory electronic cards and other examples of social engineering to shore up the Assad regime.

Across the Middle East, leaders thus have the power to define not only how the state is run but also who qualifies as a citizen of that state. That distinction is not based on law or process, it is purely arbitrary. Such arbitrary power fuels corruption.

Corruption

Political and financial corruption in the Arab world are inextricably linked. In the 1960s, 1970s, and early 1980s, Arab donors established specialist financial institutions to provide development assistance but refrained from reforming domestic economic structures. As a result, these structures have survived almost intact since independence, a state of affairs that has had significant implications for development. In particular, state corporatism—an informal partnership between the ruling elite and the business establishment—has derailed efforts at economic restructuring, transparency, and accountability. Crony capitalism is the result of this unholy alliance between power and business and it helps explain the scale of the social crisis currently afflicting Arab societies.

To begin with, most Arab states still retain greater control over economic life than other developing countries. In the 2000s, for example, the proportion of public employees of the total workforce was 30 percent in Iraq and Algeria, 33 percent in Palestine, 37 percent in Saudi Arabia, and 40 percent in Jordan. In Saudi Arabia, the employment of Saudi nationals is mostly concentrated in the service and government sectors while foreigners dominate the private production sector.[94] And this state control extends far beyond the public sector. Most governments in the Middle East dominate the private sector. In the Gulf, the ruling elites founded the private sector. Moreover, across the region, companies in the private sector are very close to the ruling elites.[95] Consequently, neither the private nor the public sector has an independent role, and boundaries between the two are blurred.

A consensus exists among writers that the rise of patronage and crony-ism has hindered economic development in the Middle East.[96] These writers trace the roots of crony capitalism and nepotism to the 1980s (lost Arab decade of development), when regimes experiencing a crisis of legitimacy moved away from state-led growth and turned to business elites to lead the private sector.[97] From the 1980s onward, the Egyptian and Syrian regimes passed laws and regulations that greatly favored busi-ness at the expense of trade unions, labor organizations, and peasant federations.[98] The corporatist state, in effect, co-opted the business elite as a vehicle for a new round of social engineering. This elite strongly emphasized urban development at the expense of rural reconstruction and prioritized nonproductive activities, consumption, and the service sector.[99] Agriculture and manufacture took a back seat and suffered a major decline.

In the past two decades, the spread of nepotism and the rise of crony capitalism have been behind weak economic growth, poor income, and even poorer wealth distribution.[100] Companies that have ties to the political elite benefit from energy subsidies and licenses, cheap land, cheap labor, and protection from competition.[101] In some countries, even if such companies perform worse than their competitors, they are still given pref-erential access to funds to borrow money.[102]

In their studies on crony capitalism in Egypt, Hamouda Chekir and Ishac Diwan provide conclusive evidence that politically connected firms are privileged at the expense of their competitors.[103] They also show that privately owned banks are dominated by actors with ties to the political elite.[104] Egyptians live with the consequences of these policies every day and many of them view the economic liberalization that started in the 1980s as a means for the business and state elites to enrich themselves at their expense. Feelings of economic marginalization and exclusion have fed resentment and discontent, culminating in bread riots, contentious politics and radicalization, and ultimately the large-scale popular upris-ings in 2011.

What happened in Egypt happened elsewhere. In the years before the 2010–2012 Arab Spring uprising, Syria and Egypt implemented a series of neoliberal reforms that made life even more difficult for everyday people.[105]

The result is increasing poverty and social polarization. Most alarmingly, these neoliberal reforms weakened an already vulnerable middle class and led to a rapid growth of the informal sector.[106]

The blurring of the lines between the executive branch, the security apparatus, and the economy lies at the heart of the widening economic injustice in the Middle East. By prioritizing closed networks, the ruling elites have empowered special interest groups and individuals in both the private and public sectors. This centralization of economic planning and development has then made it easier for officials to siphon off eye-watering sums of money into foreign bank accounts. After the 2011 Libyan revolt, credible reports suggested the ruling Gaddafi family had stolen billions of US dollars from the state's oil revenues.[107]

Similarly, Tunisian president Ben Ali had allegedly hidden $11 billion in foreign bank accounts while the Mubarak family in Egypt, along with a small inner circle of businessmen and hangers-on, pilfered the treasury of hundreds of millions of US dollars.[108]

In the Middle East, ruling families and business elites are two sides of the same coin. Patronage and cronyism permeate the public and private sectors and prevent the emergence of an independent and productive private sector that spearheads development. This unholy alliance between the ruling elite and the business elite is the most significant barrier to economic growth. The cards are stacked against independent small and big business ventures without connections to the ruling elite. This is not a level playing field.

This patron-client relationship between the state and the business elite has had a major impact on the spread of poverty and economic inequality. On the one hand, the lower-middle classes are trapped in unproductive public sector jobs that offer few prospects for career development or wage increases. On the other, the ruling elite and those with strong connections to the state are rewarded with all the economic privileges of the private sector.

A Vortex of Despair

When Mohammed Bouazizi set himself on fire in Tunisia in 2010, he helped ignite a revolution across the Arab world. As a cradle of the Arab Spring, Tunisia is often celebrated as the uprising's only success story and the country that has the best hope of realizing its aspirations for democracy and prosperity.

Yet cases of self-immolation have become more frequent in the years after the revolution.[109] In 2016, Tunisia's main burns hospital in Ben Arous, the same hospital where Mohammed Bouazizi was treated, admitted 104 patients who had set themselves on fire, a record number. Tunisia's tide of self-immolation shows no sign of slowing.[110] "I wanted to burn myself because I was burning inside," Adel Dridi, a fruit vendor, said in an interview with *the New York Times* while lying on a mattress in his family's home, where he was still recovering after pouring gasoline on his head and setting himself on fire in May 2017. "I wanted to die this way."[111]

Of all the post–Arab Spring countries, Tunisia initially made the most significant strides in terms of freedom and democratic governance. But it has fallen short on providing jobs or delivering on the hope of a better life. Tunisians represented the largest contingent of foreign fighters within IS, numbering more than 5,000. Many more thousands have abandoned the country to work abroad. Economic hardship, lack of hope, and a lingering sense of injustice pour fuel on an already raging fire in Tunisia.[112] For these reasons and others, the nascent democratic experience in Tunisia did not last. In 2021, Tunisian president Kais Saied, suspended the parliament and has ruled as a single strongman ever since. For a while Tunisia was the only the Arab Spring country to be transitioning to a parliamentary democracy and then the latest to fail.[113]

Tunisia is a microcosm of the economic and social vulnerabilities of the wider Arab world, even though the small North African country might stand a better chance to make the political transition in the mid-to-long term. There is widespread frustration at the failed promise of the first wave of Arab Spring uprisings. Breaking out in 2019 a second wave of uprisings is still unfolding in Algeria, Iraq, Lebanon, and in Sudan, where the protesters forced the military to conclude a pact to share power with a civilian government. People's lives have not improved and may even have worsened due to contentious politics, turmoil, civil wars, and the unrelenting determination of the region's old regimes to dig in and hold on, no matter what.

The reasons for the development failure and the pauperization of the Arab people are manifold. But of the many and varied factors behind the massive mismanagement of the economy, bad governance tops the list. The new elite who replaced the colonial state did not fulfill their promises to deliver prosperity, justice, and freedom. Instead of promoting transparency, accountability, social mobility, and integration, the post-colonial rulers set up one party rule and eliminated all organized opposition. They deployed state power and resources in the service of special interests and concentrated economic decision-making in the hands of a small elite. Arab rulers of all persuasions took key decisions that did not foster inclusive economic growth, productivity, or employment.

Decades of deepening authoritarianism and economic mismanagement have led to development failure. When the state fails to provide the social goods, other groups fill the gap. Unlike other parts of the postcolonial world, the Middle East has seen the emergence of a wide variety of non-state actors, some peaceful, others violent, who provide services to people the state has left behind. These social movements and radical groups have successfully mobilized resistance to the region's various forms of authoritarian government. They have also offered an ideological antithesis to the development ideology promoted and enforced by the West. In many cases, such as Hezbollah in Lebanon, they have redrawn the map of national allegiances, redefined identities, and become a state within a state. When the Arab Spring failed—or, rather, was denied the chance to succeed—and countries across the region began the slow descent into chaos, these nonstate actors stepped forward to fill the void.

9

The Nation versus the *Umma*

THE CITY OF ISMAILIYYA lies off the beaten track for most visitors to Egypt. Tourists to the country more readily make for the cosmopolitan centers of Cairo or Alexandria, the resorts of the Red Sea coast, or the pharaonic wonders of Luxor and the Valley of the Kings. But if you want to understand the modern history of Egypt, Ismailiyya is the place that matters most.

Ismailiyya owes its existence to the Suez Canal. Situated on the canal's west bank, the city was built by the Khedive Ismail in the 1860s. So important was the city to him, he gave it his name. Ismail was the grandson of the founder of modern Egypt, Muhammad Ali, and he came to power with a sense of ambition even greater than that of his famous ancestor. In the sixteen years Ismail ruled (1863–1879), he set out to modernize the country and transform the capital into the "New Paris." It was under his rule that new European-style suburbs were built across Cairo with the aim of recasting the city in a Parisian mold. "My country is no longer in Africa; we are now a part of Europe," he was fond of saying. To underline his point, he said it in French.[1]

A City by a Canal and a Man with a Mission

Even more important to Ismail than the changes to his capital was the Suez Canal. Commissioned by his uncle Said (r. 1854–1863), it fell to Ismail to see the project through to completion. The canal was to revolutionize global trade and Egypt's place in the world. Once it was operational, ships carrying goods from east to west would no longer need to make the time-consuming and costly journey round Africa to reach Europe. Everything would now pass through Egypt. Thanks to the canal, the country could reclaim the preeminent role in global trade it had lost when Vasco da Gama discovered the sea route to the east round the Cape of Good Hope in 1498. The circumnavigation of Africa was also a very severe blow to the Ottomans who saw their trade and power in the Mediterranean dwindle as a result of the operation of the Suez Canal.

With discovery of the sea route in the early modern era, the land route across Asia ceased to be economically viable. And the Egyptian exchequer suffered an immediate, and dramatic, loss of tax revenue.[2] Prior to the demise of the land route, the salt and spices from the east that were so essential for food preservation in the west had to pass through Egypt. It is no exaggeration to say that the Mamluk rulers of medieval Egypt made a profit every time someone in Western Europe put pepper on their food.

By redirecting the flow of international trade, the opening of the Suez Canal in 1869 would restore the revenue lost nearly four centuries earlier. As soon as Egypt repaid the cost of construction, the country faced a bright economic future.

But Egypt lacked the resources of a modern economy and Ismail, and his uncle Said before him, had been forced to borrow heavily from European lenders to fund their ambitions at rates that were far from favorable. Said, in particular, allowed his ambition to cloud his financial judgment. He commissioned a French engineer, Ferdinand de Lesseps, to design the canal and a French company to construct it. Under the terms of the lopsided deal Said agreed to, and under whose terms Ismail was obliged to operate, Egypt covered all the financial costs of building the canal while the French company claimed nearly all the profits of running it. The result was catastrophe. By 1876, Egypt was unable to service its debts. The country was bankrupt. Ismail was obliged to sell his stake in the canal project—around 40 percent of the shares in the company that owned the canal—and the British government, with an eye on the sea route to India, wasted no time buying them.

For Ismail, the worst was still to come. In 1879, the British and French forced him out of office. Between them, Britain and France owned the company that ran the canal. They were also the main creditors to the Ottoman sultan, Abdulhamid II, who was in the midst of his own credit crisis. They put pressure on the sultan to oust Ismail, then moved swiftly to put Ismail's young son Tawfiq on the throne. The deposed Ismail sailed away into reluctant exile in Paris, his dreams of a European Egypt in ruins. Egypt's most prized asset was now in the hands of foreigners. The country itself was in the hands of a novice.

In the midst of this turbulence, an army officer named Ahmad 'Urabi led an uprising against the British that attracted so much popular support, the Egyptian army refused to move against him. When 'Urabi was eventually arrested, the army released him and, instead of facing charges for sedition, he was appointed to the cabinet and became minister of war. But the British, having deposed Ismail, had no wish to see a popular military strongman take power. Under the flimsy pretext of protecting their investment in the Suez Canal, London deployed the full force of the British Navy against 'Urabi's uprising.[3]

The navy began shelling Alexandria on July 11, 1882. Two months later, the battle for Egypt was over. The British had control of the entire country, and they had used the Suez Canal as the means to achieve it. The mismanagement of the engineering project that was supposed to liberate Egypt financially ended up achieving the exact opposite: it brought about the country's subjugation to a foreign power. For Egyptians, British rule was a humiliation. In the words of future president Anwar al-Sadat: "Many things annoyed me.... There was, for instance, the *odious* sight of the British constable on his motorcycle tearing through the city streets day and night like a madman.... I simply loathed the sight of him."[4] Suez became a symbol of this foreign domination. The canal should have been the lifeblood of a new Egypt. Instead, it had been appropriated by a foreign power to serve foreign interests.

In Ismailiyya, the city by the canal that was home to the main British military base and the company that ran the canal, this domination was felt on a daily basis. During the reign of Ismail's grandson, King Farouq, the city became a flashpoint and played a key role in overthrowing the old order and bringing a new one to power. In early 1952, Egypt was in turmoil. King Farouq had long since lost the respect of his people.

Egyptians saw him as a British stooge. Tensions were running high across the country. On January 25, 1952, British troops opened fire on a police station in Ismailiyya after police in the local barracks refused to surrender to them. Dozens were killed. Many more were wounded. The repercussions of the attack were felt far and wide.[5] The following day, soon to be known as Black Saturday, there were riots across the country. What remained of King Farouq's authority was fatally undermined. It was the beginning of the end. Under Gamal Abdel Nasser, January 25 became a national holiday celebrating the police.

The burden of this unhappy history is one of the reasons Nasser's nationalization of the Suez Canal in 1956 was so wildly popular and why it helped cement his grip on power.[6] By openly challenging colonial Britain, he was finishing what Ahmad 'Urabi had started seventy years earlier. To the delight of Egyptians, the war that followed the nationalization saw Nasser turn the tables on Egypt's old colonial masters. His victory elevated him to hero status. Justified on the flimsy pretext of securing safe passage through the Suez Canal, the Anglo-French-Israeli attack turned into such a humiliation for Britain and France that it is still regarded as one of the United Kingdom's most disastrous foreign policy decisions.

Yet, for all their deeply ingrained differences, Ismail, Farouq, and Nasser had one key idea in common: all believed in Egypt as a *nation*. All of them looked to Egypt as their primary source of political identity. As an imagined community, Egypt was naturally equipped to lead the Arab world. Nasser's use of Arab nationalism was designed to promote Egyptian influence regionally and internationally, not to subsume the country's identity in a greater pan-Arab identity. Nasser faced pushback inside and outside. When he died of a heart attack in 1970, Nasser's political and ideological project was almost a spent force. Even before Nasser's advent to power, someone else saw things differently. And, as with so much else in modern Egypt, it was in Ismailiyya that a quiet revolution began that would change the course of modern Middle Eastern history.

In 1928, a young primary school teacher working in the canal city looked at the world around him and did not like what he saw. He did not like the British occupation. He did not like how the British lived above the law. He did not like the powerlessness and the increasing helplessness of the Egyptian people. So he decided to do something about it. He set up an organization to change society from the ground up. The young man's name was Hassan al-Banna and the organization he founded was the Jama'at al-Ikhwan al-Muslimin, the Society of Muslim Brothers or, as it came to be known: the Muslim Brotherhood.[7]

Banna, like Khedive Ismail and Nasser, was a man on a mission. He saw what was happening in Ismailiyya as a microcosm of everything that was wrong in the Arab/Islamic world, and he saw Islam as the solution. His faith had always been important to him. He came from a religiously observant family. His father had graduated from Al-Azhar University, had written a number of books on religion, and led prayers in his local mosque.[8]

At first, Banna's aim was not political. It was to harness the huge social power at the heart of Islam to change people's lives for the better. Islam is more than a religion: it is an all-encompassing way of life, a community of believers. With the faith's emphasis on communal charity and social justice, Banna believed the community of believers was more important than any one nation. This is not to say that he and his members had no sense of place or history, rather that their primary point of reference was their faith.[9] Because of that, they did not limit their outlook to Egypt alone. In this, Banna and the Brothers were fundamentally different from other contemporary political movements whose primary goal was to achieve national independence from foreign occupiers. The Brothers did not recognize borders. Their view was transnational.

The idea resonated. And resonated quickly. The concept of a Muslim Brotherhood (there was also a Sisterhood, though no longer) filled the ideological gap left by the demise of the Ottoman Empire. From the Prophet Muhammad's death in 632 to the collapse of the Ottoman Caliphate in 1924, Muslims had looked to the caliph or the sultan as the unifying symbol of their faith. Even in times of political crisis when his authority was weak, he remained the titular head of their community, providing a powerful and symbolic link back to the Prophet Muhammad. With the dismemberment of the Ottoman Empire after the First World War, that sense of continuity was broken. There was now no one single person to embody the unity of the community.[10] Because of Banna, that unity was now embodied in an *idea*. He was not the first to see Islam as the answer to society's problems. But he was the first to link the idea to an organizational structure that delivered.

By 1933, the Brotherhood's headquarters had moved from the city by the canal to the nation's capital. By 1940, the group had over 500 branches. Each one had a school, a mosque, and acted as a community hub where welfare services were provided.[11] Everything from education to medical help to job training was available for those who needed it. For people struggling to make ends meet, the Brotherhood provided more support than the state did. And it was through this network of services that the Brotherhood began its long evolution from a social movement to a state-within-a-state.

But as the Brotherhood's commitment to grassroots community projects deepened and as the number of people accessing their services grew, the question soon arose that would trouble any established order, whether royal or revolutionary, monarchist or military: What would happen if the Brotherhood decided to convert their enormous social capital into political power?

This chapter tackles this critical question by focusing on two case studies that help make sense of the dialectical relationship between political Islam and the postcolonial Middle Eastern state. Moving beyond the simplistic narrative that presents Islamism as the authentic identity of the region, the following pages will show how "secular" Arab autocrats have often nurtured Islamist activists in order to shore up their contested legitimacy. The chapter will also show how Arab rulers have turned against the Islamists as soon as the popularity of the latter threatened their monopoly power and, in doing so, they further undermined people's trust in government. The top-down, divide-and-rule strategy of colonialism (adopted later by domestic authoritarians) is perfectly complemented by the bottom-up strategy of Islamists building a state-within-a-state, both combining to undermine any hope for any other unifying vision of citizenship and inclusive/representative governance.

The big picture that this chapter highlights is that domestic autocrats have replicated the divide-and-rule playbook from the colonial era (supporting Islamists when convenient, cracking down on them when convenient). This strategy of Arab autocrats is compatible with Islamists building a state-within-a-state, actively splintering the provision of services and building sectarian tensions into the food, education, and community support available to much of the population (a vacuum in government services that incentivizes division and strife). The stronger the state-within-a-state becomes, the more justification a domestic authoritarian has in furthering military domination and brutal crackdowns. Authoritarianism persists not by eliminating the opposition but by keeping it alive in its most radical form.

Analytically, this chapter will now continue the focus of the previous chapter on the domestic relations between Arab peoples and their governments (rather than the foreign intervention that was a larger part of earlier chapters).

From Prison to the Presidency and Back Again: The Path of Political Islam in Egypt

Politics had never been far from the surface for people believing Islam was the answer to society's problems. Long before Banna founded the Brotherhood, Islamic intellectuals and religious leaders had been politically active. They supported the 'Urabi revolt in 1882 and the revolution of 1919–1922 against British rule.[12] Members of the Muslim Brotherhood also participated in the anti-colonial struggle against Britain and the Zionists in Palestine. But it was bread-and-butter issues that really allowed the Brothers to make their mark.

In the 1930s and 1940s, the inability of the secular-leaning political elite to implement reforms that would benefit the impoverished Egyptian population generated widespread distrust of the political establishment.[13] This popular disillusionment led to a return to traditional ideals, even among the literary class who had previously focused on developing semi-secular and forward-looking Islamic projects.[14]

As the political elite blundered from one mistake to another, the Muslim Brotherhood began to offer an alternative political vision based on an Islamic framework. In pursuit of their goal, the movement opened up branches all over the country and soon attracted support from the growing middle class. Before long, the Islamist movement had become the largest popular organization in the country.[15] Its branches continued to provide basic services to those in need and soon began to offer an alternative— and unofficial—political space.

Parallel to this process of providing social services was a more radical one: an armed revolutionary vanguard. Because the Muslim Brothers were officially excluded from the political process,[16] Banna and a circle of disciples decided to take more direct action and build a network of underground paramilitary cells with the aim of providing the Islamist movement with the potential for armed resistance. These structures were dominated by young elements who were becoming critical of Banna's moderate approach. Unlike Banna, they were determined to carry out high-profile assassinations in the belief that such acts would trigger a full-scale popular revolution. When the government banned the Brotherhood in 1936, these paramilitary cells spiraled out of control.

In 1948, after they assassinated Prime Minister Mahmoud al-Nuqrashi, the full force of the state came down upon them. State security forces uncovered the movement's al-Nizam al-Khass, or Special Apparatus, and in retaliation for the Nizam's murder of the prime minister, government agents killed Banna in Cairo two months later.[17]

Banna's death triggered an identity crisis within the Brotherhood that the new *Murshid* or Supreme Guide, Hassan al-Hudaybi, an outsider and a former judge, was unable to control. The movement now split between those calling for revolution and those calling for reform. Radical members vehemently opposed Hudaybi, who lacked Banna's charisma and who sought to disband the Special Apparatus. Hudaybi's answer to the crisis was to rebrand the Brotherhood as a mainstream group. But rather than alleviating the movement's internal differences, Hudaybi's project exacerbated them. Worse, it brought out into the open all the cleavages hidden below the surface during Banna's long period of leadership.

In the meantime, the Muslim Brotherhood helped the Free Officers seize power in July 1952, oust King Farouq, and put an end to the British-supported monarchy.[18] But the honeymoon between the young army officers and the Muslim Brothers did not last. By 1954, they had become bitter enemies and as Nasser consolidated his grip over the country, he clamped down on opposition movements, and the Brotherhood was banned like all the rest. After an assassination attempt on Nasser's life that he blamed on the Brothers, he turned against the Islamist organization with a vengeance. He accused them of collaborating with the forces of Western imperialism and Arab reaction. In other words, Nasser's arch-ideological enemies: the United States and Saudi Arabia.

Under Nasser, the Islamists were repressed and pushed underground. The crackdown was unrelenting. Members of the movement were arrested and often held without charge for years on end in appalling conditions.[19] Torture was routine. As a consequence, part of the movement radicalized and militarized, with the prisons becoming incubators for future jihadis. But by suppressing alternative political movements, the Nasserist state unwittingly boosted alternative religious and traditional identities. The Muslim Brotherhood's strong religious identity enabled them to turn state repression into an opportunity to frame their alternative vision for Egypt. No one personifies this journey more than the unofficial leader of the Muslim Brotherhood at this time: the poet and public intellectual Sayyid Qutb.

Sayyid Qutb inspires strong opinions. Denounced by his detractors as a terrorist, defended by his supporters as a victim of state terrorism, what cannot be denied is Qutb's ongoing influence on radical Islamist ideology. He is, without doubt, one of the most important Islamist political theorists of the twentieth century.

Detained in dreadful conditions for years, during most of which time he was seriously ill, Qutb was a prolific writer whose popular manifesto, Milestones, published in 1964, has shaped radical Islamist political thinking for decades.[20] While writing Milestones in prison, Qutb developed the concept that the Nasserist state was a Western import incompatible with Egypt's Islamic identity. From this came the idea that the Arab world was living in a time of jahiliyya, a term meaning "age of ignorance." In the Islamic tradition, jahiliyya refers back to the time of paganism in pre-Islamic Arabia. By its very definition, Islamism was on a political collision course with the nation-state. Qutb's philosophy has been—and continues to be—appropriated by those radicals who advocate the use of violence and terrorism.[21]

The idea that Egypt was in a state of *jahiliyya* (whose ruler was therefore not a Muslim) was seized upon by a young lieutenant in the Egyptian army who was then to kill Anwar Sadat in 1981.[22] After assassinating the president, Khalid al-Islambuli declared: "I killed him but I am not guilty."[23] He was able to say this because in his mind, killing pharaoh, pagan ruler, was not a crime. Modern jihadi groups have taken the idea of *jahiliyya* even further and use it to decide who does and does not belong in the community. In an Age of Ignorance, they see themselves alone as righteous and use the concept of *takfir*, calling someone an infidel, to decide who belongs to the community, and, in extreme cases, who lives and who dies.

Sayyid Qutb never saw these developments, as he was executed on August 29, 1966. His supporters believe the charges against him were fabricated and the trial was a political witch hunt rather than a genuine search for truth or justice. His detractors accuse him of a conspiracy to overthrow the Nasserist state.

In my book *Making the Arab World*, I profiled Qutb and his leadership role in al-Tanzim al-Sirri or the Secret Apparatus while he was in prison. He labored hard to subvert the existing social order, which he considered jahiliyya, and replaced it with *hakimiyya* or God's sovereignty on earth. Qutb was willing to use all means to do so, including subversion and violence. The calm way Qutb conducted himself during the trial and the dignity he showed in the face of death consolidated his standing in the Islamist movement. He is considered one of the movement's martyrs and is celebrated for his steadfast stand against an apostate order. For those who vehemently disagree with him, Sayyid Qutb is the man who opened Pandora's box and, whether he meant to or not, unleashed chaos and terror.

Following Nasser's death in 1970, Anwar Sadat came to power and moved away from his predecessor's Arab socialism in favor of economic liberalization. To sideline the Nasserist Left, which was dominant among workers and university students, Sadat turned to the Islamists. Up until the mid-1970s, Sadat allowed conservative religious forces to flourish as a counterweight to Nasserists and socialists.[24] He did so willfully, ignoring the fact that, in future, it was possible they could turn against his regime. But in the early 1970s, at the time Sadat was trying to co-opt them, the Islamist movement was still split between a mainstream pole led by Hudaybi and a more radical faction. Hudaybi preached a return to the movement's core mission—its social activities and avoidance of politics— but Qutb's followers wanted nothing less than an armed showdown with the "apostate" authorities.[25] These lines of division within the movement were blurred, and mainstream Muslim Brothers maintained contact with Qutbian splinter groups.

Sadat's strategy of "divide and conquer" succeeded in crushing the Left, but it did not work with the Islamists. By the late 1970s, the president's relationship with them had become openly contentious. The strain of eco- nomic liberalization and the reduction of state subsidies led to growing unrest, food riots, and widespread opposition to Sadat's regime.[26] The final straw was the Camp David Peace Accords, which Sadat signed with Israel in September 1978.[27]

In the eyes of Islamists, Sadat had sold out: the Accords were a com- plete betrayal of Palestinian rights. Jerusalem, the third-holiest city in Islam, the original *qibla* (direction of prayer), and the scene of the Prophet's Night Journey to heaven, was to remain under Israeli control. Reinvigorated by the Islamic Revolution in Iran and anxious to main- tain both their mass popularity and their pro-Palestine image,[28] Egypt's Islamists became more vociferous in their opposition to Sadat. For his part, the president realized too late that the Islamists had become too powerful. He retaliated by clamping down on their social and political activities.

Sadat's attempt to divide and rule failed and backfired when a radical Islamist faction grew too powerful, threatening his authoritarian hege- mony. Despite this failure, the divide-and-rule strategy is so resilient because it can work in both directions, as a way to destabilize opposition *and* as a violent program to reinforce the power of the authoritarian state. Over the past hundred years the failures of the divide-and-rule strategy became the cause for consolidated authoritarian control precisely because the divide-and-rule "balance" failed. Rather than seeing the imbalances as failures, they seem to be part of the divide-and-rule strategy itself, where the authoritarian wins when the factions stay focused on each other as well as when one grows too powerful and the state then restores balance at gunpoint.

Hopes of an Islamic revolution in Egypt failed in spite of Sadat's assassination by a militant Islamist group called Egyptian Islamic Jihad (EIJ) on October 6, 1981. His successor Hosni Mubarak was determined to escape a similar fate. During his presidency, Mubarak divided the Islamist movement into a moderate or "good" camp and a radical or "bad" one.[29] This division had nothing to do with ideology and everything to do with political expediency. It was based on each group's stance toward the government: those who refrained from doing "a Qutb" and calling the Mubarak regime "un-Islamic" were labeled as good Islamists.[30]

Mindful of how the state had treated them in the past, the Muslim Brotherhood took a conciliatory approach, but even so the movement remained proscribed. In 1982, the new murshid, Amr al-Tilmissani, officially rejected the use of violence in the service of politics and pledged to work within existing political institutions.[31] This allowed the Brotherhood to resume their activities and return to their headquarters, even though officially, they remained a banned organization.

From 1983 to 1987, most of the Brothers who had been imprisoned during the Sadat era were released and the group was able to reestablish its organization. As they still could not officially participate in the political process, they formed a coalition in 1984 with one of their former rivals: the secular Wafd Party. But as a junior coalition partner, only eight out of the fifty-eight seats won in the elections went to the Brotherhood.

The Brotherhood's backdoor entrance into the political system allowed its members to participate in elections to professional organizations.[32] The timing could not have been better. State regulations were being relaxed. The Brotherhood focused on the most important and active syndicates: the doctors, engineers, pharmacists, and lawyers' syndicates. All were managed by quasi-liberal forces in cahoots with the state or by the state itself.[33] The Brotherhood's stance on tackling endemic corruption and financial mismanagement turned it into a strong player. The stance they took revitalized the activities and symbolic power of professional organizations.[34] They used their newly acquired control of the syndicates to expand their social activities within wider society. They opened private mosques, clinics, youth houses, welfare organizations, cultural centers, and commercial and business enterprises like Islamic banks and investment companies.[35]

Under the all-seeing eye of Mubarak's police state from 1981 until 2011, the Muslim Brothers were rebuilding the state-within-a-state that would provide services to those parts of the community ignored by the official state. While Egypt witnessed a low-intensity insurgency led by militant religious activists or jihadis throughout the 1990s, the Muslim Brotherhood portrayed itself as more moderate and offered to mediate between the two warring sides. The Islamist organization also benefited from a legacy of protests and worker strikes in Egypt in the first half of 2000, becoming a force to be reckoned with in Egyptian society. For example, it gained almost a hundred seats in the parliamentary elections in 2005 after the United States had pressured Mubarak to open up the political space a little bit. The Cairo Spring did not last long because the Mubarak regime quickly tightened its grip on power, leading the Muslim Brotherhood to boycott the 2010 elections.

This was the situation in January 2011, when protests broke out in Egypt as part of the Arab Spring. Given their fragile position vis-à-vis the regime, the Muslim Brotherhood was initially reluctant to join in the protests, choosing instead to bide their time until the dust had settled on the streets. While individual Brothers and Sisters spontaneously participated in the demonstrations, they did so without the official support of their movement.[36] But once the protests gained momentum and the military refused to open fire on the protesters, the Muslim Brotherhood called its followers out on the streets.

The success of the Egyptian revolution and the election of the Muslim Brotherhood's Mohammed Morsi to the presidency in 2012 revealed the political ambitions of the organization. The state-within-the-state had evolved to run the state itself. But no sooner had the Muslim Brothers successfully turned their grassroots support into election-winning votes than their victory came to be viewed with alarm in wide sections of the population. To a large segment of the public, the Brotherhood was a closed, insular community based on networks of patron-client relationships. Egyptians who were not part of this self-declared community feared the new Brotherhood-led government would serve only the interests of its patrons and clients and exclude everyone else from access to power and resources.

There was also the issue of where Egypt's large Christian community would fit into this new status quo. Over ten million in number, the Copts had suffered systematic abuse under the old regime but their fear of the past was not enough to make them hopeful of the future. How would non-Muslims fare in an Islamist-run country?

As it turned out, Morsi's presidency did not last. What happened in the summer of 2013 in Egypt depends on whom you ask. One point of view is that President Morsi brought about his own downfall. According to this view, the military's ability to carry out a successful coup against him stemmed from a pattern of blunders committed by the Brotherhood's leadership both during and after the January 25 Revolution—mistakes that estranged many Egyptians from the Islamist movement. During their year in power, the Brotherhood's use of political, economic, social, and cultural power in a clientelist way did little to qualm public fears about the organization's hidden agenda. A feeling persisted among swathes of the public that the Brotherhood had never really abandoned the Qutbian project of establishing an Islamic state along Salafist lines; that they still believed the nation was secondary to the community and the community meant the Brotherhood.[37]

The young people who set the revolution in motion but who lacked the organizational capacity to politically profit from it had no wish to see the Brotherhood take advantage of their sacrifices to create a second Iran. They took to the streets again in the spring and summer of 2013 to protest against President Morsi. The optics of these mass protests proved too much for the military to resist.[38] In fact, increasing evidence shows that the military played an important role in organizing and financing some of these protests against Morsi and the Muslim Brotherhood. The leaders of the army saw their moment and they took it. They incited the huge anti-Morsi protests and set themselves up as the guardians of the wishes of the people. Once again, the Muslim Brotherhood was crushed and its leaders jailed. More than 800 members and supporters who staged sit-ins in Cairo and across the country were killed in one day on August 14, 2013.[39]

If you talk to members of the Muslim Brotherhood or their supporters, they will tell you a different story about what happened in that summer. They will tell you that the military, the deep state, and those who profit from it, never had any intention of allowing democracy to take root in Egypt. They were merely biding their time, waiting for an opportunity to roll back the democratic gains of the Arab Spring. Morsi's blunders and the mass protests against him gave them their opportunity. According to this view, it was not only the Egyptian military who wanted to see the Muslim Brothers fail. Regional actors, particularly Saudi Arabia and the United Arab Emirates, had no wish to see an Islamist government succeed in their neighborhood.[40] And the Americans, keen to keep Egypt signed up to the Camp David Accords, indirectly agreed with them.

In the Middle East, the consequences of ousting democratically elected Islamists from power are all too apparent, as shown by Algeria in 1992, Palestine in 2006, and Egypt in 2013. Militant Islamists like Al-Qaeda take great delight in mocking mainstream Islamists like the Muslim Brotherhood for wasting their time participating in the electoral process. In stark contrast, the jihadist message is as unequivocal as it is uncompromising. According to Abu Bakr al-Baghdadi, the leader of Islamic State, political change can only come about "through the barrel of a gun, not through the electoral box."[41]

To understand the consequences of disregarding the popular will in the Arab world and the repercussions of the battle between moderate and militant Islamists, Algeria provides a painful and prophetic lesson from history.

A Lesson from History: Nationalism
and Islamism in Algeria

After the better-known Egyptian case, Algeria is another important example of the ambiguous and contradictory relationship between the post-colonial Arab state and political Islam.

When the long and bloody Algerian War of Independence finally ended in 1962, the National Liberation Front (FLN) took control of the country.

The FLN had led the struggle against the French, and Algeria's new president Ahmed Ben Bella was a hero of the war. But independence brought new problems, and it was not long before a new power struggle was underway and Ben Bella was clashing with factions inside and outside the FLN.[42]

For the president, taking care of the groups outside the FLN was not difficult. Opposition groups were quickly banned, but tensions at the top of the revolutionary movement and, particularly, between Ben Bella and his defense minister Houari Boumedienne persisted. As Ben Bella ratcheted up pressure on Boumedienne and his allies, the latter decided to act. The man in charge of the military played his trump card—the army—and carried out a bloodless military coup that removed Ben Bella from the presidency.[43]

The repercussions of the coup were not limited to Algeria. They were felt across the region. Ben Bella had enjoyed a close working relationship with Nasser. But there soon developed strains between the new Algerian president and his Egyptian counterpart. Boumedienne refused Nasser's request to give the deposed Ben Bella a home in Egypt. The situation worsened when Algeria became suspicious of Egyptian involvement in a number of retaliatory incidents that took place after the coup. In response, Boumedienne dismissed all the Egyptian military advisers working in Algeria on grounds of national security. He dismissed and deported hundreds of Egyptian teachers for the same reason.

To reinforce the precarious foundation of his legitimacy, Boumedienne did what Anwar Sadat would later do in Egypt. He divided to conquer, using the Islamists to sideline the leftists. The national education project aimed to appropriate Islamist symbolism in the service of the secular nation-state. Linguistic Arabization was to go hand in hand with cultural Islamization.

This two-pronged approach owed much to history. The aggressive secularism of colonial France had prevented religious groups from organizing, and this resulted in the creation of a Francophone elite as the main champion of Algerian independence.[44] During the long colonial period, many schools where the curriculum was taught in French had opened across the country.

After independence, the cultural divide between French speakers and Arabic speakers widened. Many of the latter complained that most government positions went to French-educated Algerians. This accusation tarnished the image of the mainly Francophone-speaking FLN elite. In this context, Boumedienne's Arabization program aimed to establish classical Arabic as the common language and to redress the cultural bias left behind by the French. It also allowed the regime to shore up its position by co-opting the Islamist movement and displaying its religious credentials. Another goal was to fuse socialist principles with Islamic law, thereby giving a religious gloss to secular policies.

To teach in Algerian schools, Boumedienne invited teachers from Iraq and many from Egypt who belonged to the Muslim Brotherhood and were staunchly anti-Nasserist. The Muslim Brothers, with their transnational approach, were no strangers to Algeria. They had established branches there during the French occupation. But the movement's political project had not yet found fertile ground. Other Islamist groups had participated in the anti-colonial struggle, and they, too, had found it hard to make inroads into the popular imagination. This was because the secular FLN had successfully used Islamist narratives to frame the war against the French as an obligatory jihad.[45] As a result, Arabic became increasingly associated with Islamism, while leftist elements were more often French-speaking and secular.

The president did not stop there. Not content with inviting hundreds of Islamists to work in the country's schools, Boumedienne appointed one of them minister of education: Ahmed Taleb Ibrahimi. It was part of the president's policy of co-opting Islam and Islamists for his own political ends. Islam was part of the fabric of Algerian society—a reality reflected in both the 1963 and 1976 constitutions that stipulate Islam is the state religion and that the president must be Muslim—but in independent Algeria, the faith had no official place in political life. Boumedienne was changing that. But he was doing it on his own terms. Islamists were not given independent freedom of action. They were used as a pressure group and those who were not part of the government were encouraged to agitate for policy changes the regime wanted to push forward. For

Boumedienne, this approach allowed him to distinguish himself from his presidential predecessor and had the added bonus of strengthening the Salafi-inclined movement at the expense of Algeria's long-established Sufi movement. The former owed their power and prestige to the president. The latter did not.

By the 1970s, change was afoot and the Algerian government shifted focus from the re-Islamization of society toward socialism. As the Left became a potential ideological ally of the regime, the privileges on offer to the Islamists diminished. The Islamists retreated from the campuses to the mosques and sought to establish their own independent institutional frameworks free from state control. To this end, they secured nongovernment funding and built "free mosques" that operated beyond government oversight. At first, the money came from local merchants, which linked this class to the Islamist movement, who conceived of the "free mosques" as spaces where "discussion circles" could take place.

As state control deepened and expanded, Islamists successfully presented their independent space as a forum where opposition to the regime could be heard, grievances aired and publicly channeled. Moreover, these mosques served as communal and social networks for Islamists and helped spread their message through the community and across the country. Banned like their Brothers in Egypt from participating in politics, Islamists in Algeria likewise began to build a state-within-a-state. And like their Brothers in Egypt, the political power of Algeria's Islamists began to rise.

The subsequent rise of the Islamist movement as a major political force in Algeria had an unlikely ally: the new ruling regime. Under Boumedienne, the political power of Islamists had been co-opted in the service of a state project that was politically secular but had a strong Islamic cultural component. Under his successor, Colonel Chadli Ben Jedid, the renewed use of Islam as a counterweight to the Left increased the power of Islamists. When Ben Jedid succeeded Boumedienne in 1979, one of his first moves was to approve a new "family-status Code," which made concessions to Islamists, especially on the status of women.[46] Like Sadat, Ben Jedid was intent on using religiosity to shore up his power base. Consequently, his regime tolerated Islamist criticism of foreign ways, Western clothes, alcohol, and communism. Islamist organizations flourished on Algerian university campuses.[47]

In the 1980s, Islamist preachers found a new way to reach a mass audience: television and radio. This development had long-lasting implications. Their religious and partisan discourse was internalized by a large segment of the population in the region. Islamist preachers attacked imperialists and Zionists and blamed them for the pauperization of the Arab people. In the process, they aimed to deflect criticism away from Arab regimes while simultaneously setting up Islam as the only viable opposition framework to regime policies.[48] As the Algerian regime suppressed or co-opted all mainstream political opposition, Islamic forces gradually filled this vacuum. As a result, political opposition became synonymous with the most traditionalist elements in the country. And unlike other groups, Islamists could mobilize huge crowds. By doing so, they wanted to show they were in touch with the people and were the only force capable of representing their real interests.

But by the mid-1980s, the Islamist movement in Algeria was no longer just about communal charity, faith, and politics. A harder edge had emerged, and radical strands were widespread. In 1982 Mustafa Bouyali, a former FLN combatant, launched an armed group known as the Algerian Islamic Armed Movement (AIAM).[49] AIAM first targeted institutions it deemed un-Islamic, such as girls' schools, libraries, restaurants, and cinemas, and continued to call the regime un-Islamic.[50] The government finally crushed the armed group in 1987, following an ambush by the security forces in which Bouyali was killed. But the defeat of AIAM did not put an end to Islamist militancy. In the early 1990s, the return of Algerians who had participated in the war against the Soviet Union in Afghanistan in the 1980s reinvigorated the movement. During the Afghan jihad, Algerian combatants had established links with Islamists from various countries and backgrounds.

Since 1962, successive Algerian presidents had based their political legitimacy on their role in the war of independence. The state itself was presented as the embodiment of that colonial struggle and the sacrifices made in the name of Algeria's freedom. But people were angry that their liberators were now trampling on their freedom of speech and their right to protest. To defuse the rising tension, the ruling elite offered multiparty elections in the hope that mainstream political parties would prevent Islamists from gaining a majority.

Islamists, however, had other ideas and seized the occasion to become a major political force.[51] Two men were key to this process: Abassi Madani, a former FLN combatant, and Ali Belhadj, a cleric. Together, they formed the Islamic Salvation Front (FIS). Madani had received a PhD in educational psychology in London and was popular with moderates and intellectuals. Belhadj, on the other hand, was an imam who particularly appealed to the disenfranchised and unemployed youth.[52] The Algerian Islamists leveraged financial support by playing off regional powers like Saudi Arabia and Iran against each other.[53]

During the election campaign, the FIS Islamist group never published a political or economic program, and most of its discourse was full of contradictions. While Madani called for democracy, Belhadj's rhetoric undermined it. But the public wanted change. FIS won the first round of the parliamentary elections in January 1992. Their victory caught the military establishment napping and horrified Western powers. The Islamist triumph not only exposed deep fault lines in Algeria's national identity, it also revealed the shortsightedness of the state's use and misuse of political Islam as a weapon against the secular opposition.

On the eve of the second round of parliamentary elections, the military nullified the results and forced Ben Jedid to resign. Subsequent developments, including the suspension of political life in Algeria, pushed the country toward a full-fledged dictatorship and triggered a vicious civil war that killed between 50,000 and 100,000 people.[54] During the war, Islamist groups multiplied. The regime and Islamists alike carried out massacres that left deep scars on the country's psyche and ripped its social fabric apart.

After the war ended in 2002, many Islamists retreated to the mountainous region of Kabyle and to the Sahara, where they established contacts and networks with other militants. Today some of these groups have mutated and pledged loyalty to either Al-Qaeda or the Islamic State. In the meantime, the Islamization of Algeria along ultraconservative Salafist lines continues apace as the state continues to use the sacred to shore up its legitimization.

In Egypt and Algeria, a similar pattern played out: presidents who were determined to monopolize power set out to divide and conquer the opposition and used Islamists to balance the leftists. It might have seemed a clever Machiavellian plan, except for one thing: it did not work. The Islamist message resonates with sufficient numbers of people that, even when banned from the official political arena, Islamists are able to set up their own community networks that effectively form a state-within-a-state. This leaves only one option for the old order: to send in the soldiers and take back power. But such disregard for the popular will in the Arab world has galvanized a whole new genre of nonstate actors who have a radically different agenda and who play by radically different rules. Democracy is not on their radar. Their aim is global jihad.

Al-Qaeda, the Islamic State, and the Rise and Spread of Hard-Line Islamism

Groups that have weaponized Islam to oppose the secular state have done so in various ways. To begin with, they use it as the ideological basis to reject the modern nation-state. Militant Islamists seek to overthrow the entire system and replace it with a global caliphate, whereas their mainstream moderate counterparts take a more gradualist, nonviolent approach and try to change the state from within. As the cases of Egypt and Algeria show, Arab nationalist rulers, by first nurturing mainstream political Islamists and then repressing them, have unwittingly triggered the rise of militant Islamists.

For the Muslim Brotherhood in Egypt and the FIS in Algeria, the rejection of the modern state system was less clear-cut than is often assumed or claimed by the movements themselves. In Algeria, the founders of the FIS, which became the most important challenger to the FLN, were revolutionary combatants during the Algerian War of Independence and had been supporters of the FLN for decades. In Egypt, several Islamist groups, including the Muslim Brotherhood, used Islam as a vehicle for reform against the devastating effects of colonialism and its destruction of the country's social fabric. In both cases, Islamists initially aimed at changing the social and political system by working from within, even though the Muslim Brotherhood occasionally employed violence in the 1940s, 1950s, and 1960s.

Working from within had a downside, however. When Islamists were co-opted by the state, they ended up helping legitimize political authoritarianism. In Egypt and Algeria, the regimes used Islamists as a proxy tool of repression against the secular opposition and its progressive conceptualization of state and society. By using religiosity in this way—as a political tool to engage with society—it is not surprising that concepts like citizenry and civil society struggled to gain a foothold in either the popular imagination or the public arena. In addition, the use of Islamists as proxies poisoned state-society relations and created a crisis of mistrust and suspicion. In the long run, this strategy backfired on the states themselves as it allowed Islamists to accrue considerable soft power, so much so that they have become the only viable political opposition in the region.[55]

It was only after Islamists were violently excluded from politics and repressed by authoritarian regimes that they radicalized. When mainstream Islamists are persecuted, the hard-liners step in. With their uncompromising philosophy that the state is illegitimate, the ruler a pharaoh, and anyone who disagrees with them a *kafir* (an unbeliever), radical Islamists have no place for the nation-state in their worldview. They see it as a failed un-Islamic construct that must be overthrown, and they see jihad on a global scale as the way to do it.

By rejecting the state, these groups also reject nationality as a form of identity. Instead, they use an alternative set of identities to define membership of their community. The recent rise of hard-line Salafi-jihadist groups like Al-Qaeda and the Islamic State has motivated researchers to focus on the transnational aspect of the jihadist movement.[56] But this concentration on the global should not obscure the fact that both organizations use Islam as their primary site of identity. They then "layer up" their claims to legitimacy and authority by tapping into a wide range of deeply ingrained local, national, and transnational identities that have emotional resonance with the communities they are addressing.

In many cases, these local, national, and transnational identities are used simultaneously to reinforce the organization's core message. For example, since its inception in the mid-to-late 1990s, Al-Qaeda has prioritized the fight against global enemies like the United States and its European allies. But it has also linked this transnational crusade to the defeat of secular, apostate regimes in the Islamic world and the Islamization of state and society at home. The founders of Al-Qaeda, Osama bin Laden and Ayman al-Zawahiri, saw no inherent contradictions between the transnational and the local facets of their fight: each is an extension of the other and both produce the same result.

In itself, this use of multiple identities is nothing new. In the Arab world, tribal, religious, and ethnic identities have been intertwined since the beginning of Islam and even before. Islamist groups have long included several layers of sociocultural identities in their worldview. As a result, they have proven to be much more elastic in their terms of self-reference than the nation-state. Because of this flexibility, they have become adept at tailoring their message to the specific audience they are addressing, often highlighting the layers of identity that most appeal to that particular community. In the decades before and after decolonization, moderate Islamists realized the importance of the nation and therefore emphasized nationalist symbols, whereas today, radical Islamists stress a more global narrative.[57]

Even someone who so publicly identified with Islam as Osama bin Laden drew on multiple layers of identity to try and justify the attacks on the United States on September 11, 2001. In his discourse on the subject, he drew on a wide range of religious, tribal, local, and geostrategic symbols and imagery.[58] Not only did bin Laden appeal to Arabian Peninsula nationalism, he also engaged in tribal glorification by using Bedouin dialect and poetry before directly addressing the Saudi middle class and calling on them to join his jihad. More recently, in the Iraqi and Syrian conflicts, Islamic State has focused on using a mixture of local, tribal, and transnational symbols and imagery to garner support.

As well as rejecting the nation as a political construct and nationality as a form of communal identity, radical groups have another weapon in their war against the state. And it is one they have used to devastating effect: they have turned their faith into an instrument of communal division. Al-Qaeda and the Islamic State both deploy sectarianism as a means of social control. Both repeatedly portray Shia and Sunni identities as inherently incompatible with (and therefore antagonistic to) one another. In the chaos of Iraq and Syria, sectarianism has proven to be an extremely effective rallying cry for both groups and for Islamic State in particular.

This redefinition of Islam offers a powerful sense of group identity.[59] An observer of sectarianism notes: "Mythology is central to group identity on almost all levels, whether national, ethnic, religious or sectarian; myths and their symbols have the power to sustain group identity providing a sense of uniqueness and purpose for members."[60] More importantly, by dividing Islam into an "us versus them" binary, radical groups have given themselves a powerful "other," a symbolic enemy against which their own group identity can coalesce.[61]

The success of Al-Qaeda and Islamic State in playing on sectarian divisions in Iraq and Syria owes much to the fact that they tapped into something that was already there. After achieving independence, nationalism acted as a primary site of identification for most citizens in Iraq and Syria.[62] But as the two countries gradually descended into political authoritarianism from the 1950s onward, secondary identities like sectarianism started to compete with nationalist norms of inclusion, citizenship, and progress.[63] These secondary subnational identities, such as which ethnic group you belong to or which branch of Islam you practice, gained traction for another reason: they were often hijacked by the Iraqi[64] and Syrian regimes to shore up their legitimacy, to co-opt local powerholders, and provide an ideological smokescreen when popular anger erupted against them.

In recent years, the Syrian and Iraqi states deliberately privileged their sectarian coreligionists at the expense of the Sunnis. By doing so, they aggravated communal tensions, which radical groups have been quick to seize on and exploit for their own purposes. Domestic state actions, as well as foreign intervention and economic competition for resources, jobs, and money, have converged to entrench sectarian identities. Moreover, the political weight attributed to sectarian tensions by local and foreign states,

Islamist groups, as well as the media and the international community at large, has further fueled the resurgence of sectarian identities.[65]

Radical groups are clearly not the first to use sectarianism to achieve political goals. Subnational identities have been deliberately manipulated for years by authoritarian Arab regimes to deflect demands for political change and to perpetuate the power of ruling elites. From the 1970s onward, Arab rulers have intermittently turned to subnational identities like religion, tribalism, and ethnicity to consolidate their own legitimacy or to pursue a policy of divide and rule. Even regimes that defined themselves as predominantly secular, such as Syrian president Hafez al-Assad, Muammar Gaddafi of Libya, and Iraqi strongman Saddam Hussein, used religious, sectarian, and tribal symbols either narratively or as a normative instrument to divide and rule society.

The practice of pitting one community against another is therefore as old as the state system itself. Leaders used it so much, and so often, that it became an instrument of policy. But the difference between leaders like Hafez al-Assad and Saddam Hussein and radical groups like Al-Qaeda and Islamic State is that the former manipulate subnational identities to sustain their grip on the state, whereas the latter do so to destroy it. Given this fundamental difference in objectives, it is worth looking at how regimes used sectarianism in the service of the state and the consequences this strategy has had on communal cohesion. As we have seen in the case of the Islamist groups in Egypt and Algeria, the resilience of primordial identities has less to do with the unchangeable face of the region and more with the divide-and-rule practices of its autocrats.

Divide and Conquer: Sectarianism in the Service of the State

In Iraq, the men who ruled the country after independence tirelessly preached national unity and promoted pan-Arab nationalism and a unique Iraqi identity as a foundational myth. At the same time, however, they pursued divide-and-rule tactics within their population and labeled anyone who exposed their sectarian policies "enemies of the people."

At the beginning of the Iran-Iraq War in 1980, Saddam Hussein stripped thousands of Iraqi Shias of their citizenship and forced them into exile simply because they were of Persian origin. In one stroke, the Iraqi dictator created a huge opposition constituency resident in Iran that dedicated itself to his removal from power. His brutal policies also forced dissidents to flee the country in peril of their lives. Many found homes in the West, where they became bitter political dissidents who happily colluded with foreign governments in the hope of toppling Saddam and reclaiming their country.

The Iraqi ruler was relentless in the use of subnational identities to bolster his own power. He fought against his own Shia population and pushed them toward Iran. He gassed the Kurds and forced them to seek protection from foreign patrons such as the United States. By brutalizing all opposition to his rule, Saddam Hussein created the conditions that motivated Iraqi exiles in the diaspora to enlist external military intervention to bring about regime change at home.

A similar disconnect between public discourse and actual policy occurred in Syria. Hafez al-Assad preached pan-Arab nationalism but practiced sectarianism and nepotism. The Assad family controlled Syria from 1970 to 2024: first through the father, Hafez, who ruled from 1970 until 2000, then through his son, Bashar, who was overthrown in December 2024. In the fifty-four years they ruled, the Assads built a massive security apparatus with an officer corps organized along sectarian lines. It is estimated that 70 percent of officers were, like the Assads themselves, Alawite, in a country where almost 70 percent of the population are Sunnis. But the manipulation of subnational identities was not confined to the military. In their effort to strengthen their rule, the Assads frequently supported tribal and ethnic identities at the expense of inclusive nation-building.

In the past five decades, the Assads directly and indirectly helped revive subnational identities and, in doing so, they facilitated and actively encouraged the rise and proliferation of nonstate actors based on these identities. With such a narrow sectarian support base, the Assads could not claim to represent the Syrian nation. As the country descended into civil war in 2011, the state itself became the biggest militia among a multitude of nonstate actors, all of whom were fighting for power. In this regard,

Syria, unfortunately, is not the exception but the rule. Across the region, relying on a partisan support base has become the norm. Yemen is another example.

The Yemeni state under Ali Abdullah Saleh, who ruled from 1978 until 2012, mastered the art of divide and rule by playing one tribe off against another. Forced to step down by a popular uprising in 2012, Saleh had previously compared ruling Yemen to "dancing on the heads of the snakes."[66] The autocratic ruler clearly saw nothing wrong with depicting his country as a snake pit and his fellow citizens as snakes while he, Yemen's wiliest politician, danced on their heads for over three decades.

Saleh kept his own political balance by keeping rivals off theirs. Just as Bashar al-Assad turned his supporters into Syria's biggest militia, Saleh turned his tribe into Yemen's biggest tribe. And just as Bashar al-Assad strengthened the Alawite sect at the expense of the Syrian nation, Saleh strengthened his favorite tribes at the expense of the Yemeni state. Saleh also colluded with Salafi-jihadists, particularly Osama bin Laden's followers, and with their help, succeeded in subduing the south and forcing the unification of North and South Yemen in May 1990. Saleh was "elected" president of the reunited Republic of Yemen, a position he held until 2012, when he was ousted by popular uprising and replaced by his deputy, Abd-Rabbu Mansour Hadi.

Under Saleh's rule, Al-Qaeda and other like-minded factions flourished in Yemen. Furthermore, there are credible reports that Saleh instrumentalized his relationship with the Salafi-jihadists to counterbalance internal foes as well as extract foreign aid from the United States. By the time Saleh was ousted, Yemen had become home to one of the most potent Al-Qaeda affiliates in the world—Al-Qaeda in the Arabian Peninsula (AQIP)—and had become the poorest country in the Arab world. Two out of every three people in Yemen live on less than $2 per day. In contrast to this grinding poverty, Saleh spent his time in power plundering the country's resources. In February 2015, a panel of United Nations experts released a report alleging that during his thirty-three years in power Saleh had amassed a fortune somewhere between $30 and $62 billion. According to the UN report, these assets include cash, gold, property, and other commodities held under various names in at least twenty countries.[67]

As if aiding and abetting the resurgence of subnational identities and the rise of nonstate actors were not enough, Saleh left the country itself in tatters. Yemen is fast running out of water and food. Yet, even after he had left office, Saleh was not finished. He used elite army units and tribes loyal to his family to help trigger a devastating civil war that forced his successor, Hadi, into exile in Saudi Arabia.

In Yemen, as in Iraq and Syria, what started off as an authoritarian leader trying to divide and conquer his own people by privileging one group over others has spiraled out of control. Not only did this strategy turn out to be utterly self-defeating, it has had disastrous consequences for communal cohesion. With the majority of the population excluded from the state *by* the state, they had no choice but to turn elsewhere to have their needs met. Nonstate actors like the Islamic State, Al-Qaeda, and other sectarian-based militias rushed to fill the security and institutional vacuum left by development failure and state collapse.

The resurgence of religious, sectarian, tribal, and ethnic identities has occurred in states where ruling elites deliberately manipulated them to prevent the emergence of modern political identities. These modern political identities, including citizenship and political parties, threatened the survival of exclusionary authoritarian regimes in Iraq, Libya, Syria, Yemen, and beyond. The role of the state is therefore vital to understanding both the revival of subnational identities in the Middle East during the past three decades as well as the proliferation of nonstate actors. One cannot be understood without the other.

Authoritarianism and Subnational Identities

The large-scale Arab protests of 2010–2012 started with socioeconomic demands, but the brutal reaction of authoritarian regimes led to their rapid politicization. This helps explain the resurgence of centrifugal identities and their use as political tools to oppose the state and contest its sovereignty and authority. For centuries, subnational identities constituted the social fabric of Arab and Middle Eastern societies. The current revival of sectarian, ethnic, and tribal loyalties is a way for certain communities to inscribe or attempt to inscribe themselves on the internal affairs of the country they inhabit. This is reminiscent of the role political Islamism has played in countries such as Egypt, Iran, Lebanon, or Palestine since the 1950s.

Much of the journalistic and academic analysis in the aftermath of the Arab Spring uprisings has focused on how the failure to initiate a democratic transition, the deepening of authoritarianism in the region, and the pauperization of the people have led to the social and ideological fragmentation of Arab societies. But that narrative overlooks the important role the state has played, and continues to play, in the resurgence of subnational identities. While regimes in Iraq, Libya, Syria, Yemen, and others officially advocated national unity, they simultaneously carried out informal policies that sustain sectarian, tribal, ethnic, and other subnational identities.

Recent foreign military intervention and state collapse have allowed subnational identities to resurface in a manner visible to the Western eye. But they have been a vital component of the social fabric of Middle Eastern societies for centuries. Forms of identity other than the nation-state have deep roots in Middle Eastern societies and predate the establishment of the modern state system in the first half of the twentieth century. Tribes, for example, have long been part of the region's social fabric and date back far beyond the rise of Islam. These subnational identities provide groups across the Middle East with a strong sense of cohesion and the communal solidarity necessary to advance their interests.

Their recent resurgence illustrates the vacuum left by the decline of Arab nationalism and socialism as a state ideology. It is also a product of the failure to create a postcolonial order that worked. Due to a series of ruptures, from the fall of the Ottoman Empire in 1918 to the socialist revolutions in the 1950s and 1960s and the neoliberal counterrevolutions from the 1970s, the Arab world has been in a constant state of disequilibrium and disorder. These contentious shifts shook the foundation of the state system, keeping it fragmented and unstable, and authoritarian leaders, rather than constructing a system that actually worked, resorted instead to policies of divide and conquer to shore up their own authority and silence opposition. In doing so, they sowed the seeds of their own destruction and, in many cases, of the states they led.

This chapter has examined the relationship between the state and political Islam, zeroing in on the role of domestic actors as one of the three analytical keys, which were laid out previously, in an effort to understand Arab politics. In addition to the structural weaknesses and institutional fragility of the Middle Eastern state system, there is another factor at work in the proliferation of nonstate actors and the resurgence of subnational identities. Foreign powers have played a critical, if often unseen, role in the rise of alternative power blocs and alternative narratives of belonging. To understand the future of state-society relations in the Middle East, we need to shed light on this nexus between foreign powers and nonstate actors. Chapter 10 will now turn away from a strictly domestic focus and back to the world stage, reintroducing the force of foreign intervention.

10

The Subversion of the Nation from Within and Without

THE PREVIOUS CHAPTER foregrounded the relationship between authoritarian regimes and Islamist groups, highlighting how sectarianism becomes a tool for maintaining brutal autocracy. This chapter will deepen that investigation by reintroducing foreign intervention as a key force in the region and by broadening the sectarian categories to include additional religious, tribal, and ethnic identities. It will show how outside interventions and internal power disputes all deepen sectarian divides in ways that make it more difficult for modern political identities to emerge. Internal and external actors benefit from defining subnational identities in ways that actively undermine coalition-building, nation-building, and the development of an inclusive national identity. There is no fundamental law that says that these subnational identities cannot coexist within a larger national identity, as demonstrated by the fact that the Arab nationalist project was able to appeal across geographic and ethnic boundaries. Therefore, this chapter focuses on how various actors intentionally subvert larger political identities for their own shortsighted gain.

After independence, the leaders of the new Middle East had no qualms about using every means at their disposal to institutionalize their power. Across the Arab world, leaders stopped at nothing to eliminate the opposition even if it meant stirring up sectarian tensions that threatened national cohesion. Playing rivals off against each other turned into such common practice that it became an unwritten rule of politics in the region. And not just for Arab leaders. Anyone trying to influence the direction of politics in the Middle East did it.

The birth of Hamas, for example, may not have been entirely due to the tenacity and zeal of its members. A relative consensus has emerged among scholars that Israel, in a classic case of playing one enemy off against another, was pivotal in the early empowerment of the Islamist movement in Palestine. In the 1980s, Israel was looking for ways to try and weaken the popularity of Yasir Arafat in the West Bank and Gaza. The movement Arafat led, the Palestine Liberation Organization (PLO), was nationalist and secular in outlook. To offset it, the Israeli security establishment encouraged an Islamist alternative. Hamas, the Palestinian wing of the Muslim Brotherhood, fit the bill perfectly.[1] This is not to say the state of Israel in any way colluded with the activities of Hamas; rather, that in order to keep Arafat off balance, the Israeli security establishment wanted him distracted by internal opposition.

But as with so many cases of divide and conquer, the plan backfired. From 1987 onward, Hamas grew into a powerful nonstate actor and, like its Muslim Brotherhood counterpart in Egypt, developed strong networks of support in the community through its charity work and armed resistance to Israel's military occupation.[2] Then, instead of tying up Arafat's energies and neutralizing the PLO and Fatah, the movement decided to turn its attention to fighting the Israeli occupation. Israeli officials seem not to have anticipated Hamas's strategic goals would evolve in this way, even though the name of the movement—Hamas is short for Islamic Resistance Movement—was an indication of where its priorities might lie. Hamas set up an armed wing named 'Izz al-Din al-Qassam after a Palestinian rebel who fought against the British in the 1930s. The al-Qassam brigades included underground military cells that would, in time, carry out wave after wave of deadly suicide attacks across Israel in the 1990s.

Hamas has gained in popularity, winning a majority of seats in the Palestinian parliament in 2006. After Hamas seized control of Gaza from Fatah in 2007, Israel, in coordination with Egypt, has blockaded the coastal strip by land, air, and sea. Despite a suffocating blockade and frequent strikes by Israel, Hamas grew in strength and carried out a devastating attack on Israel in October 2023, which killed 1,139 Israelis, triggering Benjamin Netanyahu's onslaught on Gaza, which has killed and injured more than 150,000 Palestinians so far. Despite Israel displacing 90 percent of the population and destroying and damaging over half of all buildings, including the ecosystem, which made the strip unlivable, it has failed to subdue or defeat Hamas. In trying to pit one enemy against another, Israel allegedly ended up helping to create a more lethal adversary than the nationalist Fatah.

The following pages explore more directly the relationship between rising subnational identities, sectarianism, tribalism, and the role of the Great Powers and external intervention. In addition to encouraging and nurturing centrifugal forces, the unintended consequences of foreign interventions played a major role in the resurfacing of subnational loyalties and undermining social harmony and peace in the region. The large number of nonstate actors in the Middle East, such as Palestinian Hamas, Lebanese Hezbollah, transnational Al-Qaeda and the Islamic States, and the Kurdish PKK (Kurdistan Workers' Party), stems from the low saliency of sovereignty and limited legitimacy of the Arab state and the resilience of subnational loyalties, which are often nourished by foreign meddling. In addition to the Great Powers, Middle Eastern regimes like Iran, Israel, and Syria use nonstate actors as tools of domestic and foreign policy. Nonetheless, the stronger nonstate actors are, the less stable the regional system is.

Unintended Consequences:
Sectarianism and Nonstate Actors

It was not the first time Israel may have inadvertently created an enemy more powerful than the one it was fighting. It is doubtful if Hezbollah, the Lebanese Shia-dominated resistance organization, would have emerged if it had not been for the Israeli invasion of Lebanon in 1982.[3] Israel's subsequent two-decade-long occupation of southern Lebanon (which is largely Shia) was a direct impetus to Hezbollah.

Hezbollah (the Party of God) is now a powerful regional nonstate actor and is arguably more powerful than the Lebanese state. Both Hezbollah and Hamas are actively engaged in armed struggles against Israeli military occupation, but the two groups are also influential political players. Hamas won the 2006 Palestinian election, while Hezbollah has veto power over decisions made by the Lebanese state. Given the strength of their respective constituencies, both groups are likely to take a harder line in negotiations with Israel than their nationalist rivals would ever have done. This is one of the reasons Israel is so determined to exclude both from any future negotiations.

Israel was not alone in creating enemies more powerful than the one it was originally fighting. The United States did exactly the same in Iraq. In its attempt to turn Iraq into a client state, Washington achieved the opposite and gave a shot in the arm to any group that played on subnational identities to challenge Iraq's central authority. American patronage of the Kurds, for example, encouraged them to create an autonomous region in the north of the country and to attempt to create an independent state, thus redrawing the map of the central Middle East.

But the biggest challenge to the survival of Iraq in its current form has come from the Americans themselves. After the overthrow of Saddam, the United States dismantled all state institutions, with the exception of the oil ministry, a state of affairs that led to the collapse of the Iraqi state as a functioning entity. Even worse, it contributed significantly to the revival of subnational sectarian, ethnic, and tribal identities that had always been part of Iraq's social fabric but were often held in check by the strong arm of the state.[4]

Once the central state collapsed, tensions between Sunnis and Shia erupted and exposed a sectarian fault line that has plunged Iraq into virtual sectarian war. That fault line has been seized upon by nonstate actors, both foreign and domestic, to further their own agendas: most of the deadly sectarian attacks that kill and wound scores of civilians have been sponsored by politically based organizations, political leaders, and clerics.[5] Extremist groups such as the Islamic State (IS), Al-Qaeda, and some Shia-militias, are the chief perpetrators of sectarian killings in Iraq and the entire region. While IS and Al-Qaeda have relentlessly targeted Shia and minorities in Iraq, Syria, and beyond, Shia militias in Iraq and Syria carried out numerous attacks against Sunnis and other political opponents.

These groups of nonstate actors may have very different worldviews—Al-Qaeda and Hezbollah, for example, are sworn enemies and stand on opposite sides of the sectarian divide—but initially they shared a common approach on how to garner popular support. Both built up a solid base using anti-imperialist and anti-Zionist messages that appealed to a broad range of people. Given Israel's occupation of Palestinian lands, there is widespread popular opposition to Israel. And given the United States' preponderant support for Israel and autocratic Arab regimes, there is opposition to US foreign policy. By appealing to these core beliefs, groups like Al-Qaeda and Hezbollah have been able to transcend their sectarian base and draw support from people from a different background.

That, however, is no longer the case. Carrying supporters from your own sect is now all that matters. Hezbollah is an armed resistance movement dedicated to expelling Israel from occupied Lebanese territories. It backs the Palestinian struggle for national liberation and has been prepared to fight for it. From the 1990s until the second half of the 2000s, Hezbollah won widespread popular support in Lebanon and across the region because it was seen as an authentic religious-nationalist force that stood up to an arrogant, overreaching Israel. In 2006, Hezbollah not only withstood a relentless Israeli assault, it was credited with humbling its archenemy on the battlefield. The movement's charismatic leader, Sayyid Hassan Nasrallah, subsequently became the most popular man in the Arab world.[6]

Hezbollah's military intervention in the Syrian civil war brought an end to that. It joined the war in Syria on the regime's side, partly to defend fellow coreligionists and partly to repay Bashar al-Assad and his Iranian backers for the support they have given them over the years. But by doing Iran's bidding in an Arab country, Hezbollah squandered its hard-won popular support in the Arab arena. Now it is seen as openly partisan, a Shia-dominated group that acts only in the interests of fellow Shia. Even though its leaders repeatedly affirm the party's commitment to inclusive pan-Arab and pan-Islamic causes, Hezbollah lost the widespread support it had once enjoyed. After showing solidarity with the Palestinians after Israel's war in Gaza on October 7, 2023, Hezbollah has regained wider popular support and repaired some of the damage that it had suffered due to its intervention in the Syrian civil strife.

Al-Qaeda has also undergone a massive sectarian transformation.[7] At the beginning of its existence in the 1990s, Al-Qaeda marked a turning point in the Sunni-Salafi-jihadist worldview by shifting its focus from the near enemy, the Arab regimes, to the far enemy, the United States and other Western powers.[8] At its core, Al-Qaeda is a revolutionary antiestablishment movement and, as such, it initially acted more like a Leninist opposition movement than a sectarian militia. But Al-Qaeda morphed into a sectarian-based subversive killing machine. The group, along with like-minded affiliates, shed what they considered their pan-Islamic skin in favor of pursuing a hyper-Sunni identity.

In particular, Al-Qaeda in Iraq (AQI), established in 2004, and its successor, the IS, established in 2014, prioritize self-definition based on a sectarian Sunni identity. Because of this sectarian focus, IS has a dual purpose: to attack the far enemy in the West but also to target everyone from Shias, Christians, Kurds, and Yazidis, to fellow Sunni Muslims who refuse to submit to its rule.[9] In this, they use the practice of *takfir* (labeling someone as an infidel) to decide who belongs to their community and who does not.

Recent events in the region have facilitated this shift toward sectarian forms of identification or securitization of identity. In Iraq, the catalyst was the US-led invasion. In Syria, it was the civil war. In Iraq, after 2003, a new sense of communal identity was needed for the thousands of Sunnis dismissed from their government posts by the US-led interim authority. This was particularly the case for those in the security forces. Sunnis were politically adrift after the US invasion. As a bloc, they had no love for the old regime, but they had not welcomed the US invasion, fearing it would lead to the establishment of a Shia-dominated government.

Sectarian and tribal identity offered an important segment of Sunni society an alternative communal space for mobilization.[10] Salafi-jihadist groups like Al-Qaeda in Iraq and the Islamic State swiftly and brilliantly exploited the shifts taking place in both the social fabric and the popular imagination throughout the war-torn country. They offered an alternative worldview anchored in Sunni *asabiyya* (group or tribal solidarity) that was held together by anti-Shia and anti-Iranian ideology.

Al-Qaeda's sectarian rhetoric drew Sunni recruits from across the Islamic world to join the fight against the Iraqi government, Shia civilians, and the US-led coalition forces.[11] Abu Musab al-Zarqawi, the Jordanian who founded Al-Qaeda in Iraq, based his narrative on anti-Shia fatwas aimed at triggering civil war.[12] Al-Zarqawi almost succeeded in pushing Iraq to the brink of all-out sectarian war before he was killed in an American airstrike on an isolated safe house north of Baghdad on June 8, 2006.[13]

In Syria, the civil war amplified sectarian tensions. Sunni rebel groups have played on them to profit from the chaos and put down roots in the war-torn country. They use the fact that the Assads (both father and son) have relied on their own sect, the Alawite minority, to staff key positions in the security services and the army to depict the regime as openly sectarian and anti-Sunni. That Iran-backed militias such as the National Defense Forces, Hezbollah, and the Iraqi Asaib Ahl al-Haq—all of which are viscerally anti-Salafi[14]—fight alongside the Assad regime, they believe, only serves to underline their point.[15] As a result, radical Sunni insurgent groups like Jabhat al-Nusra, Ahrar al-Sham, and the Islamic Front deliberately use inflammatory anti-Shia rhetoric to recruit foot soldiers and gain a foothold in Sunni areas.

These groups imitate Al-Qaeda in Iraq by using a discourse that not only appeals to factions in Iraq and Syria but to the wider Islamic *umma*, the global Muslim community. Nonstate actors like these recognize no borders and make use of modern technology to reach out to potential recruits, both near and far. Via satellite television and social media, they wage a digital jihad that reverberates around the globe.[16] Their rhetorical sectarian demonization of the "other" has a long history in the Islamic world but the information age has taken it to a new level. Anti-Sunni and anti-Shia slurs have been widely popularized through television and radio, as well as sermons and speeches on the Internet by clerics only too eager to mock the other side.

This Sunni-Shia fault line is increasingly anchored in today's geopolitical rivalries. Fundamentalist Sunnis depict Shia as Safawis, or heirs to the early-modern Iranian Safavid dynasty, and therefore agents of Tehran.[17] They use other derogatory terms for Shia, including Rafidha, Majus, or Zoroastrians, all of which imply the Shia are not Muslims.[18] Leading political and religious Shia figures in Iran, Iraq, and Lebanon play the same game, referring to their Sunni foes as either *takfiris* or *Wahhabis*.[19] These two terms conflate all Sunnis with either Al-Qaeda or Saudi Arabia, as Wahhabism originated there.[20]

These words matter. This sectarian tug-of-war has turned Syria into a killing field, attracting over a hundred thousand foreign fighters from more countries than the wars in Afghanistan, Chechnya, or Bosnia combined. It has also given Al-Qaeda a chance to come back from the dead. By 2010, Al-Qaeda in Iraq was on the ropes. The organization was in retreat under US military pressure.[21] Since 2005 AQI had faced a revolt by Sunni Iraqis who, with the support of the Americans, expelled its combatants from their neighborhoods.[22] But as Syria steadily descended into civil war following the 2011 popular protests, AQI saw an opportunity. Working under the radar, the group established a base of operations in Syria. It kept its real identity hidden and blended in with other rebels. Crumbling state institutions and spiraling violence allowed armed groups to proliferate all over the country. Amid this chaos, Al-Qaeda fighters distinguished themselves on the battlefield and gained a large local following. Recruits and money poured in from neighboring countries and turned the shadowy secret organization into a mighty force.

While armed Sunni groups battled Shia militias and regime forces for control of Syria's cities, civilians were neglected and faced a daily struggle to survive. Syrians were caught in a never-ending cycle of violence and devastation. The plight of everyday Syrians was heartbreaking. More than 400,000 people were killed. Nearly two-thirds of Syrians were either refugees in neighboring countries or were internally displaced. Given such desperate conditions, it is perhaps not surprising that tens of thousands of Syrian Sunnis had joined rebel groups, including Al-Qaeda and IS.

In 2013, Al-Qaeda in Iraq took account of the deteriorating situation in both Iraq and Syria and changed tactics accordingly. It changed its name to the Islamic State in Iraq and Syria (ISIS) and strengthened its grip on

Sunni provinces in Iraq and eastern regions in Syria. In June 2014, ISIS seized Mosul, Iraq's second-largest city, and accelerated its attacks against civilians targeting not only Shia but all minorities.[23]

This was too radical even for Al-Qaeda. ISIS's repeated attacks on Sunni militias and civilians in Syria and Iraq angered the parent organization. In February 2014, the group expelled ISIS from its ranks. It made no difference. By 2013 the leader of ISIS, Abu Bakr al-Baghdadi, was more powerful than his boss, Ayman al-Zawahiri. Baghdadi had built a military apparatus and amassed billions of US dollars in assets and resources in Syria and Iraq. The roles of the top two jihadists had reversed with Baghdadi now on top. A breakup became inevitable. In July 2014 Baghdadi unilaterally formalized the split from Zawahiri's AQ by rebranding his organization the Islamic State and appointing himself caliph.

Once free of Al-Qaeda's constraints, Islamic State used sectarian identity as its weapon of choice in Syria, Iraq, and beyond. And did so to devastating effect. Baghdadi and his associates offered Sunnis in conflict zones an intoxicating mix of salvation and empowerment through a return to a tribalized pan-Sunni identity at war with the "other," by which they mainly meant the Shia. IS was thus a major beneficiary of, and contributor to, the resurgence of subnational identities in the region. The group would not have done as well as it did, had it not successfully convinced a sizable chunk of the Sunni population in Iraq and Syria that it is their defender against the minority-based regimes in Baghdad and Damascus. The civil war in Syria and the deepening sectarianism in Iraq after the US-led invasion are the fuel that powered the rise of IS. The group's ultimate downfall, in 2017 in Iraq and 2019 in Syria, is due to a number of factors: its hubris, its overestimation of its military might, and, most importantly, the sheer scale of its brutality, which turned Muslim and global opinion against it.[24]

The group also made a number of profound political miscalculations. By targeting Turkey, IS alienated the only regional power that had been neutral toward it. IS's beheading of Western hostages, together with attacks on civilians in American and European cities, led the US-led coalition to double its efforts to defeat the organization. Russia, another casualty of IS attacks, backed its old ally Syria in the fight against the group. Iran and Hezbollah also joined in, siding with the Syrian and Iraqi regimes.[25] Lacking any kind of political imagination or agenda, Baghdadi and his cohorts managed to unite the world against their blood-drenched caliphate. They will go down in history as their own worst enemies.

They would not, however, have made it as far as they did without Iraq's slide into sectarianism and Syria's descent into sectarian slaughter. Both processes are intrinsically linked. Western involvement in the former led to Western inaction on the latter. The unintended consequences of military intervention in Iraq made Americans wary of becoming bogged down in another Middle Eastern quagmire. Western powers were therefore reluctant to engage in Syria. This left Bashar al-Assad free to turn on his own people. And his people, left defenseless, turned to whoever came to help.

Alternative Forms of Identity I: Tribal Identities and War in Syria

In the chaos of war, armed rebel groups such as the Free Syrian Army, Jabhat al-Nusra, and IS offered people a form of communal protection as well as a means of identity. There is, however, another form of identity that is often ignored by outsiders even though it provides long-standing and deeply entrenched networks of solidarity: tribalism.

Tribal identity, with its focus on the local, is often viewed through an orientalist prism inherited by Western scholars from colonial times. Tribes are often described as the most primordial and yet most resilient identity in the Middle East, likened to a monolith where every tribesman abdicates personal responsibility and blithely follows the will of the sheikh. This viewpoint sees tribal identity as the primary site of identification for tribal members at the expense of all other social affiliations and associations.

Essentializing the role of Middle Eastern tribes has served an ideological function of showing the "backwardness" of the Arabs. Rather than seeing tribes as forms of social organization that have evolved throughout history, there is a dominant tendency to portray tribes as frozen in time and space, unchanged since the coming of Islam or even before. This notion served to justify the social engineering projects of both European colonialists and local modernizers. It also motivated past and present autocrats to try to replace tribalism with nationalism as an indispensable tool to strengthen the nation-state in the region, as if these concepts were always at odds with each other.

Events in Syria and Iraq show that could not be further from the truth. In both countries, tribes aligned themselves directly with the state when such an alliance served their interests. On occasions when they felt their needs were not being met, they opposed and violently resisted the authorities. Tribalism should therefore be understood as a dynamic and heterogeneous identity where fluctuations take place that mirror the material conditions of the tribes' members, their relationship to power, and the interests of the group as a whole. Far from being antagonistic to the nation-state, tribes can take on a nationalist orientation if their core interests and grievances are taken into consideration.

In Syria and Iraq, most of the tribally affiliated population have ancestors interconnected with the region known as the Syrian desert, which connects the Mashreq to the Arabian Peninsula. The term *Bedu* is used to refer to the inhabitants of the *Badia*, from Badiyat ash-Sham, the Arabic name for this large arid and semiarid steppe. The *Bedu*, or desert dweller, is the opposite of the *Hadar* or urban dweller, and Bedouin identity is thus framed in opposition to the city.[26] On an organizational level, Bedouin tribes operate on a series of alliances that represent the interests of the tribe and its survival. Most Bedouin tribes function as a collective of smaller subtribes. A subtribe is called *ashira* or *fakhdh*, and a group of these is known as a *bayt* (meaning a house) or *qawm/aqwam* (meaning people). The smallest unit of a tribe is generally constituted of a kin group. The origins of Bedouin tribes are pre-Islamic. Their pastoral way of life dates back even farther than the origins of the faith, and although pastoralism does not predate agriculture, it is an offshoot of it.

Many of the Bedouin tribes in Syria today originate from the Arabian Peninsula and migrated north from the mid-seventeenth century onward.[27] Between the seventeenth and nineteenth centuries, the Ottoman authorities adopted policies to co-opt and control these tribes and this led many of them to settle in the Badia and Jazira areas of Greater Syria. Even though a number of large tribes resisted Ottoman authority and refused to pay their taxes,[28] Istanbul did not act against them. They played too important a role in providing regional security, especially overseeing military districts and controlling important lines of communication.[29]

Between 1870 and 1900 new waves of migration brought more change to the Syrian demographic and social landscape when Circassians, Abhazi, and Chechens established themselves in agricultural settlements called *Ma'moura*.[30] In the Golan Heights, these newcomers were joined by another group with a strong sense of self-identity: the Druze. The Druze had been fighting in Mount Lebanon, and the Ottoman authorities wanted to use them to balance the power of the Bedouin tribes.[31]

Relations between the state authorities in Istanbul and the tribes in Greater Syria had generally been good. This was partly due to the legal division between state and tribe. Ottoman Syria's legal system was divided between the state law (*qanun*) and the customary law of the tribes (*'urf*).[32] But the Bedouins were rarely subjected to the authority of state law. Instead, they resolved their grievances and conflicts through their own rules and norms. In Greater Syria, Bedouin leaders succeeded in developing a close relationship with the centers of power that allowed them to preserve their nomadic style of life. That, in turn, allowed tribal leaders to maintain the support of their tribes. In the nineteenth century, a special boarding school was even set up in Istanbul for tribal leaders.[33]

Even so, the tribes were Arab Bedouin first, subjects of the sultan second. Many of them backed the Arab Revolt during World War I against the Ottomans and led by the Arab Hashemites. However, they had to adapt their position after the French defeated Emir Faisal in 1920. Faisal's defeat had important consequences for tribal cohesion. During the French Mandate, tribal leaders struggled to maintain their autonomy and relevance as different leaders adopted different stands toward the French. Many saw French rule as illegitimate. Some traveled into the neighboring British Mandate state of Transjordan to use it as a base from where they could fight the French, while others stayed in Syria to battle the colonial power at home. A third option was to play Paris off against London to try and gain leverage with French authorities.[34]

The French understood they needed Bedouin support. The tribes not only made up a third of the population of the entire mandate territory, they oversaw the important trading route to Baghdad. The French adopted a dualistic approach toward them, using a mixture of co-option and coercion to get their way.[35] Over time, this strategy caused the decline of the Bedouins' nomadic way of life. It also set them at odds with some of their fellow Syrians and caused antagonism between Bedouin tribal sheikhs and nationalist leaders. As the French consolidated their rule, they granted tribal leaders seats in the parliament. They also provided them with legal protection by integrating tribal law into the Mandate System.[36] Because of this, when Syrian nationalists called for the end of French rule, Bedouin leaders boycotted the voting session.

By the time the French were forced out of Syria in the 1940s, the relationship between the Syrian nationalist movement and Bedouin tribal leaders was tainted with distrust and suspicion.[37] The Bedouins refused to submit to the central Syrian authority. But for the newly independent nation state, the special and separate status the French had given the Bedouins clashed with a unifying national project and the desire for modernization. The 1950 constitution called for the end of nomadism and the settlement of the Bedouins.[38] In 1956 a new bill in parliament set out to dilute tribal privileges.[39] Bedouin leaders responded by setting up a coalition, the *Kilat al-asha'ir* or Tribal Bloc.[40]

This coalition forced the authorities to amend the Law of the Tribes and take tribal demands into consideration. One such demand was that a tribe could only be struck off the list of nomads if at least two-thirds of its population had settled in urban areas. In such cases, the sheikh would be elected by the tribe rather than nominated by the interior ministry. But following the union of Syria and Egypt in 1958, President Gamal Abdel Nasser repealed the Law of the Tribes and the latter lost their special judicial status.[41] Many left for Saudi Arabia or Jordan. This slow exodus lasted until 1973.

The ascension of the Baathist regime in 1963 was another blow to tribal influence.[42] Land reforms brought in by the new regime redistributed the lands among members of the tribes. In the previous decades, tribal sheikhs had often taken advantage of their position to register communal tribal lands under their names, undermining tribal bonds of loyalty. The Baathists played on these divisions to break the social powers of the sheikhs presenting tribalism as a "primitive social state." The land reforms were therefore deliberately designed to disempower them.[43]

By 1970 the Baathists had split into two factions: one focused on developing socialist policies and supporting movements like the agrarian cooperatives; the other concentrated on strengthening the Syrian state and transforming it into a regional power that could stand up to Israel.[44] Hafez al-Assad belonged to the latter camp. To broaden support for his regime, Assad advocated national unity and invited the tribes that had left the country to return home.[45] He also called for ethnic and religious minorities (but not the Kurds) to play an active role in the political, economic, and social fabric of the country.

Assad then took traditional networks of patron-client relationship and reproduced them at the political level.[46] The new president swiftly placed his fellow Alawites in key government positions and based the national redistribution of resources on calculations of loyalty to his regime.[47] As the state security apparatus and the civilian bureaucracy expanded and deepened, the state was firmly in control of all economic opportunities. A growing number of the population came to depend on the state for employment and patronage.[48]

To access resources, communities had to pledge allegiance to the Assad regime. In an effort to co-opt the Bedouins, Assad bypassed the 1958 law that stripped them of their privileged status. In complete contrast to his predecessors, he encouraged the practice of traditional customary justice.[49] An alternative system of authority now emerged, one that depended on the Assad regime for its existence. When, in the early 1980s, the Syrian Muslim Brotherhood mounted a violent insurrection against Assad,[50] the regime crushed the Muslim Brotherhood thanks to intelligence it received from tribal leaders who were monitoring the influx of arms from Iraq to the insurgents. Tribal leaders also prevented their tribesmen from sheltering the Islamists.

Assad's son, Bashar, adopted a similar policy of support and patronage to the Bedouin tribes when he became president in 2000. But he did so only on an unofficial basis. So, although the authority of the Bedouins in the *Badia* continued to expand, that progress was not codified in law. It could therefore be removed at any time and for any (or no) reason. Not that the tribes had any immediate cause for concern: Bashar appointed Bedouin leaders to high-ranking posts in the ministry of agriculture and the various presidential offices.

These unofficial arrangements paralleled the official language of the regime where the word "tribe" is often replaced with words like stakeholder or community.[51] There are no public statistics on the size of the Bedouin community in the country. While they are said to represent only 5 to 7 percent of the total pre–civil war population of Syria, in 2015 they were disproportionately represented in parliament. Twelve percent (30 out of 250 members) were Bedouins, another sign of the president's unofficial patronage.[52]

In 2012, after Defense Minister Dawoud Rajiha was assassinated in a bombing in Damascus, Bashar al-Assad appointed Fahd Jassem al-Freij, a Sunni Muslim with a tribal background, as his successor.[53] This was part of a preestablished pattern. Like his father, Bashar not only relied on Alawites to fill top regime positions but also forged alliances with tribal leaders and minorities in general. He even co-opted the tribes into the security services.[54] This investment has paid off. Although the Assad ruling family has not co-opted all the tribes, they have succeeded in establishing a patron-client relationship with some of the major ones by giving them a stake in state institutions.

The returns on the Assads' investments were substantial. As mentioned above, the tribes helped Assad Senior put down an armed rebellion against his regime by the Muslim Brotherhood in the early 1980s. In a similar vein, a number of tribes were helpful to Bashar's regime in the wake of the 2011 uprising. In the beginning, many supported the rebels in their struggle to oust him but have since rowed back from that position due to a combination of war-weariness and disillusionment with the rebels. Other tribes, however, have taken a very different view.

Tribes have been involved from the very start of the Syrian war. The beginning of the conflict can be traced back to a series of peaceful protests on March 15, 2011, that followed the detention and torture of fifteen children for writing antiregime slogans on the wall of their school in Dara'a. With tensions rising between the city's inhabitants and the security forces, a tribal delegation met with Atef Najeeb, the head of the political security branch in Dara'a. Najeeb was known for his brutality and was disliked by the people of the province.[55] As the tribal leaders awaited Najeeb's arrival, they removed their headbands as a mark of respect for him.[56] Najeeb responded by throwing them in the trash. His gesture offended the tribal leaders and epitomized the regime's disrespect for local communities.

The brutal response of the security services to the protests was filmed and watched by millions of Syrians. The murder of peaceful activists triggered more demonstrations across the country. Tribal leaders initially tried to prevent their people from participating in antiregime protests in order to protect them from police brutality. But deepening repression by the security forces provoked more anger and led to greater participation in the protests. Facing security forces armed to the teeth, protests became riots. The uprising subsequently militarized. In some provinces, members of the same tribe fought on opposite sides, a scenario that increased tensions within the tribe. Meanwhile, the Assad regime tried to co-opt tribal leaders by showering them with money, cars, and land, in a tactic that has proven particularly successful in the north and east of the country.

In contrast, the opposition represented by the Syrian National Council has refrained from using tribal networks and only rarely mentions tribes and their role in the struggle against the regime.[57] Even so, some tribal leaders who oppose Assad have organized meetings abroad with the aim of unifying the tribal movement and building up international legitimacy in case the regime falls. This tribal opposition formed a coalition known as the Syrian Arab Tribes Council to work with the Syrian National Council.[58]

Tribes opposed to Assad have long turned to their wider networks for help. As Syria, Jordan, Saudi Arabia, and Iraq witnessed cross-waves of tribal migration during the twentieth century, tribes in Syria have connections across the region. As the fighting escalated, tribes with cousins in the Gulf contacted them to ask for support.[59] They urged them to pressure their governments to intervene and provide protection to their fellow tribesmen.[60]

Qatar also set up large networks with various tribes, providing them with finance and arms, and started to use events such as the annual Palmyra camel race to expand its client network.[61] As well as help from Qatar and Saudi Arabia, Jordan and Kuwait are also said to have used tribal networks to move weapons and materials into Syria.[62] In total, Kuwaitis, Qataris, Saudis, Turks, and others, backed by the Americans, have given hundreds of millions of US dollars in aid and military hardware to the Free Syrian Army, an umbrella grouping for the nationalist opposition.[63]

Likewise, Iran and Hezbollah became involved, but for the other side. They have shed blood and treasure to prevent the collapse of the Assad regime. In this way, Syria has become a battlefield for regional powers to wage their proxy wars. The fierce rivalry between Iran and Saudi Arabia has played itself out on Syrian streets with a vengeance. Although Iran and Saudi Arabia primarily vie for influence and power, their rivalry has taken on sectarian dimensions. Both have utilized subnational identities, including the tribes, to gain strategic advantage in Iraq, Syria, Yemen, and beyond.[64]

The tribal connections that exist across the region have exacerbated tensions beyond Syria. Syrian tribes tracing their lineage to Iraq fled the violence and sought refuge in their tribal home. Some of these tribes hoped to be reunited with their distant relatives in Iraq. The Iraqi state, however, hosted them in schools and government buildings and then deployed the army and police to lay siege to the buildings. Thousands of Iraqis marched to al-Qaim to denounce the treatment of their Syrian relatives by the government in Baghdad.[65] As a compromise, the Iraqi authorities requested that families provide written guarantees they could look after their Syrian relatives.

In other instances, the stream of Syrian rebels taking refuge in Iraq has angered some tribes. In these cases, members of different tribes have killed refugees, a development that has divided the Iraqi people even further. These intertribal tensions are yet another example of how intertwined the Syrian and Iraqi conflicts are and how each one continues to impact the other.

Alternative Forms of Identity II: Tribe and State in Iraq

Iraq, like Syria, has a strong tradition of tribal identity. Three-quarters of the Iraqi people are members of one of the country's 150 tribes. Tribes have traditionally lived in rural areas and worked in agriculture and nomadic activities. For the most part, each tribe comprises around 2,000 smaller clans of varying size and influence. Their members encompass the whole of society, including Sunnis, Shia, Kurds, and other ethnic minorities.[66]

From the nineteenth century onward, branches of different tribes left the land and established themselves in the cities. This shift significantly weakened the entire tribal system. Until then, rural tribes had defined their identity in opposition to the urban way of life. In the city, tribal law no longer held sway and members were obliged to live under the writ of the central government.

It was a new twist to an old story. From the Ottoman era to the mid-1990s, every central administration in Iraq had fought hard to suppress tribal power. They were unwilling to tolerate an alternative power base, especially one that commanded such loyalty among its members. To weaken the tribes, the Ottoman Empire resorted to the tactic of divide and rule and frequently used intertribal rivalries to quell rebellions. (Aside from intertribal rivalries, there were also tensions between agricultural tribes who had settled and nomadic tribes who wanted to continue their pastoralist way of life.) The Ottoman authorities built several cities to force tribes to settle and, in doing so, made them economically dependent on the central administration.[67]

The co-option of tribal chiefs into state institutions was part of this process and gradually opened up a credibility gap between the sheikhs and their tribal members. Farmers became landless and increasingly dependent on the sheikhs who owned the land and leased it back to them for a profit. By behaving this way, the sheikhs were no longer seen as acting in the interests of their community. These Ottoman policies, along with competition over scarce resources like water, increased intertribal feuds. In this context, Shi'ism offered a new symbolic framework within which tribes could reformulate their relationships. Many saw Shi'ism as the perfect way to oppose the Ottoman policy of enforcing reliance on Sunni Islam.

In spite of these setbacks, tribes succeeded in retaining a measure of autonomy throughout the Ottoman era. The British mandate, however, was a different story. The British administration in Iraq did its best to weaken the power of tribes further. Moreover, the newly drawn borders between Iran, Iraq, Syria, and Turkey divided major Iraqi tribes and almost ended nomadism as a way of life.[68] Like the Ottomans, the British favored educated, urban Sunni Iraqis, and these well-off Sunnis started to distance themselves from their rural counterparts and, even more radically, from Shias.[69]

The cumulative effect of the centralizing policies of successive regimes was soon felt. By the time the state of Iraq was established in the 1920s, provincial tribal leaders had lost most of their influence.[70] The failure of these leaders to represent the interests of their tribal clients, along with the rising power of the urban Sunni elite, prevented them from becoming legitimate and influential political actors. Sunni tribesmen aligned instead with the Sunni elite and joined state institutions. Eventually, they would come to form the backbone of the Iraqi army and security apparatus. For them, national identity took precedence over tribal identity. Rural Sunnis soon came to the same conclusion. The professional and economic opportunities on offer to people from rural areas who worked for the state led them to emphasize the new national identity at the expense of their tribal identity. They believed their interests increasingly lay with the state.

The Shia saw it differently. To them, the army was a threat to their autonomy and most rejected being drafted to its ranks.[71] From 1935 to 1937, tribal uprisings took place in Shia areas led by sheikhs who had not gained a role in the new state following the 1920 revolution.[72] The army crushed these revolts, thus weakening the tribal system and leading many Shia to join the army and other state institutions. With the Shia integrating into the state system, the influence of the tribes as a political force decreased further. The rapid process of urbanization all but finished it off.

In the mid-twentieth century, landless peasants moved in increasing numbers to the cities. When the Iraqi Republic was declared in 1958, the tribal system had been pushed to the very margins of power. On a social level, however, tribal networks of social solidarity proved useful to the peasants migrating to the cities. These networks provided new migrants with connections, housing, financial help, and protection.

The new urbanized elite viewed the tribes as an outdated institution opposed to modernization. These prejudices were reflected in state policy. The state stopped tribal regulations and privileges and the 1958 land reforms were designed to emasculate the power of the sheikhs by depriving them of their land. But this antitribal sentiment among the newly empowered Republican elite did not last long, and the latent power of the tribes soon made itself felt.

Someone else took note of the power of the tribes: Saddam Hussein. From the late 1980s, after the devastating effects of his invasion of Iran and the bloodshed that followed had undermined the power of the Iraqi state, Saddam began a deeper process of retribalization.[73] He placed people from his own tribe, the *Al-Bu Nasir* of 'Auja in key positions, a process he accelerated after his catastrophic decision to invade Kuwait in 1990 and the defeat he suffered at the hands of the Americans in 1991. After this disastrous defeat, Saddam Hussein surrounded himself with an inner circle whom he could trust and established a network of tribal nepotism.

His retribalization process focused on staffing the security forces, including the army, the elite Republican Guard, the police, and security-related posts, with people the dictator believed were utterly loyal to him.[74] As the state struggled to perform basic services and pay its civil servants, it increasingly had to rely on tribes to provide internal security. As a result, tribes loyal to Saddam Hussein were put in charge of public order. Not all tribes, however, collaborated with the regime. In the 1990s, an alliance of tribes led by the *Jabbur*, *'Ubeid*, and *Dulaim* confederations allegedly hatched a plot to overthrow Saddam Hussein.[75]

Opportunity knocked again for the tribes after the US-led invasion and occupation of Iraq in 2003. The dismantling of state institutions, including the army, created an institutional and social vacuum the tribes could fill. Here, too, the state proved pivotal in the resurgence of tribalism. Between 2003 and 2006, tribes either fought the state or fought for it.[76]

The Bush administration recruited tribes from the Sunni triangle to expel AQI from their lands. Organized under the banner of the Sons of

Iraq or the Awakening Councils, Sunni tribes were decisive in breaking the military backbone of AQI and shoring up the fragile state. But in Baghdad, the Shia-dominated Maliki government was suspicious of these Sunni Councils and refused to honor American promises to integrate their fighters into the Iraqi security forces.[77] Maliki's discriminatory policies alienated the Sunni community, particularly those tribesmen who had risked so much to defend the state. The prime minister's decision provoked a backlash that allowed AQI to rise from the ashes and to recruit Sunni tribes into their ranks. This time, though, the target was Baghdad.

It would be misleading, however, to portray the Sunni tribes as passive spectators in the unfolding drama in Iraq or as contractors doing the bidding of foreign occupiers or insurgent groups. The tribes possess agency and act to advance the interests of their community. Known for their pragmatism and cold-blooded realism, tribesmen are steely negotiators and tough fighters who have survived centuries by warding off foes, both foreign and domestic. The tribes are survivors. They are clear-eyed about what is good and bad for their interests. Seeing the new order installed by the Americans as hostile to their community, the Sunni tribes initially welcomed armed insurgent groups with open arms and spearheaded the resistance against the coalition forces. Sunni Iraqis fought for a say in the new political order and to force the Americans to take their grievances seriously. As the tribes and insurgent groups shared the same goals of resisting foreign occupation and defending the homeland, they concluded a marriage of convenience.

But the honeymoon between the tribes and the Americans was short-lived. American military officers and diplomats in Baghdad had made promises to the tribes they knew they could not deliver. Delivery depended on the whims and ambitions of one man: the prime minister, Nuri al-Maliki, whose divisive sectarian agenda ruled out integrating the Sunnis into state institutions. By the time the Obama administration pulled all US troops out of Iraq in 2011, the Sunni tribes were on the verge of open revolt against the Maliki regime. Many tribesmen rejoined paramilitary groups, including the newly revitalized AQI, which, as we have seen, had rebranded itself as the Islamic State of Iraq in 2006. The deepening polarization of Iraq coincided with the Arab Spring uprisings in neighboring countries. By then some of the Sunni tribes had declared war on Maliki's sectarian-led regime.

The deliberate estrangement of the Sunni tribes in Iraq, together with the civil war in Syria, provided the fuel that powered the spectacular rise of the Islamic State. The Islamic State is an identity-driven organization par excellence. Sectarianism is its oxygen. Abu Bakr al-Baghdadi and his members milked Sunni grievances to their advantage and played on a sense of victimhood within the Sunni community. IS portrayed themselves as the steadfast guardians and protectors of that community.

Some of the Sunni tribes either went along for the ride or believed that Baghdadi's combatants were the most effective weapon against their nemesis in Baghdad, Nuri al-Maliki. The revival of IS caused consternation among US officials and sent them back to the drawing board, desperately trying to reassemble a tribal coalition like they had done before. But, once again, the United States faced fierce opposition from Baghdad's Shia-dominated authorities who remained wary of empowering the Sunnis.

What all of this shows is how much the political balance of power has shifted against the tribes. Pressed between the rock of the sectarian-led government in Baghdad and the hard place of the Salafi-jihadists, tribal leaders were stuck. They could no longer protect their communities and act as their interlocutor with the outside world. And even though the United States and regional powers tried to recruit them to fight IS and Al-Qaeda and to reinvigorate them as a counterweight to the Shia-dominated order in Baghdad, the obstacles to doing this are substantial. In spite of American efforts since 2014, the Sunni tribes have been much less effective in the fight against IS than they were against AQI. The spectacular rise of IS weakened the Sunni tribes and may have led to their permanent decline as a political force.

Subnational Identities and the Arab Spring Uprisings

The fracturing of the state institutions in the Arab Middle East since the 2010–2012 Arab Spring uprisings are both the reason for, as well as the consequence of, the dominance of subnational identities in the region. Subnational identities, whether religious, ethnic, or tribal, are much older than the state system itself. But these long-held identities did not wither away under the weight of the nation-state. On the contrary, they reemerged and regrouped because so many leaders of these nation-states nurtured them for their own political gain. Authoritarian regimes have been only too happy to use identities other than the nation to legitimize their rule and/or to divide society and prevent the development of a politically active population. This strategy is a virtual carbon copy of the old colonial strategy of divide and rule.

The resurgence of subnational identities is not therefore a result of people's rejection of existing borders or the nation-state. Instead, these secondary identities have been used as a tool of resistance against the state or as a means to co-opt specific groups and communities by the state. Islamist groups and nonstate actors have used religion, sectarianism, and tribalism to gain strategic advantage, including soft power (ideational and moral ascendancy) and hard power (physical strength), over their rivals. In recent years, foreign powers have also used subnational identities as a way of achieving their goals in the region.

The result of these power plays and outside interventions is that modern political identities, such as citizenship and the rule of law, have not been allowed to take hold in the Arab world. As long as the primary concern of ruling elites (and their foreign patrons) is to remain in power for life, political culture and civil society will continue to be impoverished. The use of religion, tribalism, and ethnicity has been counterproductive and even politically catastrophic: the central state is weak and Islamist groups are the only viable opposition that retain a measure of popular legitimacy and whose political program claims to transcend tribal and ethnic politics. Yet political Islamists are as tribal as their rivals.

The resurgence of tribalism in Iraq, Syria, and beyond is a part of the same pattern. Used informally by regimes and foreign powers, tribalism has provided citizens and Islamist groups with an organizational framework that proved popular and efficient because of the many national and transnational connections the tribes have. Tribes have also, when it suited them, allied with rulers, thus shoring up their legitimacy at the popular level and helping to sustain these fragile ruling elites.

At present, political identity in the Middle East and North Africa is driven both formally and informally by states, religious groups, and non-state actors. And by foreign powers who act through these groups. What all of these actors have in common is that they take agency away from the people by continuing to employ divide-and-rule tactics.

The first wave of the Arab Spring, with its calls for justice, freedom, and dignity, was supposed to change that. The protesters wanted more than the downfall of the people in the old regime. They wanted a whole new system of *ideas*. One where inclusive political concepts like citizenship and civil society, which are culturally and socially neutral, replace the divisive outdated and failed policies of divide and conquer.

11

The Arab Spring Crushed

"IF YOU DON'T SEE ME, I will burn myself."[1]

These are the words that twenty-six-year-old Mohammed Bouazizi is reported to have said as he stood outside the governor's office in his hometown of Sidi Bou Zid, Tunisia, on Friday, December 17, 2010. The act of burning, or self-immolation, has gained a symbolic weight across North Africa in recent years.[2] The term "*harraga*" (or burning) comes from the Algerian word "*harga*" (to burn). It has been used to describe the destitute young people who are willing to risk their lives to reach Europe.[3] Harraga literally means to burn the frontiers and has come to represent the idea of traveling illegally, often in makeshift boats or under a truck, and the act of burning your identity papers before leaving home.

The latter has become a ritual, a symbolic act of rebellion against a corrupt, unjust system, and the rejection of a bleak future that offers nothing. It is not only your identity papers you are burning; it is your old life, the old version of you. With daily life becoming increasingly synonymous with degradation, indignity, and hopelessness, an alarmingly large number of young people in the Arab world feel they have nothing left to lose.

The book is now turning most fully to the third key force in the book's analytical framework, the agency of the people. The Arab Spring represented a direct challenge to both foreign intervention and domestic authoritarianism. As I point out later, the very geographic breadth of the Arab Spring uprisings indicates that popular dissatisfaction transcends the sectarian identities that have been used to divide and rule the region for over a century.

The Arab Spring Revisited: The Triggers

In the wake of Mohammed Bouazizi's death, protests in his memory and against Ben Ali's corrupt police state spread across Tunisia.[4] They were a spontaneous reaction to years of political oppression, economic injustice, and systematic deprivation. In the West, Tunisia had been feted for years as a model of liberalization and secularism. But beneath the surface, Ben Ali's regime had zero tolerance for dissent and cared nothing about the grave socioeconomic plight facing the Tunisian people. After coming to power in a bloodless coup that ousted the authoritarian president Habib Bourguiba in 1987, Ben Ali promised to respect people's rights and accept constitutional limits on the length (and number) of presidential terms.

But his promises of a more open political system turned out to be short-lived.[5] By the early 1990s, he came down hard against the Islamist opposition and targeted members of the Ennahda Party. (Ennahda was the Tunisian branch of the Muslim Brotherhood, though the group has now shed its Egyptian roots and developed its own identity). Ennahda enjoyed popular support because of its work in the community. In Ben Ali's eyes, that made them a threat. Between 1990 and 1992, he had at least 8,000 of their members jailed.[6]

In 1989 and 1994, Ben Ali was the only candidate in the presidential elections. He received 99 percent of the vote. In 1999, he again obtained 99 percent in spite of allowing two minor politicians to run against him. In 2002, under his orders, parliament removed the constitutional limit of three consecutive presidential mandates and replaced it with an age limit of seventy-five years for any president. These new rules meant that if someone took office in their thirties or forties, that person would effectively become a president for life.

In 2004, Ben Ali won with 94.5 percent of the vote. (One of his hand-picked rivals declared he had voted for him.[7]) In 2009, his vote dipped slightly but still hovered just under 90 percent. When the Sidi Bou Zid protests broke out in December 2010, Ben Ali was again preparing to change the constitution in his favor so he could bypass the age limit and serve yet another term in office.[8] It would be his sixth.

Ben Ali relied on the police to crack down on any dissent. The ministry of the interior was his weapon of choice to execute his political ambitions. In contrast to the police, the Tunisian military is small and does not play a role in political life. State-sponsored killings and disappearances of dissidents were not as widespread in Tunisia as in the military regimes of Egypt, Iraq, Libya, and Syria. The Ben Ali regime focused on imprisoning political opponents for long periods of time and denying them due process. This corruption of the justice system was mirrored in political life. Nepotism and patronage pervaded the entire political system. Ben Ali milked the system for his own benefit and that of his wife and her family. He siphoned hundreds of millions of US dollars (some say billions) from state funds and hid the money in foreign bank accounts.

Social discontent had been rising in Tunisia for years before the uprising in 2010 because of the decadently luxurious life of the ruling elite, particularly those closest to the president and his wife. The gradual dismantling of the public sector, coupled with the retreat of the state from the health and education sectors, along with the burden of youth unemployment, had consolidated the gap between the political and business elite and the people.

The authoritarian regimes of the postindependence Middle East have reproduced, often using the same strategies, the repression of colonialism. The Arab Spring then can be seen as a second bubbling up of popular resentment that, it is to be hoped, prefigures a second chance to build government in the Middle East according to the principles of self-determination, representation, inclusivity, and a vision of citizenship that supersedes sectarian identity.

Indeed, the Arab Spring protests were a unifying experience. All sectors of society took part in the protests: laborers, peasants, factory workers, civil servants, intellectuals, unions, opposition parties, the middle class, even members of the security services.[9] In Tunisia, the revolts broke out in urban and rural areas where there were high concentrations of people living in severe poverty. Until this point, they had felt disempowered and disenfranchised. Working-class people in particular had suffered because of the elite's broken promises and the deteriorating economic situation. Their struggle to feed their families had become an impossible task. The protests brought these disparate groups together with a new, common purpose.

If Mohammed Bouazizi's self-immolation was the catalyst for mass protests in Tunisia, in Egypt the trigger was the death of twenty-eight-year-old Khaled Said in the Sidi Gaber area of Alexandria. Two policemen dragged Khaled from an Internet café and beat him to death because he had taken pictures of them sharing the spoils of a drug deal.[10] At first, the police tried to portray Khaled as a junkie who had died from drug ingestion.[11] But Khaled's brother managed to snap pictures of the young man's bruised and battered body in the morgue. He then circulated them online.

The pictures of Khaled Said's violated body went viral. They caused outrage and prompted protests that lasted for a year. During these protests, the slogan "We are all Khaled Said" became a powerful rallying cry because his experience resonated with a large part of the Egyptian population, especially with its sizable youth. In theory, freedom of expression is guaranteed by Egypt's constitution (Articles 45, 47, and 48), but in practice, the country had been under a state of emergency since the assassination of Anwar al-Sadat in 1981. These emergency laws were used to curtail freedom of expression, suppress civil liberties, and stifle political dissent. The massive protests in honor of Khaled spread, and inspired by events in Tunisia, they gathered enough momentum to place sustained pressure on Mubarak and force his ousting.[12]

In Syria in February 2011, protests started in Daraa, a remote, rural region near the Jordanian border known for its underdevelopment. The protests were sparked by the arrest, detention, and torture of a number of schoolchildren. They had daubed antiregime graffiti on a school wall. When their families went to the police station to obtain their release, security officials laughed at them and refused to provide any information.[13] As news of the torture of the children spread, so did popular anger. Within days, protests were organized in Daraa and Damascus. The Assads, father and son, were well known for their use of torture to deter dissent.[14] So it came as no surprise to Syrians that true to form, Bashar al-Assad, struck the protesters with an iron fist and in the process, transformed a peaceful uprising into an armed conflict.[15] The subsequent internationalization of the conflict, especially the influx of Al-Qaeda and IS combatants, led to the all-out civil war that ravaged the country.

In Libya, things also took a turn toward violence as Colonel Muammar Gaddafi's forty-two-year rule came to an end. Gaddafi used armed mercenaries to crush the peaceful revolt and sought to sow confusion and chaos in a last attempt to divide and conquer. He described protesters as "rats" and "cockroaches" who should be "slaughtered" for their disloyalty.[16] As the Libyan ruler threatened to hunt down protesters "street by street" and "alley by alley" in a speech that was meant to instill fear (but was later set to a dance track by a DJ to satirize the Libyan leader), violence spiraled across the country and triggered a UN-authorized NATO intervention to protect civilians. Gaddafi went into hiding but was eventually found by rebels and beaten up, sexually assaulted, tortured, and killed, all on camera.[17]

There is no mystery about the recent implosions of Arab countries following the Arab Spring. For decades, dictators imposed a veil of national unity on the countries they ruled. But that veil has now been ripped apart and the deep rifts between state and society and within society itself are plain to see. The lifting of repression has allowed provincial loyalties and subnational identities to resurface and compete for influence. Under the dictators, there was no strong unifying national myth around which all these competing tendencies could coalesce. A deep institutional crisis and a complete vacuum of ideas pushed these states even closer to the brink of collapse. Yemen is a case in point. Burdened by decades of dictatorship, crony capitalism, failed development, and with a social structure on the verge of disintegration, nowhere encapsulates the dynamics of the Arab uprisings the way Yemen does.

The Arab Spring Decoded: Yemen

In November 2011, President Ali Abdullah Saleh agreed to resign after months of popular protests against his thirty-two-year rule. Yemen had been in tatters long before the Arab Spring erupted. Almost from the moment of its inception, the country had been suffering from a toxic mix of severe poverty, political instability, and tribal warfare. The

Republic of Yemen was created in 1990 after the unification of the Arab Yemen Republic (North Yemen) and the People's Democratic Republic of Yemen (South Yemen). But in spite of initial hopes, reunification did not resolve the long-standing problems accumulated over decades between the two Yemens. In 1994, a brief civil war erupted between loyalists to the North and separatists from the South that resulted in the defeat of the Southern separatists and deepened the mistrust between North and South.

Internal problems in both parts of Yemen, as well as the ever-present North-South divide, complicated the political landscape even further. Immediately after reunification Saleh tried to co-opt the Southern elite, but tensions—and suspicions—lingered. In the 2000s an umbrella protest movement of Southern factions known as the *Hirak* called for regional autonomy.[18]

The situation in the North has also been problematic. In the same years, the area has seen more than its fair share of infighting as government forces and their tribal Salafi allies took on Shia Houthi insurgents. The Houthis succeeded in making important territorial gains around their ancestral home in the Sa'ada governorate.[19] But the human cost was immense: by 2010, up to 300,000 people had been displaced internally by the fighting.

Another problem was the distribution of power. The unification agreement promised a multiparty system and free elections, but Saleh, who had ruled North Yemen since 1978, hoarded power in his own hands. Throughout his thirty-two years as president, he established a complex system of patronage that took in military, tribal, clerical, and business leaders, and played the tribes off against each other. Saleh even colluded with extremist groups like Al-Qaeda to gain strategic advantage against Southern separatists and other enemies.[20] Soon, loyalists of the president could be found in all sectors of society, including government agencies, the business sector, the tribes, and the religious establishment.

Just as Syria's Hafez al-Assad had done with his son Bashar, Egypt's Hosni Mubarak had planned to do with his son Gamal, and Libya's Muammar Gaddafi with his son Saif, reports suggested Saleh was grooming his son Ahmad Ali, the commander of the elite Republican Guards, to succeed him.[21] This caused a rift with Saleh's supporters outside his family circle because, not surprisingly, they felt sidelined and disadvantaged.[22]

Politically, the General People's Congress (GPC) dominated Yemen. However, the GPC's main task was not to work on behalf of the people of Yemen but to defend the president against all enemies.[23] Members of the Congress included Arab nationalists, Islamists, tribal leaders, and public intellectuals from both the Left and the Right. Opposition parties remained marginal although many were co-opted by the regime, including the *Isla*, which was established in 1990 from a conservative coalition of tribal leaders, businessmen, and factions from the Muslim Brotherhood.

A particularly potent weapon in his arsenal to monopolize power was his relationship with the United States. After the September 11, 2011, attacks on the American homeland, Yemen became a key country in the US Global War on Terror. This allowed Saleh to extract precious resources from the Americans in return for giving the United States a free hand in Yemen to battle Al-Qaeda and its supporters. Although the Bush and Obama administrations knew Saleh was complicit in offering sanctuary to radical Islamists over the years, they turned a blind eye to his corruption and authoritarianism.[24]

When mass protests erupted against Saleh in 2011, most political parties still had a vested interest in maintaining the old order. Most of the popular dissent therefore came from informal sociopolitical movements that operated at the margins of the political system. The Houthis and the southern Hirak movement were the most active dissidents.[25] Both had decried the rise of Saleh's autocracy and lamented the lack of economic investment in their underdeveloped areas. In addition to economic and political grievances, the Houthis and Hirak had different outlooks on identity than Saleh and his cronies. The Houthis were (and still are) fiercely independent and are determined to defend their Zaydi identity, which they believe is endangered by ultraconservative Salafis operating in their area.[26]

Likewise, Southerners who make up the Hirak movement believe their identity is incompatible with the dominant tribal structure of the North. These tensions were present long before the Arab Spring. But over the years, Saleh's divide-and-rule tactics exacerbated them so much that he turned them into a time bomb just waiting for the moment to explode. The Arab Spring was that moment.

The Arab Spring protests started in Yemen after Mubarak was ousted from power in Egypt. Across the Arab world, Mubarak was seen as untouchable: the ultimate immovable object. His departure showed anything was possible. A coalition of young people, nongovernmental organizations (NGOs), and democracy activists seized the moment and took to the streets calling for Saleh to go. As was the case with the Muslim Brotherhood in Egypt, Yemen's main Islamist party, the Islah, did not initially participate in the protests. But as the protests gained momentum, more formal opposition parties like Islah joined in, even though the activists who started the protests were suspicious of their ambiguous relationship with the Saleh regime.[27] It was widely reported that Islah tried to hijack the uprisings and force the democracy activists out of the public squares. Tensions and fistfights were soon taking place between rival groups of protesters.

In June 2011, a bombing in a mosque in the presidential compound seriously injured Saleh. The president was flown to Saudi Arabia for medical treatment, leaving the country in limbo and the political crisis unresolved. His son, Ahmad, moved to the presidential palace, but anti-Saleh forces continued to organize. On March 18, 2012, military snipers killed more than fifty demonstrators and injured dozens more. The viciousness of the repression shook the political establishment out of its complacency. Within days, the number of high-level defections multiplied. Ministers of parliament (MPs), diplomats, tribal leaders, and military officers withdrew their support for the president and joined the protesters. But as the protests intensified, so too did the violence.

Three months after his injury, Saleh returned to Yemen. But with no resolution to the raging conflict in sight, his loyalists were now openly confronting opposition militias on the streets. The United States continued to send contradictory messages regarding the future of Yemen and its ruler. The Obama administration nevertheless offered him a dignified way out and immunity from prosecution, allowing him to keep the billions of US dollars he had plundered during his decades at the helm of the Arab world's poorest country.[28]

On the ground, clashes were occurring with increasing frequency, and the Gulf Cooperation Council (GCC), led by Saudi Arabia, now stepped in. The GCC, backed by the United States and the European Union (EU), pushed for a deal that would see Saleh leave. They held consultations with high-ranking figures in Yemen, including Saleh, Ali Mohsen, and members of the influential al-Ahmar tribe. The Joint Meeting Parties, an alliance of opposition parties created in 2002, was also consulted. But other parties were noticeable by their absence. Key stakeholders, like the Houthis in the north, the Hirak in the south, and democracy activists, were excluded from the negotiations. Saudi Arabia was prepared to see a change of personnel in the leadership of its southern neighbor but not a change of regime, fearing the empowerment of rival non-Sunni groups like the Houthis or democracy activists.

Saleh played for time but finally bowed to the inevitable and left in November 2011. Power was then transferred to Saleh's close ally and vice president Abd-Rabbu Mansour Hadi and elections were held in February 2012. In a move that showed how little things had really changed, Hadi was the only candidate.

In theory, a framework now existed for national dialogue. This would allow for changes to the constitution, reforms in the military and security apparatus, and new presidential elections to be held in 2014. But the GCC deal and the departure of Saleh merely reshuffled the existing political system. The only change was in the balance of power within the ruling elite. With Saleh gone, members of the political establishment and their rivals started to fight over privileges and resources. Although the Saleh camp had been weakened, its opponents did not fully capitalize on his absence. President Hadi lacked an independent power base of his own and he faced an array of enemies. His authority was fatally undermined by attacks from a number of quarters: Al-Qaeda in the Arabian Peninsula (AQAP); southern separatists; Saleh loyalists, and Houthi rebels. Economic decline and spiraling corruption were the final nails in the coffin. Hadi's already fragile presidency was unable to withstand such sustained pressure.

In September 2014, a coalition of disparate forces that included parts of the military, as well as civilians disillusioned with the GCC deal, joined

Houthi rebels from the north and stormed the capital Sa'na forcing the Hadi government to retreat.

Saudi Arabia, however, was determined to defend the GCC deal and curb what it saw as rising Iranian influence over the Houthis on its southern border in Yemen. In March 2015, the kingdom formed a coalition of Arab states and launched a military campaign to push the Shia Houthis back and restore Hadi to power. Since then, the country has been split between Houthi-controlled territory in the west and north and areas controlled by the government and its Saudi backers in the south and east.

The old North-South divide escalated into another war within the war where Southern separatists, who were part of the Saudi-led coalition, seized the city of Aden from Yemen's internationally recognized government in August 2019. Although Southern separatists battle the Houthis, they have their own agenda of establishing an independent state in south Yemen, an ambition that tears Yemen further apart.[29]

The UN and human rights organizations have accused all belligerents of committing human rights violations in the course of this war. As a result, the region's poorest country is in the process of dying a "slow death."[30] Thousands of civilians have been killed, thousands more injured, and more than two million people have been displaced. During the first two years of the conflict, a third of the deaths were children. Food is scarce. According to the United Nations Office for the Coordination of Humanitarian Affairs (OCHA), seven million people in Yemen are on the brink of starvation and 2.3 million children under the age of five are suffering from malnutrition. Infrastructure has collapsed under the weight of repeated bombings by the Saudi-led coalition. The Saudis insist they do not intentionally target civilians but their sophisticated Western-supplied military aircraft have, on a number of occasions, dropped bombs on non-military buildings. They assert the Houthis hide in plain sight among the civilian population.

The collapse of the health care system, along with an acute shortage of water and electricity, has made Yemen vulnerable to a new threat: cholera.[31] In a three-month period in 2017, cholera killed more than 2,000 people and infected half a million more, making it one of the worst outbreaks in recent memory.[32] The humanitarian situation continues to deteriorate by the day, making Yemen one of the greatest humanitarian crises in the world, the worst humanitarian crisis after World War II.

From the outset, the odds were against the Arab Spring succeeding in Yemen. Human rights and democracy activists faced insurmountable challenges in their quest for freedom and justice. Entrenched special interests within Yemen colluded with regional and international powers to thwart change. The protesters were on their own from the start. They had little or no backing from formal oppositional parties aligned with the Saleh regime. These parties were part of the problem not part of the solution. Even when the most powerful opposition party, the Islamist group Islah, belatedly joined the protests, it tried to dominate the political space and force the democracy activists out.

The Yemeni civil war has shown the detrimental effects of regional and international actors on local conflicts in the Middle East. The Gulf states were more concerned with ending the violence on the streets than with addressing calls for reform. Conservative regimes by their very nature do not encourage change. The Obama administration was also more interested in easing Saleh out of power peacefully than in facilitating any meaningful political transition. Regional and global powers alike sought to maintain the status quo. Their actions, whether by accident or design, privileged Saleh and his allies, including Hadi, and disadvantaged the young people so desperate for change who were at the mercy of the powers that be. The Houthis went on the offensive and took control of the capital Sa'na in September 2014. Ever since Yemen has become a battlefield of Saudi-Iranian geostrategic rivalry, which, in the decade following the Arab Spring uprisings, reached its peak.

If the aspirations of democracy activists and human rights advocates had been fulfilled, Yemen would not be where it is today—"The World's Worst Humanitarian Crisis"—and millions would have been spared the sort of suffering that should not be happening in the twenty-first century.[33] And Yemen would not be home to an increasingly resurgent Al-Qaeda. The recent escalation of fighting has allowed AQAP to gain more territories and influence by taking full advantage of shifting alliances, growing sectarianism, and a security vacuum. Despite the repeated killing of its top leaders by the United States, Al-Qaeda in the Arabian Peninsula is still alive today.

The Arab Spring Reinterpreted:
The End or a Beginning?

Which brings us to a very contentious question: did the Arab Spring fuel the rise of groups like Al-Qaeda in the Arabian Peninsula and the IS?

The expansion of AQAP in Yemen, as well as the rise of the IS in Syria and Iraq, is often seen as a direct result of the Arab Spring uprisings. In spite of the bravery shown by the people whose deaths triggered the protests and the courage of those who risked so much to keep them going, intellectuals, journalists, academics, and politicians alike now paint the Arab uprisings in a negative light. These opinion makers have framed the public debate in a way that makes the Arab Spring synonymous with the rise of the IS and therefore responsible for unleashing the sectarian tensions that threaten state and society across the region. Furthermore, some of these opinion makers are not content to dismiss the Arab Spring as a failure. They go further and decry the uprisings as a conspiracy hatched by external powers, particularly the United States, to control the destiny of the region.

But by caricaturing the protesters as unwitting tools of powerful external actors, they rob them of their agency. These prominent Arab poets, scholars, and public intellectuals of all persuasions belittle one of the most important moments of political emancipation in the modern Middle East.[34] Views like these, especially when expressed by well-known public intellectuals, validate the belief in conspiracy theories—a tendency already so widespread in the region that it needs no further encouragement.

This conspiratorial viewpoint not only dismisses the political will and agency of the protesters, it implicitly absolves authoritarian regimes of their responsibility in pauperizing Arab societies and sowing the seeds of extremism through their policies of divide and rule.

This crisis is not dissimilar to the current one facing the liberal elite in the West. In 2016, most of the liberal elite across the Western world did not predict the United Kingdom would vote to leave the EU or that billionaire businessman and reality TV star Donald J. Trump would win the American presidential election. In the same way that many of the opinion-forming elite in the Arab world failed to see the Arab Spring coming, their Western counterparts failed to see those results coming. And in both cases, a significant factor causing this lack of vision was the fact that the elite did not suffer from the economic problems that compelled so many people to demand political change.

In the aftermath of the Arab Spring, secularists and liberals across the Middle East have accused the Muslim Brothers and their allies of leading from behind and ultimately hijacking the revolts. Nationalists and Islamists, by contrast, see the United States behind the current turmoil. In other cases, everyone blames everyone else. Yet there is one common denominator in all these assumptions: they all agree the revolutions are responsible for the violence and civil wars that have shattered Arab lands and facilitated the rapid rise of the IS. These opinion makers draw a causal link between the popular protests and the subsequent ruptures in the region.

Nor have Western commentators proven immune to the lure of this "rise and fall" narrative. They, too, have joined the chorus lamenting the mutation of the Arab Spring into a dark, stormy Islamic Winter. In their coverage of the popular protests, the global media veered wildly from one extreme to another and dabbled in a great deal of wishful thinking and excessive expectations. When the myth of the Arab Spring (which was itself a media event) failed to materialize, Western commentators reverted to their previous binary narratives about the durability of authoritarianism and the prevalence of terrorism in the region. Context was the first casualty of the new struggle for power.

This bashing of the Arab Spring is not only misguided. It is fundamentally misleading. By their very nature, large-scale popular protests, uprisings, revolts, or revolutions, as they are interchangeably called, imply social struggle and contentious politics. The "spring" label distorts a complex reality in which millions of people had reached the end of their tether. An acute crisis of underdevelopment and decades of bad governance had pauperized a huge segment of the population and caused a rupture between them and the people who ruled over them.

Yet far from violent, the protesters distinguished themselves through their dignity and peacefulness.

And that, arguably, is the most significant fact of all. This was no jihad. There were no calls for a global caliphate. Al-Qaeda was conspicuous by its absence. Its poisonous rhetoric and slogans, including the establishment of Islamic states, were nowhere to be found. Hope, not despair, filled the air. This was a moment of great joy and even greater expectations. If the protesters could pull it off, they would prove once and for all that jihadism as a way to affect change was defunct. Their success would be Al-Qaeda's permanent failure.

It was also a moment of communal unity: a rejection of the divide-and-rule policies of old that pitted one community against another and institutionalized sectarianism. Protesters recognized the need for inclusivity. In Cairo, they carried banners proclaiming, "Not Muslim, Not Christian: Egyptian!" People were saying that a whole new kind of politics was needed.

In conclusion, the Arab Spring uprisings are *not* responsible for the mayhem in the Middle East. The reverse is true. It was the crushing of protests across the region that is responsible for today's violence and civil wars. Strongmen like Bashar al-Assad of Syria, Muammar Gaddafi of Libya, and Ali Abdullah Saleh of Yemen were the real culprits. They brutally put down popular protests, thus militarizing what was essentially a peaceful movement. By quashing any hope of peaceful change, Arab dictators sowed the seeds of today's chaos and were therefore responsible for the catastrophic consequences.

The strength and radicalism of Islamist nonstate actors is useful to domestic authoritarians, justifying their iron rule and helping them keep the popular will divided. Perhaps, rather than asking if the Arab Spring caused the rise in the IS, it is worth asking who gains from that rise? The bottom line is that the rise of the IS is only the most recent refrain in the perennial cycle of violence that keeps authoritarians in power and the people oppressed. The resurgence of the IS is a direct result of these dictators squashing the aspirations of millions of people.

But it has to be said that the dictators who trampled on the dreams of millions of their citizens and stopped democracy in its tracks could not have done it alone. Assad is a case in point. Although he and his father, Hafez, had built an ideological army and a lethal security apparatus whose core mission was to protect the Alawite minority-based regime, the son would not have survived by relying solely on his armed forces. He did not have to. The Islamic Republic of Iran, a self-styled revolutionary state, fought tooth and nail to shore him up, spending billions of dollars and losing hundreds of officers in the process. Iran also deployed highly skilled Hezbollah fighters in Syria. These battle-hardened fighters made a huge difference on the battlefield.

However, Iran on its own could not rescue Assad's sinking ship. By 2015, the opposition led by Jabhat al-Nusra (Al-Qaeda in the Levant) and Ahrar al-Sham, another Salafi-jihadist group, was on the verge of toppling Assad. They had captured territory near the heart of his ancestral home and were edging closer toward the capital Damascus when someone else came to Assad's rescue: Vladimir Putin. For a highly complex mix of historical, security, and geopolitical reasons, the Russian president decided to launch Moscow's first intervention in the Middle East since World War II. Russian military intervention tipped the scales in Assad's favor and allowed the regime and its allies to recapture key cities and towns, including Aleppo in December 2016, dealing a hard blow to the opposition and depriving it of one of its last remaining urban centers.

The United States has been no less complicit in shoring up strongmen in the Middle East and preserving the autocratic status quo at all costs.

Internal and external counterrevolutionary forces thus colluded to abort the Arab Spring uprisings, only temporarily. This caused the rupture in Iraq, Libya, Syria, Yemen, and elsewhere. This rupture opened the gates of hell and allowed nonstate actors and sectarian militias to emerge to try and fill the institutional and security vacuum. If the universal aspirations of the protesters had been fulfilled, the false promises of the IS would not have found so many receptive ears. The people are not at fault for the violent response of authoritarian elites or for the proliferation of armed gangs and terrorist groups. There is a direct correlation between the region's descent into tribalized violence and the silencing of the peaceful voices of the protesters.

As this book has tried to show throughout the history of the region, local power structures and foreign powers remain complicit in opposing self-determination and representative government for the people. In this, little has changed in a century of history.

The Arab Spring Is Not Over

The Arab state was in a mess long before Mohammed Bouazizi died in Tunisia and Khaled Said was murdered in Egypt. Likewise, Arab and Middle Eastern rulers had used sectarianism as a divide-and-control weapon in political life long before protesters took to the streets and the squares calling for the downfall of the regimes. The Arab Spring is responsible for neither. To claim otherwise is to ignore history.

The uprisings have not yet produced a truly revolutionary outcome because the demonstrators were more reformist than revolutionary. In his book *Revolution without Revolutionaries*, Asef Bayat points out the painful paradox of the Arab uprisings in coupling revolutionary mobilization with a reformist trajectory.[35] Although the protesters failed on both counts, it is far too early to pass an indictment on these titanic developments, as the triumph of the Syrian revolution against Assad in 2024 shows. The struggles of Arab youth and human rights activists are now inscribed in the collective consciousness. They cannot be wiped out or wished away. These aspirations are an integral part of the repertoire of political discourse and popular memory. They offer signposts for the next freedom wave. And the second wave of large-scale social protests, which burst out in 2019 and are still unfolding in Algeria, Iraq, Lebanon, and Sudan, are a case in point. Far from passive and dead, agency of the Arab youth is alive and well. Although the first wave was mostly crushed by the old regimes, their regional and Great Power patrons, and by radical Islamists like Al-Qaeda and the IS, it was premature to pen the obituary of the uprisings. The struggle for the political future of the Middle East, particularly Arab countries, will be long with ups and downs. Political transition is not linear. It will likely take multiple waves of revolts to bring about transformative change.

The derailment of the first wave of the Arab uprisings has extinguished the imminent possibility of a peaceful resolution to state-society rifts. It also increased the vulnerability of the Arab states to the pressures of centrifugal subnational identities such as tribalism, sectarianism, and ethnicity.

In its quest for representative government, the Arab Spring was an inspirational moment of peaceful collective action. It had the potential to reconstruct the fragile state system on a more inclusive foundation and make it more resilient. Civic and patriotic in tone, the protesters wanted a renegotiation of the social contract, not the remaking of state and society along revolutionary lines or the creation of a pan-Arab or pan-Islamic utopia. The Arab Spring uprisings showed that Middle Eastern states suffered from similar severe social, economic, and political vulnerabilities.[36] But they also showed that protesters respected national boundaries and state institutions.[37]

For the first time since the establishment of the Arab nation-state system after World War I, protesters directed their ire against Arab rulers, not foreign powers and occupiers, even though many saw undeniable links between the two. The large-scale popular protests were about citizenship and a new social contract based on the rule of law. The violence and sectarianism that have since spread across the region taint the memory of those who gave so much to stand up for freedom, justice, and dignity. They also show the moral and political bankruptcy of an order that can only sustain itself through force. The old order simply has no answer to the questions posed by the young people who took to the streets calling for change. Ironically, the protesters also did not provide a revolutionary alternative to the status quo and did not articulate a long-term strategic blueprint for real change.

Revolutions rarely succeed at the first attempt particularly the Arab Spring revolutions, which were not led by revolutionaries. Even the French Revolution, now seen as a landmark in the development of Western political culture, faced pushback in France itself and later from Europe's old order at the Congress of Vienna. The Arab Spring isn't over. This isn't the end. It is just the beginning, as the second wave of 2019 and the toppling of Assad in 2024 clearly show.

12

The End of Empire, or Is History about to Repeat Itself?

AN EMPIRE BY PROXY

THIS CHAPTER EXPLORES the role of key international actors and dissects how foreign intervention is shifting, looking at the major players on the world and regional stage. It will also focus on how fluid domestic authoritarianism fits into this picture. Is there a role for beneficial foreign intervention in the interest of the people? Or is this doomed to replicate the patronizing and ultimately disempowering interventions by colonial and postcolonial powers that weakened local institutions and indigenous state capacity?

The evidence presented below shows that there is more continuity than discontinuity in how the Great Powers have dealt with the Middle East, particularly the United States. Despite the end of the Cold War, the US war on terror, and the Arab Spring uprisings, and the implosion in Israel-Palestine, American foreign policy continued to partner with autocratic Middle Eastern rulers and Israel's settler colonialism in Palestine. While paying lip service to the promotion of human rights and democracy, US foreign policy has doggedly supported political authoritarianism in the region and used divide-and-rule tactics to maintain its Pax Americana. With few exceptions from the beginning of the Cold War to the present the United States has pursued an offensive, interventionist, realist foreign

262   THE GREAT BETRAYAL

policy toward the Middle East. Despite America's retrenchment from the Middle East after its failed invasion and occupation of Iraq in 2003, the United States retains sprawling military bases and footprints in Bahrain, Iraq, Israel, Jordan, Kuwait, Qatar, Saudi Arabia, Syria, the UAE, and beyond. As a military superpower, it provides protection for its local allies and defends the pro-Western authoritarian status quo.

There is no paradigm shift in America's approach to the Middle East, with neither human rights nor democracy promotion high on its foreign policy agenda. Nor will there ever be a paradigm shift unless there is a radical rethinking of US policy toward the region. Stability, a code word for supporting autocratic regimes, continues to be the core concern of the United States in the Middle East, though the region has never been as volatile and unstable as it is today. Israel's war in Gaza, together with the escalation of war to neighboring Iraq, Lebanon, Syria, Yemen, and the Israel-Iran direct attacks, threaten to plunge the region into all-out conflagration. The bottom line: Despite being a colossal failure, US foreign policy is resistant to change. The lives of millions of everyday people from Iraq to Palestine have been ruined. A blowback from these policies is inevitable.

Similarly, Europe's role in the Middle East has hardly changed since the end of World War II. Wherever the United States goes, Europe follows, more so in the case of Britain and Germany. Maintaining a monopoly on Middle East diplomacy, the United States has excluded Europe from any meaningful, independent engagement in the region. Europe has largely obliged, agreeing to be a banker. The old continent has not developed a coherent and unified foreign and security policy toward either the Middle East or other regions. European leaders prefer the safe comfort of following behind the United States and avoiding independent postures or actions. The Russian invasion of Ukraine in 2022 has increased Europe's dependence on the United States. Although differences emerged between the United States and some of its European allies like Belgium, Ireland, Malta, Norway, and Spain during the Israeli war in Gaza in 2023–2024, the EU faithfully adhered to the US position. For the foreseeable future, Europe will continue to defer to the United States regarding questions of war and peace in the Middle East. Now that Donald Trump has won another presidential term, Europe will have to rethink its foreign policy and chart a new autonomous defense pathway.

Of all outside powers, China has emerged as the big winner. People in the region do not see China as backing a genocide and supporting dictators. This is a Western problem, and China's vocal support for the Palestinians helps it win with public opinion. For the past few decades China has strengthened its ties with most pivotal Middle Eastern states, becoming the biggest economic partner of Iran, Saudi Arabia, and others. Unlike Russia, which has only hard power and military hardware, China possesses also soft power, including technology, the car industry, and goods and services, which are popular throughout the Middle East. When both people and the elite in the region look at the world, they see China as the future. From Turkey to Egypt to Oman, Chinese technology and investment is prized and its trade with the region exceeds that of the United States. The bottom line: China is a geoeconomic superpower in the Middle East.

That said, China has neither the desire nor the hard military power to establish an informal "empire" in the Middle East, as the West has. Unlike the United States, China is interested mainly in geoeconomics, not geopolitics so far, and it pursues transactional relations with Middle Eastern states. With the exception of brokering a rapprochement between Iran and Saudi Arabia in March 2023, however, China eschews entanglement in the region's turbulent geopolitics and focuses on transactional relations. Chinese leaders are happy to see their American counterparts embroiled (again and again) in the region's quagmire, be it in the war on terror or the recent Israeli war in Gaza and securing the flow of petroleum through the Gulf waterways. Reaping the benefits of America's costly military ventures in the region, China will continue to prioritize economics over geopolitics over the next two decades.

Unlike China, the reassertion of Russia's hard power in the Middle East has not made it as influential. Russia, like the Soviet Union before it, lacks soft power, which is a strategic handicap. With the exception of advanced arms and energy, Russia has little else to offer regional powers. Although Russia has not been able to match China's influence in the region, it has established important connections with key regional states and nonstate actors, including Iran, Libya, Saudi Arabia, Syria, Turkey, and beyond. Putin's invasion of Ukraine in February 2022 showed the endurance and resilience of Russia's ties with Middle Eastern stakeholders. The latter refused to impose sanctions on Russia as demanded by the United States and maintained a business-as-usual relationship with Moscow. Saudi Arabia coordinated energy policy with Russia, risking a rupture with the Biden administration.

The international relations of the Middle East are no longer dominated by the United States. China, Russia (and others like Brazil, India, and South Africa) compete with the United States for influence and are welcomed with open arms by Middle Eastern states. Trying to mitigate risk in a changing and highly uncertain global environment, pivotal regional actors hedge their choices and avoid taking sides in Great Power competition. Although Gulf states still rely on the United States for their security, they have diversified their economic and foreign policies. They hedge their bets. Instead of balancing and bandwagoning with either the United States or China, most regional actors keep a distance from either camp in order to mitigate risk and maximize gains.

Nonetheless, this is not a transformative moment in regional politics. The changing character of Great Powers competition does not herald a more stable balance of power or a new social contract between domestic authoritarians and everyday people. As always, the former use the new realignment in international relations to assert their control and to thwart political change at home. The rise of China and Russia won't alter the domestic power dynamics because both of them deal at a state-to-state level and eschew interference in internal affairs. Similarly, the United States and Europe will continue to pay lip service to human rights and the rule of law, but their actions betray a realist preference for stability and security. People in the region no longer take seriously Western pronouncements on human rights and the rule of law due to the West's support of Israeli war crimes and genocide in Gaza and Lebanon.

The bottom line is that from the end of World War II to today external powers have been enablers of domestic authoritarians in the Middle East. America's relative decline and retrenchment will have little effect on the relationship between rulers and citizens in the region. Or will this new development embolden autocrats and provide them with more choices and tools of repression?

From Informal Empire to Empire by Proxy

The Arab Spring took many by surprise. Not least the world's only super-power, the United States of America. US president Barack Obama was so taken aback by the popular uprisings that he reportedly sent a reprimand to the CIA for failing to predict the upheaval and warn him in advance. Obama and his political leadership were disappointed that they invested $80 billion annually in the intelligence services, yet the CIA failed to see the Arab Spring coming.

But Washington's inability to predict a democratic awakening that had been brewing for years was more than a political embarrassment; it was a monumental failure of policy. This recalls a similar moment when the United States failed to anticipate or understand the 1979 Iranian revolution. The Arab Spring, perhaps more than any event in recent history, ex-posed the contradictions at the heart of US policy in the Middle East. As historian M. E. McMillan points out in *From the First World War to the Arab Spring*, "During the Cold War, the West supported the people of the Communist Bloc against their regimes. In the Middle East, the West has done the opposite. It has supported the regimes against their people."[1] The Arab Spring showed the whole world that America had the wrong friends in the Arab world. How, for example, was Washington to react to protests calling for the downfall of the regime in Cairo when America funded, armed, and trained that regime? As vice president in January 2011, Joe Biden denied that Mubarak was a dictator.For decades, the United States had rhetorically insisted on the promotion of democracy across the globe. Their aim was nothing less than the creation of a liberal interna-tional order. In contrast to Russia and China, America has long seen its global role as based on more than economic and military power. America sees itself as the defender and promoter of freedom and democracy across the world. That belief is the ideological underpinning of its global hege-mony. But, when it comes to promoting democracy in the Middle East, there has been a yawning gap between what the United States says and what it does. And the people of the region know it. By the time the Arab Spring started in 2010, the United States had lost much of its moral capital in the region and this severely limited Washington's ability to react to and influence events.

The decline of America's soft power in the region stems from the long-standing internal conflict between its self-definition as a benevolent world power and its material interests and imperial ambitions and actions. On the one hand, the United States portrays itself as a Great Power whose goal is to promote world peace and democracy, a worldview that has allowed it to spread its soft power near and far. But on the other, the ideas behind America's soft power clash with a foreign policy that backs Middle Eastern autocrats and settler colonialism in Palestine. This dialectical tension between US values and US interests has long been at the heart of US foreign policy since the onset of the Cold War in early 1950s.

The end of the Cold War brought no conceptual shift in US strategic thinking toward the Middle East. As a result, throughout the 1990s and the first decade of the twenty-first century, the attitudes of people in the Arab world and the Middle East hardened toward the United States. Years of failure and false starts trying to resolve the Israeli-Palestine conflict diminished America's standing in the region. In addition, Washington's duplicity in casting itself as an honest broker in this conflict while repeatedly using its veto to protect Israel at the United Nations Security Council did nothing to improve relations. The US-led invasion and subsequent occupation of Iraq in 2003 made a bad situation worse. The invasion was widely viewed as a declaration of war against all Arabs. The occupation of Iraq, a country that had not attacked the United States, along with human rights atrocities committed by occupation forces in the war-torn country, marked a new low in how the Arab (and Islamic) world looked at the only surviving superpower.

And now, in the context of the Israeli wars in Gaza and Lebanon, with full-throated US backing, American standing and moral authority in the world, not just in the Middle East, has hit rock bottom. October 7, 2023, is a key turning point, or a breaking point, on this issue. As a scholar of international relations, I had never seen so much anger and rage throughout the Arab-Islamic world, Africa, and Asia directed against the United

States and Europe. More and more people in the Global South say there is one rule for "the West" and another for "the rest." More than 75 percent of respondents across the Arab world said the United States (and Israel) is "the biggest threat to the security and stability of the region," according to the first survey conducted by the reputed Doha Institute's Arab Center for Research and Policy Studies in January 2024.[2]

Over the long term, the invasion of Iraq damaged America's standing at home too. Many Americans have grown sick and tired of their leaders talking foolishly about the Middle East and squandering precious resources there. The material and ideational costs of one US misadventure in the Middle East after another have sapped the strength of American society to fight other people's wars for them. In the wake of the credit crisis of 2008, huge swathes of American society believe they need to prioritize taking care of Americans first.

The American public is therefore unlikely to support any new military engagements in the Middle East. At the start of his time in office, President Obama and his foreign policy team took note of this shift in public opinion. The new president also recognized that America's moral authority was a spent force in the wider world. The Obama administration concluded the US role in the world had dramatically changed and Washington could no longer unilaterally dictate terms to ally or enemy.[3]

From the beginning of his administration, Obama prioritized the restoration of America's soft power as a prerequisite to regaining the trust and cooperation of allies across the world. Asked why he did not order an attack on the Assad regime following its use of chemical weapons in 2013, Obama replied that the United States is not the world's policeman.[4] This new approach to foreign policy was based on multilateralism and consensus-building.

In Obama's White House, multipolarity therefore became the order of the day. Two key pillars of the realist tradition of international relations—collective security and multilateral diplomacy—gained currency in his administration. The celebrated speech in Cairo, which the president made in June 2009, inspired hope across the region for a new relationship with the United States because it repeatedly acknowledged the "mistrust" between the United States and Arab countries. The president also referred to America's own responsibilities.[5]

There was, too, the Obama factor: young, articulate, intelligent, and charismatic, the new president appealed to people across the world in a way that previous US presidents had not. As the first African American president, Obama seemed to signal a shift within US domestic politics that many people outside the United States hoped would be paralleled by a corresponding shift in US foreign policy.

But the high hopes Obama raised were dashed eighteen months later when his administration was woefully slow to support the peaceful protests in Tunisia and Egypt that called for the removal of pro-Western dictators from power.

It took American policymakers and their European counterparts weeks to come up with a coherent response to the demands of protesters in Egypt, Libya, Tunisia, and Yemen, who wanted their strongmen removed from power. The United States worked closely with the Egyptian military (which Washington financed and trained) to convince them not to fire on the protesters. But the Obama National Security Council was deeply divided about the future of longtime US ally Hosni Mubarak and took too long to address the concerns of protesters. While Washington dallied and delayed, the Obama administration sent out mixed messages and contradictory signals. None of which went unnoticed by the protesters. The result was that American soft power took another battering in the region.

Obama's eventual decision to abandon Mubarak was received badly by America's allies in the region, especially in Israel. Along with Washington's disastrous handling of postinvasion Iraq—a situation that gave Iran the green light to extend its influence in the country—the decision to dump Mubarak demonstrated America's unreliability as an ally in the eyes of the region's rulers. But as Obama subsequently conceded, he could not have saved Mubarak even if he had wanted to. His admission was a tacit acknowledgment of the limits of US influence.

In hindsight, Obama justified his reluctance to intervene and help resolve the conflicts in the Middle East and rebuild the region's failing institutions by painting a dark portrait of the region as a place frozen in time and space. In a wide-ranging interview given to *The Atlantic* at the end of his second term, Obama ascribed the region's main obstacle to progress and the source of much of its problems to the tribal structure of Middle Eastern societies. This was, he said, "a force that no president can neutralize."[6] He argued that tribalism was the reason the United States had hesitated to join the NATO-led coalition in Libya: "The degree of tribal division in Libya was greater than our analysts had expected. And our ability to have any kind of structure there that we could interact with and start training and start providing resources broke down very quickly."[7] In the same interview, Obama reportedly told a colleague from the Senate that the Libyan disaster had convinced him of the need to disengage from any and all involvement in nation-building in the Middle East.

In this famous interview, Obama failed to acknowledge US and Western culpability in the unfolding tragedy in the Middle East: that the West repeatedly propped up unpopular henchmen as rulers and Israel to protect its economic interests and repeatedly intervened militarily if those interests were threatened. To Obama's foreign policy team, the Middle East had become a burden, a place where America could not win no matter what it did. With shale gas and renewables revolutionizing America's energy needs and thus changing the fundamentals of US interests in the Middle East, the Obama team began to change direction. They focused on a general reorientation of US interests away from the war-torn region toward the rapidly expanding economies of the Asia-Pacific region, called an "Asia pivot."

The Arab uprisings, however, effectively buried any hope of a reorientation in US foreign policy, and the Obama administration was forced to shift focus away from the Middle East. The president's team now sought to limit America's engagement in the region and shield the president from any reverberations from Middle Eastern conflicts. Obama repeatedly stated that the United States had overextended itself in the Middle East to a degree far beyond what its vital national interests actually required. In line with his early commitment to "Asia First," the Middle East and Europe slipped to secondary importance for American decision-makers. This shift is part of an established pattern in US foreign policy. In the post–World War II era, US foreign policy has swung like a pendulum between East Asia and the Middle East. In the 1950s and 1960s, East Asia was the priority. In the 1970s, it was the Middle East. Obama's eight years in the White House marked the end of America's supremacy in the region, although the starting point for the retrenchment was the final years of George W. Bush's presidency.[8]

Is this shift likely to continue? Recent public opinion surveys show the US public is not interested in Middle Eastern issues. Aside from the war against Islamic State and Al-Qaeda and an "ironclad" commitment to Israel, regional issues such as the establishment of a Palestinian state as well as the wars in Libya, Syria, and Yemen, receive little attention. Respondents were more preoccupied by US immigration policy, the trade deficit, North Korea, and the rise of China as a global rival and a hegemon. These tendencies transcend party lines and point to a relative consensus on foreign policy among the US population. The Iran nuclear program was one of the only Middle Eastern issues given attention by the US public.[9]

Obama's successor, Donald J. Trump, picked up on this sense of disengagement. Acutely aware of the American public's war-weariness, President Trump seemed keen to set in motion something akin to a new "Nixon Doctrine," which would compartmentalize roles among US allies. Such a delegation of power to local allies would see a "Saudification" of US policy in the Gulf and an "Israelification" of US policy in the Near East. Both countries shared Washington's goal of containing Iran.

As a real estate tycoon, Trump views international relations through a business lens. His approach was entirely transactional. With his focus on job creation at home, he looked at foreign policy in terms of achieving maximum returns on minimum investment. Money and power are two sides of the same coin.

Armed with this "America First" doctrine, the business tycoon repeatedly reprimanded his NATO allies for not contributing adequately to NATO's military budget and leaving the United States to pick up the lion's share of the financial burden. Trump vehemently criticized both Republican and Democratic presidents for squandering trillions on wars in the Middle East, telling Congress: "With this six trillion dollars we could have rebuilt our country—twice."[10]

The concept of wasting money abroad for no return while allowing domestic infrastructure to collapse is a familiar theme for Trump. It plays well domestically. He made it clear from the start that nation-building abroad would not be part of his worldview. He pointed out, "When the world sees how bad the United States is and we start talking about civil liberties, I don't think we are a very good messenger."[11] Trump promised his audience that he will "stop trying to build new nations in far-off lands, many areas you have never even heard of these places. OK? We are going to stop."[12]

Similarly, Trump remained reluctant to engage in the Middle East. He went much further than Obama did when the latter talked of the "mistrust" between the United States and the Arab world. Trump openly admitted the United States is not entirely innocent on the world stage. When, in an interview on Fox News, Trump said he respected Vladimir Putin and was told in reply the Russian leader is "a killer," Trump responded that the United States has many of them. "What do you think? Our country's so innocent?"[13] This language carries tremendous implications for America's role in the world.

It also broke with tradition in Washington. Unlike previous presidents, Democrat and Republican alike, Trump did not even pay lip service to human rights, the rule of law, or the promotion of democracy. As his trip to Saudi Arabia in 2017 showed, concluding the deal is his top priority. He came away from that trip with reportedly billion-dollar deals that would, in his words, create thousands of jobs in the United States and secure even more. For someone who sees himself as the "jobs president," this is what matters.

Yet, it has to be said that no US president has either sanctioned a Mideast ally for human rights abuses or for not having free elections. American interests have *always* trumped American values in the Middle East. What made Trump different is that he made no pretense of promoting democracy.

The difference between the Obama approach and that of Trump was not merely one of tone. It is the fact that Obama relied on the classic realist principle of a balance of power in the region. In Obama's view, that balance of power could not occur as long as the United States backed one side against the other. Given that US interests in the Middle East are waning, the Obama administration decided to pursue a policy of relative retrenchment. But in order to avoid all hell breaking loose in the wake of US withdrawal, the Obama plan was to have Saudi Arabia on one side balancing out Iran on the other.[14]

That course of action, it was hoped, would slowly lead to a workable division of power in the region. It would also allow the United States to focus its attention elsewhere in the world while ensuring its interests in the Middle East, primarily oil and Israel, were protected. Democracy was not part of the plan. Trump turned the Obama approach on its head by reverting to America's traditional role in the Middle East—a status quo superpower—that fights terrorism and backs its allies with all means necessary, including massive arms sales and the construction of an anti-Iran coalition. The common denominator in both approaches was the unwillingness, or inability, to address the human rights deficit and the new authoritarian bulge in the Middle East, as well as an increasing popular opposition in the United States to drawn-out military adventure or investment in the region.

Despite the profound personal differences between Trump and Biden, there was more continuity than discontinuity between them on foreign policy toward the Middle East. A perfect example of this continuity is the Abraham Accords, Israeli normalization with Arab states, which both Trump and Biden championed. Unlike his predecessor, however, Biden pursued an offensive realist, militaristic foreign policy toward China and Russia, defining the clash of our time as a contest between democracies and autocracies. Biden called this challenge "a battle between the utility of democracies in the twenty-first century and autocracies" and sought to forge a united front against China and Russia.[15]

Biden's new doctrine led him initially to pivot away from conflict zones in the Middle East and elsewhere. This was on display when he ordered a withdrawal of US forces from Afghanistan, speeding up the Taliban's return to power after a twenty-year-long war. Retrenching further from the Middle East, Biden sought to orchestrate an anti-Iran regional security architecture led by Israel, Saudi Arabia, and other Arab states and buttressed by the United States. Like his predecessor Trump, Biden's preference was to lead from behind, relying on local actors and proxies to secure the regional order and maintain US interests.

But the deepening of China's economic and technological influence in the Middle East led the Biden administration to try belatedly to reestablish US regional leadership by expanding the Abraham Accords, which focused on Arab-Israeli normalization of relations—a brainchild of Jared Kushner, Trump's son-in-law. Instead of pressuring the Netanyahu government, one of the most extreme governments in Israel's history to end its occupation of Palestinian lands and support a two-state solution, Biden officials tried to bypass the Palestinian issue and pushed the Saudis to normalize relations with Israel in return for security assistance and protection. Biden's scheme was a reward to Netanyahu and his far-right coalition members to annihilate, once and for all, the possibility of a Palestinian state. "We view (normalization with Saudi Arabia) as perhaps a giant leap toward ending the Arab-Israeli conflict," stated Netanyahu.[16]

More concerned about geopolitical rivalries with China and Russia than real peace between Israelis and Palestinians, Biden accepted the Israeli narrative that the Palestine question did not matter for regional stability. The status quo was perfectly acceptable. It is no wonder that both the Biden administration and the Netanyahu government were shocked when on October 7, 2023, Hamas attacked Israel, killing 1,139 Israelis and taking more than 200 hostages. Rather than recalibrating the US policy toward the Israel-Palestine conflict, Biden used Hamas's bloody attack to double down on his failed policy. He greenlighted Netanyahu's decision to wage a "long war" in Gaza and collectively punish the Palestinians.[17] At the time of writing, more than 150,000 Palestinians have been killed or injured in Israel's military offensive on Gaza since October 7, according to the Gaza health ministry.[18] Israel's full-scale onslaught on Gaza and Lebanon threatens to escalate into a direct region-wide war with Iran.

Biden will be remembered as a president who preached democracy in Europe while backing autocracy in the Middle East. He claimed he wanted a clean break with Trump's legacy, yet in the Middle East he has not restored the nuclear deal with Iran, engineered by Obama and destroyed by Trump, and, in so doing, abandoned Obama's policy of creating a relatively stable balance of power in the region. Biden also sought to expand

Trump's legacy by ignoring the Israeli-Palestine conflict and focusing on the Abraham Accords.

More dangerously, the Gaza catastrophe unfolded on Biden's watch. It is too early to measure its full impact on regional and international security. What is certain, however, is that by fully embracing Netanyahu, Biden "owns" this war. Not unlike its ill-fated invasion and occupation of Iraq, the consequences of the bloodletting in Gaza and Lebanon will likely haunt the United States (and Israel) for years to come.[19]

Europe: A House Divided

If the United States failed to help the Middle East and North Africa advance toward representative government and the rule of law, Europe and the world at large fared no better. On March 19, 2011, NATO led a multistate coalition in a military intervention in Libya that toppled Gaddafi, but the United States and its European allies did not follow up by helping to stabilize the war-torn North African country.

From the beginning, the NATO-led military intervention in Libya exposed serious disagreements among the Western powers about what to do during the uprising and then with post-Gaddafi Libya. European powers bickered among themselves in the run-up to the UN Security Council vote over who would lead the operation: France, the United Kingdom, or NATO. These differences became public when Libya descended into lawlessness and chaos. Taking a swipe at his European allies, Obama called the European powers that had pushed for the NATO-led intervention in Libya "free riders":

> Now, option one would be to do nothing, and there were some in my administration who said, as tragic as the Libyan situation may be, it's not our problem. The way I looked at it was that it would be our problem if, in fact, complete chaos and civil war broke out in Libya. But this is not so at the core of U.S. interests that it makes sense for us to unilaterally strike against the Qaddafi regime. At that point, you've got Europe and a number of Gulf countries who despise Qaddafi or are concerned on a humanitarian basis, who are calling for action. But what

has been a habit over the last several decades in these circumstances is people pushing us to act but then showing an unwillingness to put any skin in the game.[20]

The Libyan debacle is a microcosm of a larger, structural problem. Exhaustion has set in across Western capitals. There is no appetite for an assertive or interventionist role in the Middle East or North Africa, except when it comes to defending Israel. Europe has turned inward. From the financial crisis in 2008 to post-Brexit, the EU is facing an identity crisis. It is consumed by efforts to save the Union, deal with the fallout from Brexit and put its house in order amid rising populism, lukewarm economic growth, budget deficits, and the risk of financial meltdown of some of its member states in the wake of the COVID-19 pandemic as well as Russia's invasion of Ukraine on February 24, 2022.

Europe has a habit of only waking up when direct threats from the Middle East, such as terrorism and illegal immigration, hit home. Without US leadership, European countries are reluctant to become actively engaged in the Middle East. Time and again they defer to their more powerful ally across the Atlantic. How much longer they can keep doing this remains to be seen. The global security architecture established by the United States after World War II is currently under tremendous strain. Trump questioned the relevance of both NATO and the EU. His stance has sown confusion and uncertainty among his Western allies. Should he be reelected president, this confusion and uncertainty will increase. Europe's most powerful leader at that time, German chancellor Angela Merkel, responded to the frustration felt by some of the continent's leaders by urging the EU to take care of its own security. "The era in which we could fully rely on others is over to some extent," Merkel told a crowd at an election rally in Munich in May 2017. "We Europeans truly have to take our fate into our own hands—naturally in friendship with the United States of America, in friendship with Great Britain, as good neighbors with whoever, also with Russia and other countries," she said. "But we have to know that we Europeans must fight for our own future and destiny.[21] French president Emmanuel Macron has repeatedly called on his European counterparts to achieve "strategic autonomy." In 2017, Macron declared that "what we need is a long-term economic and political strategy, [so that we] can compete with China and the United States."[22] Despite these calls, neither Merkel (or her successor, Chancellor Olaf Scholz) nor Macron has affected any real change in Europe's role in the world.

In fact, the reverse has happened. The Russian invasion of Ukraine in 2022 has amplified Europe's security dependence on the United States. The Biden administration has used the war in the heart of Europe to revive NATO and reassert its hegemony over the continent. The major European states had failed to get Russia and Ukraine to resolve their difference at the negotiating table and thus prevent the outbreak of war. Moreover, after Putin's invasion of Ukraine, Europe has been utterly incapable of developing a position of its own on the conflict different from the United States.[23] Russia's aggressiveness pushed all European capitals to turn to Washington for protection. Finland and Sweden, two EU member states with a long tradition of neutrality, joined NATO. All NATO members "finally" complied with US demands to raise their military budget to 2 percent of GDP, which shows the extent of Europe dependency.[24]

The EU's reliance on the United States is even deeper when it comes to the Middle East, due to the lack of any coherent foreign policy within the European bloc. There exists no independent European approach toward the region. Wherever the US winds blow, Europe almost blindly follows. The Libyan disaster, the Syrian conflict, the refugee crisis, the Israeli war in Gaza and Lebanon, not to mention the global financial crisis, exposed serious cleavages within the Western alliance. The slow pace with which the EU responded to the Arab Spring uprisings revealed different approaches among member states over what to do to help promote European values across its "Southern Neighborhood." It also revealed a schism over the level of engagement the bloc should have in the region. When the EU did eventually get its act together and respond, its strategies were overly bureaucratic and not entirely workable. The EU Neighborhood Policy (ENP)[25] based on the "more for more" motto, was revised in 2011 but not in a way that bestowed any real leverage on the EU, particularly in light of the dire economic problems within the Union. Many have criticized the ENP for bring really "less for less," or less for the same.[26]

The EU's stance on Tunisia during the Arab Spring is a case in point.[27] While the bloc decided to adopt a wait-and-see approach, France broke ranks and offered material support and expertise on crowd control to the Ben Ali regime.[28] The response to the Egyptian uprising was similarly incoherent. French prime minister François Fillon led a group of southern European countries that called for Mubarak to stay in power.[29] They claimed he was needed in the fight against terrorism and that the country had a better chance of carrying out a democratic transition if he remained.[30]

The international reputation of France and the United Kingdom took another hit in Libya. Both countries pushed for the NATO-led intervention in Libya, an intervention that, on paper, aimed to protect civilians, but which, in practice, was used to achieve Anglo-French foreign policy objectives. The result was increasing mistrust of their intentions in the region. It also raised suspicions among other international actors such as China and Russia. Neither of them vetoed UN Security Council Resolution (UNSC) 1973, which established a no-fly zone over Libya. In retrospect, China and Russia came to see the UNSC Resolution as a ploy designed by Paris and London to engineer regime change. Beijing and Moscow took offense with the wording used in the resolution, which called on

> Member States that have notified the Secretary-General, acting nationally or through regional organizations or arrangements, and acting in cooperation with the Secretary-General, to take all necessary measures, notwithstanding paragraph 9 of resolution 1970 (2011), to protect civilians and civilian populated areas under threat of attack in the Libyan Arab Jamahiriya, including Benghazi, while excluding a foreign occupation force of any form on any part of Libyan territory, and requests the Member States concerned to inform the Secretary-General immediately of the measures they take pursuant to the authorization conferred by this paragraph which shall be immediately reported to the Security Council.[31]

China and Russia claimed the United Kingdom and France had used the wording "all necessary measures" in their drafting of the resolution to legitimize their support for the Libyan rebels. According to this view, the aim of the no-fly zone was to facilitate the overthrow of Gaddafi and ensure that his successor(s) would be parties with whom both the United Kingdom and France would have close ties. British and French actions in Libya influenced the response of China and Russia to the Syrian conflict and the war in Ukraine. Russia and China worked in concert to veto all UN Security Council resolutions on the Syrian conflict, thus making the war even harder to resolve. Worse was to come. The war in Syria, which erupted in 2011, became almost impossible to resolve when a resurgent Russia decided to intervene militarily in the war-torn country in September 2015.

The Return of Russia to the World Stage

As Western powers, including the United States, failed to come up with a cohesive response to the Arab Spring or the subsequent civil strife in the region, tensions mounted within the EU, and between the United States and the EU. Disagreement raged over what should be done about Syria, ISIS, and the immigration crisis. The inability to decide who should shoulder the burden of the financial crises afflicting several EU member states exposed the rifts within the EU for all to see. All of this introspection left a gap on the world stage. Into this gap stepped Russia's president, Vladimir Putin.

The reassertion of Russian power reflects the country's partial recovery after the collapse of the Soviet Union in 1991. It is also a clear illustration of the changing nature of the international system. No longer is the system unipolar with the United States as the hyperpower. It is gradually shifting toward multipolarity where power is diffused worldwide. Russia's increased engagement in the Middle East is motivated by four important factors. First, Russia used its intervention in the Syrian civil war to showcase its military prowess and rebuild its reputation as a power to be feared. The reemergence of Russia as a military force to be reckoned with increases Moscow's bargaining position with the United States and the European bloc. For Moscow, this provides much-needed leverage with the West when it comes to dealing with an issue very close to Russia's heart: Ukraine and Crimea.

Second, Russia saw Syria as falling within its orbit. Syria was the Soviet Union's most reliable partner in the region. There is a large Russian community in the country, and Moscow has key assets there, including the only Russian naval base in the Mediterranean.[32] After losing major investments in Libya and the troubles in Ukraine, Russia opted for limited intervention in Syria as a way of strengthening its hand vis-à-vis the Western powers. The alliance with Assad also allowed Moscow to build closer economic and military ties with Iran. Russia's failure to defend the Assad regime in 2024 is a major setback to its regional ambitions. It is too early, however, to know the consequences of Assad's fall and the withdrawal of Russian forces from Syria on Moscow's strategic interests in the Middle East and beyond.

Third, the Middle East is strategically important to Russia because of its geographical proximity. The Russian leadership sees the region as part of its "backyard" and therefore a place where Moscow must make political alliances and develop economic opportunities, such as deals on trade, oil, gas, and arms. The Russian economy is suffering under the weight of US-led sanctions, and the Middle East offers the possibility of new commercial opportunities, especially in nuclear energy where Russia is emerging as an industry leader.

Finally, and perhaps most importantly, there was the Islamic State. Russia has been battling Islamist insurgencies along its southern borders for decades. Chechnya has become a byword for the brutality of this struggle. Due to the large Muslim population in Russia's south, Russian officials feel vulnerable to the spread of Islamist radicalism. There was a large contingent of Russians fighting with IS that Russian was the third-most spoken language in its ranks. Magazines, radio, television, and social media broadcasts produced by the group reflect this. The Kremlin takes the threat of Salafi-jihadists returning home seriously and decided it was better to preempt the movement in Syria than risk more attacks at home.

Finally, Russia has another aim in the Middle East: to promote a different worldview from the West. Russia endorses a view of the world that focuses first and foremost on sovereignty, though it violated the very same principle by invading Ukraine. By underlining the importance of territorial integrity, the Russian view stands as an alternative to the Western liberal model theoretically based on human rights and self-determination, and if need be, intervention. Russia[33] and China have repeatedly criticized Western powers for engaging in "social engineering" projects, destabilizing the region, destroying "traditional governance and security mechanisms," and promoting "the illegal spread of weapons and ammunition."[34] Both worldviews, however, often lose something in the translation from rhetoric to reality: the West has said much more about promoting democracy than it has ever done, and the Russians, as Ukraine shows, respect territorial integrity when it suits them.

To promote his worldview, Putin frequently uses the US-led invasion of Iraq and the NATO-led campaign in Libya as examples of Western duplicity and recklessness. His outlook is also driven by a fear that the same Western policies could someday be applied to Russia to topple his regime. That is why Syria and Ukraine both became red lines for him: the crises converged with major popular protests in Russia against Putin and with NATO expansionism in Russia's former sphere of influence.[35]

Russia is not alone in taking such a view of the world. China shares it. Both powers dismiss the values proclaimed by the Western powers as a ploy to advance their material interests and to impose their ideological values on other countries.[36] The Russian and Chinese narrative finds receptive ears in the Middle East because of the long and bitter legacy of Western military intervention. People in the region are deeply skeptical and cynical about the liberalism advanced by the West. The widespread distrust of the United States stems from the belief that American claims of democracy and human rights are mere window dressing. This, in turn, has increased Russia's popularity, particularly among authoritarian leaders who are becoming ever more unwilling to accept the moral preaching of their Western counterparts.

Russia's reengagement in the Middle East has brought Moscow important dividends. Russia and Iran, once enemies, now have a common aim: to protect their vital interests and keep Western powers away from their borders. Although historically the two countries have had a contentious relationship, their interests currently converge to mutual advantage. Moscow sells advanced air defense systems worth billions of US dollars to Tehran and Iranian leaders value these close links with Putin's Russia.

But after Russia's invasion of Ukraine, Iran reportedly provided drones (and allegedly ballistic missiles) to Moscow, which have proved to be effective on the Ukrainian battlefield.[37]

Russian involvement in Syria has also allowed Moscow to reset relations with other key regional powers, including Egypt, Israel, Turkey, and America's Gulf allies. Russia and Turkey have interests in improving bilateral ties, including trade, energy, and weapons sales. The diplomatic thaw continued after Putin supported Erdoğan in the wake of the botched coup against the Turkish president in July 2016. As Turkey's relations with the EU deteriorate, Russia has become a valid partner for Ankara's foreign policy. Turkey refused to join Western sanctions against Russia in both 2014 and 2022, and after Putin's invasion of Ukraine, it has increased trade and diplomatic communication with Moscow while, at the same time, remaining a full member of NATO and even selling lethal drones to Kyiv.[38] Russia has also courted Israel and Putin has established a special relationship with Benjamin Netanyahu. The two countries share mutual security issues and almost 20 percent of Israel's population is Russian-speaking. It would not be an exaggeration to argue that Russia's diplomatic and military achievements in the Middle East emboldened Putin and were a contributing driver in his ill-fated decision to invade Ukraine.

On the whole in the greater Middle East, China is mainly interested in stability, easy access to energy, and trade ties. Despite its vast economic interests and trade deals in the Gulf and the greater Middle East, Beijing has no ambitions so far to replace either US or Russian dominance in the region. On the contrary, Beijing is content to let the United States spend its time and money ensuring the security of energy supplies from the region, while Beijing reaps the economic rewards of keeping its distance from the region's fault lines. Since 2020, China has become the largest trading partner of the Gulf Cooperation Council, including Saudi Arabia and the United Arab Emirates, two wealthy economies.[39] China's foreign investment in infrastructure—part of its Belt and Road Initiative—is higher in the Middle East than in any other region in the world.[40] From Turkey to Egypt and Saudi Arabia to Iran, people in the region look at the international system and see China as the future: China as a source of advanced technology, trade, investment. To its strategic advantage, change does not carry any historical weight of aggression and imperial ambitions like that of the Western powers.

Russian and Chinese wooing of regional powers reflects the new reality of international relations in the Middle East: with the United States' retrenchment and increasingly relying on local proxies, we are now living in a decentralized, multipolar world, or conflictual multipolarity. Local players have a broader menu to choose from, and most decide to diversify their relations with outside powers as opposed to siding with only one. Local actors have become risk-averse and prefer hedging toward the Great Powers.

Does this multipolarity change the nature of Middle Eastern politics and the relationship between rulers and the ruled? The simple answer is no on both counts. Domestic authoritarians have more leverage on the global stage to maintain their grip on power and silence dissent. It is doubtful if local autocrats will allow public participation in decision-making. Rather, they will continue to use a combination of co-option and coercion as well as divide tactics to exclude everyday people from the political space.

Decentralizing Power in a Multipolar World: The Rise of Pivotal Regional Powers

In the past two decades, two very different powers have sought to spread their influence on neighboring Arab countries and establish a dominant position in the region: Turkey and Iran. The collapse of the Arab state system after the first Gulf War in 1990–1991, together with the US-led invasion of Iraq in 2003, allowed Ankara and Tehran to launch their bid for regional hegemony. The aftermath of the Arab Spring and the abject failure of Arab leaders to respond to it further facilitated the spread of Turkish and Iranian influence across the region. Israel was also a great beneficiary of the fracturing of the Arab states because civil strife and inter-Arab conflict diverted attention from the Palestine cause and weakened Arab coordination and Arab institutions further.

While one-time leaders of the region like Egypt, Iraq, and Syria have lost influence in recent years, Turkey and Iran have emerged from the current turmoil as primary regional actors. In spite of this, they have so far been unable to export their political model to neighboring Arab countries or to dominate the regional order. The Islamic Republic of Iran, for example, exercises considerable influence in Bahrain, Iraq, Lebanon, and Yemen (and in Syria until 2024), all of which have large Shia communities, but Tehran has nevertheless been unable to export its ideology of the *Wilayat al-Faqih* (the guardianship of the Islamic jurist) to any of these countries. Even Hezbollah, a key ally of Iran, has shied away from adopting the ideology. Iran's geopolitical ambitions have faced fierce resistance from other local actors, which led it to recalibrate its policies and minimize the costs of overextension. Iran's geopolitical position has weakened further following Israel's wars against Hamas and Hezbollah and the fall of the Assad regime.

Turkey has fared no better. Neo-Ottomanism has crashed at the rocks of local resistance and internal failure. The electoral success of Ennahda in Tunisia and the Muslim Brotherhood in Egypt after the Arab Spring bolstered Turkey's standing in the region. Both groups publicly acknowledged Turkey's ruling party, the Justice and Development Party (AKP), as the model by which to legitimize themselves as democratic Islamist parties. But Turkey's leadership of the postrevolutionary Middle East was short-lived. Islamists in Tunisia and Egypt have either left or been pushed out of power. Turkey's investment in Syria paid handsomely when its backed rebels overthrew Assad and expelled Iranian and Russian influence from this strategic country. Turkey is the key winner in the post-Assad Syria. Turkey, too, has been targeted by forces hostile to political Islam. The country was the scene of a military coup in July 2016 aimed at bringing down Erdoğan's democratically elected government, and before the coup had been embroiled in a fierce domestic ideological struggle that has tarnished its democratic credentials.

The Turkish experience of democratization and economic growth between 2003 and 2009 appears to have been reversed as Erdoğan turns Turkey's fragile democracy into a competitive authoritarian system.[41] The Turkish example has not only run out of steam at home but now has little appeal in the Arab world.

Erdoğan has been unable to solve the historic problems of the weakness of the Turkish lira and the high inflation, making Turkish reliance on imported energy sources increasingly expensive and problematic.[42] Moreover, Turkish export-oriented industry is extremely vulnerable to international crisis and suffers heavily any time global demand slows down as in the cases of the 2008 financial crisis and the COVID-19 pandemic and the Ukraine and Gaza wars.[43]

Nonetheless, Turkey and Iran, as the two pivotal regional powers, have managed to extend their influence across the Middle East, which means that for the first time in the contemporary history of the modern Middle East, non-Arab regional powers are active players in the Arab state system. The immunity of Arab institutions has collapsed to the degree that Arab states are now penetrable and vulnerable to, and unable to resist, external influences.

Internecine Arab warfare has allowed another key non-Arab power to consolidate its position: Israel. While Arab regimes fight their own people and each other, Israel has been busy building more settlements on Palestinian land occupied in 1967. Israel's strategic goal is to get rid of the very idea of an independent Palestinian state. They can then substitute autonomy for sovereignty.[44] Netanyahu is trying to capitalize on the incompetence and subservience of Arab leaders and the complicity of the West to put so much pressure on the Palestinians that they have no choice but to capitulate. When Hamas attacked Israel on October 7, 2023, Netanyahu and Biden acted as if they were shocked. They had thought that the status quo was tenable and that the Palestinians were manageable. Going on the offensive, Netanyahu launched all-out war, insisting on "total victory" over Hamas and killing and injuring more than 150,000 Palestinians. With full-throated US support, Netanyahu expanded the war to Lebanon and vowed to crush Hezbollah. After ordering the assassination of Hezbollah leader Hassan Nasrallah, Netanyahu declared his intention to change "the balance of power in the region for years to come." Netanyahu seems to have failed to learn the lessons of Israel's previous invasions of Lebanon and Iran and Turkey's failed attempts to fundamentally reshape the Middle East. Unlike Iran and Turkey, which use both soft and hard power in spreading their influence, Israel relies on only military means. That makes Netanyahu's wish to transform power dynamics in the region an impossible mission.

As Israel's wars in Gaza and Lebanon unfold, we could witness geopolitical shifts that increase the risks of an all-out wider regional conflict.

Before the outbreak of this current round of fighting in Gaza and Lebanon, Arab rulers, particularly in the Gulf, considered popular opposition at home and Iran as a greater threat than Israel. In fact, many Arab rulers see Israel as a partner in the fight against Iran, Turkey, and domestic uprisings. Netanyahu often boasted of expanding historical ties with Arab states while rejecting demands for a Palestinian state. In an interview with Trump's favorite television station, Fox News, Israel's longest-serving prime minister, revealed that Israel's relations with many Arab countries have undergone a profound transformation: "If you look at the Arab world as a whole, there is a change in the way many of the Arab countries perceive Israel. They no longer perceive it as their enemy, but as their indispensable ally against a common threat, and the common threat is Iran."[45] Doubling down on his outside-in approach to the Israel-Palestine conflict, in September 2023, Netanyahu declared that "There's no question the Abraham Accords heralded the dawn of a new age of peace. But I believe that we are at the cusp of an even more dramatic breakthrough, a historic peace between Israel and Saudi Arabia. . . . Peace between Israel and Saudi Arabia will truly create a new Middle East.[46]

Deprived of official Arab backing with a deeply divided leadership, the Palestinians are alone, squeezed financially, militarily and politically by Israel and the United States. The world has forsaken the Palestinians, including the Arab countries, their closest kin. By attacking Israel in October 2023, Hamas attempted to shatter the status quo and trigger a political tsunami in region. We have to wait till the dust settles on the streets of Gaza and now Lebanon to see the costs and consequences of Israel's full-scale military onslaught there as well as consequent geopolitical shifts.

As well as the rise to prominence of non-Arab powers, the post–Cold War decades saw another major change in the region's geostrategic landscape: the increasingly overt rivalry between Saudi Arabia and Iran. This clash goes back to 1979 when Iran after the Islamic Revolution sought to position itself as the guardian of authentic Islam—a role Riyadh had claimed for itself. As Iran is Shia whereas Saudi Arabia is Sunni, this struggle has taken on sectarian dimensions when, at heart, it is a battle for power. In recent years, this rivalry destabilized the entire region and opened up and exacerbated sectarian fault lines in Iraq, Lebanon, Syria, and Yemen. In fact, it became so prominent and so dangerous that it overshadowed other historical fault lines such as the Arab-Israeli conflict. Israel's supporters claim Palestine is no longer a priority for the Arabs and that Iran must be dealt with.

By the early 2020s, pivotal Middle Eastern states recalibrated their foreign policies and begun to normalize relations with each other, including Turkey, Egypt, Saudi Arabia, and the United Arab Emirates. China brokered a normalization deal between Saudi Arabia and Iran, sidelining the United States and upsetting Israel. The convergence of the COVID-19 pandemic and Russia's invasion of Ukraine wrecked the Middle Eastern economies and motivated former rivals to climb down from the tree and prioritize bilateral economic relations. Israel's war in Gaza has deepened the Saudi-Iranian thaw, a development that could bring about a new realignment of regional politics. This sudden change, while altering the geopolitics of the region, is a further sign of the growing importance and autonomy of regional powers.

Again, the growing autonomy of regional powers on the international stage does not translate into a new social contract between rulers and the ruled. The reverse is true. Domestic authoritarians have strengthened their grip on power and smothered all social protests so far.

First Tragedy, Then Farce

For analysts of the Middle East, Karl Marx's comment that history repeats itself "once as tragedy, and again as farce" is timely.[47] Is, for example, Russia's military intervention in Syria or US-China rivalry in the Middle East a sign of a new Cold War(s), and how does it differ from the old Cold War? What about the people of the region: Are their protests for justice and dignity nothing but a moment that has been quickly forgotten? Or are we truly witnessing a new beginning as ordinary citizens contest old power structures? And what about the Great Powers who have gone to war in the region and lost: could the shifts in their domestic public opinion mean we are about to witness the end of empire in the Middle East? Or will history, as Karl Marx suggested, repeat itself, but in new forms?

The aftermath of the Arab Spring uprisings and the subsequent conflicts in the region show how the international relations of the Middle East has fundamentally changed. The wars in Afghanistan, Iraq, Libya, Syria, and Yemen have influenced decision-making in Washington, Moscow, and European capitals. They have also profoundly influenced public opinion in these countries. To put it bluntly, people in Western states are tired of fighting and financing wars that cannot be won.

The Great Powers clearly no longer have the will to wage conventional wars in the Middle East the way they did in the past. Their hands are fettered by domestic concerns, regional dynamics, and shifts in the international system. Paradoxically, this change is happening at the very time new technologies allow them to wage anonymous war from the skies and cyberspace—the kind of wars that do not require boots on the ground. But although these tools enable them to be less affected by domestic political considerations, there are limits to the use of drones and special forces.

So, if the United States really is reluctant to act as the world's policeman, who might fill that role in the Middle East? Or has the sole superpower moment been replaced by new forms of control that rely on punishing economic sanctions, assassinations, and local proxies? The recent reassertion of Russia is unlikely to fill any power vacuum left by the United States. Russia may have the military and diplomatic means to frustrate US designs in Syria, but it lacks the resources to replace Washington in the region.[48] Russia blundered into war in Ukraine, and its misadventure has proved to be costly in blood and treasure and reputational damage as well. The Soviet Union's lack of soft power hindered its ability to compete effectively with the United States during the Cold War. That situation has not changed. Russia still lacks the cultural capital and the many layers of hard power, like population growth and a diversified economy—a deficit that puts it at a serious disadvantage to the United States.

The same is true of China. In the twenty-first century, China has emerged as one of the most important economic powers in the Middle East, but it continues to be politically and militarily disengaged from the region's fault lines. Despite its recent forays into mediation diplomacy between Iran and Saudi Arabia, its two regional key economic partners, China has not developed a foreign policy doctrine beyond its immediate sphere of influence in Southeast Asia and tends toward caution in international relations.

If empires, old and new, are not willing to engage fully in the Middle East, who will the new power brokers be? In their book *The Global Transformation: History, Modernity and the Making of International Relations*, Barry Buzan and George Lawson argue that the twenty-first century constitutes the beginning of a third stage in global modernity. They call it "decentered globalism."[49] The main feature of decentered globalism is that any changes to the international system will not come from a tiny core of states. Instead, they will be geographically spread out.[50] As the distribution of power becomes more diffuse, the West will lose its preeminent condition.[51] This tendency can already be seen in new sites of global governance such as the Group of Twenty (G20); new economic formations such as the intergovernmental organization comprising Brazil, Russia, India, China, South Africa, Egypt, Ethiopia, Iran, and the UAE (BRICs); and new security institutions such as the Shanghai Cooperation Organization.[52]

This spread of power means interdependence is set to increase.[53] Lawson and Buzan point out, however, that the reconfiguration of the international system does not mean the United States will be replaced by another superpower. Rather, multiple powers will operate at the core of the international system. This new system will have many regional powers but no hegemonic superpowers.[54] Two different processes currently dovetailing in the Middle East suggest that elements of this decentered globalism may already be happening. The first is the realignment of Great Power priorities. The second is the rise of local actors.

After the first wave of the Arab Spring uprisings, as peaceful popular protests escalated into armed clashes and civil wars in several countries, the United States, Europe, Russia, and China had neither the political will nor the desire to intervene directly and put an end to the spiraling conflicts in the region. When these actors ultimately intervened, they did so to pursue their own narrow interests and priorities, not those of their regional allies. Resignation and fatalism have thus dominated recent Western debates on the Middle East, along with the idea that, apart from Israel and the oil producers in the Gulf, the region should be left to its own devices until the warring factions become so exhausted they are ready to settle their own conflicts.

The rise of regional actors like Turkey, Iran, Israel, and Saudi Arabia indicates we may be witnessing the beginning of an era of greater agency for regional players. We might also be witnessing the diffusion of power away from states to broader society and nonstate actors. Middle Eastern actors—both state and nonstate—have recently become more assertive and more willing to challenge the status quo. Lebanon's Hezbollah is a case in point; Palestine's Hamas is another.

Most narratives by the interventionist superpowers have by and large failed, whether in Afghanistan, Iraq, Libya, or Syria. The age of Great Power supremacy and monopoly in the Middle East as we knew it might therefore be coming to an end. What is, however, clear is that any actor aiming to increase influence in the region will have to devise a means to sustain its power. And that will involve developing a political narrative that people accept. Because, regardless of whether the Great Powers maintain their hegemony or whether they are forced to concede more power to regional actors, all parties will have to make an effort to take the demands of the people into account.[55] This fact might help to explain the recent recalibration of regional politics and the normalization of relations among former bitter rivals. The widespread global popular opposition, including protests at home, to US almost-blind support for the Israeli war in Gaza shows clearly the new challenges facing outside powers in their attempt to impose hegemony in the region. Isolated and accused of complicity in Israel's war crimes in Gaza, the Biden administration lost its narrative and had to recalibrate its position. More than the US invasion and occupation of Iraq in 2003, the Gaza war two decades later undermined American standing and ruptured its relations with the people in the Global South. The damage to American leadership and moral authority is irreparable.

The first and second waves of the Arab Spring uprisings in 2010–2012 and 2018 have demonstrated the emerging consciousness and assertiveness of people, particularly young people. This is due, in part, to education, new technologies, the emergence of pan-Arab media, and the mobilization of certain social groups. This new development, together with the presence of powerful nonstate actors and special interests, imposes previously un-known constraints on Middle Eastern governments.

What all of this shows is that there is nothing "exceptional" or "unique" about the international relations of the Middle East. The region and its people are not isolated from, or immune to, developments at the inter-national level. Middle Eastern societies are influenced by transnational dynamics, such as globalization, technological advances, global economic disequilibrium, and shifts in food and energy supply chains. In light of the growing role of international organizations, nonstate actors, global capital flows, and waves of migration, the question is whether a state, even a former superpower, will be able to maintain power, or whether real in-fluence in international relations will depend on a state's ability to foster new and consensual multilateral governance structures on local, regional, or global levels.

Contemporary trends point to the growing role of nonstate actors, col-lective action, contentious politics, and everyday people as indispensable components in any form of global or regional governance: a sign of the complexity of today's power constellations. In this sense, because the Great Powers still control the global arena, it looks as if they will continue to play an important, though perhaps less overt, role in the Middle East. And because it is unlikely they will take unilateral action to dominate the re-gion, they will be keen to work through local proxies. It is the age of empire by proxy in the Middle East and beyond.

We are already seeing this happen in Syria, the Gulf, and Israel. The United States has been trying to set up a new security architecture in the Middle East, where local actors take care of their security, with Wash-ington leading from behind and providing intelligence, arms, and logis-tics, including an integrated regional air defense system. But even if and when local proxies are empowered to act on their behalf, this does not mean the empire by proxy will not take action to defend its vital interests. Despite its retrenchment from the Middle East after the Iraq War in 2007, the United States deployed a vast armada during the Gaza war in 2023–2024 to assist Israel in its efforts to destroy Hamas and to deter Iran and its local allies from lending a helping hand to the Palestinians. The Gaza war shows that the empire by proxy is hybrid and adaptive.

History tells us that when those interests are challenged, the Great Powers, particularly the United States, do not hesitate to step in. In the Middle East, the end of Empire has been predicted many times. In spite of the tumultuous events that have rocked the region over the past century, it has not yet happened. Empire has proven remarkably resilient. The puzzle is to determine how today's empire by proxy differs from yesterday's classical European colonialism and America's "informal" empire after World War II.

Conclusion

REIMAGINING THE MIDDLE EAST

TODAY, THERE IS a multifaceted struggle unfolding in the greater Middle East, and particularly in the Arab world, over the future of the nation-state, the role of the sacred in politics, the rising economic and social inequities, the relationship between rulers and citizens, and the continuing tragedy of the Palestinians. This struggle is more than territorial; it is ideological, cultural, and institutional. At its heart, there is an existential battle between a multitude of actors, including conservatives, progressives, Islamists, and nationalists and everyday citizens. The current all-too-apparent divisions in the Arab world between national identity and tribal, religious, and sectarian identities are contentious and violent. The latter emerged because of weak state institutions, incitement, and divide-and-conquer tactics by the ruling elites and their external backers.

Although it waned a little in the early 2020s, the fierce regional cold war between the four pivotal powers (Iran, Saudi Arabia, Turkey, and Israel) poured gasoline on this internal struggle and exacerbated it. These geostrategic rivalries undermine social and political progress in several countries, weakening progressive forces and strengthening reactionary and extremist elements.

How and in what ways could the Middle East evolve in the next two decades or so? Will we witness the further fragmentation of fragile states like Iraq, Lebanon, Libya, Sudan, Syria, and Yemen, or regime and state consolidation? Will the stakeholders in the region and their Great

Powers patrons listen to the voices of millions of everyday people who seek a dignified life free from tyranny and want? Will the Palestinians be able to exercise self-determination and have a state of their own in the coming decade, or will Israeli settler colonialism expand further?

This book has argued that the continuing partnership between local autocrats and foreign patrons is key to understanding how the Middle East has reached this lowest point after 100 years of state- and nation-building. My core argument is that the convergence of political authoritarianism with constant intervention by foreign powers, combined with the effects of prolonged conflicts, helps to explain why political change and self-determination have been constantly thwarted over the past century. The agency of everyday people has been unable to overcome this powerful internal-external partnership, which sustains the authoritarian status quo and Israel's military occupation of Palestinian lands.

From the Politics of the Past to the Politics of the Future

All of these factors and the forces at place are no more clearly on display than in Egypt, which is emblematic of the region. In the postcolonial era, Egypt had an opportunity to forge a new government with a modern political identity that would respect the dignity and agency of the people. Instead, Nasser's government gave in to its worst impulses, and the dream of Arab nationalism splintered under the weight of authoritarian consolidation. The Middle East is confronting another identity crisis today, and there is reason to hope that a new political postsectarian identity is forming, one that will only prosper if given the opportunity, which means making space for it by weakening the interdependence of foreign intervention and domestic authoritarianism. This postsectarian identity won't materialize unless the implicit partnership between US foreign policy and local autocrats is severed. The challenge facing people in the region is to find ways and means to break down the mutual interdependence of foreign intervention and domestic authoritarians.

Across the region, people want social justice, a dignified life, and freedom from oppression. These aspirations require a political culture of tolerance, openness, good governance, the rule of law, and political and economic sovereignty—none of which happened under the old system. The problem is not, therefore, with the borders and nation- states per se but with the internal dynamics of these states: the broader failures of governance and representation and continued dependency on external powers. The organic crisis in the Middle East is political and social. It is man-made. Political authoritarianism and the failures of governance are the primary drivers of the turmoil as well as constant and intense foreign intervention in the region's internal affairs. These two domestic and international dynamics overlap and interact viciously with each other. They feed the conditions that lead to the prolonged conflicts the region has become (in)famous for and which, in turn, contribute to the cycle strengthening political authoritarianism and foreign intervention. Throughout these pages, the book's analytical framework emphasized the mutually reinforcing links between foreign intervention, modes of autocratic governance, and the struggle for everyday people to reclaim their government back.

Colonialism and American meddling and intervention have undoubtedly played a significant role in sustaining the current ruling order, but local postcolonial elites cannot use the past or the Great Powers to run from their own responsibilities. They inherited the postcolonial state following World War II, and they subsequently chose to replicate similar modes of colonial rule and control vis-à-vis their citizens with backing by the Great Powers. The postcolonial elites repeatedly employed narratives about the colonial past to justify their policies and authoritarian tendencies. In doing so, they carried the toxic legacy of the colonial era into the postindependence era. And then turned these anti-colonial narratives into practices of domination to silence their own people.

If the postcolonial elites had delivered on their early promises of dignity, prosperity, and justice, the nation-state would not be as vulnerable as it is today. Instead, Middle Eastern rulers drove their countries into the ground and massively mismanaged the economies. Across the region, from the Mediterranean to the Gulf, men like the shah of Iran, Bashar al-Assad, Zine el-Abidine Ben Ali, Muammar Gaddafi, Saddam Hussein, Hosni Mubarak, and Ali Abdullah Saleh, to name but a few, pauperized large segments of their people and turned their countries into police states. While we cannot ignore the continuing legacy and impact of interference by external powers, especially the United States, local elites partnered with the outside powers in order to maintain their control and exclude their population from decision-making.

The two waves of the Arab Spring democratic uprisings in 2010–2012 and 2018–2019 clearly show the emergence of a postsectarian generation, which was fired up by the lack of good and transparent governance and inclusive citizenship, as well as foreign meddling. Millions of protesters in Algeria, Egypt, Iraq, Lebanon, Libya, Sudan, and Yemen joined ranks from across religious, sectarian, and ethnic lines and demanded representation and accountability. Everyday people of all colors, Sunni and Shia Muslims, Christians, Kurds, nationalists, leftists, and secularists, have demanded representation and accountability and jobs, surprising watchers of the contemporary Middle East, who theorized about a toxically sectarianized region. Books and articles written on the question of sectarianism as a "ticking time bomb" could fill entire libraries, but when we lift our eyes from the page and look at the world, we see instead a postsectarian identity. Across the Middle East, Sunni and Shia are defying the doomsayers and overlords by praying together and embracing each other. They are shattering sectarianism before our eyes. This nascent postsectarian identity will fill the vacuum left by the dominant ideologies like Arab nationalism and political Islam and is more inclusive and less ideological. It promises to heal the wounds and scars incurred in decades of culture wars and ideological warfare and civil strife, though this postsectarian identity has neither been conceptualized nor institutionalized. It is a work in progress.

What Is to Be Done?

Readers might sense that my story is pervaded by a sense of inconsolable despair. No, I do not present a scene of utter destruction and devastation. My goal is to show how the whole political, social, economic, and cultural landscape has failed everyday people. The bleakness of Arab and Middle Eastern politics and economics does not mean that people have given up their struggle to a better future. Despite thirteen hellish years and suffering hundreds of thousands of casualties, the Syrian people had not given up their fight for self-determination and freedom. They finally liberated their country of Assad's tyranny and sent a message of hope and optimism to other oppressed people in the region and beyond. Nor does it mean that social progress has not happened, such as improvement in rates of literacy, medical care, life expectancy, access to education, and job opportunities for young girls and women, and decreasing birth rates in most countries. But these few positive achievements are limited and uneven. The bulk of the population in the non–oil producing countries lack human security and fear for the future of their children. Despite the bleakness of various key aspects of the social fabric of Middle Eastern societies, the book's underlying core is an optimism based on the spirit of resistance and resilience of Middle Eastern people. The Palestinians are an example of a people who have shown the world that no amount of military power and settler colonialism could dampen their resistance and longing for freedom and self-determination. The multiple waves of Arab and Iranian uprisings are a clear indicator of a historical struggle for representation and justice.

The current political and economic system *must* be overhauled. Reconstructing and rebuilding state institutions on a new basis of legitimate political authority is essential. The relationship between those who rule and those who are ruled must be transformed with a new social contract based on the rule of law and the provision of public goods. This, of course, is easier said than done. It is doubtful if the reconstruction and rebuilding of state institutions could be completed in the next decade or so.

Traditionally, there are two ways in which transformative change is achieved, leadership or revolution—both of which are presently in short supply. The Arab Spring uprisings could have produced revolutionary change if a combination of local, regional, and global actors had not come together to thwart them. External efforts to institute change by force have also failed and ended up creating more instability and conflict. Afghanistan and Iraq are two cases in point.

In the Middle East, foreign intervention has not been beneficial for the interest of the people. It has served the interests of autocratic rulers and thwarted real political change. If history is a guide, foreign meddling in the region's internal affairs is doomed to replicate the patronizing and ultimately disempowering interventions by colonial and postcolonial powers that weakened local institutions and indigenous state capacity. As this book has shown, the United States and its close European allies were not often true to the values they preached. The reverse is true. From the beginning of the Cold War after World War II to the present, the United States has partnered with Middle Eastern autocrats to preserve its hegemony and access to cheap energy supplies. America and its Western partners are complicit in bolstering political authoritarianism and undermining social and political progress in the region. In this struggle for transformation in the Middle East, "the West" has been on the wrong side of history.

To rectify this historical wrong, the United States and Europe could genuinely support the self-determination of the people, starting with the Palestinians, and pressure strongmen to respect the human rights and dignity of their citizens. It is a win-win strategy for furthering the interests of both Western governments and the people of the region. But if history serves as a guide, this call will fall on deaf ears in Washington, Berlin, London, and Paris.

In the past decade, the United States built closer security ties with strongmen and potentates and promised to come to their defense if they were attacked internally, not just by external powers, though the former is implicit. Its goal is to create an empire by proxy that will replace the old "informal" American empire in the Middle East. The recent entry of China and Russia into the region will unlikely change the trajectory of Middle Eastern politics. Neither power is interested in radical political change.

I can see positive scenarios of foreign engagement like deploying peacekeeping forces to secure the peace if and when an independent Palestinian state is established. Foreign intervention could facilitate resolution of the Israel-Palestine conflict and other regional fault lines like Libya. Nonetheless, in spite of these failures, there is an urgent need to reimagine a new Middle East that offers a clear break from the colonial and postcolonial eras and will act as a counternarrative to the ideologies of extremism and settler colonialism in Palestine. This vision of self-determination and constitutionalism enshrines the rule of law and citizenship. It is consistent with the spirit of the Arab Spring uprisings that aspired to a dignified existence rooted in freedom and social justice and sought to reclaim the state from dictators.

Reimagining a new Middle East along these lines might sound like wishful thinking given the conflicts raging across the region, constant foreign meddling, the dire economic conditions of many countries, and the prevalence of extremist ideologies. But war and violence have often served as the catalysts for change. State formation in Europe was drenched in blood. The struggle for statehood lasted more than three centuries and culminated in two world wars with millions of casualties. When the violent reverberations of the French Revolution shook France in the late eighteenth and early nineteenth centuries, observers could have been forgiven for not being able to imagine a better tomorrow.

Like the Europe of old, the Middle East of today is being baptized by blood and fire. The Arab Spring uprisings showed that people can and do imagine a better tomorrow, even in the face of almost impossible odds. The popular revolts demonstrated that peaceful political change is possible. More than that, they also shattered the nonsensical (yet widely held) narratives of Arab "exceptionalism." The deliberate derailment of the first wave of the uprisings closed the door to peaceful change for the time being and ignited a range of deadly conflicts that threaten to destroy states and societies. There are close links between the crushing of the Arab Spring and the violent eruptions in Iraq, Libya, Syria, Yemen, and, more recently, Sudan.

As the swift overthrow of Assad shows, there is nothing inevitable about the current situation in the Middle East. The region is not destined to remain mired in violence, extremism, political authoritarianism, and underdevelopment. Just as other parts of the world have done in the past, the Middle East is traveling the perilous and blood-soaked journey of nation-building.[1] We might be witnessing the painful birth pangs of a new order out of the death throes of the old one: a transitional moment characterized by civil wars and contentious social struggles.

Right now, it is difficult to see what might come next. But once the dust settles on the battlefields, Middle Easterners, like their European and Asian counterparts, will have to find legal and institutional mechanisms to rebuild their shattered states and economies. It is a herculean task that will take time, resources, political will, and imagination. But there is no other way.

The social contract that governs relations between state and society in the Middle East has collapsed for good. It can only be restored along constitutional and representation lines. Since the1970s, autocrats in the region prioritized economic liberalization at the expense of political liberalization and representation, seeking to maintain control while wooing foreign investment and neglecting social security and justice. The tragedy of Arab politics since the 1970s is that the people attained neither democracy nor prosperity. A lesson learned at great costs: economic liberalization cannot succeed without political representation, citizenship, and respect for the agency of the people. The two processes are intertwined. The plundering of the Arab economies and ongoing systemic corruption and external intervention that disfranchised the Arab people might have been prevented with accountability and transparency. In spite of desperate efforts to revive political authoritarianism in Algeria, Egypt, Iraq, Sudan, Syria, Yemen, and beyond, such obsolete models of failed governance are not sustainable over the long term. This new fluid authoritarianism has already failed to deliver the public goods and freedoms to Algerians, Egyptians, and other people in the region.

The second wave of Arab Spring uprisings beginning in Algeria, Iraq, Lebanon, and Sudan in 2018 demonstrates that local agency is alive and that the struggle for representation goes on. Anyone watching what has happened in the Arab world should not focus on *when* the protesters will achieve their aims but the fact *that* they will. That is because they are taking the most important step by changing their societies at the most fundamental level: citizenship. The cry across the region is for "*almuatina*," literally translated as "citizenship," but in this case standing for a far broader appeal from the heart: "I want to be the master of my own destiny!" Despite being killed, battered, the Palestinians continue to fight to end Israeli military occupation of their lands and gain freedom. It is a moment for the political and social emancipation of the people of the Middle East.

The struggle did not begin with the first wave of the Arab Spring or the second wave; it has been carried out since the establishment of the modern state system in the Middle East. Thousands of everyday people have paid with their lives in their struggle against foreign domination, settler colonialism, political authoritarianism, and militarism. The prisons and dungeons of Saddam Hussein, the House of Assad, Gaddafi, the Islamic Republic of Iran, Israel, the monarchies in the Gulf, and other autocrats clearly show that Middle Eastern people aspire to freedom, a better life, even if the price is death. For the last 100 years, the Palestinians have been struggling and dying to gain their freedom.

The Middle East in the Global Context

Across the region, counterrevolutionary forces and authoritarian elites have won another round at the expense of those social forces struggling for change. The ability of counterrevolutionary actors to crush their opponents is due in no small measure to the support they receive from international powers like the United States and Russia, who, between them, either cling to the outdated status quo or fuel new conflicts to gain leverage on the global stage. But the Faustian pact these powers have struck with their friends in the old order is no longer tenable or acceptable. Political authoritarianism is not the guarantor of stability but is, in reality, the chief cause of instability in the Middle East.

During his two terms in office, President Barack Obama gave a few good speeches, especially his address on May 19, 2011, on the need for democracy and reform in the Middle East.[2] But he never translated his progressive rhetoric into serious policy. Moreover, by backing repressive regimes in the region, especially when so many Arabs were on the streets calling for their overthrow, the United States played into the narrative of extremists that drives Islam-West tensions. Donald Trump's actions showed contempt and disregard for the rule of law and human rights, openly and shamelessly backing autocrats and dictators. Three decades after the Islamic Revolution in Iran, Western government appear to have learned nothing from the consequences of backing the shah of Iran. Despite his rhetoric on promoting democracy and human rights, Joe Biden has pursued a similar policy to that of his predecessors—backing autocrats in the name of stability and turning a blind eye to Israeli military occupation of Palestinian territories. Biden backed Israel's military onslaught on Gaza in 2023–2024, which landed Israel before the International Court of Justice on charges of committing genocide.

The EU's view of the Middle East is equally shortsighted, though less muscular than America's and Russia's. European politicians are fixated on three goals: (1) stopping immigration from Africa and the Middle East, (2) counterterrorism, and (3) attracting foreign investment from the Gulf, particularly in the energy and arms sectors.[3] In this way, Western policies reinforce authoritarian politics. They prefer to engage with leaders in Egypt, Eritrea, Libya, Niger, Tunisia, Turkey, and elsewhere, to limit migratory movements from these countries and to combat terrorism in exchange for financial, technical, and security assistance, rather than engage with democracy activists committed to genuine change.[4]

For now, the drums of war are louder than the calls for reform and reconciliation. But when the guns eventually fall silent, and they ultimately will, the focus will shift to new patterns of governance and power. Strengthening the institutional capacity of the state, bridging the divide between government and society, empowering local authority, and providing hope for young people—all could be blueprints for the way ahead.

The Durability of the State System

A deep uncertainty hangs over the future of the region. However, we must be cautious about prematurely penning the obituary of the nation-state in the Middle East. Although weakened and made vulnerable by recent events, the Middle Eastern state has developed huge patronage networks and influence within society.

The "deep state" is indeed deep and its impact affects the lives of the majority of the population. The state is by far the biggest employer in most countries of the region with a massive bureaucracy and public sector providing jobs for millions. The security forces, particularly the military, have vested interests in the state apparatus. And because so many people directly and indirectly depend on the state for their survival, they will not easily abandon it.

As Iraq, Libya, Syria, and Yemen descended into war, the treasury continued to pay salaries of its employees even in areas under the control of armed rebels.[5] In a similar vein, the Palestinian Authority in the West Bank provides salaries for bureaucrats in Gaza under Hamas rule, at least until recently. This measure is designed to affirm state authority and patronage and co-opt people in opposition-controlled districts.

The interests of the pivotal regional powers, including Egypt, Iran, Saudi Arabia, and Turkey, lie in maintaining the current borders and preventing the emergence of new entities. These regional powers fear that once the genie is out of the bottle, their own states could disintegrate. On this issue, if on nothing else, competing powers agree: Egypt, Iran, Saudi Arabia, and Turkey are determined to maintain the territorial integrity of Iraq. The United States, Europe, China, and Russia support them on this and for the same reasons.

The Kurds of Iraq learned this to their cost after they held an independence referendum in September 2017, in which almost 93 percent of the votes favored secession. Although the Kurdistan regional government said the referendum was not binding and did not call for immediate independence, it met with opposition worldwide, including from the Kurds' long-standing patron, the United States. When Iraqi troops moved to recapture areas like Kirkuk from the Kurds in October 2017, President Trump declared, "We're not taking sides in that battle," effectively giving Iraqi prime minister Haider al-Abadi the green light to reestablish the old status quo. The irony is that Iraqi forces included pro-Iranian Shia militias, thus placing the United States and its regional nemesis, Iran, on the same side against the Kurds.

Following the US lead, the EU backed Baghdad's military action in Kirkuk. No one, not the United States, China, the EU, or Russia, has the will to draw a new map of the Middle East. They recognize the dangers and risks inherent in redrawing the borders of the region and are therefore reluctant to open Pandora's box. Building a new regional architecture is too complicated. And there is no agreement of where the new lines would be drawn.

Given this attitude, the map of the Middle East is unlikely to change. More than a hundred years after its establishment, the state system, with the exception of the creation of the State of Israel in 1948, remains in place and will mostly likely endure. The real struggle, therefore, is *within* states:

between the new ruling authoritarian populism, revolutionary or reform- ist actors, and religious activists as well as the Great Powers' continuing support to local autocrats.

Empowering Change from the Bottom Up

Rebuilding state institutions in the Middle East will take at least a couple of decades.[6] While imagining and aiming big, an intermediary effective way to institute this change is to start with small steps. This will help create trust, strengthen national unity, and build civil society. The decentraliza- tion of power to local communities would be a good place to start. That way, local communities will have a stake in the political order. Shifting resources from the center to the regions would also help allay the fears of minorities like the Kurds and disadvantaged communities.[7] But govern- ment decentralization has to guard against promoting centrifugal forces that splinter Middle Eastern states and enable nonstate actors to flourish.

Taking small steps and building from the bottom up does not mean that transformative change should be dismissed as wishful thinking. As the sec- ond wave of the Arab Spring uprisings shows, the strategic goal is to trans- form the region from authoritarianism to pluralism, from economic decline to growth, from inequality to social justice. Because sweeping reforms such as the separation of powers are difficult to realize now, the way forward about instituting change is through piecemeal initiatives and by building political and social pacts between rival factions. There is an urgent need to foster resilient institutions and open political participation as a counter- weight to sectarian and populist movements and foreign intervention.

Efforts to nurture resilience in civil society requires engagement with the ruling elite to convince them that this formula is not designed to un- dermine state-society relations but to deepen the ties that bind them together. A gradual political transition has a good chance of success because a strategy rooted in gradualism would not threaten the vital in- terests of key stakeholders or face fierce official resistance. Engagement with the ruling elite could entail providing assistance to key state insti- tutions that foster societal resilience, such as education, climate change, and renewable energy, health, the agricultural sector, and even the central bank. The challenge is to develop capacities that positively contribute to societal resilience, while making sure that any such development does not strengthen the state's coercive capacity to control society—an important distinction that is difficult to maintain in practice.[8] An active civil society, even in an illiberal democracy, can contribute to a more dynamic exchange between leaders and their populations.[9] The United Nations and other international institutions could help conflict-ridden Arab societies heal and become more socially resilient.[10]

The alternative to building societal resilience and engagement with state institutions is revolutionary action. As the Arab Spring uprisings showed, revolutionary action in Libya, Syria, and Yemen—and more recently in Sudan—often ended up empowering exclusionary groups and bringing ruin to millions of everyday people. In Egypt, counterrevolutionary forces were able to hijack the peaceful uprising because they were better organized than the protesters. The millions of peaceful demonstrators who called for political accountability, participation, democracy, and justice lacked the revolutionary zeal and vision, and seemed unable and reluctant to articulate modes of governance and institutions different from those against which they were revolting. It is no wonder these reformist protesters proved to be no match for the established networks of the Islamists or the old regime and the deep state.[11] The high hopes of the Arab Spring crashed on the realities of the balance of power, which favored identity-based groups and, ultimately, the military, with strong links to external powers.[12] The success of the Syrian revolution in 2024 is an exception to the rule, and it is too early to know its future trajectory.

Looking at the past often sheds light on the present and future. Iran witnessed a long-lasting social revolution in the late 1970s. The country then had an important middle class, a dynamic intelligentsia, and a strong communist party called the Tudeh. After the shah fell, the odds favored the progressives. Yet, a coalition of religiously conservative small traders and the clerical establishment were able to hijack the revolution. Why? Simply put, the Islamists were better organized. They possessed a wide network of mosques, had a charismatic leader, and were willing to use force to crush their rivals. Moreover, the Islamists successfully deployed and politicized religion to rally people to their cause. Nationalists, liberals, and left-wing groups could not compete. The clerics in Iran systemically

Islamized the revolution and brutally purged leftists and secularists. What began as a democratic revolution ended as an Islamist one.[13]

Although the millions of protesters in the two Arab waves of uprisings called for a more pluralistic and representative system of governance, on the whole the formal Arab opposition is a mirror image of the existing despotic order: illiberal and insular. Organized opposition groups have been unable or unwilling to establish broad-based coalitions to defend a common set of values, and they have not resisted the temptation to collude with the authorities and turn on each other. Revolutionary action will therefore most likely produce a similarly oppressive system to the current one, though we will have to wait and see how the Syrian revolution plays itself out in the future. While critics might dismiss this scenario as fantastical because the present situation is so dire, it is hard to believe it could possibly get worse, but as the rise of the IS in 2014 indicates, there is no limit to how bleak the situation can become.

For real, transformative change to happen, there must be organized constituencies, parties, and social movements that believe in it and are willing to struggle and sacrifice to bring it about. As the two waves of the Arab Spring uprisings have demonstrated, civil society in the Arab world does not have the organizational and institutional capacity to operationalize its demands. Across the region, the overwhelming majority of people want change. But they are not organized or unified enough to make it happen, which is part of the repressive political context they inhabit. It is hoped the Syrian people might surprise the world with their ingenuity, resourcefulness, and ability to institute peaceful political change.

The region is undergoing a painful rebirth. The people of the Middle East have endured years of foreign intervention, settler colonialism, authoritarian rule, political violence, and humanitarian catastrophes. When the fog of war eventually lifts, the map of the Middle East will remain more or less the same, but the social contract between the people and the powerful will never be the same. The future of the region now depends on negotiating a new contract between rulers and citizens that is based on the rule of law, freedom, social justice, and representation. The struggle to achieve this will be prolonged, costly, and uncertain, just as it was in the long struggle for representative government in Western societies.

However, as Leo Tolstoy reminded us in *War and Peace*, his masterful chronicle of Russian life during the Napoleonic Wars, history's great protagonists, its drivers, are the ordinary people whose political will and struggle shape events. The application of Tolstoy's golden rule underscores the need to take seriously everyday people in the Middle East. Time and again, the people in the region have surprised the world by their actions and universal strivings for freedom, dignity, and justice. Although most of the world had declared that Bashar al-Assad had won the war and the that the Syrian people had lost, the latter roared to life in 2024 and reclaimed their nation from the dictator-for-life. The future of the Middle East will ultimately be determined by society below, not by the kings, emirs, and strongmen above.

NOTES

Introduction

1. Leo Tolstoy, *War and Peace*, trans. from the Russian by Richard Pevear and Larissa Volokhonsky (New York: Vintage Classics, 2008), pp. 823, 1179.

2. Tolstoy, *War and Peace*, p. 1179.

3. These historians and others broke new conceptual ground by studying history from below. See E. P. Thompson, *The Making of the English Working Class* (London: Penguin, 2013); Christopher Hill, *The English Revolution, 1640*, new ed. (London: Lawrence & Wishart, 1987); Eric Hobsbawm's trilogy about what he called the "long nineteenth century": *The Age of Revolution: Europe 1789–1848*; *The Age of Capital: 1848–1875*; and *The Age of Empire: 1875–1914*; and Howard Zinn, *A People's History of the United States* (New York: HarperCollins, 2015).

4. F. Gregory Gause III, "Why Middle East Studies Missed the Arab Spring: The Myth of Authoritarian Stability," *Foreign Affairs* 90, no. 4 (2011): 81–84, 85–90.

5. G.W.F. Hegel, *The Philosophy of History*, trans. J. Sibree (New York: Dover, 1956), p. 52, italics in original.

6. In his book *Imperialism and the Developing World*, Atul Kohli compares British formal empire during the nineteenth century with America's informal empire in the twentieth. While formal empires imply direct control of territory, *informal empires are based on "an alliance* in which elites in the imperial country allow elites on the global periphery to share in economic growth in exchange for establishing stable but ultimately subservient governments there." Kohli cites the US relationship with the shah of Iran during the global Cold War as a "classic . . . example" of an informal empire. See Atul Kohli, *Imperialism and the Developing World: How Britain and the U.S. Shaped the Global Periphery* (Oxford: Oxford University Press, 2020), pp. 4, 6.

7. Timothy Mitchell, *Colonising Egypt* (Berkeley: University of California Press, 1991).

8. Yezid Sayigh and Avi Shlaim, eds., *The Cold War and the Middle East* (Oxford: Oxford University Press, 1997).

9. L. Carl Brown, *International Politics of the Middle East: Old Rules, Dangerous Game* (Princeton, NJ: Princeton University Press, 1984), p. 16.

10. Nadine Sika, "The Political Economy of Arab Uprisings," European Institute of the Mediterranean, March 2012, https://www.iemed.org/publication/the-political-economy-of-arab-uprisings/.

11. United Nations Economic and Social Commission for Western Asia (ESCWA), "ESCWA: 31 Arab Billionaires Own as Much Wealth as Half of the Region's Population," June 3,

2020, https://www.unescwa.org/news/escwa-31-arab-billionaires-own-much-wealth-half
-region%E2%80%99s-population.

12. Zahra Babar and Suzi Mirgani, eds., *Food Security in the Middle East* (Oxford: Oxford University Press, 2014).

13. Hedrick Smith, "Nasser, Angered by Criticism, Says U. S. Can 'Jump in Lake'; Asserts Cairo Would Refuse Aid Rather Than Accept Dictation of Policy," *New York Times*, December 24, 1964, https://timesmachine.nytimes.com/timesmachine/1964/12/24/97694404.html.

14. Smith, "Nasser, Angered by Criticism."

15. Smith, "Nasser, Angered by Criticism."

16. "Low Oil Prices: The End of Gulf-Style Five-Star Socialism?," *Fanack Newsletter*, January 13, 2016, https://fanack.com/politics/features-insights/low-oil-prices~62404/.

17. Nancy A. Youssef, Vivian Salama, and Michael C. Bender, "Trump, Awaiting Egyptian Counterpart at Summit, Called Out for 'My Favorite Dictator,'" *Wall Street Journal*, September 13, 2019, https://www.wsj.com/articles/trump-awaiting-egyptian-counterpart-at-summit -called-out-for-my-favorite-dictator-11568403645.

18. As the United States pressed Saudi Arabia to end its oil price war with Russia at the height of the COVID-19 pandemic in April 2020, Trump gave Crown Prince Mohammed bin Salman an ultimatum. He warned King Salman's son that unless the Organization of the Petroleum Exporting Countries (OPEC) started cutting oil production, he would basically withdraw US troops from the Kingdom. The Saudi crown prince obliged and slashed the oil supply. Asked if he told the crown prince that the United States might pull its forces out of Saudi Arabia, Trump arrogantly retorted, "I didn't have to tell him." See Timothy Gardner, Steve Holland, Dmitry Zhdannikov, and Rania El Gamal, "Special Report: Trump Told Saudi: Cut Oil Supply or Lose U.S. Military Support—Sources," Reuters, April 30, 2020, https://www .reuters.com/article/us-global-oil-trump-saudi-specialreport-idUSKBN22C1V4.

19. Alex Emmons, Aída Chávez, and Akela Lacy, "Joe Biden, in Departure from Obama Policy, Says He Would Make Saudi Arabia a 'Pariah,'" The Intercept, November 21, 2019, https:// theintercept.com/2019/11/21/democratic-debate-joe-biden-saudi-arabia/.

20. United Nations Economic and Social Commission for Western Asia (ESCWA), *Rethinking Inequality in Arab Countries*, no. 2, 2019, https://www.unescwa.org/sites/www .unescwa.org/files/publications/files/rethinking-inequality-arab-countries-english.pdf.

21. Statistics on violence worldwide show the Middle East and North Africa (MENA) region still ranks as highest for political violence and deaths and conflict. See Armed Conflict Location & Event Data Project (ACLED), *Year in Review 2019*, 2019, https://acleddata.com/acleddatanew /wp-content/uploads/dlm_uploads/2020/03/ACLED_AnnualReport2019_WebV2020.pdf.

22. See MERIP's double issue devoted to the "Return to Revolution," *Middle East Report and Information Project* (MERIP), nos. 292–293 (Fall/Winter 2019), https://merip.org/2019 /12/return-to-revolution/.

23. See the excellent book by Asef Bayat, *Life as Politics: How Ordinary People Change the Middle East*, 2nd ed. (Stanford, CA: Stanford University Press, 2013).

24. Bessma Momani, *Arab Dawn: Arab Youth and the Demographic Dividend They Will Bring* (Toronto: University of Toronto Press, 2016).

25. For good studies of Arab public opinion, see Arab Pulse—Abdul-Wahab Kayyali, "The Arab World's Trust in Government and the Perils of Generalization," *Arab Barometer*,

June 23, 2020, https://www.arabbarometer.org/2020/06/the-arab-worlds-trust-in-government-and-the-perils-of-generalization/.

26. A new generation of scholars are writing original accounts of popular activism in the Middle East. For an impressive sample, see Asef Bayat, *Life as Politics* (Stanford, CA: Stanford University Press, 2010); and John Chalcraft, *Popular Politics in the Making of the Modern Middle East* (New York: Cambridge University Press, 2016).

27. UNESCWA, IMF, and the World Bank painted a gloomy picture of the effects of the COVID-19 pandemic on the regional economy, although they acknowledged there was substantial uncertainty around this projection. Economic activity in the MENA region contracted sharply (by 4.2 percent) in 2020, as consumption, exports, oil prices, and the services sector (e.g., tourism) were severely disrupted by COVID-19. More than 1.7 million jobs were expected to be lost in 2020. Unlike in the aftermath of the global 2008 financial crisis, employment is expected to be affected across all sectors. The services sector, the region's main employment provider, is particularly hit due to "social distancing." Estimates pointed to a reduction by half of service sector jobs. Russia's invasion of the Ukraine in February 2022 and Israel's war in Gaza in October 2024 have had adverse effects on the region's economies in terms of inflation, capital flow, debts, unemployment, and poverty (more of this in subsequent chapters). See IMF, "Confronting the COVID-19 Pandemic in the Middle East and Central Asia, April 2020," https://www.imf.org/en/Publications/REO/MECA/Issues/2020/04/15/regional-economic-outlook-middle-east-central-asia-report; see also World Bank, "Middled East and North Africa," in *Global Economic Prospects*, June 2020, http://pubdocs.worldbank.org/en/950801588788414569/Global-Economic-Prospects-June-2020-Analysis-MENA.pdf; and UNESCWA, "At Least 1.7 Million Jobs Will Be Lost in the Arab Region Due to the Coronavirus Pandemic," March 18, 2020, https://www.unescwa.org/news/least-17-million-jobs-will-be-lost-arab-region-due-coronavirus-pandemic; for the full report, see UNESCWA, "COVID-19: Economic Cost to the Arab Region," September 2020, https://www.unescwa.org/sites/www.unescwa.org/files/escwa-covid-19-economic-cost-arab-region-en.pdf.

28. "In the past decade, the MENA has experienced the largest increase of mass protests in the world, an increase by an annual average of 11.5 percent. The two waves of the Arab Spring uprisings were not an isolated phenomenon but rather an acute manifestation of a broadly increasing global trend. Analysis of the drivers of these global protests, particularly in the MENA, suggests they will continue and could increase in 2020 and beyond. While each protest has a unique context, common grievances overwhelmingly center on perceptions of ineffective governance and corruption." See Center for Strategic and International Studies, *The Age of Mass Protests: Understanding an Escalating Global Trend*, March 2, 2020, https://www.csis.org/analysis/age-mass-protests-understanding-escalating-global-trend. See also ACLED, *Year in Review 2019*.

Chapter 1: The Original Sin

1. Roxanne Lynn Doty, *Imperial Encounters: The Politics of Representation in North-South Relations* (Minneapolis: University of Minnesota Press, 1996), p. 3.

2. Malcolm Yapp, *The Making of the Modern Near East, 1792–1923* (London: Longman, 1993), p. 278.

3. Yapp, *The Making of the Modern Near East*, p. 279.

4. Jean-Pierre Filiu, *Les Arabes, leur destin et le nôtre* (Paris: La Découverte, 2018), p. 55.

5. Reinhard Schulze, *A Modern History of the Islamic World* (New York: New York University Press, 2002), p. 55.

6. Husayn's letter dated July 14, 1915, in George Antonius, *The Arab Awakening* (London: J. B. Lippincott, 1939), p. 414.

7. Husayn specifies that these Arab countries "are bounded: on the north, by the line Mersin-Adana to parallel 37 degrees N. and thence along the line Birejik-Urfa-Mardin-Midiat-Jazirat (ibn Umar)—Amadia to the Persian frontier; on the south, by the Indian Ocean (with the exclusion of Aden whose status will remain as at present); on the west, by the Red Sea and the Mediterranean Sea back to Mersin."

8. Husayn's letter dated July 14, 1915, in Antonius, *The Arab Awakening*, p. 414.

9. Antonius, *The Arab Awakening*, p. 164.

10. Sir Henry McMahon's letter, dated August 30, 1915, in Antonius, *The Arab Awakening*, p. 416.

11. Sharif Husayn's letter, dated September 9, 1915, in Antonius, *The Arab Awakening*, p. 417.

12. Sir Henry McMahon's letter, dated October 24, 1915, in Antonius, *The Arab Awakening*, p. 419.

13. Elizabeth Monroe, *Britain's Moment in the Middle East* (London: Chatto and Windus, 1981), p. 32.

14. Husayn's letter written on January 1, 1916, in Antonius, *The Arab Awakening*, p. 425.

15. The Dardanelles campaign refers to a British naval operation against the Dardanelles in the Ottoman Empire. It lasted from February 1915 till March 1915. The Royal Navy was supported by France, and to a lesser extent Russia.

16. David Fromkin, *A Peace to End All Peace: Creating the Modern Middle East 1914–1922* (London: Penguin Books, 1991), p. 146.

17. Fromkin, *A Peace to End All Peace*, p. 147.

18. Fromkin, *A Peace to End All Peace*, p. 146.

19. Fromkin, *A Peace to End All Peace*, p. 147.

20. Fromkin, *A Peace to End All Peace*, p. 149.

21. Yapp, *The Making of the Modern Near East*, p. 277.

22. Yapp, *The Making of the Modern Near East*, p. 277.

23. Yapp, *The Making of the Modern Near East*. See also M. E. McMillan, *From the First World War to the Arab Spring: What's Really Going on in the Middle East?* (New York: Palgrave Macmillan, 2016), pp. 70–76.

24. Fromkin, *A Peace to End All Peace*, p. 190.

25. The report was written by Senator Etienne Flandin, a member of the pressure group Amis de l'Orient (Friends of the East).

26. David K. Fieldhouse, *Western Imperialism in the Middle East: 1914–1958* (Oxford: Oxford University Press, 2006), p. 49.

27. Jennifer M. Dueck, *The Claims of Culture at Empire's End: Syria and Lebanon under French Rule* (London: British Academy, 2009). See also Idir Ouahes, *Syria and Lebanon under the French Mandate: Cultural Imperialism and the Workings of Empire* (London: I. B. Tauris, 2018).

28. See McMillan, *From the First World War to the Arab Spring.*

29. Ironically, the Alawites in Syria were then drawn to the anti-imperialist rhetoric of the pan-Arabist Baath Party in the interwar period. Indeed, the Baath made big inroads in the military, and thus was able to recruit many members from the Alawi community. The late president Hafez Al-Assad, for example, was imbued with an anti-French sentiment in his youth when he joined the Baath. See Patrick Seale, *Asad of Syria: The Struggle for the Middle East* (London: I. B. Tauris, 1988). So there is an irony there for the French that their "clients" in Syria turned against them. This shows the complexity of the colonial relationship with the minorities.

30. Eugene Rogan, *The Arabs: A History* (London: Penguin Books, 2011), p. 455.

31. On this, see the work of Hanna Batatu on both Syria and Iraq. See Hanna Batatu, *The Old Social Classes and the Revolutionary Movement in Iraq: A Study of Iraq's Old Landed and Commercial Classes and of Its Communists, Ba'thists and Free Officers* (Princeton, NJ: Princeton University Press, 1978); and Hanna Batatu, *Syria's Peasantry, the Descendants of Its Lesser Rural Notables, and Their Politics* (Princeton, NJ: Princeton University Press, 1999).

32. Fromkin, *A Peace to End All Peace*, p. 189.

33. Fromkin, *A Peace to End All Peace*, p. 189.

34. Antonius, *The Arab Awakening*, p. 246.

35. Filiu, *Les Arabes*, p. 59.

36. See Fieldhouse, *Western Imperialism in the Middle East*; and Raja Shehadeh and Penny Johnson, *Shifting Sands: The Unravelling of the Old Order in the Middle East* (London: Profile Books, 2015).

37. For more on Britain's legacy, see Anthony Parsons, *They Say the Lion: Britain's Legacy to the Arabs—A Personal Memoir* (London: Jonathan Cape, 1986).

38. Robin Wright, "How the Curse of Sykes-Picot Still Haunts the Middle East," *New Yorker*, April 30, 2016, http://www.newyorker.com/news/news-desk/how-the-curse-of-sykes-picot -still-haunts-the-middle-east.

39. David Fromkin, *A Peace to End All Peace: The Fall of the Ottoman Empire and the Creation of the Modern Middle East*, with new afterword (New York: Henry Holt, 2009), p. 191.

40. Monroe, *Britain's Moment*, p. 32.

41. Filiu, *Les Arabes*, p. 61.

42. Monroe, *Britain's Moment*, p. 34.

43. Monroe, *Britain's Moment*, p. 160.

44. Quoted in Charles D. Smith, *Palestine and the Arab-Israeli Conflict*, 10th ed. (Boston: Bedford, 2020), p. 75.

45. For more on the relationship between David Lloyd George and the Zionist movement, see Leonard Stein, *The Balfour Declaration* (New York: American Council of Learned Societies, 2008), pp. 137–146.

46. See Avi Shlaim in Wm. Roger Louis, ed., *Yet More Adventures with Britannia: Personalities, Politics and Culture in Britain* (London: I. B. Tauris, 2005), pp. 251–270. For more on the Bafour Declaration, see Fromkin, *A Peace to End all Peace*; and Joseph Mary Nagle Jeffries, *Palestine: The Reality: The Inside Story on the Balfour Declaration 1917–1983* (Northampton, MA: Olive Branch Press, 2017).

47. In an interview with Al Jazeera, prominent historian Avi Shlaim points out that the concept of "national home" does not exist under international law, making the institutionalization

of the Balfour Declaration within the context of international law all the more bankrupt. See Mersiha Gadzo, "Balfour: UK Government 'Should Hang Its Head in Shame,'" *Al Jazeera*, October 29, 2017, https://www.aljazeera.com/news/2017/10/balfour-uk-government-hang -head-shame-171028084045226.html.

48. Edward W. Said, *Reflections on Exile and Other Essays* (Cambridge, MA; Harvard University Press, 2000), pp. 431–432.

49. See Rashid Khalidi, *Palestinian Identity: The Construction of Modern National Consciousness* (New York: Columbia University Press, 1997). See also "From Balfour to Boris: Britain's Broken Promises in Palestine," *The New Arab*, October 16, 2017, https://english.alaraby .co.uk/english/comment/2017/10/16/from-balfour-to-boris-britains-broken-promises-in -palestine.

50. Rashid Khalidi, *The Hundred Years' War on Palestine: A History of Settler Colonialism and Resistance, 1917–2017* (New York: Metropolitan Books, 2020).

51. It is worth noting that the colonial powers did not create all borders of the Arab states: some states had existed roughly within the same borders for a millennium like Egypt. As a Middle East state, Iran had not been formally colonized. As in Europe, some countries were formed either through local military conquests like Saudi Arabia, or through dealmaking among elites such as the central fertile crescent area. It wasn't the entire Arab Middle East that fell victim to the Sykes-Picot Agreement. Much as in pre–World War I Europe, especially in the Balkans, what writer S. B. Cohen in his book *Geography and Politics in a World Divided* calls a "shatterbelt": this consists of internally divided multiethnic states, as those partially inspired by Sykes-Picot in the fertile crescent, which are used as a battlefield for major regional and extraregional powers. See Saul Bernard Cohen, *Geography and Politics in a World Divided*, 2nd ed. (New York: Oxford University Press, 1973).

Chapter 2: The Great Betrayal

1. Susan Pedersen, *The Guardians: The League of Nations and the Crisis of Empire* (Oxford: Oxford University Press, 2015), p. 22.

2. See Zachary Lockman, *Contending Visions of the Middle East: The History and Politics of Orientalism* (Cambridge: Cambridge University Press, 2010); Edward Said, *Orientalism* (London: Pantheon Books, 1978); see also Thomas McCarthy, who traces the foundations of civilizational and racial hierarchies in *Social Darwinism and Enlightenment Thought: Race, Empire and the Idea of Human Development* (Cambridge: Cambridge University Press, 2009), p. 69.

3. William Cleveland and Martin Bunton, *A History of the Modern Middle East* (Boulder, CO: Westview Press, 2009), p. 125.

4. Elizabeth Monroe, *Britain's Moment in the Middle East* (London: Chatto and Windus, 1981), p. 19.

5. Monroe, *Britain's Moment in the Middle East*, p. 15.

6. Monroe, *Britain's Moment in the Middle East*, p. 19.

7. Cleveland and Bunton, *A History of the Modern Middle East*, p. 125.

8. Monroe, *Britain's Moment in the Middle East*, p. 125.

9. Monroe, *Britain's Moment in the Middle East*, p. 76.

10. Walter Reid, *Empire of Sand: How Britain Made the Middle East* (Edinburgh: Birlinn, 2011), p. 339.

11. Jean-Pierre Filiu, *Les Arabes, leur destin et le nôtre* (Paris: La Découverte, 2018), p. 67.

12. Filiu, *Les Arabes*, p. 67.

13. Eugene Rogan, *The Arabs: A History* (London: Penguin Books, 2011), p. 316. The first part of the twentieth century witnessed the rise of the Arab nationalist intellectuals in the Ottoman Empire, many of whom had been educated in Paris and London and Europe more generally. These intellectuals were inspired by German nationalism, eulogized the West to a certain extent, and were highly critical of the Ottoman Empire. Very often this intellectual movement coincided with, or inspired, political activism by Arab inhabitants within the Ottoman Empire. See Sylvia Kedourie, *Arab Nationalism: An Anthology* (Berkeley: University of California Press, 1962).

14. Quoted in Rogan, *The Arabs*, p. 318.

15. Rogan, *The Arabs*, p. 319.

16. Rogan, *The Arabs*, p. 324.

17. Rogan, *The Arabs*, p. 327.

18. Rogan, *The Arabs*, p. 328.

19. Elizabeth F. Thompson, How the West Stole Democracy from the Arabs: The Syrian Congress of 1920 and the Destruction of its Historic Liberal-Islamic Alliance (New York: Atlantic Monthly Press, 2020).

20. Woodrow Wilson's Fourteen Points were presented in a speech on January 8, 1919, at the League of Nations. They espoused the principle of self-determination but were welcomed skeptically by Britain and France as they were seen to contradict the imperial powers' interests in the Middle East.

21. L. Carl Brown, *International Politics and the Middle East: Old Rules, Dangerous Games* (Princeton, NJ: Princeton University Press, 1984), p. 89.

22. For good references that detail the revolts in Syria and Iraq, see Phillip Khoury, *Syria and the French Mandate: the Politics of Arab Nationalism, 1920–1945* (London: I. B. Tauris, 1987), esp. chap. 7; Aula Hariri, "The Iraqi Independence Movement: A Case of Transgressive Contention, 1918–1920," in *Contentious Politics in the Middle East: Popular Resistance and Marginalized Activism beyond the Arab Uprisings*, ed. Fawaz A. Gerges (New York: Palgrave Macmillan, 2015), pp. 97–124.

23. Cleveland and Bunton, *A History of the Modern Middle East*, p. 168.

24. Quoted in Charles D. Smith, *Palestine and the Arab-Israeli Conflict*, 10th ed. (Boston: Bedford, 2020), p. 80.

25. Smith, *Palestine and the Arab-Israeli Conflict*, p. 81.

26. David K. Fieldhouse, *Western Imperialism in the Middle East 1914–1958* (Oxford: Oxford University Press, 2006), pp. 151–219; Jeremy Salt, *The Unmaking of the Middle East: A History of Western Disorder in Arab Lands* (Berkeley: University of California Press, 2008), pp. 121–148; Baruch Kimmerling and Joel S. Migdal, *The Palestinian People: A History* (Cambridge, MA: Harvard University Press, 2003). See their introduction, which outlines the colonial mentality that underpinned British and Zionist approaches to the "Palestinian question."

27. On the Israeli point of view, see Amos Elon, *Founders and Sons* (New York: Holt, Rinehart, and Winston, 1971); and Ari Shavit, *My Promised Land: The Triumph and Tragedy of Israel* (New York: Spiegel and Grau, 2015).

28. Rashid Khalidi, *Palestinian Identity: The Construction of Modern National Consciousness* (New York: Columbia University Press, 1997), p. 213. Ilan Pappé also discusses the "erasure" of Palestinians from political discourse in Western academia in the introduction to *The Israel/Palestine Question: A Reader*, 2nd ed. (New York: Routledge, 2007).

29. See Adam Garfinkle, "The Bullshitstory of 'Sykes-Picot,'" *The American Interest*, May 16, 2016, http://www.the-american-interest.com/2016/05/16/the-bullshistory-of-sykes-picot/; Adam Garfinkle, "The Origins of the Palestine Mandate," *Foreign Policy Research Institute*, November 2014, http://www.fpri.org/docs/garfinkle_-_hi_-_palestine_mandate.pdf.

30. An Islamic ruling issued by a high authority or religious leader.

31. Eliezer Tauber, *The Formation of Modern Iraq and Syria* (Portland, OR: Frank Cass, 1994), p. 301.

32. On this see Kathryn Tidrick, *Heart Beguiling Araby: The English Romance with Arabia* (London: I. B. Tauris Parke Paperbacks, 2009).

33. Jean-Pierre Filiu, *Les Arabes, leur destin et le nôtre* (Paris: La Découverte, 2018), pp. 70–71.

34. For more discussion by Arabic writers on the role of the Great Powers in undermining the territorial integrity of the Arab region, see Gerges Fathallah, *Nazarat Fil Qawmiyya al-Arabiyya Hatta 'Am 1970* [An overview on Arab nationalism till 1970], Part I (Erbil: El-Jamal, 2012).

35. "64 Years Later, CIA Finally Releases Details of Iranian Coup," *Foreign Policy*, June 20, 2017, https://foreignpolicy.com/2017/06/20/64-years-later-cia-finally-releases-details-of-iranian-coup-iran-tehran-oil/.

36. Both Arab public intellectuals and state discourse often assert that Iran and Turkey behave toward the Arab countries in similar ways to the colonialists and constantly seek to weaken the territorial integrity of neighboring Arab states. See the analysis of Iran's image in the school textbooks in Arab states, Talal Al-Atrisi, *Al-Jumhuriyya al-Sa'ba: Iran fi Tahwulatiha al-Dakhiliaa wa Siyassatiha al-Iqlimiyya* [The difficult republic: Iran's internal transformation and regional policies] (London: Al-Saqi, 2006), pp. 121–169.

37. It is worth mentioning that the term "Middle East" itself is a Western construction, a constant reminder to the people of the region of the preponderant role that the Western powers have played in the construction of the state system. For millions of Arabs, they substitute the "Arab world" for the "Middle East," signifying rejection of the foreign term.

38. Here are examples of this scepticism of some Western commentators: David Siddhartha Patel, "Repartitioning the Sykes-Picot Middle East? Debunking Three Myths," Middle East Brief 103, Brandeis University, November 2016, https://www.brandeis.edu/crown/publications/meb/MEB103.pdf; Steven A. Cook and Amr T. Leheta, "Don't Blame Sykes-Picot for the Middle East's Mess," *Foreign Policy*, May 13, 2016, http://foreignpolicy.com/2016/05/13/sykes-picot-isnt-whats-wrong-with-the-modern-middle-east-100-years.

39. "Abbas on Trump Peace Plan: 'Conspiracy Deal Won't Pass," BBC, January 28, 2020, https://www.bbc.co.uk/news/av/world-middle-east-51288022/abbas-on-trump-peace-plan-conspiracy-deal-won-t-pass.

Chapter 3: Rhetoric versus Reality

1. The United Kingdom opposed the rise of genuine Arab nationalism and Arab unity because such a step "could run against its own interests" and "would endanger its existing policies." See Youssef Choueiri, *Bayna al-Nas wal Hamesh: Derasa fi al-Tarikh wal-Qawmiyya wal-Deen* [Between text and margin: A study about history, nationalism and religion] (London: Riad El-Rayyes Books, 1988), p. 98.

2. Fred Halliday, *The Middle East in International Relations: Power, Politics and Ideology* (Cambridge: Cambridge University Press, 2005), p. 49.

3. William Roger Louis, "The Era of the Mandates System and the Non-European World," in *The Expansion of International Society*, ed. Hedley Bull and Adam Watson (Oxford: Oxford University Press, 1984), pp. 201–213.

4. League of Nations Covenant, Article 22, paras. 1–2.

5. See Ali Afifi Ali Ghazi, "Misr wal Harb Al-'Alamiyya al-Ulla bayna 1914–1918" [Egypt and World War I—1914–1918], in *Al-Tariq ella Sykes-Pictot, Al-Harb al-A'lamiyya al-Ula be U'youn Arabiyya* [The road to Sykes-Picot: World War I through Arab eyes], ed. Rachid Khashana (Doha: Aljazeera Centre for Studies, 2016), pp. 117–148. In his chapter, Ghazi also explores sociopolitical changes, including those related to shifts in the class system.

6. This section on Egypt relies on chapters 1 and 2 of my book *Making the Arab World: Nasser, Qutb and the Clash That Shaped the Middle East* (Princeton, NJ: Princeton University Press, 2018).

7. Marius Deeb, *Party Politics in Egypt: The Wafd and Its Rivals, 1919–1939* (London: Ithaca Press for the Middle East Centre, St Antony's College, Oxford, 1979), p. 320.

8. Israel Gershoni and James P. Jankowski, *Redefining the Egyptian Nation* (Cambridge: Cambridge University Press, 1995), pp. 11–12.

9. Jacques Berque, *Egypt: Imperialism and Revolution* (London: Faber, 1972), p. 418.

10. Gershoni and Jankowski, *Redefining the Egyptian Nation*, p. 1.

11. Gershoni and Jankowski, *Redefining the Egyptian Nation*, pp. 1–2.

12. See Abdel-Azeem Ramadan, *Tatawur al-Haraka al-Wataniyya fi Misr 1918–1936* [The development of the nationalist movement in Egypt, 1918–1936], vol. 1 (Cairo: Al-Hayaa al-Misriyya al-'Ama Leil Kitab, 1998).

13. Gerges, *Making the Arab World*, chaps. 1 and 2.

14. Eugene Rogan, *The Arabs: A History* (London: Penguin Books, 2011), p. 376.

15. Rogan, *The Arabs*, p. 377.

16. Rogan, *The Arabs*, p. 383.

17. Albert Hourani, Philip Shukry Khoury, and Mary Christina Wilson, eds., *The Modern Middle East: A Reader* (Berkeley: University of California Press, 1993), p. 513.

18. Hourani, Khoury, and Wilson, *The Modern Middle East*.

19. Hourani, Khoury, and Wilson, *The Modern Middle East*.

20. Fanar Haddad, *Sectarianism in Iraq: Antagonistic Visions of Unity* (Oxford: Oxford University Press, 2011), p. 42.

21. Haddad, *Sectarianism in Iraq*.

22. Walter Reid, *Empire of Sand: How Britain Made the Middle East* (Edinburgh: Birlinn, 2011), p. 566.

23. Reid, *Empire of Sand*, 593.

24. Reid, *Empire of Sand*, 594.

25. Rogan, *The Arabs*, p. 456.

26. Rogan, *The Arabs*, p. 456.

27. Phillip Khoury, *Syria and the French Mandate: The Politics of Arab Nationalism, 1920–1945* (London: I. B. Tauris, 1987), p. 136.

28. Khoury, *Syria and the French Mandate*, 483.

29. Khoury, *Syria and the French Mandate*, 483.

30. Khoury, *Syria and the French Mandate*, p. 486.

31. David McDowall, *A Modern History of the Kurds* (London: I. B. Tauris, 2007), p. xi.

32. "1988: Thousands Die in Halabja Gas Attack," BBC, accessed April 15, 2017, http://news.bbc.co.uk/onthisday/hi/dates/stories/march/16/newsid_4304000/4304853.stm.

33. "Stateless Kurds in Syria Granted Citizenship," CNN, April 8, 2011, http://edition.cnn.com/2011/WORLD/meast/04/07/syria.kurdish.citizenship/.

34. "Stateless Kurds in Syria Granted Citizenship."

35. William Cleveland and Martin Bunton, *A History of the Modern Middle East* (Boulder, CO: Westview Press, 2009), p. 170.

36. Kjetil Selvik and Stig Stenslie, *Stability and Change in the Modern Middle East* (London: I. B. Tauris, 2011), p. 43.

37. The Syrian Legion, also known as the Army of the Levant, was an armed force organized, trained, and managed by the French authorities in Syria. It contained mostly men from minority communities in Syria.

38. See Gerges, *Making the Arab World*.

39. See Salma Botman, *The Rise of Egyptian Communism, 1939–1970* (Syracuse, NY: Syracuse University Press, 1988), p. 20.

40. Gamal Abdul Nasser, *Falsafat Al-Thawra* [The philosophy of the revolution], 9th ed. (Cairo: Dar al-Sha'ab, n.d.), p. 11.

41. Mohammed Ayoob, *The Many Faces of Political Islam* (Ann Arbor: University of Michigan Press, 2007).

42. Steven Heydemann, *Authoritarianism in Syria: Institutions and Social Conflict, 1946–1970* (Ithaca, NY: Cornell University Press, 1999).

43. M. Valbjorn and A. Bank, "The New Arab Cold War: Rediscovering the Arab Dimension of Middle East Regional Politics." *Review of International Studies* 38, no. 1 (2012): 3–24.

Chapter 4: Life after Independence

1. Bassam Yousef, *Human Development in Iraq: 1950–1990* (Oxford: Routledge, 2012).

2. Thomas R. Mockaitis, *The Iraq War: A Documentary and Reference Guide* (Santa Barbara, CA: Greenwood Press, 2012), p. 33.

3. David Kashki, "Syrian Oil and Gas: Little-Known Facts on Syria's Energy Resources and Russia's Help," *International Business Times*, April 9, 2013, http://www.ibtimes.com/syrian-oil-gas-little-known-facts-syrias-energy-resources-russias-help-1402405.

4. Armin Rosen, "The Industry behind the World's 9th-Largest Proven Oil Reserves Has All but Collapsed," Business Insider UK, February 17, 2105, http://uk.businessinsider.com/libya

-has-48-billion-barrels-of-oil-but-its-industry-has-almost-entirely-collapsed-2015-2?r
=US&IR=T.

5. William Wager Cooper and Piyu Yue, *Challenges of the Muslim World: Present, Future and Past* (Amsterdam: Elsevier, 2008), p. 58.

6. Jack G. Kaikati, "The Economy of Sudan: A Potential Breadbasket of the Arab World?," *International Journal of Middle East Studies* 11, no. 1 (February 1980): 99.

7. Arthur Goldschmidt, *Historical Dictionary of Egypt*, 4th ed. (Lanham, MD: Scarecrow Press, 2013), p. 124.

8. Younan Labib Rizq, "Al-Guzour al-Tarikihia leil Ahzab al-Misriyya" [The historical roots of the Egyptian parties], in *Al-Ahzab al-Misriyya: 1922–1953* [The Egyptian parties: 1922–1953], ed. R. A. Hamed (Cairo: Markaz al-Ahram li-l-Dirasat al-Siyasiyya wa-l-Istratijiyya, 1995), p. 35.

9. No Author, *Al-Dasatir al-Misriyya, 1805–1971: Nusus wa tahlil* [The Egyptian constitutions, 1805–1971: Texts and analysis] (Cairo: Markaz al-Tanzim wa al-Microfilm, 1977), pp. 79, 159–160.

10. Marius Deeb, *Party Politics in Egypt: The Wafd and Its Rivals, 1919–1939* (London: Ithaca Press for the Middle East Centre, St Antony's College, Oxford, 1979), p. 124; No Author, *Al-Dasatir al-Misriyya*, pp. 162–165.

11. The Editors of Encyclopedia Britannica, "Wafd," *Enyclopedia Britanniaca*, accessed November 1, 2013, http://www.britannica.com/EBchecked/topic/633823/Wafd.

12. Eugene Rogan, *The Arabs: A History* (London: Penguin Books, 2011), p. 579. For more on Black Saturday, see also Arthur Goldschmidt, Amy J. Johnson, and Barak A. Salmoni, *Re-envisioning Egypt 1919–1952* (Cairo: American University in Cairo Press, 2005), p. 108.

13. Rashid Khalidi, Lisa Anderson, Muhammad Muslih, and Reeva S. Simon, eds., *The Origins of Arab Nationalism* (New York: Columbia University Press, 1991), p. vii.

14. Adeed Dawisha, *Arab Nationalism in the Twentieth Century: From Triumph to Despair* (Princeton, NJ: Princeton University Press, 2003), p. 2. See also Adeed Dawisha, "A Requiem for Arab Nationalism," *Middle East Quarterly* 10, no. 1 (2003); Hilal Khashan, *Arabs at the Crossroads: Political Identity and Nationalism* (Gainesville: University Press of Florida, 2000); James G. Mellon, "Pan-Arabism, Pan-Islamism and Inter-State Relations in the Arab World," *Nationalism and Ethnic Politics* 8, no. 4 (2002): 1–15; Bassam Tibi, *Arab Nationalism: Between Islam and the Nation-State* (Houndmills, UK: Palgrave Macmillan, 1980); Aparajita Gogoi and Gazi Ibdewi Abdulghafour, *Arab Nationalism: Birth, Evolution and the Present Dilemma* (New Delhi: Lancer Books, 1994).

15. Dawisha, *Arab Nationalism in the Twentieth Century*, p. 2.

16. Zeine N. Zeine, *The Emergence of Arab Nationalism* (Beirut: Khatay, 1966), p. 83.

17. Khalidi et al., *The Origins of Arab Nationalism*, p. x; Gogoi and Abdulghafour, *Arab Nationalism*. See also Israel Gershoni and James P. Jankowski, *Redefining the Egyptian Nation* (Cambridge: Cambridge University Press, 1995).

18. Khalidi et al., *The Origins of Arab Nationalism*, p. xi.

19. Stephen Humphreys, *Between Memory and Desire: The Middle East in a Troubled Age* (Berkeley: University of California Press, 2001), p. 64.

20. Jasmine Gani, "Arab Nationalism in Praxis: A Conceptual and Historical Reassessment," in *Ashgate Research Companion on Middle East Politics*, ed. Raymond Hinnebusch (London: Routledge, 2018).

21. Humphreys, *Between Memory and Desire*, p. 64.

22. See Rashid Khalidi, *Palestinian Identity: The Construction of Modern National Consciousness* (New York: Columbia University Press, 1997). See also contributions in James Jankowski and Israel Gershoni, eds., *Rethinking Nationalism in the Arab Middle East* (New York: Columbia University Press, 1997).

23. Rogan, *The Arabs*, p. 570; Khashan, *Arabs at the Crossroads.*

24. For a more detailed background on the various forms of collective identity, including pan-Islamism, territorial nationalism, Arab nationalism, and communism and socialism in the region at the time, see Ilham Khuri-Makdisi, "Levantine Trajectories: The Formulation and Dissemination of Radical Ideas in and between Beirut, Cairo, and Alexandria, 1860–1914" (PhD thesis, Harvard University, 2003), pp. 1–25; Albert Hourani, *Arabic Thought in the Liberal Age, 1798–1939* (Cambridge: Cambridge University Press, 1983), pp. 341–343; and Tibi, *Arab Nationalism.*

25. Albert Hourani, *A History of the Arab Peoples* (London: Faber and Faber, 1991), p. 586.

26. Cited in Dawisha, *Arab Nationalism*, p. 1.

27. Gamal Abdel Nasser, *Falsafat al-Thawra* [The philosophy of the revolution] (Cairo: Matab'i al-Dar al-Qawmiyya, n.d.), p. 64.

28. Nasser, *Falsafat al-Thawra*, p. 57.

29. Gerges, *Making the Arab World.*

30. Nasser, *Falsafat Al-Thawra*, p. 11.

31. Gerges, *Making the Arab World.*

32. One of the first foreign acts of Ayatollah Khomeini after the revolution that toppled the shah of Iran in the late 1970s was to invite the leader of the Palestine Liberation Organization (PLO), Yasir Arafat, to Tehran and hand him the key to the Israeli embassy. Designed to appeal to the Islamic imagination, Khomeini's symbolic-political deed spoke to the resonance of Palestine in distant Muslim lands, not just the Arab lands.

33. M. Fayek, interview by Fawaz Gerges in Cairo, November 26, 2006.

34. Elie Podeh and Onn Winckler, *Rethinking Nasserism: Revolution and Historical Memory in Modern Egypt* (Gainesville: University Press of Florida, 2004), p. 23.

35. See Lliya F. Harik, *The Political Mobilization of Peasants* (Bloomington: Indiana University Press, 1974).

36. Sami A. Hanna and George H. Gardner, eds., *Arab Socialism: A Documentary Survey* (Leiden, the Netherlands: E. J. Brill, 1969), p. 10.

37. Alan Richards, "Egypt's Agriculture in Trouble," *Middle East Research and Information Project* 84, no. 10 (January/February 1980), http://www.merip.org/mer/mer84/egypts -agriculture-trouble.

38. Anouar Abdel Malek, *Egypt: Military Society: The Army Regime, the Left, and Social Change under Nasser* (New York: Vintage Books, 1968), p. 61.

39. Peter Mansfield, *Nasser's Egypt* (Harmondsworth, UK: Penguin Books, 1965), pp. 174–178.

40. See also Hanna and Gardner, *Arab Socialism.*

41. For more on the land reform, see Ninette S. Fahmy, *The Politics of Egypt: State-Society Relationship* (London: Routledge, 2002), pp. 198–220.

42. John Waterbury, *The Egypt of Nasser and Sadat: The Political Economy of Two Regimes* (Princeton, NJ: Princeton University Press, 1983), p. 263; Mansfield, *Nasser's Egypt*, p. 267.

43. Eleanore Hargreaves, "The Diploma Disease in Egypt: Learning, Teaching and the Monster of the Secondary Leaving Certificate," *Assessment in Education: Principles, Policy & Practice* 4, no. 1 (1997): 161–176.

44. Rosarri Griffith, *Education in the Muslim World: Different Perspectives* (Oxford: Symposium Books, 2006), p. 16.

45. See Gerges, *Making the Arab World*.

46. Fayek, interview.

47. M. E. McMillan, *From the First World War to the Arab Spring: What's Really Going on in the Middle East?* (New York: Palgrave Macmillan, 2016), p. 152.

48. Fawaz A. Gerges, *Obama and the Middle East: The End of America's Moment?* (New York: Palgrave Macmillan, 2012).

49. Malcom H. Kerr, *The Arab Cold War: Gamel 'Abd Al-Nasir and His Rivals, 1958–70* (Oxford: Oxford University Press, 1972), p. 8.

50. Mohamed Naguib, *Kuntu Ra'isan li-Misr* [I was the president of Egypt] (Cairo: al-Maktab al-Misry al-Hadith, 1984), pp. 178–180.

51. Wm. Roger Louis and Roger Owen, eds., *Suez 1956: The Crisis and Its Consequences* (Oxford: Clarendon Press, 1989). For more on the invasion and then withdrawal, see Anthony Gorst and Lewis Johnman, *The Suez Crisis* (London: Routledge, 1997). For more on the impact of the crisis, see Israel Gershoni and James P. Jankowski, *Nasser's Egypt, Arab Nationalism, and the United Arab Republic* (Boulder, CO: Lynne Rienner, 2002), p. 83.

52. Gershoni and Jankowski, *Nasser's Egypt*, p. 83.

53. Gershoni and Jankowski, *Nasser's Egypt*, pp. 104–105.

54. Patrick Seale, *The Struggle for Syria*, new ed. (London: I. B. Tauris, 1986), p. 154; Sylvia Kedourie, *Arab Nationalism: An Anthology* (Berkeley: University of California Press, 1962), p. 69.

55. Hourani, *A History of the Arab Peoples*, p. 584. For more on the Baath Party, see Robert W. Olson, *The Ba'th and Syria, 1947–1982: The Evolution of Ideology, Party and State* (Princeton, NJ: Kingston Press, 1982).

56. Hourani, *A History of the Arab Peoples*, p. 584; Kedourie, *Arab Nationalism*; and Olson, *The Ba'th and Syria*.

57. Patrick Seale, *Asad of Syria: The Struggle for the Middle East* (London: I. B. Tauris, 1988), p. 154.

58. Seale, *Asad of Syria*. For more on Nasser's vision of Arab unity, see Hanna and Gardner, *Arab Socialism*.

59. Gershoni and Jankowski, *Nasser's Egypt*, p. 104.

60. Gershoni and Jankowski, *Nasser's Egypt*, p. 104; Elie Podeh, *The Decline of Arab Unity: The Rise and Fall of the United Arab Republic* (Brighton, UK: Sussex Academic Press, 1999), emphasis added.

61. Kamal Mohieddin, interview by Fawaz Gerges in Cairo, December 12, 2006.

62. Dawisha, *Arab Nationalism*, p. 199; Seale, *Asad of Syria*, p. 323.

63. Seale, *Asad of Syria*, p. 319. See also Podeh, *The Decline of Arab Unity*.

64. Seale, *Asad of Syria*, p. 318; Podeh, *The Decline of Arab Unity*.

65. Gamal Abdel Nasser, *President Gamal Abdel-Nasser's Speeches and Press-interviews* (Cairo: United Arab Republic–Information Department, 1961), p. 56; Michael Sharnoff, "Looking Back: Nasser's Inter-Arab Rivalries: 1958–1967," *Al-Arabiya*, July 30, 2011, http://www.alarabiya.net/articles/2011/07/30/160027.html.

66. See Phebe Marr, *The Modern History of Iraq*, 4th ed. (Boulder, CO: Westview Press, 2016).

67. Marr, *The Modern History of Iraq*; Geoff Simons, *Iraq: From Sumer to Post-Saddam* (New York: Palgrave Macmillan, 2003), pp. 156, 252.

68. Tripp, *A History of Iraq*, pp. 139–143.

69. For a masterly account of the social struggle in Iraq, see Hannah Batatu, *The Old Social Classes and the Revolutionary Movement of Iraq: A Study of Iraq's Old Landed and Commercial Classes and of Its Communists, Ba'thists and Free Officers* (Princeton, NJ: Princeton University Press, 1978).

70. Raymond A. Hinnebusch, *The International Politics of the Middle East* (Manchester, UK: Manchester University Press, 2003), p. 26.

71. This point is argued by Humphreys as well as Dawisha: Humphreys, *Between Memory and Desire*; Dawisha, *Arab Nationalism*.

Chapter 5: The Collapse of the Foundational Myth

1. Patrick Seale, *Asad of Syria: The Struggle for the Middle East* (London: I. B. Tauris, 1988), p. 325.

2. Seale, *Asad of Syria*, p. 325.

3. Mohamed Hassanein Heikal, *Sanawat al-Ghalayan* [Years of turmoil] (Cairo: Ahram, 1988), pp. 258, 266. On the Eisenhower Doctrine, see Abdul Latif Tibawi, *A Modern History of Syria, Including Lebanon and Palestine* (London: Macmillan, 1969), pp. 399–401; Elie Podeh and Onn Winckler, *Rethinking Nasserism: Revolution and Historical Memory in Modern Egypt* (Gainesville: University Press of Florida, 2004), pp. 213–214; Rami Ginat, *Syria and the Doctrine of Arab Neutralism* (Brighton, UK: Sussex Academic Press, 2005), pp. 119, 123.

4. *Arba'una 'Aman 'ala al-Wihda al-Misriyya al-Suriyya* [40 Years after the Egyptian-Syrian unity]. The document is the outcome of a seminar held on February 22–23, 1998 (Cairo: Ahram, 1998), p. 204.

5. *Arba'una 'Aman 'ala al-Wihda al-Misriyya al-Suriyya*.

6. Syed Aziz-al Ahsan, "Economic Policy and Class Structure in Syria: 1958–1980," *International Journal of Middle East Studies* 15, no. 3 (1984): 301–323.

7. Hanna Batatu, *Syria's Peasantry, the Descendants of Its Lesser Rural Notables, and Their Politics* (Princeton, NJ: Princeton University Press, 1999), pp. 38–53. See also Ahsan, "Economic Policy and Class Structure in Syria."

8. Kamal Deeb, *Tarikh Suriya al-Mu'asir: Min al-Intidab al-Faransi hatta Sayf 2011* [Syria's modern history from the French protectorate until summer 2011] (Beirut: Al-Nahar, 2011), pp. 1985–1986.

9. For more on the land reform in Syria, see Eva Garzouzi, "Land Reform in Syria," *Middle East Journal* 17, no. 1/2 (January 1963): 85–86.

10. Tabitha Petran, *Syria* (New York: Praeger, 1972), p. 136.

11. See Raymond A. Hinnebusch, *Peasant and Bureaucracy in Ba'thist Syria: The Political Economy of Rural Development* (Boulder, CO: Westview Press, 1989); Batatu, *Syria's Peasantry*, pp. 38–53; Ahsan, "Economic Policy and Class Structure in Syria," p. 304.

12. Ahsan, "Economic Policy and Class Structure in Syria." See also Raymond A. Hinnebusch, *Authoritarian Power and State Formation in Ba'thist Syria* (Boulder, CO: Westview Press, 1990).

13. See Raymond A. Hinnebusch, *Syria: Revolution from Above* (London: Routledge, 2001); Ahsan, "Economic Policy and Class Structure in Syria"; and Petran, *Syria*, pp. 138–139.

14. Ahsan, "Economic Policy and Class Structure in Syria." See also Elie Podeh, *The Decline of Arab Unity: The Rise and Fall of the United Arab Republic* (Brighton, UK: Sussex Academic Press, 1999).

15. Ahsan, "Economic Policy and Class Structure in Syria," pp. 304–305; Podeh, *The Decline of Arab Unity*.

16. Ahsan, "Economic Policy and Class Structure in Syria, p. 305. See also Ziad Keilany, "Socialism and Economic Change in Syria," *Journal of Middle Eastern Studies* 9, no. 1 (January 1973): 65–66.

17. After the failure of the talks, Nasser released the transcripts and went in for the kill, saying: "We do not consider that the UAR is bound to the present Fascist regime in Syria by any common aim. This . . . is impossible when the other regime is built on fraud and treachery, is nonunionist and non-socialist, but rather secessionist, inhuman and immoral." Malcom H. Kerr, *The Arab Cold War: Gamel ʿAbd Al-Nasir and His Rivals, 1958–70* (Oxford: Oxford University Press, 1972), p.117. This citation is also in "Khitāb ar-ra' īs fī alʿ īd al-hādiyaʿashara li-ath-thawra· 22 yuliyu 1963" (Speech of the resident on the occasion of the anniversary of the revolution), in *Kitāb at-tahrīr: Hadīth al-batal az-zaʿīm JamālʿAbdannāsir ilā al-umma. Al-juz' ar-rābiʿ 1961–1963, al ʿadad 47–48*, (n.p., n.d.), pp. 550–556.

18. "The major point of controversy was the political and democratic structure of the proposed state. Our delegation insisted on the necessity for a parliamentary regime based on representation proportionate to the population of each regime. When the question of political representation came up, the Egyptian side insisted on equal representation for all unionist forces. When the Syrian side demanded the inclusion of all unorganised unionist elements in certain groups, this was rejected. The Egyptian side in turn emphasized the privileges and power of the President. We finally agreed to all these demands so as to avoid disruption of the talks, and in order not to disappoint the hopes of the Arabs. . . . Unity soars above party and personalities. It is a historical destiny whose disruption constitutes a historical crime." Kerr, *The Arab Cold War*, p. 118.

19. Kerr, *The Arab Cold War*, p. 120.

20. Raymond A. Hinnebusch, *Egyptian Politics under Sadat: The Post-Populist Development of an Authoritarian-Modernizing State* (Cambridge: Cambridge University Press, 1985), p. 35.

21. Eugene Rogan and Tewfik Aclimandos, "The Yemen War and Egypt's War Preparedness," in *The 1967 Arab-Israeli War: Origins and Consequences*, ed. William Roger Louis and Avi Shlaim (Cambridge: Cambridge University Press, 2012), p. 149; Jesse Ferris, *Nasser's Gamble: How the Intervention in Yemen Caused the Six-Day War and the Decline of Egyptian Power* (Princeton, NJ: Princeton University Press, 1972).

22. Rogan and Aclimandos, "The Yemen War," p. 150; Ferris, *Nasser's Gamble*.

23. A. Al-Baydani, *Azmat al-Umaa al-Arabiyya wa Thawrat al-Yemen* [The crisis of the Arab nation and the Yemen revolution] (Cairo: al-Maktab al-Misri al-Hadith, 1984), p. 192. See also *Tarikh al-Yemen al-Mua'sser: 1917–1982* [The modern history of Yemen: 1917–1982] (Cairo: Madbouli, 1990); Rogan and Aclimandos, "The Yemen War," p. 150.

24. Eugene Rogan, *The Arabs: A History* (London: Penguin Books, 2011), pp. 419–420.

25. Rogan, *The Arabs*.

26. Fawaz A. Gerges, *The Superpowers and the Middle East: Regional and International Politics* (Boulder, CO: Westview Press, 1994), p. 214.

27. Yezid Sayigh, "Escalation or Containment? Egypt and the Palestine Liberation Army, 1964–67," *International Journal of Middle East Studies* 30, no. 1 (February 1998): 97–116.

28. Avi Shlaim, *The Iron Wall: Israel and the Arab World* (London: Penguin Books, 2001), pp. 232–284.

29. M. E. McMillan, *From the First World War to the Arab Spring: What's Really Going on in the Middle East?* (New York: Palgrave Macmillan, 2016), pp. 180–184.

30. El-Gamsy cited in Rogan and Aclimandos, "The Yemen War," p. 163.

31. Seale, *Asad of Syria*, p. 126; Adeed Dawisha, *Egypt in the Arab World: The Elements of Foreign Policy* (London: Macmillan, 1976), p. 47.

32. David W. Lesch, "Syria: Playing with Fire," in Louis and Shlaim, *The 1967 Arab-Israeli War*, p. 92.

33. Lesch, "Syria."

34. Lesch, "Syria."

35. Gerges, *The Superpowers and the Middle East*, pp. 205, 214.

36. Ferris, *Nasser's Gamble*.

37. Gerges, *The Superpowers and the Middle East*, pp. 214–215.

38. Podeh and Winckler, *Rethinking Nasserism*, pp. 218–220.

39. See Robert McNamara, *Britain, Nasser and the Balance of Power in the Middle East, 1952–1967: From the Egyptian Revolution to the Six Day War* (London: Frank Cass, 2003).

40. Albert Hourani, *A History of the Arab Peoples* (London: Faber and Faber, 1991), p. 300.

41. See A. Al-Shuqayri, *Al-Hazima al-Kubra: ma' al-Muluk wa-l-Ru'sa min Bayt 'Abdel Nasser ila Ghorfat al-'Amalyat* [The great defeat: With the kings and presidents from the house of Abdel Nasser to the operations center] (Beirut: Dar al-Awda, 1973), pp. 8–9; G. Tarabishi, *Al-Muthaqqafun al-'Arab wa-l-Turath: al-Tahlil al-Nafsi li-'Isab Jama'i* [Arab intellectuals and heritage: A psychological analysis of a collective neurosis] (London: Riad el-Rayyes, 1991), pp. 22, 39–40; and T. Al-Hakim, *The Return of Consciousness*, trans. B. Winder (New York: Macmillan, 1985).

42. Hinnebusch, *The International Politics of the Middle East*, p. 30.

43. Walt Rostow to the President, no. 299 (June 7, 1967), and Department of State to Embassy Paris, no. 209550 (June 8, 1967), in Gerges, *The Superpowers and the Middle East*, p. 230.

44. Raymond A. Hinnebusch, *The International Politics of the Middle East* (Manchester, UK: Manchester University Press, 2003), p. 31.

45. For more on the role of Palestine in internal Arab affairs, see Walid Kazziha, "The Impact of Palestine on Arab Politics," in *The Politics of Arab Integration*, ed. Ghassan Salamé and Giacomo Luciani (London: Croom Heim, 1988), pp. 300–318.

46. Kerr, *The Arab Cold War*.

47. See Michael Barnett, *Dialogues in Arab Politics: Negotiations in Regional Order* (New York: Columbia University Press, 1998).

48. Fred Halliday, "The Middle East and Conceptions of 'International Society,'" in *International Society and the Middle East: English School Theory at the Regional Level*, ed. Barry Buzan and Ana Gonzalez-Perez (New York: Palgrave, 2009), p.15.

49. Barnett, *Dialogues in Arab Politics*, p. 158.

50. Raymond A. Hinnebusch, "The Foreign Policy of Egypt," in *The Foreign Policies of Middle East States*, ed. Raymond A. Hinnebusch and Anoushiravan Ehteshami (Boulder, CO: Lynne Rienner, 2014), pp. 91–114.

51. See John Waterbury, *The Egypt of Nasser and Sadat: The Political Economy of Two Regimes* (Princeton, NJ: Princeton University Press, 1983); Dieter Weiss and Ulrich Wurzel, *The Economics and Politics of Transition to an Open Market Economy: Egypt, Development Centre Studies* (Paris: OECD, 1998), https://doi.org/10.1787/9789264163607-en.

52. Waterbury, *The Egypt of Nasser and Sadat*, pp. 76–78.

53. Anette Ranko, *The Muslim Brotherhood and Its Quest for Hegemony in Egypt: State Discourse and Islamist Counter-Discourse* (Wiesbaden, Germany: Springer VS, 2015), p. 47; Waterbury, *The Egypt of Nasser and Sadat*, p. 82.

54. Maha Abdelrahman, *Egypt's Long Revolution: Protest Movements and Uprisings* (London: Routledge, 2015), chap. 3, especially the section on Nasser and corporatism.

55. Nazih Ayubi, *Overstating the Arab State: Politics and Society in the Middle East* (London: I. B. Tauris, 1995), p. 25.

56. Ayubi, *Overstating the Arab State*, p. 25.

57. Ayubi, *Overstating the Arab State*, p. 25.

58. Ayubi, *Overstating the Arab State*, pp. 246–247.

59. Ayubi, *Overstating the Arab State*, pp. 246–247.

60. *Muzakerat al-Rayees al-Qadi Abdel-Rahman Bin Yehia al-Iryani* [Memoirs of President Abdel Rahman bin Yehia al-Iryani], 2nd vol. (Cairo: Al-Hayaa al-Masriyya al-'Ama leil Kitab, n.d.), p. 582.

61. Al-Shuqairy, *Al-Hazima al-Kubra*, p. 138.

62. See chapters 7 and 8 on the Six-Day War and Sadat in Fawaz A. Gerges, *Making the Arab World: Nasser, Qutb and the Clash That Shaped the Middle East* (Princeton, NJ: Princeton University Press, 2018).

63. Abridged translation of Nizar Qabbani's poem "When Will They Announce the Death of the Arabs," published in 1994. Translation in Riad Nourallah, *Beyond the Arab Disease: New Perspectives in Politics and Culture* (London: Routledge, 2006), p. 4.

64. Jasmine Gani, *The Role of Ideology in Syrian-US Relations: Conflict and Cooperation* (New York: Palgrave Macmillan, 2014), pp. 15–18. See also Adeed Dawisha, *Arab Nationalism in the Twentieth Century: From Triumph to Despair* (Princeton, NJ: Princeton University

Press, 2003); Rashid Khalidi, Lisa Anderson, Muhammad Muslih, and Reeva S. Simon, eds., *The Origins of Arab Nationalism* (New York: Columbia University Press, 1991), p. x; and Aparajita Gogoi and Gazi Ibdewi Abdulghafour, *Arab Nationalism: Birth, Evolution and the Present Dilemma* (New Delhi: Lancer Books, 1994).

65. See David Hirst, *Beware of Small States: Lebanon, Battleground of the Middle East* (New York: Nation Books, 2011), or Robert Fisk, *Pity the Nation* (New York: Nation Books, 2002).

66. Pierre Razoux, *La Guerre Iran-Irak* (Paris: Perrin, 2013).

67. Eberhard Kienle's book *Ba'th vs Ba'th: The Conflict between Syria and Iraq, 1968–1989* (London: I. B. Tauris, 1990) is a good account of inter-Baath rivalry, though it is plausible that Syria sided with Iran against Iraq because of Iran's anti-US stance, more so than because of Syria's animosity with Iraq.

68. Dawisha, *Arab Nationalism*, p. 3.

69. Dawisha, *Arab Nationalism*, p. 3.

Chapter 6: From Colonialism to the Cold War

1. Fred Halliday, "The Middle East, the Great Powers and the Cold War," in *The Cold War and the Middle East*, ed. Yazid Sayigh and Avi Shlaim (Oxford: Clarendon Press, 1997), p. 10.

2. See Fred Halliday, *The Middle East in International Relations: Power, Politics and Ideology* (Cambridge: Cambridge University Press, 2005), p. 124.

3. For a comparison between the old and the new forms of imperialism, see Atul Kohli, *Imperialism and the Developing World: How Britain and the U.S. Shaped the Global Periphery* (Oxford: Oxford University Press, 2020).

4. Alex Lubin and Marwan M. Kraidy, *American Studies Encounters the Middle East* (Oxford: Oxford University Press, 2016). See also Nathan J. Citino, *Envisioning the Arab Future: Modernization in US-Arab Relations, 1945–1967* (Cambridge: Cambridge University Press, 2017).

5. Fawaz A. Gerges, *What Really Went Wrong: The West and the Failure of Democracy in the Middle East* (New Haven, CT: Yale University Press, 2024).

6. Ussama Makdisi, *Faith Misplaced: The Broken Promise of U.S.-Arab Relations: 1820–2001* (New York: Public Affairs, 2011).

7. Halliday, "The Middle East, the Great Powers and the Cold War," p. 9.

8. Halliday, "The Middle East, the Great Powers and the Cold War," pp. 6–26.

9. "Contextualizing the Arab Revolts: The Politics behind Three Decades of Neoliberalism in the Arab World," *Middle East Critique* 22, no. 3 (October 22, 2013): 231–234, https://www.tandfonline.com/doi/full/10.1080/19436149.2013.814945?src=recsys; or "The IMF in the Arab World: Lessons Unlearnt," in *Bretton Woods Project* (November 2015), https://eurodad.org/files/pdf/56b075f5395dd.pdf.

10. "Final Communique of the Asian-African Conference of Bandung (24 April 1955)," *European Navigator*, p. 9, http://franke.uchicago.edu/Final_Communique_Bandung_1955.pdf.

11. "Final Communique of the Asian-African Conference," p. 9.

12. "Final Communique of the Asian-African Conference," p. 3.

13. Fawaz Gerges, *The Superpowers and the Middle East: Regional and International Politics, 1955–1967* (Boulder, CO: Westview Press, 1994), p. 21.

14. Hugh Wilford, *America's Great Game: The CIA's Secret Arabists and the Shaping of the Modern Middle East* (New York: Basic Books, 2013), pp. 133–145. See also Hazem Kandil, *Soldiers, Spies and Statesmen: Egypt's Road to Revolt* (London: Verso, 2014).

15. On the historical importance of this point and of the views of the Dulles brothers, see Richard H. Immermann, *John Foster Dulles: Piety, Pragmatism, and Power in U.S. Foreign Policy* (Wilmington, DE: Scholarly Resources, 1999); and John D. Wilsey, *God's Cold Warrior: The Life and Faith of John Foster Dulles* (Grand Rapids, MI: William B. Eerdmans, 2021).

16. Raymond A. Hinnebusch, *The International Politics of the Middle East* (Manchester, UK: Manchester University Press, 2003), p. 22.

17. Halliday, "The Middle East, the Great Powers and the Cold War," p. 8.

18. Christopher de Bellaigue, *Patriot of Persia: Muhammad Mossadegh and a Very British Coup* (London: Vintage Books, 2013).

19. Malcom H. Kerr, *The Arab Cold War: Gamel 'Abd Al-Nasir and His Rivals, 1958–70* (Oxford: Oxford University Press, 1972).

20. Adeed Dawisha, "Egypt," in Sayigh and Shlaim, *The Cold War and the Middle East,* p. 31.

21. Halliday, "The Middle East, the Great Powers and the Cold War," p. 17.

22. Albert Hourani, *A History of the Arab Peoples* (London: Faber and Faber, 1991), p. 401.

23. Gerges, *The Superpowers and the Middle East,* p. 24.

24. See Rashid Khalidi: "The Superpowers and the Cold War in the Middle East," in *The Middle East and the United States: History, Politics and Ideologies,* 5th ed., ed. David W. Lesch and Mark L. Haas (Boulder, CO: Westview Press, 2012), chap. 10. See also Rashid Khalidi, *Sowing Crisis: The Cold War and American Dominance in the Middle East* (Boston: Beacon Press, 2009), chap. 5.

25. Jonathan Nitzan and Bichler Shimshon, *The Global Political Economy of Israel* (London: Pluto Press, 2002), p. 217. On the 1973 oil crisis and its resolution—setting in motion the petro-dollars affairs and continuing the modernization theory—see Andrea Wong, "The Untold Story behind Saudi Arabia's 41-Year U.S. Debt Secret," Bloomberg, May 31, 2016, https://www.bloomberg.com/news/features/2016-05-30/the-untold-story-behind-saudi-arabia-s-41-year-u-s-debt-secret; Raymond Close, "Nixon and Faisal: If Arabs Mistrust America, There's Good Reason," *New York Times,* December 19, 2002, http://www.nytimes.com/2002/12/19/opinion/nixon-and-faisal-if-arabs-mistrust-america-theres-good-reason.html.

26. In September 1953, President Dwight D. Eisenhower dined at the White House with Said Ramadan, a leader of the Muslim Brotherhood, the popular Islamist group, which since the late 1940s has been known for its extensive ties to radicals and assassins in the Middle East. Melanie Colburn, "America's Devil's Game with Extremist Islam," *Mother Jones,* January/February 2006, http://www.motherjones.com/politics/2006/01/americas-devils-game-extremist-islam. See also Benjamin Schett, "US Sponsored 'Islamic Fundamentalism': The Roots of the US Wahhabi Alliance," Global Research, September 7, 2012, http://www.globalresearch.ca/us-sponsored-islamic-fundamentalism-the-roots-of-the-us-wahhabi-alliance/5303558.

27. Halliday, "The Middle East, the Great Powers and the Cold War," pp. 8–14.

28. Patrick Seale, "Syria," in Sayigh and Shlaim, *The Cold War and the Middle East,* p. 48.

29. Seale, "Syria," p. 48.

30. Seale, "Syria," p. 50.

31. Tareq Y. Ismael, *The Communist Movement in the Arab World* (London: Routledge, 2004); Rashid Khalidi, "Arab Views of the Soviet Role in the Middle East," *Middle East Journal* 39, no. 4 (Autumn, 1985): 716–732.

32. Halliday, "The Middle East, the Great Powers and the Cold War," p. 16.

33. Halliday, "The Middle East, the Great Powers and the Cold War," p. 16.

34. See Khalidi, *Sowing Crisis*.

35. Halliday, "The Middle East, the Great Powers and the Cold War," p. 23.

36. Dawisha, *Egypt*, p. 30.

37. Gerges, *The Superpowers and the Middle East*, p. 15.

38. For further reference on this subject, see Richard W. Bulliet, *The Case for Islamo-Christian Civilization* (New York: Columbia University Press, 2004).

39. Rashid Khalidi, *Resurrecting Empire: Western Footprints and America's Perilous Path in the Middle East* (London: I. B. Tauris, 2004).

40. M. E. McMillan, *From the First World War to the Arab Spring: What's Really Going on in the Middle East?* (New York: Palgrave Macmillan, 2016), p. 224.

41. Pierre Razoux, *La guerre Iran-Irak* (Paris: Perrin, 2013).

42. "Exclusive: CIA Files Prove America Helped Saddam as He Gassed Iran," *Foreign Policy*, August 26, 2013, https://foreignpolicy.com/2013/08/26/exclusive-cia-files-prove-america-helped-saddam-as-he-gassed-iran/.

43. See Steve Coll, *Ghost Wars: The Secret History of the CIA, Afghanistan and Bin Laden* (New York: Penguin, 2005); Lawrence Wright, *The Looming Tower: Al Qaeda's Road to 9/11* (New York: Penguin, 2007).

44. Nazih Ayubi, *Overstating the Arab State: Politics and Society in the Middle East* (London: I. B. Tauris, 1995).

Chapter 7: The Winter of Discontent

1. See M. E. McMillan, *Fathers and Sons: The Rise and Fall of Political Dynasty in the Middle East* (New York: Palgrave Macmillan, 2013), pp. 1–3.

2. Rania Abouzeid, "Bouazizi: The Man Who Set Himself and Tunisia on Fire," *Time*, January 21, 2011, http://content.time.com/time/magazine/article/0,9171,2044723,00.html.

3. Abouzeid, "Bouazizi." See also Alcinda Honwana, *Youth and Revolution in Tunisia* (London: Zed Books, 2013), pp. 1–2, 74; Shelly Culbertson, *The Fires of Spring: A Post-Arab Spring Journey through the Turbulent New Middle East, Turkey, Iraq, Qatar, Jordan, Egypt, and Tunisia* (New York: St. Martin's Press, 2016). It is worth noting that many of the personal details involving Mohammed Bouazizi are not conclusive, reflecting lack of solid information and contested accounts.

4. See Ira William Zartman, ed., *Tunisia: The Political Economy of Reform* (Boulder, CO: Lynne Rienner, 1991).

5. See the chapter by Rami Zurayk and Anne Gough, "Bread and Olive Oil: The Agrarian Roots of the Arab Uprisings," in *The New Middle East: Protest and Revolution in the Arab World*, ed. Fawaz A. Gerges (New York: Cambridge University Press, 2014), pp. 107–131. See

also Mohamed Elmeshad, "Rural Egyptians Suffer Most from Increasing Poverty," *Egypt Independent*, September 28, 2011, www.egyptindependent.com/node/199833; "Rural Poverty Portal: Syria," International Fund for Agricultural Development (IFAD), accessed March 23, 2017, http://www.ruralpovertyportal.org/web/rural-poverty-portal/country/home/tags/syria; "Tunisia: Data," the World Bank, accessed March 23, 2017, http://data.worldbank.org/country /tunisia#cp_wdi; "The State of Food Security and Nutrition in Yemen: Summary and Overview," World Food Programme, June 2012, http://documents.wfp.org/stellent/groups/public /documents/ena/wfp247833.pdf; "Improving Food Security in Arab Countries," World Bank, FAO, and IFAD, January 2009, http://siteresources.worldbank.org/INTMENA/Resources /FoodSecfinal.pdf. For a critical study, see Habib Ayeb, "The Marginalization of the Small Peasantry: Egypt and Tunisia," in *Marginality and Exclusion in Egypt*, ed. Ray Bush and Habib Ayeb (London: Zed Books, 2012). See also Saker el Nour, "National Geographical Targeting of Poverty in Upper Egypt," in Bush and Ayeb, *Marginality and Exclusion in Egypt*; Mohammad Pournik, "Por un crecimiento inclusivo en la region Arabe," *Afkar/Ideas* 33 (Spring 2012); Gerges, *The New Middle East*, p. 12.

6. McMillan, *Fathers and Sons*, p. 1.

7. Basma Barakat, "Bouazzizi's Family: He Wanted to Join the Army and Died of Injustice," *al-Araby*, December 16, 2014.

8. Jean-Pierre Filiu, *The Arab Revolution: Ten Lessons from the Democratic Uprising* (London: C. Hurst, 2011), pp. 15, 20.

9. McMillan, *Fathers and Sons*, p. 2.

10. Filiu, *The Arab Revolution*, p. 21.

11. Clemens Höges, "Meeting the Man Who Helped Trigger the Arab Spring," *Spiegel International*, January 21, 2016, http://www.spiegel.de/international/world/self-immolation -survivor-looks-back-at-arab-spring-a-1072814.html.

12. "Algerian Dies in Self-Immolation, Echoing Tunisia," Reuters, January 16, 2011, http://af .reuters.com/article/worldNews/idAFTRE70F0UL20110116. See also "Algeria at the Crossroads, between Continuity and Change" (Rome: Istituto Affari Internazionali, September 28, 2011), http://www.iai.it/sites/default/files/iaiwp1128.pdf.

13. Tarik M. Youssef, "Development, Growth and Policy Reform in the Middle East and North Africa since 1950," *Journal of Economic Perspectives* 18, no. 3 (Summer 2004): 91–116.

14. Andre Gunder Frank, "The Development of Underdevelopment," *Monthly Review* 18, no. 4 (September 1966): 17–31.

15. Gerges, *The New Middle East*, p. 14n28.

16. For more on the Nasser/Sadat comparison, see Hamid Ansari, *Egypt: The Stalled Society* (Albany: State University of New York Press, 1986), pp. 11–12.

17. Derek Hopwood, *Egypt: Politics and Society, 1945–1990*, 3rd ed. (London: Routledge, 2002), p. 105. See also Raymond A. Hinnebusch, *Egyptian Politics under Sadat: The Post-Populist Development of an Authoritarian-Modernizing State* (Cambridge: Cambridge University Press, 1985).

18. Ibrahim Hassan El-Issawy, "Interconnections between Income Distribution and Economic Growth in the Context of Egypt's Economic Development," in *The Political Economy*

of Income Distribution in Egypt, ed. Jūdah 'Abd al-Khāliq and Robert L. Tignor (New York: Holmes and Meier, 1982), p. 100.

19. El-Issawy, "Interconnections between Income Distribution and Economic Growth," p. 100.

20. Hopwood, *Egypt*, pp. 106–107.

21. Hopwood, *Egypt*, p. 108. For more on the war and Sadat's foreign policy toward Israel, see Mohamed Ali Hussein, "The War and Peace of President Sadat: A Study in Egypt's Foreign Policy towards Israel, 1970–81" (PhD thesis, London School of Economics, 1987).

22. See Kirk J. Beattie, *Egypt during the Sadat Years* (New York: Palgrave, 2000).

23. See Ninette S. Fahmy, *The Politics of Egypt: State-Society Relationship* (London: Routledge, 2002).

24. For more on the war and Sadat's vision, see Anwar el-Sadat, *In Search of Identity* (London: Collins, 1978); and Anwar el-Sadat, *President Anwar el-Sadat's Policy* (Cairo: State Information Service, 1971).

25. Ali E. Hilal Dessouki, "The Politics of Income Distribution in Egypt," in *The Political Economy of Income Distribution in Egypt*, ed. Gouda Abdel-Khalek and Robert Tignor (New York: Holmes and Meier, 1982), p. 77. See also Fouad Ajami, "Retreat from Economic Nationalism: The Political Economy of Sadat's Egypt," *Journal of Arab Affairs* 1, no. 1 (October 1981): 27–52.

26. Dessouki, "The Politics of Income Distribution in Egypt," pp. 65–81.

27. Dessouki, "The Politics of Income Distribution in Egypt," p. 81; Ajami, "Retreat from Economic Nationalism," pp. 27–52.

28. Dessouki, "The Politics of Income Distribution in Egypt," p. 81. See also Arthur Goldschmidt, *A Brief History of Egypt* (New York: Checkmark Books, 2008), pp. 198–199. For more on the impact of the Infitah on Egyptian society, and women more specifically, see Nadje Al-Ali, *Secularism, Gender and the State in the Middle East: The Egyptian Women's Movement* (Cambridge: Cambridge University Press, 2000), pp. 71–74.

29. Dessouki, "The Politics of Income Distribution in Egypt," p.77.

30. "Sadat's Half-Brother Is Sentenced to Jail," *New York Times*, February 13, 1983, http://www.nytimes.com/1983/02/13/world/sadat-s-half-brother-is-sentenced-to-jail.html.

31. "Sadat's Half-Brother Is Sentenced to Jail."

32. "Sadat's Half-Brother Is Sentenced to Jail."

33. "Sadat's Half-Brother Is Sentenced to Jail." For more on Rashad Osman, see Robert Roccu, *The Political Economy of the Egyptian Revolution: Mubarak, Economic Reforms and Failed Hegemony* (New York: Palgrave Macmillan, 2013), p. 61.

34. Dessouki, "The Politics of Income Distribution in Egypt," p. 79. For more on the bread riots, see Ram Sachs, "On Bread and Circuses: Food Subsidy Reform and Popular Opposition in Egypt," Center for International Security and Cooperation Stanford University, May 21, 2012, pp. 25–45.

35. Dessouki, "The Politics of Income Distribution in Egypt," p. 79.

36. Hopwood, *Egypt*, p. 109.

37. See Abdullah Al-Arian, *Answering the Call: Popular Islamic Activism in Sadat's Egypt* (Oxford: Oxford University Press, 2014).

38. Gilles Kepel, *The Prophet and Pharaoh: Muslim Extremism in Egypt* (London: Al Saqi Books, 1985), p. 192; Hopwood, *Egypt*, p. 184.

39. "Egypt's Parliament Speaker Is Assassinated by Gunman," *New York Times*, October 13, 1990, http://www.nytimes.com/1990/10/13/world/mideast-tensions-egypt-s-parliament-speaker-is-assassinated-by-gunmen.html.

40. Roccu, *The Political Economy of the Egyptian Revolution*, p. 59. See also Alia al-Mahdi and Ali Rashed, "The Changing Economic Environment and the Development of Micro and Small Enterprises in Egypt," in *The Egyptian Labour Market Revisited*, ed. Ragui Assaad (Cairo: American University in Cairo Press, 2009).

41. McMillan, *Fathers and Sons*, pp. 4–5.

42. Alaa Al-Aswany, *On the State of Egypt: What Caused the Revolution* (Edinburgh: Canongate, 2011), p. 7.

43. Roccu, *The Political Economy of the Egyptian Revolution*, p. 61.

44. Roccu, *The Political Economy of the Egyptian Revolution*, p. 63.

45. Roccu, *The Political Economy of the Egyptian Revolution*, p. 63.

46. Roccu, *The Political Economy of the Egyptian Revolution*, p. 63. For more on the fiscal crisis and the state policies under Mubarak, see Samer Soliman, *The Autumn of Dictatorship: Fiscal Crisis and Political Change in Egypt under Mubarak* (Redwood City, CA: Stanford University Press, 2011), p. 150.

47. Roccu, *The Political Economy of the Egyptian Revolution*, p. 63.

48. Roccu, *The Political Economy of the Egyptian Revolution*, p. 63; see also Tareq Osman, *Egypt on the Brink: From Nasser to the Muslim Brotherhood* (New Haven, CT: Yale University Press, 2010), pp. 115–116.

49. Roccu, *The Political Economy of the Egyptian Revolution*, p. 64.

50. Soliman, *The Autumn of Dictatorship*, p. 150; Roccu, *The Political Economy of the Egyptian Revolution*, p. 65.

51. Roccu, *The Political Economy of the Egyptian Revolution*, p. 65. See also Lisa Blaydes, *Elections and Distributive Politics in Mubarak's Egypt* (New York: Cambridge University Press, 2011); and Robert Springborg, *Mubarak's Egypt: Fragmentation of the Political Order* (Boulder, CO: Westview Press, 1989).

52. Roccu, *The Political Economy of the Egyptian Revolution*, p. 65.

53. Roccu, *The Political Economy of the Egyptian Revolution*, p. 67. See also Charles Tripp and Roger Owen, eds., *Egypt under Mubarak* (London: Routledge, 1990).

54. Roccu, *The Political Economy of the Egyptian Revolution*, p. 67.

55. Roccu, *The Political Economy of the Egyptian Revolution*, p. 66. See also Soliman, *The Autumn of Dictatorship*, pp. 145–146.

56. Roccu, *The Political Economy of the Egyptian Revolution*, p. 66.

57. Shana Marshall, "The Egyptian Armed Forces and the Remaking of an Economic Empire," Carnegie Middle East Center, April 2015, https://carnegieendowment.org/files/egyptian_armed_forces.pdf. See also Reuters Staff, "From War Room to Boardroom. Military Firms Flourish in Sisi's Egypt," Reuters, May 16, 2018, https://www.reuters.com/investigates/special-report/egypt-economy-military/; "The Economic Empire of the Egyptian Army," *Middle East Observer*, June 21, 2018, https://www.middleeastobserver.org/2018/06/21/the-economic-empire-of-the-egyptian-army/.

58. See the critical analysis by Ali Kadri, *The Cordon Sanitaire: A Single Law Governing Development in East Asia and the Arab World* (New York: Palgrave Macmillan, 2017).

59. Wei Lu and Marcus Chan, "In Global Innovation Race, Taiwan Is Tops in Patents, Israel Leads in R&D," Bloomberg, January 23 2014, https://www.bloomberg.com/news/2014-01-22 /in-global-innovation-race-taiwan-is-tops-in-patents-israel-leads-in-r-d.html.

60. "Korea Is the Most Innovative Country: Bloomberg," Korea.net, January 27, 2014, http:// www.korea.net/NewsFocus/Business/view?articleId=117310.

61. For an overview, see Marc Sullivan "Who Has the Smartest Math and Science Students? Singapore," Forbes, November 30, 2016, https://www.forbes.com/sites/maureensullivan /2016/11/30/who-has-the-smartest-math-and-science-students-singapore/#48cebe4f1913; Sean Coughlan, "Pisa Tests: Singapore Top in Global Education Rankings," BBC, December 6, 2016, http://www.bbc.co.uk/news/education-38212070; Matthew Speiser, "The 10 Smartest Countries Based on Math and Science," Business Insider UK, May 13, 2015, http://www .businessinsider.com/the-10-smartest-countries-based-on-math-and-science-2015-5; Deidre McPhillips, "The Best Students in the World," US News & World Report, December 6, 2016, https://www.usnews.com/news/best-countries/articles/2016-12-06/2015-pisa-scores-are-no -surprise; Abby Jackson and Andy Kiersz, "The Latest Ranking of Top Countries in Math, Reading, and Science Is Out—and the US Didn't Crack the Top 10," Business Insider UK, December 16, 2016, http://www.businessinsider.com/pisa-worldwide-ranking-of-math-science -reading-skills-2016-12; "HKU Faculty of Dentistry Ranked No.1 in the World," Hong Kong University, March 22, 2016, http://www.hku.hk/press/news_detail_14311.html; "Top Dental Schools in 2017," Topniversities.com, March 23, 2017, https://www.topuniversities.com/university -rankings-articles/university-subject-rankings/top-dental-schools-2017; Sammy Said, "Top 10 Best Health Care Systems in the World," The Richest.com, July 30, 2013, http://www.therichest .com/expensive-lifestyle/lifestyle/top-10-best-health-care-systems-in-the-world/.

62. A qualification is in order. The oil-producing Arabian Gulf states have done much better economically than the non-oil producing republics. With their wealth and small populations, Saudi Arabia, United Arab Emirates, Qatar, and Kuwait have provided their citizens with social goods and benefits to keep them satisfied. Although these conservative monarchies eschew political liberalization, they have not faced large-scale protests and revolts along the lines of the Arab Spring in 2010–2012. It remains to be seen if the Gulf sheikdoms could keep the peace, given that a majority of their populations are young, educated, and aspiring.

63. For a thought-provoking analysis, see Daron Acemoglu and James A. Robinson, *Why Nations Fail: The Origins of Power, Prosperity and Poverty* (New York: Crown Business, 2012).

Chapter 8: How and Why Did the Middle East Fail to Achieve Its Potential?

1. See John Isbister, *Promises Not Kept: Poverty and the Betrayal of Third World Development*, 7th ed. (Bloomfield, CT: Kumarian Press, 2006).

2. Marwan Muasher, "Arab Fractures: Citizens, States and Social Contracts," Carnegie Endowment, December 2016, https://carnegieendowment.org/2017/02/01/arab-fractures -citizens-states-and-social-contracts-pub-66612. See also Hedi Larbi, *Rewriting the Arab Social Contract: Toward Inclusive Development and Politics in the Arab World*, Middle East Initiative, Belfer Center, May 2016, https://www.belfercenter.org/publication/rewriting-arab-social

-contract; Amr Hamzawy, "The Arab World Needs a New Social Contract," Carnegie Endowment, September 22, 2016, https://carnegieendowment.org/2016/09/22/arab-world-needs-new -social-contract-pub-64667; Marwan Muasher, "The Next Arab Uprising: The Collapse of Authoritarianism in the Middle East," Carnegie Endowment, October 16, 2018, https:// carnegieendowment.org/2018/10/16/next-arab-uprising-collapse-of-authoritarianism-in -middle-east-pub-77512.

3. Marcus Noland and Howard Pack, *Arab Economies in a Changing World* (Washington, DC: Peterson Institute for International Economics, 2007), p.160.

4. Noland and Pack, *Arab Economies in a Changing World*, p. 161.

5. Noland and Pack, *Arab Economies in a Changing World*, p. 161. See also William Joseph Burns, *Economic Aid and American Policy toward Egypt, 1955–1981* (Albany: State University of New York Press, 1985), p. 192.

6. Noland and Pack, *Arab Economies in a Changing World*, p. 161. See Dina Jadallah, *US Economic Aid in Egypt: Strategies for Democratisation and Reform in the Middle East* (London: I. B. Tauris, 2016).

7. United Nations Development Programme, *Arab Human Development Report 2016: Youth and the Prospects for Human Development in a Changing Reality*, November 29, 2016, p. 26, https://www.undp.org/iraq/publications/arab-human-development-report-2016.

8. Ishaan Tharoor, "Sudan's War Has No End in Sight, as Atrocities and Abuses Mount," *Washington Post*, August 30, 2023, https://www.washingtonpost.com/world/2023/08/30/sudan -civil-war-atrocities-abuse/.

9. Tyler Durden, "The US War on Terror Has Cost $5 Trillion and Increased Terrorism by 6,500%," Zero Hedge, September 2016, https://www.zerohedge.com/news/2016-09-15/us-war -terror-has-cost-5-trillion-and-increased-terrorism-6500. See also Kit O'Connell, "Deaths from Terrorism Increased 4,500% since Beginning of War on Terror: between 2007 and 2011, Almost Half the World's Terror Attacks Took Place in Iraq and Afghanistan—Two Countries under Active Occupation by the United States," MPN News, December 2015, https://www .mintpressnews.com/212244-2/212244/; "US 'War on Terror' Has Killed over Half a Million People: Study," *Al Jazeera*, November 9, 2018, https://www.aljazeera.com/news/2018/11/wars -terror-killed-million-people-study-181109080620011.html?fbclid=IwAR2CH-7g4YP2uLCl -4ztxUyUeoate_Ujalc67dScM_PziwZ27FU5BUKddgI.

10. Durden, "The US War on Terror Has Cost $5 Trillion."

11. Economic and Social Commission for Western Asia, *Survey of Economic and Social Developments in the Arab Region 2015–2016*, November 2016, p. 7, https://www.unescwa.org/sites /www.unescwa.org/files/uploads/summary-survey-economic-social-development-arab -region-2015-2016-english.pdf. See also R. Alaaldin, A. Baabood, S. Colombo, A. Dessi, M. Kerrou, J. Mouawad, V. Ntousas, et al., *The EU, Resilience and the MENA Region* (Rome: Foundation for European Progressive Studies and Istituto Affari Internazionali, 2017), p. 166, https://feps-europe.eu/wp-content/uploads/2018/03/The-EU-Resilience-and-the -MENA-Region.pdf.

12. "MENA: COVID-19 Amplified Inequalities and Was Used to Further Ramp Up Repression," Amnesty International, April 7, 2021, https://www.amnesty.org/en/latest/press-release /2021/04/mena-covid-19-amplified-inequalities-and-was-used-to-further-ramp-up -repression/.

13. Nan Tian, Diego Lopes da Silva, Xiao Liang, Lorenzo Scarazzato, Lucie Béraud Su-dreau, and Ana Carolina de Oliveira Assis, "Trends in World Military Expenditure," SIPRI Fact Sheet, 2022, https://www.sipri.org/sites/default/files/2023-04/2304_fs_milex_2022.pdf.

14. Noland and Pack, *Arab Economies*, p. 161. See also Steffen Hertog, *Princes, Brokers, and Bureaucrats: Oil and the State in Saudi Arabia* (Ithaca, NY: Cornell University Press, 2010); Hossein Askari and Babak Dastmaltschi, *Saudi Arabia's Economy: Oil and the Search for Economic Development* (Greenwich, CT: JAI Press, 1990).

15. Noland and Pack, *Arab Economies*, p. 161. See also Sheikh Rustum Ali, *Saudi Arabia and Oil Diplomacy* (New York: Praeger, 1976).

16. United Nations Development Programme (UNDP), *Arab Human Development Report 2009: Challenges to Human Security in the Arab Countries*, May 26, 2009, https://www.undp.org/publications/arab-human-development-report-2009.

17. UNDP, *Arab Human Development Report 2009*.

18. UNDP, *Arab Human Development Report 2009*.

19. UNDP, *Arab Human Development Report 2009*. See also Clement M. Henry and Robert Springborg, *Globalization and the Politics of Development in the Middle East* (Cambridge: Cambridge University Press, 2010), p. 46.

20. UNDP, *Arab Human Development Report 2009*; Henry and Springborg, *Globalization and the Politics of Development*.

21. UNDP, *Arab Human Development Report 2009*; Henry and Springborg, *Globalization and the Politics of Development*.

22. UNDP, *Arab Human Development Report 2009*; Henry and Springborg, *Globalization and the Politics of Development*.

23. Henry and Springborg, *Globalization and the Politics of Development*, p. 46.

24. Henry and Springborg, *Globalization and the Politics of Development*.

25. "Foreign Direct Investment, Net Inflows (BoP, Current US$)—Middle East & North Africa," World Bank Data, 2023, https://data.worldbank.org/indicator/BX.KLT.DINV.CD.WD?locations=ZQ.

26. "Foreign Direct Investment, Net Inflows."

27. "Foreign Direct Investment, Net Inflows."

28. "Dubai's Emaar Launches $3 Bln Project in Iraqi Kurdistan," Reuters, October 23, 2013, http://uk.reuters.com/article/emaar-iraq-idUKL5N0IH0HU20131027; see also Lucy Barnard, "Bloom Properties Delays Plan for Homes in Iraq," *The National*, November 18, 2015, http://www.thenational.ae/business/property/bloom-properties-delays-plan-for-homes-in-iraq.

29. Barnard, "Bloom Properties Delays Plan for Homes in Iraq."

30. Samuel Wandel, "Has Foreign Investment Helped Jordanian SMEs and Entrepreneurs?," Wamda, March 28, 2016, https://www.wamda.com/2016/03/has-foreign-investment-helped-jordanian-smes-entrepreneurs.

31. Wandel, "Has Foreign Investment Helped Jordanian SMEs and Entrepreneurs?"

32. "Foreign Direct Investment, Net Inflows."

33. Henry and Springborg, *Globalization and the Politics of Development*, p. 46.

34. Henry and Springborg, *Globalization and the Politics of Development*, p. 48.

35. Henry and Springborg, *Globalization and the Politics of Development*, p. 48.

36. Henry and Springborg, *Globalization and the Politics of Development*, p. 48.

37. See Kannaa Ambalam, "Reallocation of Water Resources in the Arab Region: An Emerging Challenge in Water Governance," *European Journal of Sustainable Development* 3, no. 3 (2014): 283–298. See also Ernie Jowsey, "The Changing Status of Water as a Natural Resource," *International Journal of Sustainable Development and World Ecology* 19 (2012): 433–441.

38. Ambalam, "Reallocation of Water Resources," p. 289; UNDP, *Arab Human Development Report 2009*.

39. Hannah Summers, "Yemen on Brink of 'World's Worst Famine in 100 Years' If War Continues," *The Guardian*, October 15, 2018, https://www.theguardian.com/global-development/2018/oct/15/yemen-on-brink-worst-famine-100-years-un.

40. Declan Walsh and Somini Sengupta, "For Thousands of Years, Egypt Controlled the Nile. A New Dam Threatens That," *New York Times*, February 9, 2020.

41. Ambalam, "Reallocation of Water Resources."

42. Ambalam, "Reallocation of Water Resources," p. 286.

43. Ambalam, "Reallocation of Water Resources," p. 286.

44. Ambalam, "Reallocation of Water Resources," p. 290.

45. Ambalam, "Reallocation of Water Resources," p. 291.

46. Achref Chibani, "Water Politics in the Tigris-Euphrates Basin" (Washington, DC: Arab Center, May 30, 2023), https://arabcenterdc.org/resource/water-politics-in-the-tigris-euphrates-basin/.

47. Daniela Sala and Bart von Laffert, "Iranian Dams Cut Off Iraqi Water Supplies," *Deutsch Welle*, August 16, 2021, https://www.dw.com/en/tensions-rise-as-iranian-dams-cut-off-iraqi-water-supplies/a-58764729.

48. UNDP, *Arab Human Development Report 2009*, p. 54.

49. UNDP, *The Arab Cities Resilience Report, 2021*, pp. 10–13; United Nations Development Programme, *UNDP Annual Report 2021*, https://www.undp.org/publications/undp-annual-report-2021.

50. "One-Third of Arab World's Population Suffers from Hunger: UN," *Al Jazeera*, December 16, 2021, https://www.aljazeera.com/news/2021/12/16/third-of-arab-worlds-population-suffers-from-hunger-un.

51. Michelle Nichols, "Is There Famine in Gaza? Here's What We Know," Reuters, March 18, 2024, https://www.reuters.com/world/middle-east/famine-looms-gaza-how-will-world-know-it-has-arrived-2024-03-05/. See also "Joint Statement on Conflict-Induced Hunger in Gaza," Save the Children, February 14, 2024, https://www.savethechildren.net/news/joint-statement-conflict-induced-hunger-gaza.

52. UNDP, *Arab Development Report 2016*, p. 31.

53. UNDP, *Arab Development Report 2016*, p. 31.

54. UNDP, *Arab Development Report 2016*, p. 31.

55. UNDP, *Arab Development Report 2016*, p. 31.

56. Mark Habeeb, "The Middle East Leads the World in Income Inequality: During the Period 1990–2016, the Top 10% of the Population in the Middle East Enjoyed about 60–66% of the Region's Income," *Arab Weekly*, January 14, 2018, https://thearabweekly.com/middle-east

-leads-world-income-inequality. See also F. Alvarado, L. Assouad, and T. Piketty, "Inequality in the Middle East," VOX, August 13, 2018, https://voxeu.org/article/inequality-middle-east.

57. Madaniya, *Injustice in the Arab Region and the Road to Justice* (2017), p. 119, https://www.madaniya.info/wp-content/uploads/2017/06/version-anglaise.pdf.

58. Madaniya, *Injustice in the Arab Region and the Road to Justice*, p. 119.

59. Madaniya, *Injustice in the Arab Region and the Road to Justice*, p. 119.

60. "Roadblocks Still in Place for Saudi Women after Five Years of Driving," France 24, July 7, 2023, https://www.france24.com/en/live-news/20230707-after-five-years-of-driving-roadblocks-remain-for-saudi-women-1.

61. Madaniya, *Injustice in the Arab Region and the Road to Justice*, p. 120.

62. Madaniya, *Injustice in the Arab Region and the Road to Justice*, p. 119.

63. Madaniya, *Injustice in the Arab Region and the Road to Justice*, p. 120.

64. Madaniya, *Injustice in the Arab Region and the Road to Justice*, p. 120.

65. Zena Tal-ahhan, "'Historic Day' as Jordanian Parliament Repeals Rape Law," *Al Jazeera*, August 1, 2017, http://www.aljazeera.com/indepth/features/2017/08/day-jordanian-parliament-repeals-rape-law-170801103929836.html?xif=.

66. UNDP, *Arab Development Report 2016*, p. 33.

67. UNDP, *Arab Development Report 2016*, p. 80.

68. UNDP, *Arab Development Report 2016*, p. 80.

69. UNDP, *Arab Development Report 2016*, p. 80.

70. UNDP, *Arab Development Report 2016*, p. 80.

71. United Nations, *Times of Crisis, Times of Change: Science for Accelerating Transformations to Sustainable Development, Global Sustainable Development Report 2023* (New York: United Nations, 2023), https://sdgs.un.org/sites/default/files/2023-09/FINAL%20GSDR%202023-Digital%20-110923_1.pdf.

72. Paul Rivin, *Arab Economies in the Twentieth-Century* (Cambridge: Cambridge University Press, 2009), p. 220.

73. UNDP, *Arab Development Report 2016*, p. 31.

74. Nader Kabbani, "Youth Employment in the Middle East and North Africa: Revisiting and Reframing the Challenge" (Policy Briefing, Brookings Doha Center, February 2019), https://www.brookings.edu/wp-content/uploads/2019/02/Youth_Unemployment_MENA_English_Web.pdf.

75. International Labour Organization, "Global Employment Trends for Youth 2022: The Arab States" (Geneva: International Labor Organization, 2023), https://www.ilo.org/resource/brief/global-employment-trends-youth-2022-arab-states.

76. UNDP, *Arab Development Report 2016*, pp. 22–23.

77. UNDP, *Arab Development Report 2016*, pp. 22–23.

78. UNDP, *Arab Development Report 2016*, p. 27.

79. UNDP, *Arab Development Report 2016*, p. 27.

80. UNDP, *Arab Development Report 2016*, p. 171.

81. UNDP, *Arab Development Report 2016*, p. 171.

82. UNDP, *Arab Development Report 2016*, p. 171.

83. UNDP, *Arab Development Report 2016*, p. 171.

84. UNDP, *Arab Development Report 2016*, p. 31.

85. UNDP, *Arab Development Report 2016*, pp. 141–193.

86. Jacob Powell, "Climate Change May Make Middle East and North Africa Uninhabitable," *Middle East Eye*, June 29, 2017, https://www.middleeasteye.net/news/climate-change-may-make-middle-east-and-north-africa-uninhabitable; "Gulf Will Be Too Hot for Humans by 2070: Study," *Gulf News*, October 27, 2015, https://gulfnews.com/uae/environment/gulf-will-be-too-hot-for-humans-by-2070-study-1.1608055; Baher Kamal, "Middle East, Uninhabitable? Accessible Freshwater Has Fallen by Two-Thirds," Meer, March 14, 2017, https://www.meer.com/en/24280-middle-east-uninhabitable; and "Climate Change Is Making the Arab World More Miserable," *The Economist*, May 31, 2018, https://www.economist.com/middle-east-and-africa/2018/05/31/climate-change-is-making-the-arab-world-more-miserable.

87. Peter Hergersberg, "Hot Air in the Orient," *Max Planck Research*, no. 4 (2016): 63–68, https://www.mpg.de/10856695/.

88. Madaniya, *Injustice in the Arab Region and the Road to Justice*, p. 107.

89. Madaniya, *Injustice in the Arab Region and the Road to Justice*, p. 107.

90. Madaniya, *Injustice in the Arab Region and the Road to Justice*, p. 107.

91. Madaniya, *Injustice in the Arab Region and the Road to Justice*, pp. 107–111.

92. Madaniya, *Injustice in the Arab Region and the Road to Justice*, p. 115.

93. Madaniya, *Injustice in the Arab Region and the Road to Justice*, p. 116.

94. Rivin, *Arab Economies*, p. 221.

95. UNDP, *Arab Human Development Report 2009*, p. 91.

96. See Yahya M. Sadowski, *Political Vegetable? Businessmen and Bureaucrats in the Development of Egyptian Agriculture* (Washington, DC: Brookings Institution, 1991); Steven Heydemann, *Networks of Privilege in the Middle East: The Politics of Economic Reform Revisited* (New York: Palgrave Macmillan, 2004); Bassam Haddad, "Syria, the Arab Uprisings, and the Political Economy of Authoritarian Resilience," *Interface* 4, no. 1 (2012): 113–130.

97. Hamouda Chekir and Ishac Diwan, "Crony Capitalism in Egypt," *Journal of Globalization and Development* 5, no. 2 (2014): 179.

98. Haddad, "Syria, the Arab Uprisings, and the Political Economy of Authoritarian Resilience," p. 80; See also Joel Beinin, *Workers and Peasants in the Modern Middle East* (Cambridge: Cambridge University Press, 2001).

99. Timothy Mitchell, "Society, Economy, and the State Effect," in *State/Culture: State-Formation after the Cultural Turn*, ed. George Steinmetz (Ithaca, NY: Cornell University Press, 1999), p. 89.

100. See Heydemann, *Networks of Privilege in the Middle East*; Haddad, "Syria, the Arab Uprisings, and the Political Economy of Authoritarian Resilience"; Henry and Springborg, *Globalization and the Politics of Development*.

101. Madaniya, *Injustice in the Arab Region and the Road to Justice*, p. 178.

102. Madaniya, *Injustice in the Arab Region and the Road to Justice*, p. 178.

103. Chekir and Diwan, *Crony Capitalism in Egypt*.

104. Chekir and Diwan, *Crony Capitalism in Egypt*.

105. Haddad, "Syria, the Arab Uprisings, and the Political Economy of Authoritarian Resilience," p. 80.

106. Haddad, "Syria, the Arab Uprisings, and the Political Economy of Authoritarian Resilience," p. 80; see also Friedrich Schneider and Dominik H. Enste, *The Shadow Economy: An International Survey* (Cambridge: Cambridge University Press, 2002).

107. Tom Bawden and John Hooper, "Gaddafi's Hidden Billions: Dubai Banks, Plush London Pads and Italian Water," *The Guardian*, February 22, 2011, https://www.theguardian.com/world/2011/feb/22/gaddafi-libya-oil-wealth-portfolio.

108. Eileen Byrne, "Tunisia Struggles to Trace Up to £11Bn Hidden Abroad by Ben Ali Regime," *The Guardian*, January 13, 2002, https://www.theguardian.com/world/2012/jan/13/tunisia-11bn-hidden-funds-ben-ali.

109. Lillia Blaise, "Self-Immolation: Catalyst of the Arab Spring, Is Now a Grim Trend," *New York Times*, July 9, 2017, https://www.nytimes.com/2017/07/09/world/africa/self-immolation-catalyst-of-the-arab-spring-is-now-a-grim-trend.html.

110. Blaise, "Self-Immolation." See also Mehdi Ben Khelil, Amine Zgarni, Mounir Ben Mohamed, Mohamed Allouche, Anis Benzarti, Ahmed Banasr, and Moncef Hamdoun, "A Comparison of Suicidal Behavior by Burns Five Years before and Five Years after the 2011 Tunisian Revolution," *Burns Journals* 43, no. 4 (June 2017): 858–865.

111. Blaise, "Self-Immolation"; Khelil et al., "A Comparison of Suicidal Behavior."

112. Blaise, "Self-Immolation"; Khelil et al., "A Comparison of Suicidal Behavior."

113. Sihem Bensedrine, "A Poisonous Dictatorship Has Been Built in Tunisia, the Birthplace of the Arab Spring," *The Guardian*, March 31, 2023, https://www.theguardian.com/global-development/commentisfree/2023/mar/31/dictatorship-tunisia-kais-saied-sihem-bensedrine.

Chapter 9: The Nation versus the *Umma*

1. Peter Mansfield, *Nasser's Egypt* (Harmondsworth, UK: Penguin Books, 1965), p. 20.

2. Philip K. Hitti, *A History of the Arabs*, 10th ed. (Basingstoke, UK: Palgrave Macmillan, 2002), pp. 727–728.

3. For more on the 'Urabi revolt, see Juan R. Cole, *Colonialism and Revolution in the Middle East: Social and Cultural Origins of Egypt's Urabi Movement* (Princeton, NJ: Princeton University Press, 1992); Thomas S. Mayer, *The Changing Past: Egyptian Historiography of the Urabi Revolt, 1882–1983* (Gainesville: University of Florida Press, 1988); R. Al-Sa'id, *al-Asas al-Ijtima'i Leil Thawra al-Urabiyya* [The social basis of the 'Urabi revolution] (Cairo: Maktabat Madbouli, 1967), p. 69; A. 'Urabi, *'Urabi: Kashf al-Sitar 'an Sirr al-Asrar fi al-Nahda al-Misriyya al-Mashhura bi al-thawra al-'Urabiya* [Unveiling the lid or the cover? On the secret of the secrets on the Egyptian renaissance known as the 'Urabi revolution], *Al-Jumi'i, A. M. I.* 1 (Cairo: Dar al-Kutub wa al-Watha'iq al-Qawmiyya, 2005): 485–587.

4. Derek Hopwood, *Egypt: Politics and Society, 1945–1990*, 3rd ed. (London: Routledge, 2002), p. 13.

5. Bernard Reich, *Political Leaders of the Contemporary Middle East and North Africa: A Biographical Dictionary* (Westport, CT: Greenwood Press, 1990), p. 377.

6. Anthony Gorst and Lewis Johnman, *The Suez Crisis* (London: Routledge, 1997).

7. For more on Banna's founding of the Muslim Brotherhood, see Richard P. Mitchell, *The Society of the Muslim Brothers* (Oxford: Oxford University Press, 1969), chap. 1.

8. Dilip Hiro, *Islamic Fundamentalism* (London: Paladin, 1988), p. 60.

9. Carrie Rosefsky Wickham, *The Muslim Brotherhood: Evolution of an Islamist Movement* (Princeton, NJ: Princeton University Press, 2013), pp. 22–24.

10. Wickham, *The Muslim Brotherhood*, pp. 22–25.

11. Hiro, *Islamic Fundamentalism*, pp. 61–62.

12. Cole, *Colonialism and Revolution*; see also Fawaz A. Gerges, *Making the Arab World: Nasser, Qutb and the Clash That Shaped the Middle East* (Princeton, NJ: Princeton University Press, 2018), chap. 1; and G. Baer, "Islamic Political Activity in Modern Egyptian History: A Comparative Analysis," in *Islam, Nationalism, and Radicalism in Egypt and the Sudan*, ed. Gabriel R. Warburg and Uri M. Kupferschmidt (New York: Praeger, 1983), p. 39.

13. See Panayiotis J. Vatikiotis, *The Modern History of Egypt* (London: Butler and Tanner, 1969).

14. See, Nadav Safran, *Egypt in Search of Political Community: An Analysis of the Intellectual and Political Evolution of Egypt, 1804–1952* (Cambridge, MA: Harvard University Press, 1961).

15. Mitchell, *The Society of the Muslim Brothers*, pp. 180–183, 200–205.

16. Marius Deeb, *Party Politics in Egypt: The Wafd and Its Rivals, 1919–1939* (London: Ithaca Press for the Middle East Centre, St Antony's College, Oxford, 1979); Israel Gershoni and James P. Jankowski, *Redefining the Egyptian Nation* (Cambridge: Cambridge University Press, 1995), pp. 11–12.

17. For more on the organizational structure of the group, see Z. Munson, "Islamic Mobilization: Social Movement Theory and the Egyptian Muslim Brotherhood," *Sociological Quarterly* 42, no. 4 (1972): 487–510. For more on the special apparatus, see S. al-Hakim, *Asrar al-'Alaqa al-Khassa bayna 'Abd al-Nasir wa-l-Ikhwan* [The secrets of the special relationship between Abdel Nasser and the Brothers] (Cairo: Markaz al-Hadara al-'Arabiyya li-l-I'lam wa-l-Nashr, 1996), p. 8.

18. See Gerges, *Making the Arab World*.

19. Israel Gershoni and James P. Jankowski, *Nasser's Egypt, Arab Nationalism, and the United Arab Republic* (Boulder, CO: Lynne Rienner, 2002), pp. 23–24.

20. For more on Sayyid Qutb, see James Toth, *Sayyid Qutb: The Life and Legacy of a Radical Islamic Intellectual* (Oxford: Oxford University Press, 2013).

21. See John Calvert, *Sayyid Qutb and the Origins of Radical Islam* (London: C. Hurst, 2010), and Gerges, *Making the Arab World*.

22. Mohammed Qutb, *Jahiliyayat al-Qarn al-'Ishrin* [The ignorance of the twentieth century] (Cairo: Dar al-Shurouk, 1980). See also Sayyid Qutb, *Ma'lim fil Tariq* [Signposts] (Cairo: Dar al-Shurouk, 1979), pp. 17–18.

23. Hopwood, *Egypt*, p. 183.

24. See Abdullah Al-Arian, *Answering the Call: Popular Islamic Activism in Sadat's Egypt* (Oxford: Oxford University Press, 2014).

25. See Barbara H. E. Zollner, *The Muslim Brotherhood: Hasan al-Hudaybi and Ideology* (New York: Routledge, 2009); Omar Ashour, *The De-Radicalization of Jihadists: Transforming Armed Islamist Movements* (London Routledge, 2009), p. 66.

26. For more on the food riots, see Hamid Ansari, *Egypt: The Stalled Society* (Albany: State University of New York Press, 1986), chap. 8.

27. See William B. Quandt, *Camp David: Peacemaking and Politics* (Washington, DC: Brookings Institution, 1986).

28. Akbar S. Ahmed and Hastings Donnan, "Islam in the Age of Postmodernity," in *Islam, Globalization and Postmodernity*, ed. Akbar S. Ahmed and Hastings Donnan (London: Routledge, 1994). See also Fred Halliday, "The Politics of Islamic Fundamentalism: Iran, Tunisia, and the Challenge to the Secular State," in *International Colloquium on the History of the Central Mediterranean* (University of Malta, December 13, 1989 [Unpublished]), pp. 95–99; and Sami Zubaida, *Islam, the People and the State: Essays on Political Ideas and Movements in the Middle East* (London: Routledge, 1989), pp. 64–83; for background on the Iranian opposition, see Asef Bayat, ed., *Post-Islamism: The Changing Faces of Political Islam* (Oxford: Oxford University Press, 2013), pp. 35–71.

29. Anette Ranko, *The Muslim Brotherhood and Its Quest for Hegemony in Egypt: State Discourse and Islamist Counter-Discourse* (Wiesbaden, Germany: Springer VS, 2015), p. 79.

30. Ranko, *The Muslim Brotherhood*, p. 79.

31. Ranko, *The Muslim Brotherhood*, p. 80.

32. For more on the Brotherhood's foray into the political system, see Wickham, *The Muslim Brotherhood*, pp. 46–76.

33. Ranko, *The Muslim Brotherhood*, p. 83.

34. Ranko, *The Muslim Brotherhood*. See also Ninette S. Fahmy, "The Performance of the Muslim Brotherhood in the Egyptian Syndicates: An Alternative Formula for Reform?," *Middle East Journal* 52, no. 4 (Fall 1998): 554–556.

35. Ranko, *The Muslim Brotherhood*, p. 86.

36. Wickham, *The Muslim Brotherhood*, pp. 154–195. See also Mohammed Zahid, *The Muslim Brotherhood and Egypt's Succession Crisis: The Politics of Liberalisation and Reform in the Middle East*, rev. ed. (London: I. B. Tauris, 2012).

37. This viewpoint is misleading, assert supporters of the Muslim Brotherhood. See Neil Ketchley, "How Egypt's Generals Used Street Protest to Stage a Coup," *New York Times*, July 3, 2017, http://wapo.st/2syKa6C?tid=ss_mail&utm_term=.b0012367b7de.

38. David M. Kirkpatrick, "Recordings Suggest That Emirates and Egyptian Military Pushed Ousting of Morsi," *New York Times*, March 1, 2015, https://www.nytimes.com/2015/03/02/world/middleeast/recordings-suggest-emirates-and-egyptian-military-pushed-ousting-of-morsi.html. See also Neil Ketchley, "How Egypt's Generals Used Street Protests to Stage a Coup," *Washington Post*, July 3, 2017, https://www.washingtonpost.com/news/monkey-cage/wp/2017/07/03/how-egypts-generals-used-street-protests-to-stage-a-coup/.

39. Patrick Kingsley, "Egypt's Rabaa Massacre: One Year On," *The Guardian*, August 16, 2014, https://www.theguardian.com/world/2014/aug/16/rabaa-massacre-egypt-human-rights-watch.

40. M. E. McMillan, *From the First World War to the Arab Spring: What's Really Going on in the Middle East?* (New York: Palgrave Macmillan, 2016), pp. 230–232.

41. Fawaz A. Gerges, *ISIS: A History* (Princeton, NJ: Princeton University Press, 2016), p. 212.

42. See Benjamin Stora, "La différenciation entre le F.L.N. et le courant messaliste (été 1954–décembre 1955). Contribution à l'histoire intérieure de la révolution algérienne," *Cahiers de la Méditerranée* 26, no. 1 (1983): 15–82.

43. Stora, "La différenciation."

44. Laurie A. Brand, *Official Stories: Politics and National Narratives in Egypt and Algeria* (Stanford, CA: Stanford University Press, 2014), p. 137. The French refused to acknowledge negotiators with religious affiliation, preferring the francophone elite who they saw as a more "rational agent." Colonial France tried to divide and conquer the nationalist movement by playing off religious and secular activists. However, the FLN, the vanguard party, and the francophone elite joined forces with the Islamists. As such, the FLN was more heterogeneous than homogenous.

45. Addi Lahouari, "De la permanence du populisme Algerien," *Peuples Mediterraneens* 46 (1990): 3, 37–46.

46. Frédéric Volpi, *Islam and Democracy: The Failure of Dialogue in Algeria* (London: Pluto Press, 2003), p. 32.

47. See Ahmed Rouadja, *Les Freres et la mosque: Enquete sur le movement Islamiste en Algerie* (Paris: Editions Karthala, 1990).

48. Rouadja, *Les Freres et la mosque.*

49. Rouadja, *Les Freres et la mosque*, p. 129.

50. Rouadja, *Les Freres et la mosque*, pp. 129–131.

51. Martin Evans and John Phillips, *Algeria: Anger of the Dispossessed* (New Haven, CT: Yale University Press, 2007), p. 146.

52. Omar Carlier, *D'une guerre à l'autre: Le redéploiement de la violence entre soi* (Paris: Presse de Sciences Po, 1995), pp. 135–150.

53. Ray Takeyh, "Iran's New Iraq," *Middle East Journal* 62, no. 1 (2008): 13–30.

54. For a detailed background on the Algerian civil war, see Louis Martinez, *La Guerre civile en Algerie, 1990–1998* (Algiers: Karthala, 1998); see also Evans and Phillips, *Algeria*, chap. 6.

55. For more on the concept of symbolic power, see Pierre Bourdieu, *Language and Symbolic Power* (Cambridge, MA: Harvard University Press, 1991).

56. See Fawaz A. Gerges, *The Far Enemy: Why Jihad Went Global* (Cambridge: Cambridge University Press, 2005); Fawaz A. Gerges, *The Rise and Fall of Al Qaeda* (Oxford: Oxford University Press, 2011); and Fawaz A. Gerges, *ISIS: A History*, 2nd ed. (Princeton, NJ: Princeton University Press, 2021).

57. Ira M. Lapidus, "Between Universalism and Particularism: The Historical Bases of Muslim Communal, National, and Global Identities," *Global Networks* 1 (2001): 3.

58. Denis McAuley, "The Ideology of Osama Bin Laden: Nation, Tribe and World Economy," *Journal of Political Ideologies* 10, no. 3 (2005): 269–287.

59. Fanar Haddad, *Sectarianism in Iraq: Antagonistic Visions of Unity* (Oxford: Oxford University Press, 2011), p. 28.

60. Haddad, *Sectarianism in Iraq.*

61. A minority of adherents has a disproportionately high impact due to the Islamic State's (IS) strategy to maximize destruction. The symbiosis with the global media that has in the first two years of its existence—2014–2016—at least offered the perfect platform for IS to indirectly publicize its rhetoric and actions. The impact of IS can also act as a vehicle for moderation, in a paradoxical way. Such is the anger against IS for "hijacking" their religion, many Sunni Muslims may emphasize a message of moderation more than they might have to counter the negative image that IS has produced. Or indeed, as has been the case with many Syrians,

they have chosen to renounce religion altogether, having been deeply disillusioned by the likes of IS and other so-called Islamist groups. Thus, it is worth noting the variety and complexity of the impact of IS on the wider Sunni community.

62. It is worth mentioning that this was a work in progress; most people still had localized identities, but the new postcolonial state was trying to develop a new national identity and bridge the rural-urban divide.

63. See Fanar Haddad's chapter on "Sectarian Relations before 'Sectarianization' in pre-2003 Iraq," in *Sectarianization: Mapping the New Politics of the Middle East*, ed. Nader Hashemi and Danny Postel (Oxford: Oxford University Press, 2017).

64. Ranj Alaaldin, "Fragility and Resilience in Iraq" (Rome: Istituto Affari Internazionali, November 2017), http://www.iai.it/sites/default/files/iaiwp1733.pdf.

65. Haddad, *Sectarianism in Iraq*, p. 24.

66. See "Newsmaker: Yemen's Saleh, Dancing on the Heads of Snakes," Reuters, September 23, 2011, www.reuters.com/article/us-yemen-saleh-idUSTRE78M20X20110923.

67. See "Ali Abdullah Saleh Fast Facts," CNN Library, March 20, 2017, http://edition.cnn.com/2013/07/08/world/meast/ali-abdullah-saleh-fast-facts/index.html; Peter Salisbury, "Yemen's Former President Ali Abdullah Saleh behind Houthis' Rise," *Financial Times*, March 26, 2015, https://www.ft.com/content/dbbc1ddc-d3c2-11e4-99bd-00144feab7de.

Chapter 10: The Subversion of the Nation from Within and Without

1. For more on Hamas, see Sarah M. Roy, *Hamas and Civil Society in Gaza: Engaging the Islamist Social Sector* (Princeton, NJ: Princeton University Press, 2011); and Khaled Hroub, *Hamas: Political Thought and Practice* (Washington, DC: Institute for Palestine Studies, 2000).

2. Mohammed Ayoob, *The Many Faces of Political Islam* (Ann Arbor: University of Michigan Press, 2007), p. 117. For background on the Muslim Brotherhood and Hamas, see Katerina Dalacoura, *Islamist Terrorism and Democracy in the Middle East* (New York: Cambridge University Press, 2011), pp. 66–96.

3. For more on Hezbollah, see Hamzeh Ahmad Nizar, *In the Path of Hizbullah* (Syracuse, NY: Syracuse University Press, 2004); Joseph Elie Alagha, *Hizbullah's Documents: From the 1985 Open Letter to the 2009 Manifesto* (Amsterdam: Pallas, 2011); and Simon Haddad, "The Origins of Popular Support for Lebanon's Hezbollah," *Studies in Conflict and Terrorism* 29, no. 1 (2006): 21–34.

4. Fanar Haddad, *Sectarianism in Iraq: Antagonistic Visions of Unity* (Oxford: Oxford University Press, 2011), pp. 117–142; see also Eric Davis, "Introduction: The Question of Sectarian Identities in Iraq," *International Journal of Contemporary Iraqi Studies* 4, no. 3 (2010): 229–242.

5. Haddad, *Sectarianism in Iraq*, pp. 117–142; Davis, "Introduction."

6. Shibley Telhami, "The 2011 Arab Public Opinion Poll," Brookings, November 21, 2011, https://www.brookings.edu/research/the-2011-arab-public-opinion-poll/.

7. For more on Al-Qaeda and the transformation of the Islamist movement, see Fawaz A. Gerges, *The Far Enemy: Why Jihad Went Global* (New York: Cambridge University Press, 2005); and Jean-Pierre Filiu, *From Deep State to Islamic State: The Arab Counter-Revolution and Its Jihad Legacy* (London: Hurst & Company, 2015).

8. Fawaz A. Gerges, *The Rise and Fall of Al-Qaeda* (Oxford: Oxford University Press, 2014); and Gerges, *The Far Enemy*.

9. Fawaz A. Gerges, *ISIS: A History*, 2nd ed. (Princeton, NJ: Princeton University Press, 2021).

10. Aymenn Jawad al-Tamimi, "The Dawn of the Islamic State of Iraq and ash-Sham," *Current Trends in Islamist Ideology*, January 27, 2014, www.meforum.org/3732/islamic-state-iraq-ash -sham.

11. Thomas Hegghammer, "Global Jihadism after the Iraq War," *Middle East Journal* 60, no. 1 (Winter 2006): 11–32.

12. Hegghammer, "Global Jihadism after the Iraq War."

13. Abu Musab al-Zarqawi and Abu Bakr al-Baghdadi, the self-appointed IS caliph, tried to fill an institutional and security vacuum in the area. Perhaps even more importantly from their point of view, they have tried to fill an identity void. They have successfully tapped into the clash of identities that is ravaging the Arab world as a direct result of the implosion of national identity in Iraq, Syria, and beyond. By contrast, the first generation of jihadists like Osama bin Laden and Ayman al-Zawahiri were not obsessed with sectarian identity. In fact, Bin Laden and al-Zawahiri repeatedly pleaded with their subordinate, Zarqawi, to stop attacking Shia and concentrate instead on the US-led coalition forces. Both Zarqawi and his successor Baghdadi recognized that appealing to Sunni *asabiyya* was a successful strategy. By portraying themselves as the defenders of persecuted Sunnis, their goal was to ignite a sectarian war and reap the political rewards of such a doomsday scenario. What has so far saved Iraq from complete disintegration is that the majority of Iraqis do not accept Al-Qaeda's binary narrative portraying the Shia majority as an existential threat to Iraq's Sunnis. Furthermore, key figures in the Shia religious establishment have refused to retaliate. Iraq's well-respected Grand Ayatollah, Ali al-Sistani, has exerted a moderating influence on his community and called for restraint.

14. A detailed profile of Asaib Ahl is available online. See Mapping Militant Organizations, "Asa'ib Ahl al-Haq," last modified June 1, 2021, https://mappingmilitants.org/node/336/.

15. A detailed profile of the organization Kata'ib Hezbullah is available online. See Mapping Militant Organizations, "Kata'ib Hezbollah," last modified June 1, 2021, https:// mappingmilitants.org/node/427/. For more on the Syria-Iran diplomatic ties, see Jubin M. Goodarzi, *Syria and Iran: Diplomatic Alliance and Power Politics in the Middle East* (London: I. B. Tauris, 2009).

16. Gerges, *ISIS*, pp. 74, 107, 179.

17. For example, see Angus McDowall, "Saudi Opposition Clerics Make Sectarian Call to Jihad in Syria," Reuters, October 5, 2015, www.reuters.com/article/us-mideast-crisis-saudi-clerics -idUSKCN0RZ1IW20151005.

18. See "Sunni-Shia Divide," Council on Foreign Relations, accessed June 24, 2017, www .cfr.org/peace-conflict-and-human-rights/sunni-shia-divide/p33176#!/?cid=otr-marketing _url-sunni_shia_infoguide.

19. Gerges, *ISIS*, pp. 148–151.

20. Gerges, *ISIS*, pp. 148–151.

21. Toby Dodge, *Iraq from War to New Authoritarianism* (London: Routledge, 2013), pp. 75–114; Gerges, *ISIS*, pp. 50–98.

22. Dodge, *Iraq from War to New Authoritarianism*, pp. 75–114; Gerges, *ISIS*, pp. 50–98.

23. Gerges, *ISIS*, pp. 46–48.

24. Ashley Fantz and Michael Pearson, "Who's Doing What in the Coalition Battle against ISIS," CNN, February 28, 2015, edition.cnn.com/2014/10/06/world/meast/isis-coalition-nations/.

25. Jasmine Gani, "Contentious Politics and the Syrian Crisis: Internationalisation and Militarisation of Conflict," in *Contentious Politics in the Middle East: Popular Resistance and Marginalized Activism beyond the Arab Uprisings*, ed. Fawaz A. Gerges (New York: Palgrave Macmillan, 2015).

26. Dawn Chatty, "Bedouin Tribes in Contemporary Syria: Alternative Perceptions of Authority, Management and Control," in *Tribes and States in a Changing Middle East*, ed. Uzi Rabi (New York: Oxford University Press, 2016), p. 4.

27. Antony Toth, "The Transformation of a Pastoral Economy: Bedouin and States in Northern Arabia, 1850–1950" (PhD thesis, Oxford University, 2000). See also Dick Douwes, *The Ottomans in Syria: A History of Justice and Oppression* (London: I. B. Tauris, 2000), p. 29.

28. See, for example, Douwes, *The Ottomans in Syria*, p. 40.

29. Jonathan Rae, "Tribe and State: Management of the Syrian Steppe" (PhD thesis, University of Oxford, 1999), p. 64.

30. See Gertrude Bell, *Syria: The Desert and the Sown* (London: Heinemann, 1907).

31. Chatty, *Bedouin Tribes*, p. 2.

32. Chatty, *Bedouin Tribes*, p. 8.

33. Douwes, *The Ottomans in Syria*, p. 40.

34. For more on the role of demographics from World War I, see Hanna Batatu, *Syria's Peasantry, the Descendants of Its Lesser Rural Notables, and Their Politics* (Princeton, NJ: Princeton University Press, 1999), chap. 1.

35. John Glubb, *Handbook of the Nomads, Semi-Nomads, Semi-Sedentary Tribes of Syria* (London: GSI Headquarters, 9th Army, 1942); Philip Shukry Koury, *Syria and the French Mandate: The Politics of Arab Nationalism, 1920–1945* (Princeton, NJ: Princeton University Press, 2014), p. 206; and Patrick Seale, *Asad of Syria: The Struggle for the Middle East* (London: I. B. Tauris, 1988), p. 20.

36. Katharina Lange, "'Bedouin' and 'Shawaya': The Performative Constitution of Tribal Identities in Syria during the French Mandate and Today," *Journal of the Economic and Social History of the Orient* 58, nos. 1–2 (April 2015): 200–235.

37. For more on the relationship between the peasants and the political establishment, see Batatu, *Syria's Peasantry*, chaps. 9 and 10.

38. The Syrian 1950 constitution is available in Arabic at www.righttononviolence.org/mecf/wp-content/uploads/1950/09/1950Syria.pdf, accessed, July 15, 2017.

39. See also Kheder Khaddour and Kevin Mazur, "Eastern Expectations: The Changing Dynamics in Syria's Tribal Regions," Carnegie Endowment, February 18, 2017, carnegie-mec.org/2017/02/28/eastern-expectations-changing-dynamics-in-syria-s-tribal-regions-pub-68008.

40. Chatty, *Bedouin Tribes*, p. 2.

41. Chatty, *Bedouin Tribes*, pp. 19–22.

42. Batatu, *Syria's Peasantry*, chap. 11; Hanna Batatu, *The Egyptian, Syrian, and Iraqi Revolutions: Some Observations on Their Underlying Causes and Social Character* (Washington, DC: Georgetown University, Center for Contemporary Arab Studies, 1984), pp. 9–11.

43. Chatty, *Bedouin Tribes*, pp. 19–22.

44. Chatty, *Bedouin Tribes*, p. 2. See also Seale, *Asad of Syria*, p. 145.

45. For more on Assad and the Baath, see Batatu, *Syria's Peasantry*, chap. 13.

46. Seale, *Asad of Syria*, p. 441.

47. Bassam Haddad, *Business Networks in Syria* (Stanford, CA: Stanford University Press, 2012).

48. Chatty, *Bedouin Tribes*, p. 2.

49. Chatty, *Bedouin Tribes*, p. 2.

50. Chatty, *Bedouin Tribes*, p. 2.

51. Chatty, *Bedouin Tribes*, p. 2.

52. Chatty, *Bedouin Tribes*, p. 2.

53. Haian Dukhan, "Tribes and Tribalism in the Syrian Uprising," *Syrian Studies* 6, no. 2 (2014): 10.

54. Dukhan, "Tribes and Tribalism," p. 17.

55. Phi Sands, Justin Vela, and Suha Maayeh, "The Man Who Ignited the Syrian Revolution," *The National*, March 17, 2014, www.thenational.ae/world/syria/the-man-who-ignited-the-syrian-revolution.

56. Dukhan, "Tribes and Tribalism," p. 10.

57. The SNC does so perhaps in an attempt to emulate state mechanisms and to portray themselves as government-in-waiting modeled on a Western state. In an indication of just how complicated the war in Syria has become since 2015, Arab tribes from the Syrian desert and the Jazeera region were encouraged by the US-led anti-ISIS coalition to join forces with the Kurdish Democratic Union Party (PYD) in the newly established Syrian Democratic Forces (SDF). While this alliance was essential to defeat ISIS and recapture its capital in Raqqa, it is extremely unstable, partly because of the Syrian regime's and Turkey's attempts to sow dissent between the Arab tribes and Kurdish forces as well as the profound incompatibility between the social conservatism of the tribes and the radical outlook of the Kurdish group.

58. For background, see Nicholas A. Heras and Carole A. O'Leary, "The Tribal Factor in Syria's Rebellion: A Survey of Armed Tribal Groups in Syria," *Terrorism Monitor* 11, no. 13 (June 2013), jamestown.org/program/the-tribal-factor-in-syrias-rebellion-a-survey-of-armed-tribal-groups-in-syria/.

59. These requests came particularly from tribes in Deir Ezzor and Homs that were facing the full force of the Assad regime. The Saudis had already established a patron-client relationship with the *Aneza* tribe in Syria before the uprising began. They provided them with financial support during King Abdullah's visit to Syria in 2010.

60. Dukhan, "Tribes and Tribalism," p. 17.

61. Dukhan, "Tribes and Tribalism," p. 17.

62. Dukhan, "Tribes and Tribalism," p. 17.

63. Rania Abouzeid, "Syria's Secular and Islamist Rebels: Who Are the Saudis and the Qataris Arming?," *Time*, September 18, 2012, world.time.com/2012/09/18/syrias-secular-and-islamist-rebels-who-are-the-saudis-and-the-qataris-arming/.

64. Meanwhile, allies on the same side have seen their interests diverge in Syria, particularly Saudi Arabia and Qatar. In July 2013, Saudi Arabia and Qatar competed over the election of the president of the Syrian National Coalition. While Riyadh supported Ahmad al-Jarba, a tribal leader who traces his ancestry to Saudi Arabia, Qatar backed Riad Hijab, a candidate from a different tribe. Thus, in Syria, tribes continue to be pitted against each other in the competition for other people to gain influence.

65. Dukhan, "Tribes and Tribalism," p. 19.

66. Iraqi tribes are divided into segments and the smallest unit is the *bayt* or extended family. Several extended families form a cluster known as a *fakhd*. A *fakhd* acts as a subtribe, and solidarity among its members is very strong. Several *fakhds* form an *'ashira*, which is a tribe headed by a sheikh. Several *'ashira* form a confederation of tribes known as *qabila*, which is headed by a *sheikh al-mashaikh* or paramount sheikh. The qabila was set up as a political arrangement to facilitate intertribe relations. Most Sunni and Shia tribes define their tribal affiliation through their bloodline. Kurdish tribes, on the other hand, define their affiliation by their territory. For more background, see Charles Tripp, *A History of Iraq*, 3rd ed. (Cambridge: Cambridge University Press, 2007), pp. 8–19.

67. Tripp, *A History of Iraq*, pp. 8–13. On tribal rebellions, see P. Luizar, "La Confederation des Muntafik: Une representation en miniature de la question Iraquienne," *Monde Arabe Maghreb-Machrek* 147 (January–March 1995): 72–92.

68. For more background on the tensions between Iraq and Turkey, see Toby Dodge, *Inventing Iraq* (New York: Columbia University Press, 2003), p. 51.

69. Dodge, *Inventing Iraq*, pp. 1–40.

70. Sami Zubaida, "The Fragments Imagine the Nation: The Case of Iraq," *International Journal of Middle East Studies* 34 (2002): 205–215.

71. Ronen Zeidel, "Tribes in Iraq: A Negligible Factor in State Formation," in *Tribes and States in a Changing Middle East*, ed. Uzi Rabi (Oxford: Oxford University Press, 2016), p. 10.

72. Zeidel, *Tribes in Iraq*, p. 11.

73. Zeidel, *Tribes in Iraq*, p. 13. See also Haddad, *Sectarianism in Iraq*, pp. 94–103; for more background, see Faleh A. Jaber "Sheikhs and Ideologues: Deconstruction and Reconstruction of Tribes under Patrimonial Totalitarianism in Iraq, 1968–1998," in *Tribes and Power: Nationalism and Ethnicity in the Middle East*, ed. Abdul-Jabar and Hosham Dawod (London: Saqi, 2003).

74. Amatzia Baram, "Neo-Tribalism in Iraq: Saddam Hussein's Tribal Policies, 1991–96," *International Journal of Middle East Studies* 29, no. 1 (February 1997): 1–31.

75. See, "The Iraqi Tribes, Their Identity and Role in Internal Security," *The Iraqi Inquiry*, declassified politico-military memorandum, accessed August 3, 2017, www.iraqinquiry.org.uk/media/210995/2002-06-06-briefing-dis-politico-military-memorandum-the-iraqi-tribes-their-identity-and-role-in-internal-security.pdf.

76. Gerges, *ISIS*, p. 104.

77. Juan R. Cole, "Top 10 Mistakes of Former Iraq PM Nouri al-Maliki (That Ruined His Country)," *Informed Comment*, August 15, 2014, https://www.juancole.com/2014/08/mistakes

-maliki-country.html; Faleh A. Jabar, Renad Mansour, and Abir Khaddaj, *Iraq on the Brink: Maliki's Unraveling* (Beirut: Iraq Institute for Strategies Studies, 2014); Faleh A. Jabar, Renad Mansour, and Abir Khaddaj, *Maliki and the Rest: A Crisis within a Crisis* (Beirut: Iraq Institute for Strategic Studies, 2012).

Chapter 11: The Arab Spring Crushed

1. David Sharrock, Jack Shenker, and Paul Harris, "Egypt: How the People Span the Wheel of Their Country's History," *The Guardian*, February 12, 2011, https://www.theguardian.com /world/2011/feb/12/egypt-cairo-street-protests-tunisia-mubarak-obama. It is worth mentioning that there are conflicting elements in the story surrounding the burning of Bouazizi. Like all mythologized figures, Bouazizi has become a powerful symbol in a power struggle in Tunisia and the larger Arab world.

2. Yasmine Ryan, "Exodus from North Africa Full of Perils," *New York Times*, September 8, 2009, http://www.nytimes.com/2009/09/09/world/africa/09iht-algeria.html.

3. See Boualem Sansal's novel *Harraga* for a poignant account of the life and pain of Harragas. Boualem Sensal, *Harragas* (London: Bloomsbury, 2014).

4. For more on the Tunisian uprising see, Michael J. Willis, "Revolt for Dignity: Tunisia's Revolution and Civil Resistance," in *Civil Resistance in the Arab Spring: Triumphs and Disasters*, ed. Adam Roberts, Michael J. Willis, Rory McCarthy, and Timothy Garton Ash (Oxford: Oxford University Press, 2016).

5. Olfa Lamloum and Bernard Ravenel, *La Tunisie de Ben Ali: La société contre le régime* (Paris: Harmattan, 2002).

6. "Background on Political Prisoners in Tunisia," Human Rights Watch, April 2005, https:// www.hrw.org/reports/2005/tunisia0405/3.htm.

7. M. E. McMillan, *Fathers and Sons: The Rise and Fall of Political Dynasty in the Middle East* (New York: Palgrave Macmillan, 2013), p. 3; and Jean-Pierre Filiu, *The Arab Revolution: Ten Lessons from the Democratic Uprising* (London: C. Hurst, 2011), p. 15.

8. Amy Alsen Kallander, "Tunisia's Post-Ben Ali Challenge," in *Middle East Research and Information Project* 281 (Winter 2016), http://www.merip.org/mero/mero012611.

9. See Asaad al-Saleh, *Voices of the Arab Spring: Personal Stories from The Arab Revolutions* (New York: Columbia University Press, 2015), for various accounts from protesters of different countries.

10. For more on Khaled Said's background and death, see Juan R. Cole, *The New Arabs: How the Millennial Generation Is Changing the Middle East* (New York: Simon and Schuster 2014), p. 385.

11. Cole, *The New Arabs*, p. 387.

12. Peter Hessler, "Egypt's Failed Revolution," *New Yorker*, January 2, 2017, http://www .newyorker.com/magazine/2017/01/02/egypts-failed-revolution. See also M. Cherif Bassiouni, *Chronicles of the Egyptian Revolution and Its Aftermath: 2011–2016* (Cambridge: Cambridge University Press, 2017).

13. Joe Sterling, "Daraa: The Spark That Lit the Syrian Flame," CNN, March 1, 2012, http:// edition.cnn.com/2012/03/01/world/meast/syria-crisis-beginnings/index.html.

14. Garence Le Caisne, "They Were Torturing to Kill: Inside Syria's Death Machine," *The Guardian,* October 1, 2015, https://www.theguardian.com/world/2015/oct/01/they-were -torturing-to-kill-inside-syrias-death-machine-caesar.

15. For more on the militarization and internationalization of the conflict, see Jasmine Gani, "Contentious Politics and the Syrian Crisis: Internationalisation and Militarisation of Conflict," in *Contentious Politics in the Middle East: Popular Resistance and Marginalized Activism beyond the Arab Uprisings,* ed. Fawaz A. Gerges (New York: Palgrave Macmillan, 2015).

16. For more on the Libyan uprising, see Christopher S. Chivvis, *Toppling Qaddafi: Libya and the Limits of Liberal Intervention* (Cambridge: Cambridge University Press, 2013); and Jason Pack, *The 2011 Libyan Uprisings and the Struggle for the Post-Qadhafi Future* (London: Palgrave Macmillan, 2013).

17. Peter Beaumont and Chris Stephen, "Gaddafi's Last Words as He Begged for Mercy: 'What Did I Do to You?,'" *The Guardian*, October 23, 2011, https://www.theguardian.com /world/2011/oct/23/gaddafi-last-words-begged-mercy.

18. Ibrahim Fraihat, *Unfinished Revolutions, Yemen, Libya, and Tunisia after the Arab Spring* (New Haven, CT: Yale University Press, 2016), pp. 42–45; Thomas Juneau, "Yemen and The Arab Spring," in *Beyond the Arab Spring: The Evolving Ruling Bargain in the Middle East*, ed. Mehran Kamrava (Oxford: Oxford University Press, 2014), p. 381.

19. Kamrava, *Beyond the Arab Spring*, p. 395.

20. See, for example, Evan Hill and Laura Kasinof, "Playing a Double Game in the Fight against AQAP," *Foreign Policy*, January 21, 2015, http://foreignpolicy.com/2015/01/21/playing -a-double-game-in-the-fight-against-aqap-yemen-saleh-al-qaeda/. See also Fawaz A. Gerges, *The Rise and Fall of Al-Qaeda* (Oxford: Oxford University Press, 2011), p. 146.

21. See Hugh Naylor, "A Key Player in Yemen's Political Chaos? A Strongman Ousted in 2012," *Washington Post*, February 11, 2015, https://www.washingtonpost.com/world/middle_east/a -key-player-in-yemens-political-chaos-a-strongman-ousted-in-2012/2015/02/10/15ff6a9c -b124-11e4-bf39-5560f3918d4b_story.html?utm_term=.897844b9b8ae; see also Fawaz A. Gerges, ed., *The New Middle East: Protest and Revolution in the Arab World* (New York: Cambridge University Press, 2014), p. 288.

22. Gerges, *The New Middle East*, p. 288.

23. Noel Brehony, *Yemen Divided: The Story of a Failed State in South Arabia* (London: I. B. Tauris, 2011), pp. 181–191.

24. Bruce Riedel, "A Brief History of America's Troubled Relationship with Yemen," Brookings, October 22, 2018, https://www.brookings.edu/blog/order-from-chaos/2018/10/22/a-brief -history-of-americas-troubled-relationship-with-yemen/.

25. For more on the Arab uprising, see Gerges, *The New Middle East*, pp. 289–308. For a more detailed perspective on the uprising in the South, see Frances S. Hasso and Zakia Salime, eds., *Freedom without Permission: Bodies, Space in the Arab Revolutions* (Durham, NC: Duke University Press, 2016), pp. 80–104.

26. For more on the Houthis' political claims, see Ibrahim Fraihat, *Unfinished Revolutions*, pp. 45–49.

27. Gerges, *The New Middle East*, p. 293.

28. Daniel Byman, "No More Half Measures: A Compromise Solution That Removes Syria's Bashar al-Assad but Replaces Him with a Crony Is Now Fully Off the Table. It's Time for

Washington to Back the Opposition," *Foreign Policy*, June 14, 2012, https://foreignpolicy.com/2012/06/14/no-more-half-measures/. See also Michele Kelemen, "Weighing the 'Yemen Option' for Syria," NPR, May 30, 2012, https://www.npr.org/2012/05/30/154002166/weighing-the-yemen-option-for-syria; "After Massacre, 'Yemen Option' May Be Too Late," *The National*, May 28, 2012, https://www.thenational.ae/after-massacre-yemen-option-may-be-too-late-1.403536?videoId=5771275459001; Rami G. Khouri, "The Logic of Kofi Annan's Syria Strategy," *Daily Star*, June 2, 2012, http://www.dailystar.com.lb/Opinion/Columnist/2012/Jun-02/175462-the-logic-of-kofi-annans-syria-strategy.ashx#axzzlxD4YeXN2.

29. "The War within the War: Southern Separatists Are Tearing Yemen Apart," *The Economist*, August 15, 2019.

30. Shuaib Almosawa, Ben Hubbard, and Troy Griggs, "'It's a Slow Death': The World's Worst Humanitarian Crisis," *New York Times*, August 23, 2017.

31. Almosawa, Hubbard, and Griggs, "It's a Slow Death."

32. Almosawa, Hubbard, and Griggs, "It's a Slow Death."

33. Almosawa, Hubbard, and Griggs, "It's a Slow Death."

34. "Asim Sheikh Historians: Arab Spring a US Plot to Serve Israel," May 12, 2014 [in Arabic], http://alwafd.org/; Leo Messi, "Nabil al-Awadi, International Conspiracy against Syria," YouTube, August 21, 2011, www.youtube.com/watch?v=um6eCDFpHlM; Tariq Ramadan, *Islam and the Arab Awakening* (New York: Oxford University Press, 2012), pp. 6–22.

35. Asef Bayat, *Revolution without Revolutionaries: Making Sense of the Arab Spring* (Stanford, CA: Stanford University Press, 2017).

36. See, for instance, Maria Cristina Paciello, "The Arab Spring: Socio-Economic Challenges and Opportunities," trans. Andrea Dessì (Rome: Istituto Affari Internazionali, December 2011), http://www.iai.it/sites/default/files/iai1115e.pdf.

37. See Shibley Telhami in Andrea Dessì, "Re-Ordering the Middle East?" (Rome: Istituto Affari Internazionali, July 31, 2016), p. 5, http://www.iai.it/en/pubblicazioni/re-ordering-middle-east.

Chapter 12: The End of Empire, or Is History about to Repeat Itself?

1. M. E. McMillan, *From the First World War to the Arab Spring: What's Really Going on in the Middle East?* (New York: Palgrave Macmillan, 2016), p. 224.

2. "Arab Public Opinion about the Israeli War on Gaza," Doha Institute, Arab Center for Research and Policy Studies, January 10, 2024, https://www.dohainstitute.org/en/News/Pages/arab-public-opinion-about-the-israeli-war-on-gaza.aspx#.

3. Fawaz A. Gerges, *Obama and the Middle East: The End of America's Moment?* (New York: Palgrave Macmillan, 2012). See also Jeffrey Goldberg, "The Obama Doctrine," *The Atlantic*, April 2016, https://www.theatlantic.com/magazine/archive/2016/04/the-obama-doctrine/471525.

4. See "America Is Not the World's Policeman Says Barack Obama on Syria," *The Australian*, September 11, 2013, http://www.theaustralian.com.au/in-depth/middle-east-in-turmoil/america-is-not-the-worlds-policeman-says-barack-obama-on-syria/news-story/3fc9f1b0300f3e27638985f8fa74d5ee.

5. The word "mistrust" is repeated four times in the speech.

6. Goldberg, "The Obama Doctrine."

7. Goldberg, "The Obama Doctrine."

8. See Gerges, *Obama and the Middle East*.

9. Shibley Telhami, "American Attitudes toward the Middle East and Israel: A Public Opinion Poll," Center for Middle East Policy at Brookings, November 2015, https://www.brookings.edu/wp-content/uploads/2016/07/2015-Poll-Key-Findings-Final-1.pdf. See also Shibley Telhami in Andrea Dessì, "Re-Ordering the Middle East? Peoples, Borders and States in Flux" (Rome: Istituto Affari Internazionali, July 31, 2016), pp. 4–7, http://www.iai.it/en/pubblicazioni/re-ordering-middle-east.

10. Alan Yuhas, "Fact-Checking Donald Trump's First Presidential Address to Congress," *The Guardian*, March 1, 2017, https://www.theguardian.com/us-news/2017/mar/01/donald-trump-congress-address-fact-check.

11. David E. Sanger and Maggie Haberman, "Donald Trump Sets Conditions for Defending NATO Allies against Attack," *New York Times*, July 20, 2016, https://www.nytimes.com/2016/07/21/us/politics/donald-trump-issues.html?_r=0.

12. "Trump Says Would Rebuild 'Badly-Depleted' US Military," *Business Standard*, December 16, 2016, http://www.business-standard.com/article/pti-stories/trump-says-would-rebuild-badly-depleted-us-military-116121601381_1.html.

13. "Trump's Response to Being Told Putin Is 'a Killer': The U.S. Isn't 'So Innocent,'" *Fortune*, February 6, 2017, http://fortune.com/2017/02/05/trump-putin-us-not-so-innocent/.

14. "Trump's Response to Being Told Putin Is 'a Killer.'"

15. Hal Brands, "The Emerging Biden Doctrine: Democracy, Autocracy, and the Defining Clash of Our Time," *Foreign Affairs*, June 29, 2021; Steven Lee Myers, "An Alliance of Autocracies? China Wants to Lead a New World Order," *New York Times*, March 29, 2021.

16. Sheldon Kirshner, "Netanyahu Still Strives for Saudi Normalization," *Times of Israel*, April 21, 2023.

17. Simon Tisdall, "Toxic Netanyahu Could Drag Biden Down in His Fight for Political Survival," *The Guardian*, October 10, 2023, https://www.theguardian.com/world/commentisfree/2023/oct/21/toxic-netanyahu-could-drag-biden-down-in-his-fight-for-political-survival.

18. "32,490 Palestinians Killed in Gaza since Oct. 7, Health Ministry Says," Reuters, March 27, 2024, https://www.reuters.com/world/middle-east/32490-palestinians-killed-gaza-since-oct-7-health-ministry-says-2024-03-27/.

19. Tisdall, "Toxic Netanyahu Could Drag Biden Down."

20. Goldberg, "The Obama Doctrine."

21. Giulia Paravicini, "Angela Merkel: Europe Must Take 'Our Fate' into Own Hands," *Politico*, May 28, 2017, https://www.politico.eu/article/angela-merkel-europe-cdu-must-take-its-fate-into-its-own-hands-elections-2017/.

22. "President Macron Gives Speech on New Initiative for Europe," Élysée, September 26, 2017, https://www.elysee.fr/en/emmanuel-macron/2017/09/26/president-macron-gives-speech-on-new-initiative-for-europe.

23. Heidi Maurer, Richard G. Whitman, and Nicholas Wright, "The EU and the Invasion of Ukraine: A Collective Responsibility to Act?," *International Affairs* 99, no. 1 (2023): 219–238, https://doi.org/10.1093/ia/iiac262.

24. Juuko Alozious, "NATO's Two Percent Guideline: A Demand for Military Expenditure Perspective," *Defence and Peace Economies* 33, no. 4 (2022): 475–488, https://doi.org/10.1080/10242694.2021.1940649.

25. "A New and Ambitious European Neighbourhood Policy," European Commission, May 25, 2011, https://ec.europa.eu/commission/presscorner/detail/en/IP_11_643; "Joint Communication to the European Parliament, the Council, the European Economic and Social Committee and the Committee of the Regions: Review of the European Neighbourhood Policy," European Commission, November 18, 2015, http://eeas.europa.eu/archives/docs/enp/documents/2015/151118_joint-communication_review-of-the-enp_en.pdf.

26. See, for instance, Daniela Huber and Maria Cristina Paciello, "Overhauling EU Policy in the Mediterranean towards More Inclusive, Responsive and Flexible Policies," IAI Working Paper 35 (September 2015), http://www.iai.it/sites/default/files/iaiwp1535.pdf; Richard Youngs, "Europe's Flawed Approach to Arab Democracy," Centre for European Reform Essays, October 2006, http://cer-live.thomas-ppaterson.co.uk/sites/default/files/publications/attachments/pdf/2011/essay_youngs_arab_democracy-1423.pdf; Richard Youngs, "Full Circle in the Middle East," Judy Dempsey's Strategic Europe—Carnegie Europe, October 16, 2014, http://carnegieeurope.eu/strategiceurope/56940.

27. The ENP was revised in 2015 after the uprising in Tunisia, and ever since the EU has tried to prioritize the North African country in its documents.

28. Tobias Schumacher, "The EU and the Arab Spring: Between Spectatorship and Actorness," *Insight Turkey* 13, no. 3 (Summer 2011): 115, https://www.insightturkey.com/news/the-eu-and-the-arab-spring-between-spectatorship-and-actorness.

29. Schumacher, "The EU and the Arab Spring."

30. Schumacher, "The EU and the Arab Spring."

31. United Nations Security Council, Resolution 1973, adopted on March 17, 2011, http://www.nato.int/nato_static/assets/pdf/pdf_2011_03/20110927_110311-UNSCR-1973.pdf.

32. Frank Gardner, "How Vital Is Syria's Tartus Port to Russia?," BBC, June 27, 2012, http://www.bbc.co.uk/news/world-middleeast-18616191. See also "New Report on Russian Interests in Syria, Part 2: Russian Arms Sales," *Russian Military Reform*, June 29, 2012, http://russiamil.wordpress.com/2012/06/29/new-report-on-russian-interests-in-syria-part-2-russian-arms-sales/; Ekaterina Stepanova, "Russia and Conflicts in the Middle East: Regionalisation and Implications for the West," *The International Spectator* 53, no. 4 (October 10, 2018): 35–57.

33. A. Dessì and E. Greco, "Search for Stability in Libya OSCE's Role between Internal Obstacles and External Challenges" (Rome: Istituto Affari Internazionali, 2018), http://www.iai.it/sites/default/files/iairs_1.pdf.

34. "The Foreign Policy Concept of the Russian Federation," approved by President of the Russian Federation Vladimir Putin on November 30, 2016, https://www.rusemb.org.uk/rp_insight/.

35. Benjamin Haddad and Hannah Thoburn, "Putin Aims at Syria—and Strikes Europe," *Foreign Policy*, October 2, 2015.

36. "The Foreign Policy Concept of the Russian Federation."

37. Jeff Mason and Steve Holland, "Russia Received Hundreds of Iranian Drones to Attack Ukraine, US Says," Reuters, June 10, 2023, https://www.reuters.com/world/europe/russia-has-received-hundreds-iranian-drones-attack-ukraine-white-house-2023-06-09/.

38. Mansur Mirovalev, "Turkish Neutrality: How Erdogan Manages Ties with Russia, Ukraine amid War," *Al Jazeera*, September 28, 2023, https://www.aljazeera.com/news/2023/9/28/turkish-neutrality-how-erdogan-manages-ties-with-russia-ukraine-amid-war.

39. "China-UAE Bilateral Trade Rises 28% to Exceed $64 Bn during 1st 8 Months of 2022: Chinese Envoy," Emirates News Agency WAM, November 11, 2022.

40. Mohammad Eslami and Maria Papageorgiou, "China's Increasing Role in the Middle East: Implications for Regional and International Dynamics," *Georgetown Journal of International Affairs*, June 2, 2023, https://gjia.georgetown.edu/2023/06/02/chinas-increasing-role-in -the-middle-east-implications-for-regional-and-international-dynamics/.

41. R. Alaaldin, A. Baabood, S. Colombo, A. Dessì, M. Kerrou, J. Mouawad, V. Ntousas, et al., *The EU, Resilience and the MENA Region* (Rome: Foundation for European Progressive Studies and Istituto Affari Internazionali, 2017), pp. 109–126, https://feps-europe.eu/wp-content /uploads/2018/03/The-EU-Resilience-and-the-MENA-Region.pdf.

42. Stefanie Glinski, "Turks Are Running Out of Cash—and Patience," *Foreign Policy*, September 7, 2023, https://foreignpolicy.com/2023/09/07/turkey-economy-inflation-erdogan-lira -interest-rate-tourism/.

43. Brad W. Setser, "Turkey's Increasing Balance Sheet Risks," Council on Foreign Relations, June 6, 2023, https://www.cfr.org/blog/turkeys-increasing-balance-sheet-risks.

44. Seth Anziska, *Preventing Palestine: A Political History from Camp David to Oslo* (Princeton, NJ: Princeton University Press, 2018). See also Seth Anziska, "Neither Two States nor One: The Palestine Question in the Age of Trump," *Journal of Palestine Studies* 46, no. 3 (2017): 57–74.

45. "Netanyahu on Israel's relationship with the Arab World," Fox News, May 19, 2018, https://www.foxnews.com/transcript/netanyahu-on-israels-relationship-with-the-arab-world.

46. Louis Casiano, "Israeli PM Netanyahu Tells Bret Baier 'We're Getting Closer to Peace Every Day That Passes' with Saudi Arabia," Fox News, September 22, 2023, https://www .foxnews.com/world/israeli-pm-netanyahu-tell-bret-baier-getting-closer-peace-every-day -passes-saudi-arabia.

47. Original: "Hegel says somewhere that great historic facts and personages recur twice. He forgot to add: "Once as tragedy, and again as farce." From "The 18th Brumaire of Louis Bonaparte by Karl Marx" (1852).

48. Aside from arms deals and economic ties and some attempts at political mediation in the region, Russia's real influence in the Middle East is in actuality limited to Syria (and maybe only within Syria, mainly the northwestern areas close to the military base and in the outskirts of Damascus).

49. Barry Buzan and George Lawson, *The Global Transformation: History, Modernity and the Making of International Relations* (Cambridge: Cambridge University Press, 2015), p. 274.

50. Buzan and Lawson, *The Global Transformation*, p. 276.

51. Buzan and Lawson, *The Global Transformation*, p. 276.

52. Buzan and Lawson, *The Global Transformation*, p. 276.

53. Buzan and Lawson, *The Global Transformation*, p. 275.

54. Buzan and Lawson, *The Global Transformation*, p. 277.

55. It is worth mentioning the declining state capacity both in the region and at the global level: we are very much looking at a state-centric piece, while part of the conflictual multipolarity taking place in the region also derives from the actions of nonstate or quasi-state actors in the good and bad realm. As the COVID-19 pandemic wrecked humanity, state capacity

emerged as an important policy priority. The state was seen as the first and last line of defense of panicky citizenry weighed down by this pandemic.

Conclusion

1. This does not mean that the region will either follow the same path as other regions or produce similar results.

2. "Remarks by the President on the Middle East and North Africa," The White House, May 19, 2011, https://obamawhitehouse.archives.gov/the-press-office/2011/05/19/remarks -president-middle-east-and-north-africa.

3. For example, Italian arms exports to the region have grown by 250 percent over the last two decades; Germany has increased its arms exports by 500 percent and so has France— mostly to the states of the Arabian Gulf. See A. Sanford and M. Jamet, "US and European Arms Sales to Middle East Soar amid Widespread Conflict," EuroNews, March 12, 2018, https://www .euronews.com/2018/03/12/us-and-european-arms-sales-to-middle-east-soar-amid -widespread-conflict. See also A. Fleurant, A. Kuimova, N. Tian, and T. S. Wezeman, "Trends in International Arms Transfers, 2017," SIPRI, March 2018, https://www.sipri.org/sites/default /files/2018-03/fssipri_at2017_0.pdf.

4. For more on this, see the EU Trust Fund for Africa, which collects EU funding toward Africa and has increasingly been used for border control and security sector training as opposed to developmental assistance. Indeed, much of the funds have been taken from the EU Development Fund and are now being used for migration control—this has been heavily criticized by many in Europe and the EU Parliament. See, for instance, Luca Barana, "The EU Trust Fund for Africa and the Perils of a Securitized Migration Policy," Istituto Affari Internazionali, December 20, 2017, http://www.iai.it/it/pubblicazioni/eu-trust-fund-africa-and-perils -securitized-migration-policy. See also "The Joint Africa-EU Strategy" (Directorate-General for External Policies, European Union, 2017), http://www.europarl.europa.eu/RegData/etudes /STUD/2017/603849/EXPO_STU(2017)603849_EN.pdf.

5. In the case of Libya, see Florence Gaub, "Libya: The Struggle for Security," EUISS Brief, June 2013, https://www.ciaonet.org/attachments/23879/uploads; Andrea Dessì, "Re-Ordering the Middle East?" (Rome: Istituto Affari Internazionali, July 31, 2016), pp. 13–14, http://www.iai.it/en/pubblicazioni/re-ordering-middle-east; Andrea Dessì, "A Multilateral Approach to Ungoverned Spaces: Libya and Beyond," *IAI Documenti* 15, no. 10 (June 2015), http://www.iai.it/en/node/4262.

6. See these monographs: Lorenzo Kamel, ed., *The Frailty of Authority: Borders, Non-State Actors and Power Vacuums in a Changing Middle East* (Rome: Edizioni Nuova Cultura, 2017), http://www.iai.it/en/pubblicazioni/frailty-authority, esp. chap. 1; and Pierre Cammack, Michelle Dunne, Amr Hamzawy, Marc Lynch, Marwan Muasher, Yezid Sayigh, and Maha Yahya, *Arab Fractures: Citizens, States, and Social Contracts* (Washington, DC: Carnegie Endowment for International Peace, 2017), https://carnegieendowment.org/files/Arab_World _Horizons_Final.pdf, esp. chaps. 1 and 2.

7. See Daniela Huber and Lorenzo Kamel, *Arab Spring and Peripheries: A Decentering Research Agenda* (New York: Routledge, 2016).

8. Andrea Dessì, "Crisis and Breakdown: How Can the EU Foster Resilience in the Middle East and North Africa?," Istituto Affari Internazionali (IAI), Working Paper 17/37, December 2017, pp. 15–18, https://www.iai.it/en/pubblicazioni/crisis-and-breakdown-how-can-eu -foster-resilience-middle-east-and-north-africa.

9. Florence Gaub, ed., "WHAT IF . . . ? 14 Futures for 2024," Chaillot Paper 157 (Paris: European Union Institute for Security Studies, January 2020).

10. See Dessì, "Crisis and Breakdown"; R. Alaaldin, A. Baabood, S. Colombo, A. Dessì, M. Kerrou, J. Mouawad, V. Ntousas, et al., *The EU, Resilience and the MENA Region* (Rome: Foundation for European Progressive Studies and Istituto Affari Internazionali, 2017), https:// feps-europe.eu/wp-content/uploads/2018/03/The-EU-Resilience-and-the-MENA-Region.pdf.

11. Asef Bayat, *Revolution without Revolutionaries: Making Sense of the Arab Spring* (Stanford, CA: Stanford University Press, 2017).

12. See Marc Lynch, *The New Arab Wars: Uprisings and Anarchy in the Middle East* (New York: Public Affairs, 2016).

13. See Nikki R. Keddie, *Modern Iran: Roots and Results of Revolution*, updated ed. (New Haven, CT: Yale University Press, 2006); and Ervand Abrahamian, *A History of Modern Iran* (Cambridge: Cambridge University Press, 2008).

INDEX

Abadi, Haider al-, 302
Abdulhamid II (Ottoman sultan), 192
Abed, Mohammed Ali Bey al-, 62
Abraham Accords, 272–274, 285
Abu Dhabi, 173
Afghanistan, 128, 132, 138, 167, 272, 287, 296
Aflaq, Michel, 64, 81, 83
agency of the people: Americans and,
    128; asymmetrical encounters and, 23;
    authoritarianism and, 15–17, 146, 165,
    293; colonial powers and, 33, 36, 42,
    45, 48, 57; divide-and-rule tactics, 243;
    imperial ambitions and, 10; power of, 5,
    20, 29, 244; protesters and, 255; revolu-
    tionary governments and, 90, 106
agricultural sector problems, 175
Ajami, Fouad, 22
Algeria: African independence movement,
    105; Arab Spring second wave, 17, 259;
    armed conflicts in, 165–166; bloodless
    military coup, 205; civil war in, 209;
    domestic violence offenses, 179; Egypt
    and Nasser, 205; foreign direct invest-
    ment in, 173; Islam and Islamists, 206–210;
    Islamic Salvation Front (FIS), 209–210;
    linguistic Arabization, 205–206; marriage
    permission, 178; Muslim Brotherhood
    and, 206; National Liberation Front
    (FLN), 204–206, 208–210, 339n44;
    natural gas resources in, 69; postcolonial
    and political Islam, 204; self-immolations
    in, 146; television and radio preachers,
    208; War of Independence (1954–1962),
    166, 204, 208, 210

Algerian Islamic Armed Movement
    (AIAM), 208
Ali, Muhammad, 190
Ali, Rashid, 56, 58
Allenby, Edmund, 38–39
Al-Qaeda: failure of, 257; Iraq and, 341n13;
    ISIS and, 228; jihadist movement,
    211–212; as nonstate actor, 139, 222–224;
    pan-Islamism and, 129, 204, 209–210,
    259; sectarianism of, 213; September 11
    and, 137–138; state system and borders,
    4, 214, 217; Sunni recruits, 226–227;
    transformation of, 225; tribal leaders
    and, 241; United States and, 270;
    war against, 248–249; in Yemen, 216,
    250, 254
Al-Qaeda in Iraq (AQI), 225–227, 239–240,
    341n13
Amer, Abdel Hakim, 99
American University in Beirut (AUB),
    132
American University in Cairo (AUC),
    132
Amis de l'Orient (Friends of the East),
    310n25
Ammar, Rashid, 144
Arab Charter on Human Rights, 184
Arab Cold War, 103–104, 126, 128
Arab history, 22–23
Arab Human Development Report (UNDP),
    178, 180–182
Arabism. *See* pan-Arab nationalism
Arab League, 103
Arab Middle East, 46, 48, 50, 62, 163, 241

Arab nationalism: authoritarianism and, 293; Baath Party and, 81; British opposition, 315n1; colonialism response, 70; Communism and, 130; decline and failure of, 22, 92–93, 105–106, 109–111, 218; definition of, 71; ethnic minorities and, 73; German nationalism and, 313n13; intellectuals and journalists and, 73; Kurds and, 61; Nasser and, 82, 100, 127; origins and rise during 1960s, 60, 72, 90; radical force of, 64; sectarianism and, 295; United States and, 128–129, 135; use by autocrats, 113. *See also* pan-Arab nationalism

Arab Revolt (1916–1918), 39–40, 56, 58

Arab Spring revolt (2010–2012): Arab counterrevolutionary forces and, 16; Bashar al-Assad and, 11; authoritarianism and, 217, 244–246, 256, 260; beginning of, 141, 145–146; blame and understanding of, 256–257; citizenship and, 4; elite politics and, 2; exclusionary groups and ruin, 304; foreign powers and, 10, 17, 256, 287; Nasser and, 146–147; ordinary people and, 15–17, 256–257, 289; pan-Arab nationalism, 260; postsectarian generation, 294, 298; self-immolations (harraga), 144–146, 188, 244, 247; subnational identities and, 218. *See also* Egypt, Mubarak era; Libya; Syria; Tunisia; Yemen

Arab Spring revolt (2018–2019): authoritarianism to pluralism, 303; local agency and, 299; postsectarian generation, 294; second wave of, 17, 19, 146, 259

Arab state structure, 8, 16, 47, 66

Arab Summit, Khartoum (1967), 108

Arafat, Yasir, 221, 318n32

Arif, Abdel Salam, 84

armed conflicts, 165–167

Asquith, Herbert Henry (H. H.), 30

Assad, Bashar al-: Alawites and, 234; Arab Spring and, 11; authoritarian regime of, 113; Bedouins and, 233–234; brutality of, 229, 257; global powers and, 16; Hezbollah and, 224; Kurds and, 61; military of, 144;

pauperized the people, 294; sectarianism of, 229; tribes and, 234–235, 343n59

Assad, Hafez al-: Alawites and, 233; Baath Party and, 311n29; Bedouins and, 233; divide-and-rule tactics, 214; Israelis and, 100; revolts against, 169; sectarianism of, 215; Syrian Legion and, 62; top-down decision-making, 163; tribes and Muslim Brotherhood, 234

Assad family, 10, 109, 215, 226, 247, 258

Aswany, Alaa al-, 157

Atlantic, The, 269

authoritarianism: Arab culture and, 22; Arab rulers and, 104, 106, 119–120, 122, 294, 299; attention diversion tactic, 113; Cold War and, 140; colonial methods, 246; constitutional monarchies, failure of, 64; Dawlat al-Mukhabarat (intelligence-dominated state), 163, 165; economic liberalism and, 299; economics and, 160, 189; foreign intervention and, 9–10, 20, 23, 36, 65, 261, 293; Great Powers and, 7, 14, 29, 45, 51–52, 264, 297, 303; hope to end, 68; instability and, 300; Iraq and Syria and, 213; Islamists and, 211, 257; Kurds and, 61; man-made crisis of, 294; Middle Eastern leaders and, 88; multipolarity of politics and, 282; Nasser and, 79, 99, 148; oil and gas resources financing, 168–169; pan-Arab nationalism device, 87; pauperized societies, 255; postcolonial governments and, 90, 93; Russia and, 280; Sadat and, 154, 200; state-within-a-state, 196; top-down decision-making, 107; violent conflict and, 5; weapons imports and, 128; Western policies and, 8, 301

Azerbaijan, 114–116

Azmah, Yusuf, 42

Baath Party: Egypt and Syria merger, 82; founding of, 81; Kurds and, 60; Shia Iraqis and, 56

Badr, Zaki, "Iron Fist," 156

Baghdadi, Abu Bakr al-, 85, 204, 228–229, 241, 341n13
Bahrain, 16, 179, 283
Balfour, Arthur, 32–33, 44
Balfour Declaration (1917), 31–33, 41, 44, 312n47
Bandung Conference (1955), 122–123
Banna, Hassan al-, 64, 194, 196–197
Battle, Lucius D., 12
Bedouins, 212, 230–234
Begin, Menachem, 154
Belhadj, Ali, 209
Ben Ali, Zine El Abidine, 143–145, 147, 163, 187, 245–246, 277, 294
Ben Bella, Ahmed, 205
Ben Jedid, Chadli, 207–209
Biden, Joe, and Biden administration, 13–14, 49, 264–265, 272–274, 276, 289, 300–301
bin Laden, Osama, 138–139, 212, 216, 341n13
Bitar, Salah al-Din al-, 64, 83
Bloom, 172–173
Bouazizi, Mohammed, 141, 143–147, 180, 188, 244–245, 247, 259, 326n3, 345n1
Boumedienne, Houari, 205–207
boundaries: effect of, 33–34, 51; Egypt and Syria merger proposal, 82; historical borders, 312n51; Mandate period and negotiations, 43; partitioning of Middle East, 36–38; permanence of, 4, 302. *See also* McMahon-Husayn correspondence
Bourguiba, Habib, 143, 245
Bouyali, Mustafa, 208
British Desiderata in Asiatic Turkey Committee, 26
Brzezinski, Zbigniew, 128
Bush, George H. W., 166–167
Bush, George W., and Bush administration, 239, 250, 270
Buzan, Barry, 288

Cairo Unity Talks, 94–95, 321nn17–18
Camp David Accords, 150, 200, 204
Carter, Jimmy, 125, 128, 138

Chamoun, Camille, 85
Chekir, Hamouda, 186
China: Belt and Road Initiative, 281; economy of, 160; Gulf Cooperation Council (GCC) and, 281; Middle East influence, 263–264, 286; Middle East policy and, 281–282, 287; worldview of, 280
Churchill, Winston, 45
Clemenceau, Georges, 39
Cohen, S. B., 312n51
Cold War: asymmetric relationships, 119; beginning of, 114; effect on Middle East, 117–118, 136, 139–140; global rivalry and financial aid, 166; informal empire during, 307n6; legacy of, 6; Middle East impact of, 6, 119–120; neoimperialism and, 121–122; transactional relationships, 134; Western influence, 125–127; Western model for modernization, 121; Western or Soviet influence, 130, 132, 134–135
colonialism: Arab resistance to, 23, 45, 51; asymmetrical encounters, 23; continued influence of, 65–67, 164, 294; end of an era, 68; independence of Middle Eastern states, 116–117; local rulers and external patrons, 36; Mandate System and, 35–36, 49; missionary aim, 36; postcolonial structural deficits, 69–70; post–Ottoman Empire, 22–23; "post-Ottoman syndrome," 22; post–World War II, 7, 11; toxic legacy of, 6; Westphalian model and, 63
Comité de l'Afrique Française, 27
Communism, 60, 130, 132, 138
constitutionalism, 46, 52, 54–55, 61, 63–65, 71, 169, 245, 297, 299
corporatism, 107, 185
counterrevolutionaries, 16, 258, 300, 304
COVID-19 pandemic, 9, 18–19, 167, 180, 275, 284, 286, 308n18, 309n27, 350n55
Cromer, Evelyn Baring, 51–52, 70

Dahoud, Yavoub Ould, 146
de Lesseps, Ferdinand, 191

Diwan, Ishac, 186
Dridi, Adel, 188
Druze, 28, 58, 231
Dulles, Allen, 86, 124–126
Dulles, John Foster, 124–125, 127

economic mismanagement and youth
 unemployment, 145–147
Eden, Anthony, 127
Egypt: British rule in, 51–52, 63, 192;
 constitutional process in, 54–55; cotton
 price collapse (1920s), 53; Egyptian
 ruling family, 52, 54–55; historical
 border, 312n51; living standard, 53;
 military of, 70; nationalism in, 73–74;
 political elite and, 53–54; post–World
 War I, 52; revolutionary groups in, 54;
 United States and, 12–13; Wafd ruling
 party, 53–55, 63, 71, 201
Egypt, Mubarak era (1981–2011): Arab
 Spring in, 247, 251, 259; Cairo Spring,
 202; crony capitalism and corruption,
 157–158, 185–187; economic status of,
 155; Mubarak family thefts, 187; Sadat's
 policies and, 155; social unrest and
 government response, 155–156
Egypt, Nasser era (1954–1970): Aswan Dam
 financing, 126; Black Saturday (January 1952), 71, 76–77, 79–80, 124, 193;
 Cold War and defense pacts, 126; Egypt
 and Syria merger proposal, 82–83;
 Egyptian Constitution of 1956, 77; Israel
 and, 76; land reform, 77–78; Middle
 East Defense Organization, 124; right-
 wing development, 133; Six-Day War
 (1967), 96–102, 105, 112, 163; Soviet
 Union and, 128, 130–131, 133–134; Syria,
 political union, 89–93, 232; United States
 and, 123–124; Western or Soviet influence, 130–131; Yemen and military
 intervention, 93, 96, 100, 105. See also
 Free Officers Movement; Suez Canal
Egypt, postcolonial period: authoritarianism in, 294; British role, 71, 196; limited

independence (1922), 70–71; military
 coup (1952), 71; political culture and
 economic affairs, 70; Wafd ruling party,
 71; Yemen and military intervention, 95
Egypt, Sadat era (1970–1981): bread riots,
 152, 169; corruption of, 151–152; economic problems and discontent, 149;
 emergency laws in, 247; "Infitah" (Open
 Door Policy), 150–151, 158; Ministry
 of Trade and Industry, 158; peace
 with Israel and peace dividend, 166;
 Pyramids Plateau Project, 151; secret
 police and Mukhabarat, 183–184; United
 States and, 150
Egypt, al-Sisi era (2014–): climate change
 and, 182; COVID-19 pandemic in, 18;
 domestic violence offenses, 179; education and, 181; foreign direct investment
 in, 173; poverty of, 178; water security in,
 174; youth unemployment, 180
Egyptian-American Businessman Council,
 157
Egyptian Islamic Jihad (EIJ), 201
Eisenhower, Dwight D., 125, 127, 325n26
Emaar Properties, 172
Ennahda Party (Muslim Brotherhood), 283
Erdoğan, Recep Tayyip, 10, 47, 281, 283
Ethiopia, 174, 288
Euphrates River, 174–175
European Union (EU): Arab Spring and,
 277; arms sales to Middle East, 301,
 351n3; EU Neighborhood Policy (ENP),
 276, 349n27; EU Trust Fund for Africa,
 351n4; internal crises, 275; Kurds and,
 302; liberal elites of, 255; Middle East
 policy and, 301; United States and, 262,
 275–276; Yemen and, 252

Faisal (emir of Syria, later king of Iraq),
 38–42, 43, 45, 55–56, 60, 84, 231
Faisal (king of Saudi Arabia), 8, 12–13, 108
Falsafat al-Thawra (The philosophy of the
 revolution) (Nasser), 75
Farouk (king of Egypt), 63, 71, 192–193, 197

Fayek, Mohammad, 79
Fillon, François, 277
Flandin, Etienne, 310n25
foreign direct investment (FDI), 150, 155, 165, 171–173
foreign powers, 4–9, 220, 222, 293, 296–298
formal and informal empires, 4, 307n6
Four Asian Tigers, 160
Fox News, 285
France: Algeria and, 165–166, 205, 339n44; arms sales to Middle East, 351n3; Britain and, 28; Lebanon and, 11, 29, 38, 41–42; Morocco and, 37; Ottoman Empire and, 27–28; Syria and, 38–39, 41, 58, 60, 311n29; Tunisia and, 143, 277. *See also* Great Powers
Franco-British Boundary Agreements (1933), 44–45
Frank, Andre Gunder, 147
Free Officers Movement: Aswan Dam and, 126; Egypt independence and, 79; Iraqi Free Officers, 84–86; land reform laws, 77; Mubarak and, 159; Muslim Brotherhood and, 197; Nasser and, 71; Palestine defeat and, 76; Sadat and, 148; United States and, 124; Yemen and military intervention, 96
Free Syrian Army, 229, 236, 340n62
Freij, Fahd Jassem al-, 234
Fromkin, David, 30
From the First World War to the Arab Spring (McMillan), 265

Gaddafi, Muammar, 11, 113, 163, 187, 214, 248–249, 257, 274, 278, 294, 300
Gamasy, Abdel Ghani el-, 100
gender inequality, 178–180
Geography and Politics in a World Divided (Cohen), 312n51
Georges-Picot, François, 27–30
geostrategic rivalries, 3, 6–7, 16, 59, 85, 94, 103, 254, 285, 292
Gerges, Fawaz A., 6, 76, 199
Germany, 24, 37

Global South, 3, 6, 9, 127, 130, 132, 266–267, 289
Global Transformation, The (Buzan and Lawson), 288
Grand Ethiopian Renaissance Dam, 174
Great Britain: Dardanelles campaign, 26, 310n15; De Bunsen Committee, 29; entente cordiale, 37; formal empire of, 307n6; India and, 27, 29–30; Iraq and, 27–28, 30; Palestine and, 29–31; World War I and, 24–26. *See also* Great Powers
Great Powers (Britain and France): agenda implementation, 23–24; autocrats and, 303; Balfour Declaration and, 32–33; change of, 261; Cold War and, 139; colonialism and, 294; competition of, 264; continuity of policies, 261–262; conventional wars and, 287; decentered globalism and, 288; dependence on, 228; divide-and-rule strategy, 28–29; influence in Middle East, 50–51, 164, 264, 282, 286, 289–291; intervention and secret agreements, 9, 24, 34, 36, 43, 47–49; liberal constitutionalism and, 63; listing of, 12; missionary aim, 36, 42, 51; Ottoman Empire and, 38, 40; role in Middle East, 7; role of, 222; strategic assets and, 3, 36; supremacy ending, 289. *See also* France; Great Britain
Gulf Cooperation Council (GCC), 252–253, 281
Gulf War (1990–1991), 136, 138, 166, 170, 282

Hadi, Abd-Rabbu Mansour, 216–217, 252–254
Halliday, Fred, 115
Hamadah, Abdou Abdel-Monaam, 146
Hamas (Islamic Resistance Movement), 2, 17–18, 112, 221–223, 273, 283, 284–285, 289–290, 302
Hamdi, Fayda, 143
Hanunu, Ibrahim, 58
Hegel, Georg, 4, 350n47
Heikal, Mohamed, 89
Henry, Clement Moore, 174

Herzl, Theodor, 44

Hezbollah (Party of God), 112, 189, 222–224, 226, 229, 236, 258, 283–284

Hijab, Riad, 344n64

History of the Arab Peoples (Hourani), 102

Hourani, Albert, 101

Hudaybi, Hassan al-, 197, 200

Human Rights Watch, 183

Husayn Ibn Ali, Sharif, 24–26, 30–31, 310n7

Husri, Sati' al-, 72, 111

Hussein (king of Jordan), 85, 105

Hussein, Abdullah ibn, 45

Hussein, Ahmed, 64

Hussein, Saddam: authoritarianism of, 10, 113, 166; Baath Party and, 60; corruption of, 294; death of, 8; dissidents called traitors, 10; divide-and-rule tactics, 214; Kurds gassing, 60, 136, 183; Kuwait and Iraq invasions, 111, 136, 139, 163, 239; neoliberal policies of, 109; on Palestine, 76; Reagan administration and, 136; retribalization, 239; Saudi Arabia and, 170; Shias exiled, 215; United States and, 8; violence of, 85

Ibrahimi, Ahmed Taleb, 206

Ikhwan. *See* Muslim Brotherhood; Nasser, Gamal Abdel

Imperialism and the Developing World (Kohli), 307n6

intelligentsia, pessimism and fatalism, 15

International Court of Justice, 300

International Monetary Fund (IMF), 3, 9, 122, 146, 152, 156, 309n27

Iran: Arab fight against, 283; climate change and, 182; colonial behavior of, 314n36; Islamic Republic of Iran, 76, 258; mandate resistance, 46; oil resources and Western countries, 12, 47; as primary regional actor, 282–283; regime change goal, 7; Saudi Arabia and, 285; Shia and Safavid dynasty, 227–228, 285; social revolution in (1970s), 304; Syrian civil war and, 236

Iranian Revolution (1979), 2, 12, 265, 285

Iran-Iraq War (1980), 136, 163, 166, 170, 215

Iraq: Anglo-Iraqi Treaties (1922, 1930), 45–46; Arab Spring second wave, 259; armed conflicts in, 167; Assyrians in, 56–57; Bagdad coup (1958), 84–85; Baghdad Pact, 85; border permanence, 4; British control of, 57–58, 85; British mandate (Mesopotamia), 43, 45–46, 55–57, 238; chemical weapons, 136; constitution (1921), 56; divide-and-rule tactics, 214; education and, 181; Farhud pogrom, 57; fatwa demanding rights, 45, 314n30; foreign direct investment in, 172; former Ottoman military officers in, 60; Halabja chemical weapons attack (1988), 60, 136, 183, 267; Hashemite monarchy in, 55, 57, 84, 231; honor killing and, 179; Iraqi Free Officers, 84–86; Iraqi Republic (1958), 238; Iraqi revolt (1920–1921), 45; Islam, Sunnis and Shi'ism, 56, 215, 237–241, 341n13; Jews in, 56–57; Kurdistan Democratic Party, 64; Kurds in, 60, 215, 223; Law for the Election of the Constituent Assembly (1922), 56; Mosul and, 28, 30, 39, 228; national army formation, 56; oil resources in, 56, 68; "original" and "non-original" Iraqis, 56; second wave, 17; sectarianism in, 229; Shia Dawa Party, 64, 184; Sons of Iraq or Awakening Councils, 239–240; terrorism and political violence, 167; treaty granting independence (1932), 55; tribalism in, 230, 237–241, 344n66; United States and, 223; water security in, 174–176

Iraq and Iran conflict (1980–1988), 111

Islambuli, Khalid al-, 154, 199

Islamic State (IS): boundary remaking, 4; colonial inheritance and, 85; downfall of, 228–229; economic impact of, 172–173; goal of, 139; impact of, 339nn61–62; militia of, 16; nonstate actors and, 139, 209, 217, 222; offer of protection, 229; resurgence of militia, 16; reworking Middle East, 4; Salafi-jihadist group, 211–212; sectarian identity, 223, 225, 228; sectarianism of, 213; split from Al-Qaeda, 228; subnational identity and, 214; Sunni grievances and, 241; terrorism and political violence, 167; Yazidis and, 183

Islamic State in Iraq and Syria (ISIS), 227–228, 278, 343n57

Islamism: answer to society's problems, 196–197; *jahiliyya* ("age of ignorance"), 198–199; radical and revolutionary ideologies, 8; Sadat and, 200; Sunni-Shia split, 8, 56, 213, 223, 226–228, 285–286, 295; unifying symbol of faith, 194–195; varieties of, 110; Wahhabism, 228. *See also* Algeria; Sadat, Anwar al-

Ismailiyya, Egypt, 190, 192–194

Israel: Abraham Accords, 272–274, 285; Arab defeat (1948), 65; Arab-Israeli War (1973), 120–121, 150; Arab-Israeli wars and, 121; Arab states and, 44, 93; Europe, defense of, 275; Gaza war (2023–2024), 49, 177, 183, 221–222, 273, 289, 300–301, 309n27; Hamas and, 221, 273, 284–285; Iran and, 285; Israeli-Palestinian conflict, 166; Lebanon and, 273, 284; Saudi Arabia and, 273; settlements in occupied territory, 283; Six-Day War (1967), 96–102, 163; United States, special relationship with, 101–103; water security in, 176

Jabhat al-Nusra (Al Qaeda in the Levant), 226, 229, 258

Jarba, Ahmad al-, 344n64

Johnson, Lyndon B., 12, 102, 125

Jordan: British mandate (Transjordan), 45–46; COVID-19 pandemic in, 18; domestic violence offenses, 179; foreign direct investment in, 173; honor killing and, 179; marriage permission, 178; oil price volatility, 171; Six-Day War (1967), 105; tribal networks of, 236; water shortage in, 176; youth unemployment, 180

Kalaya, Hosni, 146

Kemal, Mustafa (Atatürk), 46

Kennedy, John F., 125

Kerr, Malcolm H., 103

Khalidi, Rashid, 33

Khedive Ismail, 190–194

Khomeini, Ayatollah, 76, 318n32

King-Crane Commission, 40–41

Kissinger, Henry, 12, 136

Kitchener, Horatio Herbert, 25, 27, 30, 38

Kohli, Atul, 307n6

Kurds: foreign powers and, 11; Halabja chemical weapons attack (1988), 60, 136, 183, 215; in Iraq, 56, 223, 302; lack of statehood, 56, 59–60; minority status of, 47; in Syria, 60–61, 184–185

Kushner, Jared, 273

Kuwait, 111, 136, 139, 163, 167, 170–171, 173, 236

Lawson, George, 288

League of Nations, 31, 35–36, 40, 42–46, 48, 51, 55–57, 232, 313n20

Lebanon: Arab Spring second wave, 259; armed conflicts in, 166; COVID-19 pandemic in, 18; domestic violence offenses, 179; economic center, 69; France and, 11, 38, 45–46; Hezbollah, 112, 189, 222–224, 226, 229, 236, 284, 289; honor killing and, 179; Lebanese civil war, 111; second wave, 17

Lenin, Vladimir, 114

Lewis, Bernard, 22

Libya: Arab Spring in, 248–249, 268, 298; armed conflicts in, 167; border permanence, 4; civil strife and wars, 16; Gaddafi family thefts, 187; NATO involvement in, 10–11, 248, 269, 274, 277, 280; oil resources in, 69; Russia and, 130–131, 264; Saif Gaddafi and, 249; terrorism and political violence, 167; United States and, 270; UN Security Council Resolution (UNSC), 277–278

Lloyd George, David, 32, 39

Macron, Emmanuel, 275–276

Madani, Abassi, 209

Mahgoub, Rifaat al-, 155

Making the Arab World (Gerges), 76, 199

Malek, Anouar Abdel, 77

Maliki, Nuri al-, 240–241

Maronite Christians, 28

Marx, Karl, 286, 350n47

Masri, Aziz al-, 54

Mauritania, 146, 177

Max Planck Institute, 182

McMahon, Henry, 24–26, 31

McMahon-Husayn correspondence, 24–26, 30–31, 35, 39, 310n7

McMillan, M. E., 265

MENA (Middle East and North Africa) region: climate change and, 182–183; corporatist state, 107, 186; crony capitalism and corruption, 185–187; economic activity disruptions, 309n27; education and, 181–182; failures of, 188–189; foreign direct investment and, 172–173; genocides and political killings, 183–184; mass protests, 309n27; minority discrimination, 184; poverty of, 177; state control of economic life, 185; violent conflict and, 167; water scarcity in, 175; youth unemployment, 180

Merkel, Angela, 275

Middle East: colonial origins of states, 4; nation building, 298, 351n1; state system of, 219, 301–302; terminology of, 314n37

Milestones (Qutb), 198

Misr al-Fatat (Young Egypt), 54, 64; al-Qumsan al-Khadra' (the Green Shirts), 64

Mohsen, Ali, 252

Morocco, 37, 178–179

Morsi, Mohammed, 202–204

Mossadegh, Mohammad, 7–8, 11–13, 47, 118, 126, 135

Mubarak, Gamal, 157–158, 249

Mubarak, Hosni: authoritarianism of, 113; corporatism and, 107; crony capitalism and corruption, 156, 158, 294; economic mismanagement of, 163; France and, 277; Islamists and, 201; military and, 154, 159; Muslim Brotherhood and, 202; neoliberal economic policies, 109, 157; ousted from power, 247, 251; "rentier" state, 155; United States and, 13, 167, 265, 268. *See also* Egypt, Mubarak era

Muhammed bin Salman (MBS), 13–14, 171, 178, 308n18

Muslim Brotherhood: al-Nizam al-Khass, 64, 197; al-Tanzim al-Sirri, 199; Arab Spring and, 256; armed revolutionary vanguard, 197; banned by government (1936), 197; Copt Christian community and, 203; in Egypt, 148, 153, 283; with Eisenhower at White House, 325n26; founding of, 74; Hamas and, 221; Islamic framework of, 196–198, 203; Islamists and, 204; modern state rejection, 210; Qutb splinter groups and, 200; Saudi Arabia and, 206; social activities of, 201–202; state-within-a-state, 195, 202; status in Egypt, 201; Syria and, 184, 233–234; transnationalism of, 194; Wafd Party and, 201; working from within, 211; Yemen and, 250–251

Najeeb, Atef, 235

Napoleonic Wars, 1, 306

Nasrallah, Sayyid Hassan, 224, 284

Nasser, Gamal Abdel: Algeria and, 105; anti-colonial struggle and, 64–65, 67, 193; Arab nationalism and, 75–76, 79–80, 94, 193; assassination attempt, 198; authoritarianism of, 3, 79, 148; Baath Party, 81; Free Officers Movement and, 70–71; Iraqi coup and, 85–86; Israel and, 98–99; Israel, war with (1967), 13; land reform and, 78, 90, 148; Law of the Tribes repealed, 232; leader of Arab nations, 80; Muslim Brotherhood and, 197–198; nationalization of industries, 78–79;

nonaligned foreign policy, 8, 12–13; Non-Aligned Movement and, 123; on Palestine, 75–76; popularity of, 82; populism of, 162; progressive social agenda of, 77–79, 106; radio speeches, 104; rivalry with Qasim, 87; Soviet Union and, 128, 130–131; Syria and Baath Party, 94–95, 97; United Arab Republic and, 83–84, 89, 95–96, 321n17; United States and, 7, 12, 126; Yemen, military intervention in, 96–97. *See also* Arab nationalism; Egypt, Nasser era

Nazif, Ahmed, 158

Nehru, Jawaharlal, 123

neocolonialism, 122, 124

Netanyahu, Benjamin, 222, 273–274, 281, 284–285

New York Times, 188

Nicolson, Arthur, 29

Nixon, Richard, 125

Nkrumah, Kwame, 123

Non-Aligned Movement, 122–123, 166

nonstate actors: Ahrar al-Sham, 258; Arab Spring and, 258; Assad family, encouragement of, 215; avoidance of, 303; China and, 263–264; conflictual multipolarity, 350n55; global jihad, 210; global powers and, 137; Iraq and, 223; popular support of, 224; proliferation of, 219; religious groups, 111; tools of resistance, 242–243. *See also* Al-Qaeda; Hamas; Hezbollah; Islamic State; Jabhat al-Nusra

North Atlantic Treaty Organization (NATO), 11, 248, 269–270, 272, 274–277, 280–281. *See also* Libya

Nuqrashi, Mahmoud al-, 197

Obama, Barack, and Obama administration: Arab Spring and, 265; *The Atlantic* interview, 269; balance-of-power principle, 271–273; Cairo speech (2009), 267; Iraq and, 240; on Libya and NATO, 274; Middle East policy and, 267–270, 300;

Mubarak and, 268; Saudi Arabia and, 13; Yemen and Saleh, 250–251, 254

oil and gas resources, 12, 47, 56, 68, 108, 114–115, 164, 168–171

oil-producing states, success of, 160, 330n62

ordinary people, 11, 14–15, 18, 296

Organization of the Petroleum Exporting Countries (OPEC), 128, 308n18

Oslo Accords, 176

Ottoman Empire: Arab Revolt, 31, 39–40, 56, 58, 231; defeat of, 21–22; nationalist intellectuals in, 313n13; partition of, 27–28; "post-Ottoman syndrome," 29, 56, 73; tribalism and, 231; World War I and Germany, 24, 26. *See also* McMahon-Husayn correspondence

Pahlavi, Shah Mohammad Reza, 7–8, 10–12, 47, 119, 128, 169, 294, 300, 307n6, 318n32

Pakistan, 132, 138, 167

Palestine: Arab lack of assistance, 112; British mandate, 32, 43–46; capture of Jerusalem, 38; denial of statehood, 59; domestic violence offenses, 179; Great Britain and Jewish claims, 29, 43; honor killing and, 179; marriage permission, 178; optimism for, 296; Orthodox Russian Empire claim, 29; Palestine War (1947–1948), 111; two-state solution, 273; water shortage in, 176. *See also* Balfour Declaration

Palestine Liberation Army (PLO), 108, 221, 318n32

Palestinian Authority, 302

pan-Arab nationalism: Arab cold war and, 105; cultural unity and, 66; Egypt and, 73–74, 94, 96, 103–104, 193; failure of, 97, 106; Hezbollah and, 224; ideology of, 110; Iran and, 214; Ottoman Empire and, 72–73; promises of, 74; resistance and disagreements, 86–87; Syria and, 215; territorial nationalism alternative, 108; Wafd ruling party (*see* United Arab Republic); Western intervention and, 85 pan-Islamism, 66, 74, 103–104, 109–110, 129, 133–135, 139, 224–225, 260

Pasha, Cemel, 40

Paulet-Newcombe Agreement (1933), 44–45

Peace to End All Peace, A (Fromkin), 30

petro-dollars, 7, 20, 108–110, 133

proxy wars, 6, 103, 107, 111–112, 116, 120, 138, 166, 236, 254

Putin, Vladimir, 258, 264, 271, 276, 278, 280–281

Qabbani, Nizar, 109

Qasim, Abd al-Karim, 131

Qasim, Abdel Karim, 84, 86–87

Qatar, 180, 236, 262, 344n64

Quandt, William, 137

Qutb, Sayyid, 198–201

Quwatli, Shukri al-, 60

Rabin, Yitzhak, 99

Rajiha, Dawoud, 234

Ramadan, Said, 325n26

Reagan, Ronald, 125, 136, 138

regional actors, 122, 164, 166, 204, 264, 283, 289–290

religious nationalism, 73

"rentier" states, 155, 167, 169, 171

Rostow, Walt, 102

Rothschild, Walter, 32

ruling elites: British and French and, 23; cronyism of, 15, 308n21; failure to adopt democracy, 22; future choices, 18–19, 309n28; global capitalism of, 50; Mandate System and, 36; politics and, 2; representative government possibilities, 20; rhetoric of, 113; securitization of, 112–113; superpower support, 9, 14; wealth of, 9

Russia: Chechnya and, 279; entente cordiale, 37–38; geographic proximity and, 279; Iran and, 280; Islamic State (IS) and Islamist radicalism, 279; Israel and, 281; Middle East influence, 263–264; Middle East policy and, 278, 282, 286–287; Syria and, 279, 281, 350n48; Turkey and, 281; Ukraine invasion and, 168, 262, 264, 276, 279, 287, 309n27; worldview of, 279–280. *See also* Soviet Union

Sadat, Anwar al-: Arab-Israeli war (1973), 150; assassination and funeral, 153–154, 199, 201, 247; "Believer President," 152, 199; British and, 192; corporatism and, 107; economic mismanagement, 163; Egypt and United States, 13; Free Officers and, 148; Islamists and leftists, 153, 200, 205, 207, 211; Mubarak and, 157–159; Nasser and, 148–149; Nobel Peace Prize, 150; petro-dollar politics and pan-Islamism, 108–109, 133; Soviet military advisors expelled, 149; United States and, 134, 166–167. *See also* Egypt, Sadat era

Sadat, Esmaat al-, 152

Sa'dun, Abdul Muhsin al-, 62

Said, Khaled, 247, 259

Said, Nuri al-, 57, 62, 84–85, 87

Saied, Kais, 188

Salafi-jihadism: anti-Salafis and, 226; Arab nationalism and, 110; global jihad and, 138, 203; Russia and, 279; Saleh and, 216; tribal leaders and, 241, 249; untraconservatism of, 128, 209, 211, 225, 250

Saleh, Ahmad Ali, 249–251

Saleh, Ali Abdullah, 163, 216–217, 248–252, 254, 257, 294

Saudi Arabia: climate change and, 182; COVID-19 pandemic in, 308n18; domestic violence offenses, 179; Iran and, 285; marriage permission, 178; Muslim Brotherhood and, 204; oil resources in, 108, 169–171; pan-Islamism of, 110; Sunni Islam, 285; Syrian civil war and, 236; tribalism, 344n64; United States and, 13–14, 128–129, 308n18; Yemen and Egyptian military intervention, 96; youth unemployment, 180

Sawt al-Arab (Voice of the Arabs) (radio station), 80, 104–105

Seale, Patrick, 89, 131

sectarianism: Arab nationalism alternative, 74; autocracy and, 220; divide-and-rule tactic, 259; foreign powers' tool, 93; Islamic State (IS) and, 228–229; Islam incompatability with, 2; jihadism and US-led coalition forces, 341n13; means of social control, 213–214; postsectarian identity, 292, 294; subnational identities and, 222; Sunni identity and, 225, 241–242; in Syria, 215

Shirazi, Muhammad Taqi al-Ha'iri, 45

Shlaim, Avi, 311n47

Shuqari, Ahmed al-, 108

Sisi, Abdel al-Fatah al-, 13, 107

Sistani, Ali al-, 341n13

Soviet Union, 6, 10, 97, 114–116, 118, 129–134. *See also* Russia

Springborg, Robert, 174

Stalin, Joseph, 115

Stark, Freya, 59

subnational identities: authoritarian regimes and, 213–215; competition among, 248; external intervention and, 218, 222; Iran and Saudi Arabia, 236; in Iraq, 223; Islamic State (IS) and, 228; proliferation of, 219; repression of minorities and, 184; resurgence of, 139, 218, 241–242, 259; use by autocrats, 220; Yemen and, 217

Sudan: Arab Spring second wave, 17, 259; armed conflicts in, 167; Darfur genocide, 183; discrimination in, 179; marriage permission, 178; natural resources of, 69; water security in, 174

Suez Canal: British and, 29, 37, 191–192; importance of, 191; Israel attack (1967), 101; nationalization of (1956), 71, 80, 193; project of, 190–191; Suez Crisis (1956), 76, 80, 97, 118, 130; 'Urabi's uprising, 192, 196. *See also* Ismailiyya, Egypt

Sukarno, 123

supranationalism, 66, 104

Sykes, Mark, 26–27, 29–30

Sykes-Picot Agreement (1916), 10, 30, 33–36, 38–39, 41–42, 48–49, 312n51

Syria: Alawites, 28, 58, 62, 215, 234, 258, 311n29; Arab Spring in, 247–248; armed conflicts in, 167; Army of the Levant, 316n37; Baath Party, 61, 87, 92, 94–95, 232–233, 311n29; Battle of Maysalun (1920), 41–42; Bedouins in, 230–231; border permanence, 4; boundary of, 81; civil strife and war, 16, 228–229, 234–235; constitutional monarchy of, 55; COVID-19 pandemic in, 18; crony capitalism and corruption, 186–187; Declaration of Independence, 41; Egypt and Syria, 83, 90–93; former Ottoman military officers in, 60; France and, 28, 38–39, 41; Free Syrian Army, 229, 236, 340n62; French mandate, 43, 45–46, 58–60, 62, 231–232; Hezbollah, 258; history of, 92; honor killing and, 179; independent Arab state after World War I, 38–39; internal partition, 58–59; King-Crane Commission and, 40–41; Kurdish Democratic Union Party (PYD), 343n57; Kurds in, 60–61, 184–185; land reform and, 90–91; Law of the Tribes, 232; living conditions in, 18; marriage permission, 178; mass "politicide," 183; Muslim Brotherhood of, 64, 184; nationalization of Syrian industries, 92; oil resources in, 68; revolt against French occupation, 58; Russia and, 258; sectarian tensions in, 226; Six-Day War (1967), 100; Soviet Union and, 131; Sunnis and Shias in, 226–227; Syrian Arab Tribes Council, 235; Syrian Democratic Forces (SDF), 343n57; Syrian Great Revolt, 59; Syrian Legion, 62, 316n37; Syrian National Council (SNC), 235, 343n57, 344n64; terrorism and political violence, 167; tribalism in, 230–236, 343n59; United Arab Republic and, 95, 321n17; water security in, 174–175. *See also* Assad family; Bedouins

Syrian Communist Party, 81

Tawfiq, 192

territorial nationalism, 73–74, 104, 108

Thompson, Elizabeth, 42

Tigris River, 174–176

Tilmissani, Amr al-, 201

Tito, Josip, 123

Tolstoy, Leo, 1, 4, 306

Transjordan, 40, 44–46, 231

Treaty of Lausanne (1923), 46

Treaty of Sèvres (1920), 46

tribalism, 74, 214, 229–230, 237–238, 242, 344n66. *See also* Iraq; Syria

Truman, Harry S., 125

Truman Doctrine, 115

Trump, Donald, 13, 49, 256, 262–263, 270–275, 285, 300, 302, 308n18

Tunisia: Arab Spring in, 141, 144, 188, 247, 259; Ben Ali family thefts, 147, 187; corruption in, 143, 245–246; COVID-19 pandemic in, 18; domestic violence offenses, 179; economic mismanagement, 18, 142–143; Ennahda Party (Muslim Brotherhood), 245; self-immolations, 146, 188; Sidi Bou Zid protests, 141, 244–245; state funds in foreign banks, 145; Western policies and, 268, 277, 301; women's education in, 78; youth unemployment, 145, 180. *See also* Ben Ali, Zine El Abidine

Turkey: authoritarianism in, 282; colonial behavior of, 314n36; Committee of Union and Progress, 72; economics of, 282–284; Justice and Development Party (AKP), 282; mandate resistance, 46; migratory journey to, 18; military coups and attempts, 47, 282; as primary regional actor, 282–283; "Turkification" policy, 24, 72; water security in, 174–176

UN Convention on the Elimination of All Forms of Discrimination against Women, 178

United Arab Emirates (UAE), 172, 204, 262, 281, 286, 288, 330n62

United Arab Republic (UAR), 83–84, 86, 88–90, 92–96, 99, 321n17

United Nations, 9, 101–102, 183, 216, 304

United Nations Development Programme (UNDP), 177, 180

United Nations Economic and Social Commission for Western Asia (ESCWA), 15, 167, 309n27

United Nations Office for the Coordination of Humanitarian Affairs (OCHA), 253

United Nations Security Council, 121, 135–136, 266

United States: Afghanistan and, 129; "America First" doctrine, 270; Arab-Israeli war (1973) and, 120–121; Arab nationalism resistance, 86; arms industry, 127–128, 136; Asia policy, 269–270; Central Intelligence Agency (CIA), 13, 100, 265; Cold War and, 115–116, 124–125, 137; Cold War and defense pacts, 117–118, 126; Eisenhower Doctrine (1958), 89; empire by proxy, 297; food exports to Middle East, 13; foreign policy of, 261–262, 266, 287; Gaza War and, 290, 300; Global War on Terror and, 159, 250; informal empire, 135; Iran and, 265, 273; Iraqi coup and, 86; Islam and conservative monarchies, 127, 196–197; Israel and Palestinians, 135; legacy of imperial control, 12–13; liberal international order and, 265–266; Middle East policy and, 267–270, 287; Middle East strategy, 102; Muslim Brotherhood and, 132; National Security Council, 267; "Nixon Doctrine," 270; Pakistan and, 132; proxy empire of, 7; Saudi Arabia and, 103, 132; September 11, 2001, 137–138, 212, 250; spread of "godless communism," 128, 132, 138; US-Soviet proxy war, 112

Universal Declaration of Human Rights, 184

'Urabi, Ahmad, 192–193

War and Peace (Tolstoy), 1, 306

water security, 9, 143, 174–176, 183

Weizmann, Chaim, 44

Western imperialism, 3, 6, 17, 45, 49, 139, 198

What Really Went Wrong (Gerges), 6

"When Will They Announce the Death of the Arabs" (Qabbani), 109

Wilson, Woodrow, 35, 40–43, 48, 125, 313n20

Wingate, Reginald, 31

World Bank, 3, 9, 122, 146, 156–157, 172, 309n27

World War I: Allied powers, 27; King-Crane Commission, 40–41; Ottoman Empire disposition, 40–42; Paris Peace Conference (1919), 39; San Remo Conference, 36, 38–39, 42

Yassin, Sayyed, 75

Yemen: Al-Qaeda in the Arabian Peninsula (AQAP), 216, 252, 254–255; Arab Spring in, 248, 250–251, 254–255; armed conflicts in, 166–167; border permanence, 4; civil strife and wars, 16–17, 254; discrimination in, 179; education and, 182; General People's Congress (GPC), 250; health care system collapse, 253–254; Hirak movement, 249–250, 252; honor killing and, 179; Houthis and, 249–250, 252–254; humanitarian crisis in, 253–254; Islah party, 251, 254; Joint Meeting Parties, 252; marriage permission, 178; "Nasser's Vietnam," 96; nonstate actors and, 217; North-South divide, 253; oil price volatility, 171; poverty of, 143, 177–178, 216; proxy war between Egypt and Saudi Arabia, 107; reunification of, 249–250; Saudi Arabia and, 252–253; Saudi royalists and Egyptian fighting, 93, 95–96; terrorism and political violence, 167; tribalism of, 216; United States and, 250; water crisis, 143, 174, 217, 253

youth unemployment, 180

Zarqawi, Abu Musab al-, 226, 341n13

Zawahiri, Ayman al-, 138, 212, 228, 341n13